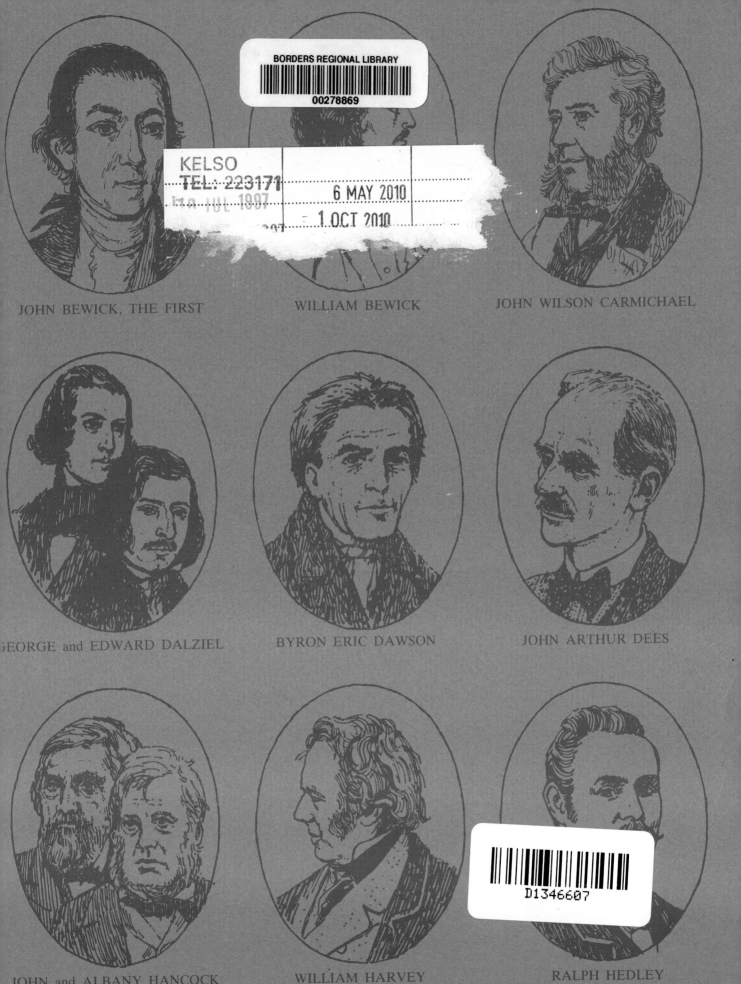

JOHN BEWICK, THE FIRST

WILLIAM BEWICK

JOHN WILSON CARMICHAEL

GEORGE and EDWARD DALZIEL

BYRON ERIC DAWSON

JOHN ARTHUR DEES

JOHN and ALBANY HANCOCK

WILLIAM HARVEY

RALPH HEDLEY

The Artists of
Northumbria

an Illustrated Dictionary

John Wilson Carmichael: Sunderland Harbour, 1864.
Oil 24×36. *Tyne & Wear County Council Museums,*
Sunderland Art Gallery & Museum.

Thomas Bewick 1753-1828.
Portrait by William Nicholson. Oil 49½×39½.
Tyne & Wear County Council Museums,
Laing Art Gallery.

The Artists of
Northumbria

**an illustrated dictionary
of Northumberland, Newcastle upon Tyne,
Durham and North East Yorkshire
painters, sculptors, draughtsmen and engravers
born between 1625 and 1900**

by Marshall Hall

Artists of the Regions Series: Volume One

MARSHALL HALL ASSOCIATES

26 Jesmond Road, Newcastle upon Tyne NE2 4QP

Dedicated to the memory of
Byron Eric Dawson
Artist
my tutor in art
and friend for more than a decade

First published 1973
New 2nd edition revised and enlarged 1982

ISBN 0 903858 02 9

Printed in Great Britain by Titus Wilson and Son Ltd.,
28 Highgate, Kendal.

Contents

Acknowledgements   vi

Introduction   vii

The Artists   1

Bibliography   203

Map of Northumbria   205

Exhibiting organisations   206

*Notes: * at the beginning of an artist's entry indicates that his, or her work, is illustrated; # following a reference in an entry to a particular work, or type of work, produced by an artist, signifies that this work is illustrated; all dimensions shown in captions are given in inches, height preceding width. All Northumbrian place names mentioned in the Introduction, and in artists' entries, have been set in capitals for ease of identification, thus: ALNWICK. For NEWCASTLE, wherever it appears in an artist's entry, please read: NEWCASTLE UPON TYNE.*

Acknowledgements

The assistance of the following art galleries, organisations and individuals in the preparation and illustration of this revised and enlarged edition of *The Artists of Northumbria*, 1973, is hereby gratefully acknowledged.

Abbey Antiques & Arts, Hemel Hempstead; James Alder Ltd., Newcastle upon Tyne; Anderson & Garland, Newcastle upon Tyne; Art Gallery of South Australia, Adelaide, Australia; Berwick Art Gallery, Berwick-upon-Tweed; Bowes Museum, Barnard Castle; Bristol Museum & Art Gallery, Bristol; Darlington Art Gallery, Darlington; The Dean & Chapter of Durham Cathedral; Dean Gallery, Newcastle upon Tyne; J. C. Featonby, Whitley Bay; Hancock Museum, Newcastle upon Tyne; Hatton Gallery, University of Newcastle upon Tyne; Hexham Antiques, Hexham; Laing Art Gallery, Newcastle upon Tyne; Literary & Philosophical Society, Newcastle upon Tyne; Lyndhurst Antiques, Newcastle upon Tyne; Macdonald Fine Art, Newcastle upon Tyne; Manx Museum and National Trust, Douglas, Isle of Man; Roy Miles Gallery, London; Morgan & Brown, Newcastle upon Tyne; Moss Galleries, Hexham; National Portrait Gallery, London; National Trust, Beckenham; Natural History Society of Northumbria, Newcastle upon Tyne; Netherlands Institute for Art History, The Hague; Newcastle upon Tyne City Libraries; Northumberland County Council, Morpeth; N. R. Omell Gallery, London; Pannett Art Gallery, Whitby; Port of Tyne Authority, Newcastle upon Tyne; Scottish National Gallery, Edinburgh; Scottish National Portrait Gallery, Edinburgh; Scottish & Newcastle Breweries Ltd., Newcastle upon Tyne; Shipley Art Gallery, Gateshead; Simon Carter Gallery, Woodbridge; Sotheby, King & Chasemore, Pulborough, Sussex; South Shields Museum & Art Gallery, South Shields; Stone Gallery, Newcastle upon Tyne; State Library of Victoria, Melbourne, Australia; Sunderland Museum & Art Gallery, Sunderland; Tate Gallery, London; Tyne & Wear County Council Museums, Newcastle upon Tyne; Victoria & Albert Museum, London; Walker Art Gallery, Liverpool; Westgate Antiques, Newcastle upon Tyne; Christopher Wood Ltd., London.

My special thanks are due to several individuals for drawing my attention to artists omitted from the 1973 publication, or for assisting me with my further research into those originally presented. Among the former I should like to single out Dr. Raymond Layton, Tynemouth, and Gill Hedley, Laing Art Gallery, Newcastle upon Tyne, while the latter include Iain Bain, Baldock, Hertfordshire; June Crosby, Durham; Tom Faulkner, Newcastle upon Tyne; Dr. E. D. Mackerness, Sheffield; Dr. Sheila Murray, Newcastle upon Tyne, and James Rush, Newcastle upon Tyne.

Others whom I should like to thank in the above respects are the descendants of many of the artists now presented, and the Local Studies Librarians, Reference Librarians, and County Archivists throughout Northumbria, who patiently dealt with my hundreds of enquiries.

Finally, my thanks must be expressed to all the art galleries in Northumberland, Durham, Tyne & Wear, and Cleveland, for their immense help and encouragement throughout my mammoth task, and in particular to Tyne & Wear County Council Museums, the Gray Art Gallery & Museum, Hartlepool, Darlington Art Gallery, and the Dean Gallery, Newcastle upon Tyne, for providing the bulk of the photographs reproduced in this volume.

Marshall Hall

Introduction

The area now popularly known as "Northumbria" (see map page 205) stretches from a few miles beyond Berwick-upon-Tweed, Northumberland, in the north, to just short of Staithes, North Yorkshire, in the south; from the North Sea Coast in the east, to the borders of Berwickshire, Roxburgh and Cumbria in the west.

It is an area which has long been associated with some of the best known names in British Art – Thomas Bewick, Clarkson Stanfield, John Martin and Myles Birket Foster, to mention only four. But in addition to these well known artists there were literally hundreds whose associations with the area have hitherto remained poorly documented.

Many were artists who remained in Northumbria throughout their careers, and though once well known, have faded into oblivion; some were artists who left the area of their birth to become leading painters elsewhere in the world, and have long been regarded in their adopted countries as American . . . Canadian . . . Australian . . . South African, their connections with Northumbria almost forgotten; surprisingly many belonged to that universally underrated and therefore poorly recorded category of artist – the amateur; yet others were immigrant artists who settled in Northumbria, leaving little evidence of their one-time presence apart from a number of intriguing paintings and drawings.

This dictionary presents not only those artists whose connections with Northumbria are already well known, but the many more whom the author's long and wide ranging research has brought to light. They total more than 650, and include some of the most talented painters, sculptors, draughtsmen and engravers associated with any area of Britain.

These are some of the fields of art in which Northumbrian artists notably distinguished themselves . . .

Marine painting

As one of Britain's oldest shipbuilding areas, and with a number of ancient and busy seaports strung along its coastline, it is not surprising that Northumbria has produced some of the finest marine painters in the country. Clarkson Stanfield and Charles Napier Hemy – both Royal Academicians – drew their earliest inspi-

ration from the ship arrivals and departures, the shipbuilding activity, and talk of naval men which were a daily part of their lives, the one at SUNDERLAND, the other at NEWCASTLE, and later NORTH SHIELDS.

These were only two of Northumbria's many fine marine artists, however, outstanding as they undoubtedly were. Long before either of them were born the multi-talented Francis Place had turned down an offer of £500 a year from Charles II, to paint the King's Ships, and throughout their respective careers there were many other artists from the area whose work in marine painting was among the best the country could claim.

One of the earliest of these artists was John Wilson Carmichael, born a scant six years after Stanfield, yet destined to commence his career in marine painting at much the same time as his older contemporary; Stanfield after some years as a scenic painter for the Theatre; Carmichael after an apprenticeship in the shipbuilding industry.

Stanfield then quickly made his name in London. Carmichael remained on Tyneside, his struggle to establish himself as its leading marine painter initially challenged by the excellent work of fellow Northumbrians George Balmer and John Wilson Ewbank. These two men did not, however, have Carmichael's intimate knowledge of his subject, and his dogged determination to succeed in his chosen profession, and soon went their respective ways – Balmer to paint river and coastal scenes; Ewbank to flourish briefly at Edinburgh as one of its leading marine and landscape painters before succumbing to the temptations of drink.

But even Carmichael could not remain fully employed as a marine painter during his long period at NEWCASTLE. What he did produce in this field, however, helped to establish a local demand for ship portraits, and marine works generally, of which others were able to take advantage when he left for London in 1846. His pupil John Scott; contemporaries Mark Thompson, Robert F. Watson, James Warkup Swift and James Stokeld, rapidly filled the vacuum left by his departure.

The shipping scene which Carmichael left behind him in Northumbria began to change rapidly in the immediately following years of the mid-19th century. Shipbuilding, mainly for the coaling trade, accelerated dramatically, and several Northumbrian seaports were developed considerably to accommodate the increasing number of ships engaged in this trade and in the expanding North Sea fishing industry.

To this later scene along the rivers and coast of Northumbria were attracted the brothers of Charles Napier Hemy – Thomas Marie Madawaska staying several years before following his elder brother to the South of England; Bernard Benedict plodding away in the area until his death.

The second half of the 19th century inevitably witnessed a substantial increase in the number of Northumbria's marine artists, in line with this expansion in shipbuilding and seaport facilities, and each place of activity had its resident masters of the art, as well as a host of artists who occasionally turned their hands to painting ships and coastal scenes with shipping. NEWCASTLE had its Robert Jobling ... SUNDERLAND its Stuart Henry Bell ... NORTH SHIELDS its John Chambers ... SOUTH SHIELDS its Robert F. Watson ... BERWICK-UPON-TWEED its John Wallace, Senior ... HARTLEPOOL its John William Howey ... the tiny fishing port of CULLERCOATS, not only a surprising number of resident artists, but dozens of seasonal and other artist visitors, including the now famous American painter Winslow Homer.

With the rapid decline in the use of sail which came with the beginning of the 20th century the number of Northumbrian marine artists dwindled rapidly. Steam ships lacked the glamour of their predecessors, at least as far as the general public was concerned, and those marine artists who did continue to practise survived by either drawing on their earlier compositions featuring sailing ships, or were at pains to include examples of the relatively few that were still to be seen. Among these latterday artists were Bernard Benedict Hemy and William Thomas Nichols Boyce, both of whom remained dedicated to the local shipping scene until their deaths, while among those who carried on to paint the age of steam were Charles de Lacy, Frank Watson Wood, and Frank Henry Mason – the last named one of Britain's best marine painters of this century.

Landscape painters

Although Northumbria has produced only a few landscape painters whose names are widely familiar, they were each outstanding in their respective periods.

Francis Place of DINSDALE, near DARLINGTON, has been acknowledged as the first British artist whose main preoccupation was landscape, and was among the first of those topographers who set out to explore and record the landscape of Britain in the 17th century; Thomas Bewick, of NEWCASTLE, towards the close of the 18th century produced watercolours of the local landscape for his wood engravings which are unique of their period for their scale, draughtsmanship and content; Myles Birket Foster, born at NORTH SHIELDS, was the most prolific and successful landscape painter in Britain in the 19th century, and the work of George Horton of NORTH SHIELDS is now being recognised as among the most distinctive produced by any British artist in the present century.

For three quarters of a century after Francis Place finally settled at York, in 1692, almost the only landscapes painted in Northumbria, or of Northumbrian subjects, were those executed by visiting artists. Not until the last quarter of the 18th century did local artists begin to produce local views, and then ones mainly inspired by the vogue for the "Picturesque" which was then at its height. Notable among these early local landscape painters were John Bailey, Luke Clennell, George Fennel Robson, and William Andrews Nesfield, all of whom except the first named became distinguished water-colourists practising mainly in the South of England. But perhaps the best known Northumbrian view of this period, painted by a local artist, was by an artist usually devoted to animal and sporting painting – Joseph Atkinson – whose "Tanfield Arch" is familiar to students of the Industrial Revolution around the world. That there was little demand for the services of a full-time resident professional landscape painter in Northumbria in the early years of the 19th century is evidenced by the abruptness with which William Nicholson switched to portrait painting after only a brief time at NEWCASTLE painting local scenes. But with the changes which shortly afterwards came to the area via its industrial development there also came a demand to record these changes; town scenes showing the destruction of the old and the building of the new; river scenes showing the activity of shipyard and glassworks; landscapes pin-pointing the whereabouts of coal mine and railway line; pastoral scenes incorporating the homes of those now rich through the industry of the area.

One of the first local landscape painters to benefit from this demand was Thomas Miles Richardson, Senior, of NEWCASTLE, about whom grew the area's earliest landscape school, comprising himself, Henry Perlee Parker, John Wilson Carmichael, and later his sons George Richardson, Edward Richardson, and Thomas Miles Richardson, Junior. These were followed by the sons of his second marriage; pupils James Burrell Smith and John Storey, and several young converts to landscape painting including John Henry Mole.

By the middle of the century the area could boast some three dozen accomplished landscape painters, several of whom had established reputations elsewhere in Britain. With Richardson's death in 1848, however, it lost the greatest of those landscape painters who had chosen to remain in the area of their birth, and interest in the art visibly faltered until the arrival of William Cosens Way at the Government School of Design, NEWCASTLE, in 1862, when once again young local artists gained someone from whom they could learn the rudiments of the art.

In the second half of the 19th century Northumbria experienced massive increases in the populations of its industrial towns, principally those on the Tyne, Wear and Tees, and with these increases came a demand from the middle class comfortably ensconced in their town houses and suburban villas, for pure landscapes uncluttered by the products of the industrial development which had made their wealth possible. Belonging to this later period of landscape painting in the area were several artists who found their subject matter elsewhere in Britain; Edward Train and George Blackie Sticks travelled the Highlands of Scotland; John Surtees formed an attachment for the wild scenery of Wales; James Peel painted the Lake District, and the lush pastures of the South of England and John Atkinson made painting forays into the dales of North Yorkshire. But a surprising number of local artists found their inspiration in the river valleys, hill country and coastal stretches of their native Northumbria, and art exhibitions at Newcastle in the late 19th and early 20th centuries bulged with views of the upper Tyne, Tees, Wear and Coquet, the castles along the coast, and the sheep-dotted Cheviot Hills.

Those local artists who distinguished themselves in landscape painting in this later period are too numerous to mention. Outstanding, however, were John Atkinson, Ralph Hedley and John Falconar Slater, in the early part of this century; George Horton, James Walker Tucker and John Richardson Gauld, more recently.

Portrait painting

It is perhaps significant that Northumbria's earliest portrait painter of note – Sir Ralph Cole – was a man of independent means who was able to indulge his artistic tastes unfettered by the need to earn a living from them. Northumbria in the middle of the 17th century, when Cole was in London receiving lessons from Van Dyck, could not have been a very encouraging place for a professional portrait painter, and it was not until almost half a century after Cole's death that the first Northumbrian artists were born who were able to practise as such. These men – Nicholas Farrer and William Bell – were fortunate, however, the former gaining the patronage of the Duke of Richmond; the latter that of Lord Delaval. It was not, in fact, until Northumbria in the later years of the 18th century developed into one of the fastest growing industrial areas in Britain that opportunities for the portrait painter really began to present themselves, attracting first George Gray – ordinarily devoted to fruit painting – then a succession of able portraitists including William Nicholson, James Ramsay, and Henry Perlee Parker.

Nicholson, the first professional portrait painter to try his success in Northumbria, left Newcastle about 1814, before its opportunities for his skills had fully ripened, and later made his name in Edinburgh. Ramsay, making his first professional visit to the area shortly after Nicholson's departure, was not immediately impressed by its prospects and did not, indeed, become so until much later in his life. Parker, on the other hand, deemed its prospects bright, and though obliged to paint many other types of work than portraits while at Newcastle, dominated the local portrait painting scene for almost a quarter of a century. His dominancy did not go unchallenged, however, several young Northumbrian artists returning to the area to paint portraits after periods in London; William Bewick, Andrew Morton, Thomas Sword Good and Edward Hastings, to name only a few.

With the foundation of the Northumberland Institution for the Promotion of the Fine Arts, at Newcastle, a shop window was suddenly provided for the work of local portrait painters, its first exhibition in 1822 including work by both professionals such as Ramsay, and amateurs like Barrodail Robert Dodd. By the time that the Institution was succeeded by the Northern Academy of Arts in 1828 portraits of local celebrities and men of wealth had become regular features of local exhibitions, many also making their appearance at the Royal Academy, and the Scottish Academy.

But while the demand for the services of portrait painters in Northumbria mushroomed in the first half of the 19th century, keeping pace with its growth in prosperity, it was only in the later years of this period that Ramsay, after exploring his chances of success in Edinburgh, decided he could afford to settle here. His move came late in his life, however, and following his death at Newcastle in 1854, portrait painting continued in the hands of artists trained in new ideas about art – those of the town's Government School of Design, under William Bell Scott. From this School in time emerged such portrait painters as Henry Hetherington Emmerson and Ralph Hedley, among many fine practitioners of the art.

The late 19th century saw the number of Northumbrian portrait painters reach its highest level, some settling elsewhere in Britain, or abroad, to further their careers; others, like Thomas Bowman Garvie, William Irving and John Hodgson Campbell, working on Tyneside until photography virtually extinguished the art. Of those who lived on to serve the much reduced demand for portrait painting of the present century none distinguished himself more than Royal Academician Richard Jack, of Sunderland, who died in 1952, while in John Thomas Young Gilroy, Northumbria can claim one of the most accomplished portrait painters working in Britain today.

Historical, religious and subject painters

Probably no British artist is better known for his work as an historical, religious and subject painter than John Martin, of Haydon Bridge. His work astonished his generation, was vilified in the half century following his death, and now stands higher in the esteem of art historians than ever before. But another such man was Sir Robert Ker Porter, of Durham, who, while his work has been consistently admired since his death, left so much of it that only today are we able to see that his accomplishment places him with Martin among the top half-dozen exponents of drama in art this country has produced.

Martin and Porter were Northumbria's most visibly successful painters of historical and religious themes; many other such artists from the area flourished less conspicuously. In the late 17th and early 18th centuries there was Thomas Whittle, who wandered the villages of South Northumberland painting altar pieces for local churches; in the late 18th century both William Bell and Robert Watson, of Newcastle, achieved success with their exhibits at the Royal Academy; in the early 19th century poor Luke Clennell went mad in his efforts to portray a particularly difficult subject, while later in this same century William Bell Scott completed his magnificent series of scenes from Northumbrian history for Wallington Hall, near Cambo, and Louisa Anne, Marchioness of Waterford, her biblical studies for the school she had built at FORD; later still, Frederic James Shields and Thomas Ralph Spence decorated churches throughout Britain, and John Charlton recorded some of the country's great state occasions.

The present century has witnessed a sharp decline in the volume of historical, religious and subject paintings produced by Northumbrian artists, although several have distinguished themselves as painters of contemporary history, particularly in the context of the First World War, of which John Charlton and Joseph Gray produced many moving images of land warfare, and Frank Henry Mason, and Frank Watson Wood, the war at sea. But in the more traditional line of history painting a rare opportunity was provided for several leading Northumbrian artists by Newcastle Corporation in 1930, to paint themes from the history of the area to decorate the Laing Art Gallery, NEWCASTLE, and this type of work was continued for many years subsequently by Byron Eric Dawson, Robert John Scott Bertram and Thomas William Pattison. In religious and subject painting, two of the area's most outstanding artists this century have been Ernest Procter and Frederick Appleyard, works by whom are now in several important public collections.

Sculptors, stonemasons and wood carvers

When George Bowes commissioned Christopher Richardson to sculpture a figure of "Liberty" for the park of his home at ROWLANDS GILL, near GATESHEAD, in the middle of the 17th century, Richardson had long been working outside Northumbria so little was the demand for his skills. The few commissions in sculpture there were in this period were handled by stonemasons – most sculptors, indeed, first serving an apprenticeship as such before branching out into statuary.

Not until the late 18th century, and with the expansion of many towns in Northumbria, was there enough work for the full-time sculptor, and then mainly on statues for the graves of the wealthy, and memorial tablets for churches. Among the earliest such professionals were Isaac Jopling, Junior, of GATESHEAD, John Priestman of DARLINGTON, and Christopher Tate of NEWCASTLE. All three were working at their respective places of birth when John Graham Lough, ambitious to develop the skills as sculptor which he had acquired while working for a stonemason near his home at GREENHEAD, near CONSETT, came to NEWCASTLE to work on carvings for the facade of the town's new Literary and Philosophical Society building, and he quickly divined that there would be little work of other kinds for him should he remain.

Indeed, there was little work for the professional sculptor in Northumbria throughout the 19th century, though very much for the gifted stonemason, and even more for the wood carver, in the train of the fashion for highly decorated furniture which blossomed in the 1840's, only to expire some twenty or so years later. In fact Northumbria produced some of Britain's most talented wood carvers in this period, Gerrard Robinson, for instance, becoming recognised internationally for the excellence of his work. The area also produced a school of wood carvers, based at ALNWICK, where John Brown, among several fine artists in wood worked on

the interior decoration of Alnwick Castle under the supervision of Bulletti of Florence.

As the fashion for large, ornate pieces of furniture died, the interest in the neo-Gothic style of architecture quickened, providing work for many wood carvers who would otherwise have become idle. Thomas Ralph Spence and Ralph Hedley – both gifted easel painters – did much distinguished work for the interiors of churches built in this style, others such as William Robinson and Henry Thomas Robinson carrying on this type of work until well into the present century.

With the demand for war memorial work which came in the late 19th and the early 20th centuries several Northumbrian sculptors were able to find full employment, and to produce accomplished work – Francis W. Doyle Jones and Thomas Eyre Macklin gracing many public places in the area with their works in bronze, and Master of Sculpture John W. M. Reid giving us at NEWCASTLE a rare example of his work in his St. George and the Dragon, for the grounds of St. Thomas, in the city's Haymarket.

Draughtsmen and engravers

Northumbria's draughtsmen and engravers deserve a volume of their own so numerous and talented were those who practised as such, and could claim the area as their birthplace. In many instances the draughtsman was his own engraver, as with Northumbria's earliest artists of note of both kinds – Francis Place and Thomas Bewick. In others the work produced by pencil, pen or burin was as much as the artist was able or interested to do, others more skilful than he taking responsibility for the complementary activity.

This division between the activity of drawing, and its translation into a means by which it could be reproduced, became greater as time progressed, until etching became popular in the middle of the 19th century. Then, as in the days of Place and Bewick, the two once more became popularly combined, and have remained so ever since.

Outstanding among Northumbria's draughtsmen were Place, John Wykeham Archer, George Balmer, John Wilson Carmichael, Thomas Miles Richardson, Senior, John Dobson, Joseph Crawhall, The Third, John Scott Bertram and Byron Dawson. Its distinguished engravers included, again Place and Bewick, various of Bewick's pupils, John Scott, William Chapman, William Collard, Joseph Crawhall, The Second, the Dalziels, George Fennel Robson and Andrew Reid. Its etchers, Place, William Nicholson, Thomas Hope McLachlan, Robert Spence, John Atkinson, Arthur Heslop and Joseph Henry Kirsop.

The area's greatest draughtsman it would be difficult to single out, but there is little doubt who was its greatest engraver. Bewick took wood engraving when it was at its lowest ebb in Britain, and through his skill and artistry made it the most popular means of printing illustrations and moveable type simultaneously for more than a hundred years . . .

The Artists

*ADAMS, Mrs. Laura Gladstone (née Clark, Laura Annie) (1887-1967)

Miniature painter. The daughter of Joseph Dixon Clark, Senior (q.v.), and sister of Joseph Dixon Clark, Junior (q.v.), and John Stewart Clark (q.v.), she was born at BLAYDON, near GATESHEAD, and later practised as a successful painter of portrait miniatures. She exhibited her work at the Royal Academy, the Paris Salon, the Walker Art Gallery, Liverpool, and at various other provincial galleries, including the Laing Art Gallery, NEWCASTLE, whose Artists of the Northern Counties exhibitions she contributed to for many years. Her miniature on ivory portraying herself and infant son Dennis Gladstone Adams, entitled: *The Green Necklace,#* was given the place of honour in the miniature section of the Royal Academy exhibition of 1923, between portraits of King George V and Queen Mary. She spent all of her life on Tyneside, marrying master photographer and inventor of the car windscreen wiper Gladstone Adams, and working as a colourist in her husband's studios at NEWCASTLE and WHITLEY BAY. In addition to being an accomplished artist she was a talented musician and composer; an operetta which she composed was recorded, Laura acting as pianist, Hubert Dunkerley of the Carl Rosa Opera Company providing the vocal accompaniment. She died at the Jubilee Infirmary, TYNEMOUTH, after living for many years at MONKSEATON.

ADAMSON, Charles Murray (1820-1894)

Amateur bird illustrator. He was born at NEWCASTLE, the son of solicitor, scholar, antiquary, author of the *Life of Camoens*, and translator of Portuguese sonnets, John Adamson. He also became a solicitor, later taking up the appointment of Clerk to the Commissioners of Taxes at NEWCASTLE, and developing in his spare time a keen interest in studying and sketching birds. He was

a founder member of the Tyneside Naturalists' Field Club, and became such an authority on birds that he was frequently consulted about the habits of different species, and had his observations published in the correspondence columns of *The Field*. He also published several books on bird life, among these: *Sundry Natural History Scraps*, 1879, *More Scraps About Birds*, 1880-81, *Studies of Birds*, 1881, and *Some More Illustrations of Wild Birds*, 1887, illustrating all save the first named publication himself. He died at NEWCASTLE. He was the younger brother of William Adamson (q.v.).

ADAMSON, William (1818-1892)

Amateur architectural and coastal painter in watercolour. He was born at NEWCASTLE, the son of solicitor, scholar, antiquary, author of the *Life of Camoens*, and translator of Portuguese sonnets, John Adamson. He

Laura Gladstone Adams: The Green Necklace. Miniature 3×5. *Mr. & Mrs. Dennis Gladstone Adams.*

1

succeeded to his father's business, and later took a keen interest in antiquarian and natural history matters, becoming a member of the Society of Antiquaries, NEWCASTLE, and the town's Literary and Philosophical Society, as well as a close friend of the brothers Albany Hancock (q.v.), and John Hancock (q.v.). On his retirement he settled at CULLERCOATS, a place for which he had formed an attachment earlier in his life, and while visiting which, according to William Weaver Tomlinson, in *Historical notes on Cullercoats, Whitley and Monkseaton*, 1893, he had "made, about 1839 and 1842, a number of water-colour sketches of the village, of Sparrow Hall, Garden House, Whitley Rocks etc., which, though crude in execution, enable us to form a good impression of the place as it was half a century ago". Tomlinson also noted that "Mr. Adamson compiled and edited 'Notices of the Services of the 27th Northumberland Light Infantry Militia', to which corps he was appointed senior captain and honorary major in 1877". He died at CULLERCOATS. He was the elder brother of Charles Murray Adamson (q.v.), and grandfather of Sophia Mildred Atkinson (q.v.).

ADYE, General Sir John (1819-1900)

Amateur landscape painter in watercolour; architectural draughtsman; illustrator. This artist was born at Sevenoaks, Kent, and enjoyed a distinguished military career, culminating in his promotion to General in 1884. He was a keen spare-time painter throughout his service, and in 1888 exhibited two of his works, described as portraying "fortresses", at the New Water Colour Society (later the Royal Institute of Painters in Water Colours). In 1889, his daughter Winifreda Adye, married William Henry Armstrong Fitzpatrick Watson-Armstrong, later First Baron Armstrong of Bamburgh and Cragside, and Adye, now having retired from the Army, joined his daughter at the Armstrong family home at Cragside, ROTHBURY. Here, and at BAMBURGH, he produced many watercolour and monochrome studies of local subjects, some of which are now on display at Cragside, courtesy of the National Trust. He also illustrated a volume of autobiographical reminiscences, and some of his Northumbrian work was sold in the form of prints. He died at ROTHBURY.

ALDERSON, Elizabeth Mary, and Dorothy Margaret (b. 1900)

Animal and landscape painters in oil and watercolour. These two sisters were born at NEASHAM, near DARLINGTON, descendants of William Etty, the Royal Academician, and in 1919 began to collaborate in the production of paintings, usually featuring horses. Their first commissions of importance came from Sir William Nussey, of Melmerby, Cumberland, and they have since received hundreds of other commissions, many as a consequence of their attendance of the Harewood Trials, and other sporting events. They have exhibited their work in London, and at various provincial exhibitions, including the Artists of the Northern Counties exhibitions at the Laing Art Gallery, NEWCASTLE, and for many years the Darlington Society of Arts exhibitions. Represented: Darlington A.G.; Middlesbrough A.G.

ALEXANDER, Joseph (fl. late 18th, early 19th cent.)

Landscape painter in oil; draughtsman. This artist practised at BERWICK-UPON-TWEED in the late 18th, and early 19th centuries. His *View of the Barracks and Parade from the Walls above the Cow Port*, and *East View of the Governor's House &c of Berwick*, were engraved by R. Scott, for *The History of Berwick upon Tweed*, by John Fuller, M.D. of BERWICK-UPON-TWEED, published in 1799. This work was reprinted by Frank Graham in 1973.

ALTSON, Daniel Meyer (1881-1965)

Portrait and decorative painter in oil; etcher. He was born at MIDDLESBROUGH, and studied at the National Gallery of Victoria, Melbourne, Australia, where he was awarded a scholarship at the age of sixteen. He later studied at the Ecole des Beaux Arts, and at Colarossi's, Paris, settling in London by 1925. He spent the remainder of his life in London, and exhibited his work at the Royal Academy, the Paris Salon, and in the provinces. He died in London. His brother ABBEY ALTSON, was a successful portrait painter and widely exhibited his work.

ANDERS, T. (fl. early 19th cent.)

Landscape painter in oil. This artist painted a landscape featuring salmon netters on the Tyne, entitled: *Close House, Wylam, from Ryton Willows*, in the 1830's. An example of his work was included in the "Exhibition of Paintings and other Works of Art", at the Town Hall, NEWCASTLE, in 1866, described as: *Landscape and figures*. He is believed to have been a native of NEWCASTLE.

ANDERSON, Charles Goldsborough (1865-1936)

Portrait painter in oil. Born at TYNEMOUTH, Anderson studied at the Royal Academy Schools before practising as a professional artist. He first began exhibiting his work by sending three portraits to the Royal Academy in 1888. He sent a further sixteen works to the Academy before his death in 1936, and also exhibited at the Royal Institute of Oil Painters, the Royal Society of British Artists, and at various London and provincial galleries. In 1901 and 1904 exhibitions of his work were held at the Grafton Galleries, London. One of his major works was the panel which he painted for the Royal Exchange, in 1910. He worked most of his life in London, but appears to have spent his final years at Rustington, Sussex. The Laing Art Gallery, NEWCASTLE, has his portrait of his wife, which was exhibited at the Royal Academy in 1900.

ANDERSON, John (b. 1778)

Wood engraver. The son of Dr. James Anderson of Edinburgh, editor of *The Bee*, and a customer of Thomas Bewick (q.v.), he was an apprentice of Bewick from 1792 until 1799. He engraved the illustrations for the first edition of Bloomfield's *The Farmer's Boy*, 1800, and Maurice's *Grove Hill*, 1799. After spending some time in London he is believed to have emigrated to South America, or Botany Bay, in 1803 or 4, and was lost to wood engraving.

2

ANDERSON, William S. "Jock" (1878-1929)
Amateur landscape, interior, flower and still-life painter in watercolour; etcher. Born at Kilsyth, near Glasgow, Anderson painted from his early childhood, though frequently admonished by his parents for wasting time on this practice. Early in his life, however, he had the good fortune to meet Alexander Roche, the Royal Scottish Academician, who took an interest in his work and encouraged him to develop it further. By the end of the First World War Anderson had moved to HEXHAM, and began to exhibit his work, showing examples at the Royal Scottish Academy, the Royal Scottish Society of Painters in Water Colours, the Goupil Gallery, London, and at the Artists of the Northern Counties exhibitions at the Laing Art Gallery, NEWCASTLE. He remained an exhibitor at NEWCASTLE all his life, in later years becoming a member of the city's Pen & Palette Club, and regularly showing at its exhibitions. His work encompassed a wide variety of subjects, but he was especially fond of interiors, and is said to have been greatly influenced by the work of the Dutch Masters in this field, particularly Vermeer of Delft. The Laing Art Gallery has his oils: *Lustre*, and *Still-life*.

ANDERTON, Mrs. Mary Margaret (née East) (d. 1931)
Landscape, architectural and flower painter in watercolour. She was the daughter of Canon East, sometime Vicar of St. Andrew's, NEWCASTLE, and trained as a teacher before becoming, in 1896, the first wife of Basil Anderton, City Librarian 1894-1935. While still unmarried she contributed two watercolour works to the Suffolk Street Gallery (1873/4) entitled: *A Dead Duck* and *Wild Flowers and Nest*. She followed this by showing one work at the Arts Association exhibition, NEWCASTLE, in 1878, and thereafter showed her work regularly at the Bewick Club in the city, almost from its foundation. Following her marriage she continued to exhibit at the Bewick Club, and in 1899 sent one work to the Society of Women Artists' exhibition in London. She later became a frequent exhibitor at the Artists of the Northern Counties exhibitions at the Laing Art Gallery, NEWCASTLE, showing a wide range of British and continental landscape and architectural subjects. She was a member of the Royal Drawing Society, and an occasional illustrator. Some of her work was reproduced in *Fragrance among old volumes*, written by her husband, and published by Kegan Paul in 1910.

ANDREWS, James (fl. 19th cent.)
Portrait and genre painter in oil. This artist practised at NEWCASTLE in the 1840's, listing himself in trade directories of this period, and exhibiting his work both in the town, and at Carlisle. He exhibited ten works at the North of England Society for the Promotion of the Fine Arts, NEWCASTLE, in 1842, which included portraits of the Rev. J. C. Bruce, and Mrs. Bruce. He exhibited at the Society's exhibition in the following year, and in 1846 sent two works to Carlisle Athenaeum: *The Little Shepherdess*, and *Portrait of Thomas H. Graham Esq., Edmond Castle*. He may have been the James Andrews who practised at Maidenhead in 1868, and sent a portrait entitled: *Ernest Andrews* to the Royal Academy in that year.

*ANGAS, George French (1822-1886)
Topographical and natural history illustrator; lithographer. He was born at NEWCASTLE, the eldest son of George Fife Angas, Tyneside mahogany and wood merchant, and later one of the founders of South

George French Angas:
The City of Adelaide from
the Torrens, *c.* 1844-5.
Watercolour 9¾×12. *Art
Gallery of South Australia.*

3

Australia. Following his general education his father placed him in a London office, but he left this employment after a year to study for a time under Waterhouse Hawkins, a natural history artist. At nineteen he toured the Mediterranean, and in 1842 published his first major illustrative work: *A Ramble in Malta and Sicily in the Autumn of 1841*. The illustrations took the form of lithographs drawn by him on the stone. In 1843 he exhibited for the first time, showing a drawing: *West Side of the Quadrangle of the British Museum*, at the Suffolk Street Gallery. Shortly after this he went to Australia, spending a few months there in 1844, before moving on to New Zealand. In the following year he returned to Australia for six months, during this period showing at Adelaide and Sydney, watercolours made during various trips into the Australian interior. After a tour of New South Wales he set sail for England via Cape Horn, stopping off briefly at Rio de Janeiro, where he made several watercolour drawings.

In 1847 he exhibited in London a number of the watercolours from his Sydney exhibition, and in this year published three of his most important works: *South Australia Illustrated*, *The New Zealanders Illustrated* (both large folios), and *Savage Life & Scenes in Australia & New Zealand*. Most of the lithographs for the first two of these works were executed, and subsequently coloured, by Angas himself, and he was also responsible for much of the texts. He next travelled in South Africa, and in 1849 published in London the third of his large folios of hand-coloured lithographs: *The Kaffirs Illustrated*. In the same year he also published *Description of the Balarossa Range*; this was illustrated with six hand-coloured plates drawn "from nature on the stone", by Angas. Some time later he was appointed naturalist to the Turko-Persian Boundary Commission, but caught a fever in Turkey and was invalided back to England. In 1849 he married, and in 1850 moved back to Australia, where in 1851 he published two works on the country's gold fields. In 1853 he was appointed secretary to The Australian Museum in Sydney, holding this position until 1860, when he retired to South Australia. In 1863 he left with his family for London, where he remained until his death in 1886. He exhibited on only one further occasion following his return to London, this being when he sent his *Constantinople looking over the Sea of Mamora*, to the Royal Academy in 1873. He published two further works after his return to Britain: *Australia, a Popular Account*, 1865, and *Polynesia, a Popular Description*, 1866. Represented: British Museum; The Art Gallery of South Australia, Adelaide; The Australian Museum, Sydney.

*APPLEYARD, Frederick, R. W. A. (1874-1963)
Landscape, genre and portrait painter in oil. Born at MIDDLESBROUGH, Appleyard studied art at Scarborough School of Art under Albert Strange. He later attended the Royal College of Art, and the Royal Academy Schools, at which latter he won the Creswick prize for landscape painting. He began exhibiting at the Royal Academy in 1900, showing: *The Incoming Tide*, and a wall decoration entitled: *Spring driving out Winter*. He left London in 1910 to work in South Africa, returning to the city in 1912, where he resumed exhibiting at the Royal Academy, and later began exhibiting at the Royal West of England Academy, and at various London and provincial galleries, including the Artists of the Northern Counties exhibitions of the Laing Art Gallery, NEWCASTLE. His work: *A Secret*,# was purchased for the Tate Gallery by the Chantrey Bequest, in 1915, and in 1926 he was elected a member of the Royal West of

Frederick Appleyard: A Secret. Oil 36×48½. *Tate Gallery*.

4

England Academy. He died at Alresford, Hampshire, where he had lived for many years. The Laing Art Gallery, NEWCASTLE, has his oils: *Portrait of a Lady*, and *Roses*.

ARCHER, John Wykeham (1806-1864)
Architectural draughtsman and painter in watercolour; animal and figure painter in oil; engraver; etcher. Born at NEWCASTLE, the son of a tradesman, Archer displayed a gift for drawing at an early age and was permitted by his family to enrol as a pupil of John Scott (q.v.), the well known London engraver. Returning to his birthplace in his late teens, he became a partner of William Collard (q.v.), producing in 1827 a series of large etchings of Fountains Abbey, Yorkshire, after John Wilson Carmichael (q.v.), and four plates for Mackenzie's *Durham*. Also while at NEWCASTLE, he began exhibiting at the town's Northern Academy, showing as his first work in 1828: *Quagger pursued by a Lion*. A short period in Edinburgh followed, during which he made a large collection of drawings of old buildings in the city, then he returned to London to develop his skill as an engraver with the engraver and publisher brothers Finden.

Archer spent the remaining thirty-odd years of his life mainly in London, and during this period became a regular exhibitor at the New Water Colour Society (later the Royal Institute of Painters in Water Colours), showing some sixty-three works from his election as member in 1842, until his death. He also in this period produced drawings of "ruins, curios, and other objects of antiquarian interest" on the estates in Northumbria of the Fourth Duke of Northumberland, and thirty-seven etchings for his folio volume: *Vestiges of Ancient London*, 1851. A few more works in oil were produced while he was in London, but he was principally interested in drawing, later colouring his work or reproducing it in the form of engravings or etchings. Among his engraving work after others were many plates for *Views on the Newcastle to Carlisle Railway*, engraved on steel after Carmichael, and wood engravings for the *Illustrated London News*, and Blackie's *History of England*. Following his death in London, a small volume of his poems was published by his son. Archer was a close friend of George Balmer (q.v.), during the latter's period in London, and contributed a lengthy tribute to the memory of his friend in the *Art Union*, October, 1846, a few months after Balmer's death. Represented: British Museum; Victoria and Albert Museum; Laing A. G., Newcastle.

ARMSTRONG, Charles, A.B.W.S. (b.1864)
Landscape painter in oil and watercolour. He was born at SUNDERLAND, and studied at the Royal College of Art, and at the Academie Julian, Paris, before serving at the former in the capacity of examiner for some eleven years. He later worked as Headmaster of Peterborough School of Art, and the City of London School of Art, painting in his spare time. He painted several works in Switzerland and Italy, but exhibited sparingly. He exhibited two works at the Royal Hibernian Academy in the period 1901-2, and various works at the British Water Colour Society (of which he was an associate), and at miscellaneous London and provincial galleries in subsequent years. He lived for a number of years at Ramsgate, Kent.

ARMSTRONG, George (fl. early 19th cent.)
Engraver. This engraver practised at NEWCASTLE in the early 19th century, where one of his most notable works was the engraving of the *Principal Eccentric Characters of Newcastle upon Tyne, c.* 1818, of Henry Perlee Parker (q.v.). It was published by Emerson Charnley of NEWCASTLE, who had the painting exhibited to obtain subscribers. The popularity of the subject is said to have contributed much to Parker's later success in the town. Armstrong sometimes collaborated in his engraving work with James Walker (q.v.), and, indeed, is believed to have been in business with Walker for several years.

ARMSTRONG, John (1772-1847)
Engraver. This engraver practised at NEWCASTLE in the early 19th century. He died at NEWCASTLE. Little is known of his work.

ARMSTRONG, John (fl. late 18th, early 19th cent.)
Wood engraver. Armstrong was the last apprentice of Thomas Bewick (q.v.), and probably carried out some of the less complicated wood engraving work in the Bewick workshop. He later practised as a wood engraver in London.

ARTHUR, Alice E. (c.1885- after 1940)
Landscape painter in watercolour. She was born at NEWCASTLE, the daughter of Samuel Arthur, chemist, and part owner of a firm of city druggists. Details of her early artistic education are not known, but by the age of about twenty she began exhibiting her work at the Artists of the Northern Counties exhibitions at the Laing Art Gallery, NEWCASTLE. She remained a regular exhibitor at these exhibitions for some thirty years, showing a wide range of English and continental landscape and architectural studies, frequently of high standard in execution. She died at NEWCASTLE. Her sister GERTRUDE ARTHUR was also artistically gifted and showed her work at the Artists of the Northern Counties exhibitions.

ASH, Donald (1890-1964)
Amateur landscape painter in oil and watercolour. Ash was born at Leicester, but moved with his family from Birmingham to GATESHEAD at the turn of the century. On leaving school he went into engineering, becoming first a locomotive engineer, later a manufacturers' agent. Throughout his career in engineering Ash was a keen spare-time painter of landscapes, exhibiting many examples of his work at the Artists of the Northern Counties exhibitions at the Laing Art Gallery, NEWCASTLE, and showing three examples of his work at the North East Coast Exhibition, Palace of Arts, in 1929. He shared an exhibition at the Shipley Art Gallery, GATESHEAD, with John Arthur Dees (q.v.), and contributed three examples of his work to this gallery's "Contemporary Artists of Durham County" exhibition in 1951, in connection with the Festival of Britain; these comprised two views of Durham, and one view of the

Cray Valley, Kent. Ash spent his early life on Tyneside at GATESHEAD and NEWCASTLE, later moving to MONKSEATON, where he died in 1964. He was the younger brother of John Willsteed Ash (q.v.) and Sidney Ash (q.v.). One of his spare-time interests was modelling sailing ships in bone, several examples of his work in this field finding their way into Tyneside public and private collections. Represented: Laing A. G., Newcastle.

ASH, John Willsteed (1872-1946)

Landscape painter in oil and watercolour; decorative artist; art teacher. He was born at Leicester, and by the time that he was in his twenties had become a regular exhibitor at the Royal Society of Artists, Birmingham. Following his move with his family from Birmingham to GATESHEAD, at the turn of the century, he maintained a studio at WYLAM for some years, but did not continue to exhibit his work. In the early twenties of the century he emigrated to New Zealand to take up the position of Head of the School of Art, Auckland, remaining there until his retirement. He died at Auckland. He was the elder brother of Sidney Ash (q.v.), and Donald Ash (q.v.).

*ASH, Sidney (1884-1959)

Amateur landscape painter in watercolour; architectural draughtsman. He was born at Leicester, the elder brother of Donald Ash (q.v.), and younger brother of John Willsteed Ash (q.v.). His family moved from Birmingham to GATESHEAD at the turn of the century, and here he embarked on a career in art by enrolling as a student at the School of Art, NEWCASTLE. At the outbreak of the First World War he enlisted in the Artists' Rifles, and on his demobilisation decided to

become an architect, qualifying for the profession at Armstrong College (later King's College; now Newcastle University). He practised for some years with Thomas Harrison (q.v.), as his partner, continuing on his own after Harrison's retirement from the practice. Ash remained interested in painting and drawing throughout his life, and exhibited his work at the Artists of the Northern Counties exhibitions at the Laing Art Gallery, NEWCASTLE, for many years, showing a wide variety of North Country landscapes. Much of his later work included bird and architectural studies, and he was also a skilled designer of jewellery. He lived at NEWCASTLE for much of his life, and was a member of the Newcastle Society of Artists, and the city's Pen & Palette Club. He died at NEWCASTLE.

*ATKIN, William Park "Gabriel" (1897-1937)

Landscape, architectural and figure painter in oil and watercolour; draughtsman; illustrator. Born at SOUTH SHIELDS, Atkin received his first artistic training at Armstrong College (later King's College; now Newcastle University), under Richard George Hatton (q.v.), and later at the Slade and in Paris. He later lived in London for many years, showing one work at the London Salon in 1919, and regularly sending work to the Artists of the Northern Counties exhibitions at the Laing Art Gallery, NEWCASTLE. Although mainly a painter of landscapes in watercolour, he was a capable artist in line and prepared many book illustrations. He died suddenly at NEWCASTLE after living for some ten years in the Jesmond area of the city, and remaining a regular exhibitor at the Artists of the Northern Counties exhibitions, mainly showing continental views. He was the husband of authoress Mary Butts, who also died in 1937. A major loan exhibition of his work was held at

Sidney Ash: On Boulmer Beach, Northumberland. Watercolour 10×13. *David Ash.*

6

the Laing Art Gallery in 1940, for which his friend of many years, Osbert, later Sir Osbert Sitwell, wrote the Foreword. Although christened William Park Atkin, he preferred to be called "Gabriel Atkin", and signed his work using this name. The Laing Art Gallery, NEWCASTLE, has a large collection of his watercolours.

ATKINSON, George Clayton (1808-1877)

Topographical draughtsman. He was born at NEWCASTLE, the eldest son of Matthew Atkinson of Carr's Hill, GATESHEAD. His youth was spent at the family home, and at the vicarage at OVINGHAM at which Thomas Bewick (q.v.), had been educated, and following his own education at St. Bees, Cumberland, and Charterhouse, he formed a close friendship with the great wood engraver. His association with Bewick led to a deep interest in natural history, and the encouragement to sketch birds and their habitats. Following Bewick's death in 1828, Atkinson divided his time between his natural history studies and the business to which his father had introduced him in 1831. In the year in which he joined this business – the Tyne Iron Company, at LEMINGTON, near NEWCASTLE – he undertook the first of three major natural history expeditions, visiting the Hebrides and St. Kilda with his two brothers, and artist Edward Train (q.v.). On his subsequent expeditions, to the Shetlands in 1832, and Iceland in 1833, he travelled without the company of an artist to sketch to his request, and made his own sketches. These were later worked up into watercolours by Thomas Miles Richardson, Senior (q.v.), for the purpose of illustrating Atkinson's manuscript work on his discoveries. Following his expeditions Atkinson lived in the West Denton area of NEWCASTLE for some years, then lived at WYLAM for some twenty years. His final years were spent at NEWCASTLE, where he died in 1877. He is mainly remembered for being one of the earliest biographers of Bewick, his *Sketch of the Life and Work of the late Thomas Bewick*, appearing in 1831. His only son Matthew Hutton Atkinson (q.v.), and granddaughter, Sophia Mildred Atkinson (q.v.), were both talented artists.

ATKINSON, James (fl. 18th cent.)

Portrait painter. William Hylton Dyer Longstaffe (q.v.), in his *History and Antiquities of the Parish of Darlington*, published in 1854, records Atkinson as ". . . a young house-painter, the son of a woolcomber . . ." who ". . . painted portraits, strong likenesses, and at London published a series of letters on art addressed to Barry". Longstaffe also tells us that a "gentleman found him the means to become a surgeon, and secured him a post in India, where by the aid of his taste for the higher accomplishments in life he pushed his fortune, and sent his aged parents £200 a year for their lives".

*ATKINSON, John (1863-1924)

Animal and landscape painter in oil, tempera and watercolour; etcher; illustrator; inn-sign designer. Atkinson was born at NEWCASTLE, the son of a hostelry owner and Freeman of the town, and it was not until he had spent many years as a telegraphist, draughtsman,

William Park Atkin: Venice in August. Watercolour 11½×9. *Private collection.*

and finally secretary to industrialist, art patron and father of Charles William Mitchell (q.v.), Dr. Charles Mitchell, that he turned to a full-time career in art. Meanwhile, to advance his abilities as an artist, he had attended classes at the School of Art, NEWCASTLE, and is said to have studied briefly under Wilson Hepple (q.v.). In 1900, however, and after establishing something of a reputation for his work by frequently exhibiting at the Bewick Club, NEWCASTLE, he decided to become a full-time professional artist, and moved to an area which had increasingly attracted him in the immediately preceding years, North Yorkshire. From Sleights, North Yorkshire, in 1901, he sent his first work for exhibition to the Royal Academy: *A Winter's Morning*, subsequently deciding to make his home at nearby Glaisdale. Here he lived with his family until just before the First World War, forming many friendships with artists then painting in the area around Staithes, and becoming considerably influenced in his style of painting, particularly in oil. On returning to NEWCASTLE about 1914 he took a studio in the city, and practised there almost uninterruptedly until his death ten years later.

Atkinson's work both before and after turning professional was mainly animal portraiture, with a particular emphasis on horses (he was a lifelong supporter of the R.S.P.C.A., and supplied the Society with many illustrations for its publicity purposes). He also painted many landscapes, however, showing a special fondness for haymaking,# hunting, and other countryside activities. In addition to showing his work at the Royal

Academy, Atkinson also exhibited at the Royal Scottish Academy, the Royal Institute of Painters in Water Colours, and at the exhibitions of several provincial galleries, including the Laing Art Gallery, NEWCASTLE, whose Artists of the Northern Counties exhibitions he contributed to from their foundation, until his death. He also exhibited with the Yorkshire Union of Artists, receiving a Bronze Medal in 1915 for his watercolour work. He was for some time an art teacher at Ushaw College, near DURHAM, and the Grammar School, at MORPETH. During the First World War years he also worked on the art staff of the *Newcastle Chronicle*. One of his most interesting commissions as a professional artist was that of painting the King's Drummer Horse, in 1911. After the War he increasingly turned to designing inn-signs, earning praise from the Duke of York for those which he designed for villages along the Thames. He was a member of the Bewick Club almost from its foundation, and was also a member of the Newcastle Society of Artists, and the Pen & Palette Club, NEWCASTLE. He died at GATESHEAD, and was buried in the town's Saltwell Cemetery. A major exhibition of his work was held at the Moss Galleries, HEXHAM, in 1981. Represented: Laing A.G., Newcastle; Middlesbrough A.G.; Pannett A.G., Whitby; Shipley A.G., Gateshead; South Shields Museum & A.G.; Sunderland A.G.

*ATKINSON, Joseph (1776-1816)

Animal and landscape painter in oil and watercolour. Born at NEWCASTLE, Atkinson is principally known for his *View of Tanfield Arch*, near GATESHEAD, reproduced as an aquatint engraving by J. C. Stadler in 1804.# The subject was commissioned by his patron, Sir Matthew White Ridley, of Blagdon Hall, near SEATON BURN. Thomas Oliver (q.v.), in his *A New Picture of Newcastle upon Tyne*, 1831, states that Atkinson "excelled in animal painting". Robert Robinson, in his *Thomas Bewick – his life and times*, 1887, notes that Thomas Bewick (q.v.), was responsible for two engravings on wood, and an etching on copper, after Atkinson's paintings, for *A Short Treatise on that Useful Invention called the Sportsman's Friend, or the Farmer's Footman . . .*, 1801, by Henry Utrick Reay of KILLINGWORTH, near NEWCASTLE. According to T. Hugo, in *The Bewick Collector*, 1866-68, Reay was a "patron of the famous Stubbs, and had several horses painted by him . . . The black pony, the bay and the white were all painted by Stubbs and from these paintings our 'Newcastle Atkinson' reduced the drawings for the engraver." The Science Museum, London, has Atkinson's watercolour of Tanfield Arch from which Stadler's aquatint was derived, and his oil of the same subject was on the London art market in 1964. He was possibly the "J. Atkinson, Painter", who contributed one work to the Royal Academy in 1796, entitled: *Portraits of a Horse and a Dog*.

ATKINSON, Matthew Hutton (1843-1917)

Amateur landscape and figure painter in watercolour. The only son of George Clayton Atkinson (q.v.), he was born at NEWCASTLE, and after his education remained in business most of his life, only painting in his spare time. He served an apprenticeship as an engineer with Armstrong Mitchell & Co., and in his twenties went to Egypt as a torpedo instructor to the Egyptian Government. From 1891 until his death he was a director of the Newcastle & Gateshead Water Company, and took a keen interest in local affairs, but for some years prior to his death lived in virtual retirement,

John Atkinson: Hay-time in a Yorkshire Dale, 1911. Watercolour 22×30½. *Moss Galleries.*

(Right) Joseph Atkinson: View of Tanfield Arch. Aquatint 16×24. *Private collection.*
(Below) Sophia Mildred Atkinson: Spring in the Rockies. Watercolour 14×10. *Private collection.*

occasionally occupying himself by painting in watercolour. A considerable body of his work survives in the hands of his family, including examples of the watercolours which he produced while working in Egypt. He died at NEWCASTLE. His daughter, Sophia Mildred Atkinson (q.v.), was a talented painter in watercolour.

*ATKINSON, Sophia Mildred (1876-1972)
Landscape painter in oil and watercolour; art teacher. She was born at NEWCASTLE, the daughter of Matthew Hutton Atkinson (q.v.), and granddaughter of George Clayton Atkinson (q.v.), and William Adamson (q.v.). Following her general education she studied art under Richard George Hatton (q.v.), at Armstrong College (later King's College; now Newcastle University), and later at Bushey, Herts, at the school of Sir Hubert Von Herkomer. After her training under Herkomer she practised as an artist at NEWCASTLE, and in 1905 showed one work at the Royal Institute of Painters in Water Colours, and three works at the Artists of the Northern Counties exhibition at the Laing Art Gallery, NEWCASTLE. She remained a regular exhibitor at the Laing Art Gallery until the First World War, in the middle of this period showing several oils and watercolours of the Island of Corfu, on which she had spent a year preparing notes and illustrations for her book: *An Artist on Corfu*, published 1911. Between the outbreak of the War, and making her first trip to Canada in 1925, she painted in India, Denmark, England, Bavaria, the Southern Tyrol, and the Mission Country of California, U.S.A., also enjoying a special one-man exhibition at the Hatton Gallery, at NEWCASTLE, in 1924.

In Canada in 1925 she toured widely throughout British Columbia, taking a special interest in Rocky Mountain scenery,# and in the following year staged her first exhibition in that country, at Montreal. A

period of talks and exhibitions in Canada followed, after which she returned to England and was given a special section for her Canadian work at the North East Coast Exhibition, Palace of Arts, in 1929. She returned

9

to Canada about 1932, and settling at Victoria, British Columbia, painted widely in the area under the sponsorship of the Canadian Pacific Railway. On leaving Canada some years later, she lived at Edinburgh until 1948, continuing to paint throughout her sojourn in the Scottish capital, and producing many studies of historic buildings and gardens. On returning to Canada in 1948 she settled at Revelstoke, British Columbia, where she lived for twenty years, teaching art, lecturing, painting, and running the Revelstoke Art Club, which she had founded. In this period, exhibitions of her work were held at Vernon, British Columbia, in 1951 and at the Hatton Gallery, NEWCASTLE, in 1953. In 1967 she left Revelstoke and moved back to Edinburgh, where she died five years later. Her work is highly regarded in Canada; several examples have been included in the National Archives.

ATKINSON, William (1773-1839)

Architectural draughtsman. Born at BISHOP AUCKLAND, Atkinson began life as a carpenter, but with the assistance of Bishop Barrington was sent to London, and became an apprentice of James Wyatt, the architect and Royal Academician. He entered the Royal Academy Schools, and first began to exhibit his architectural drawings in 1796, when he sent three designs for buildings to the Royal Academy. He remained an occasional exhibitor at the Academy until 1811, showing designs for a variety of buildings ranging from monuments to mansions. In 1797 he gained the Academy gold medal for his designs for a Court of Justice. He was "both in theory and practice a clever architect", it has been remarked, and held the office of architect to the Board of Ordnance; he was also the inventor of "Atkinson's Cement", and in 1805 published: *Views of Picturesque Cottages*. He died at Cobham, Surrey.

BACKHOUSE, Edward (1808-1879)

Amateur landscape painter in watercolour. He was born at DARLINGTON, but about 1816 his parents moved to SUNDERLAND to establish a branch of the Backhouse

John Bailey: Newcastle in 1781. Engraving after sketch by the artist, in Brand's "History and Antiquities of Newcastle", 1789.

banking firm. Here he later became a leading public figure, well known for his philanthropic work and wide cultural interests. He travelled extensively throughout his life, combining an interest in landscape painting with natural history. On his death at Hastings a large collection of shells and butterflies which he had assembled on these travels was bequeathed to Sunderland Museum. His home at SUNDERLAND later became the premises of Sunderland School of Art & Design. Sunderland Art Gallery has his watercolour: *Vevey, Lake Geneva*.

BACKHOUSE, James Edward (1845-1897)

Amateur landscape painter in watercolour. He was born at SUNDERLAND, and educated at University College, London, before entering the family banking business in the town. In 1869 he became a partner in the firm and moved from SUNDERLAND to CROFT, near DARLINGTON, living with his uncle until his own future home, Hurworth Grange, was completed. Backhouse was a keen spare-time painter from his youth and in later years frequently visited Italy, where he had a villa, to paint the local scenery. He exhibited his work at the New Water Colour Society (later the Royal Institute of Painters in Water Colours), from 1886 until 1891. He died at Hurworth Grange, DARLINGTON. Represented: Darlington A.G.

*BAILEY, John (1750-1819)

Topographical painter in watercolour; draughtsman; engraver. Bailey was born at BOWES, and after showing a considerable talent for drawing as a child was placed as a pupil of the engraver, Godfrey. On leaving Godfrey he went to live with his uncle by marriage, George Dixon, of COCKFIELD, near BARNARD CASTLE, acting as tutor to Dixon's children, and drawing and engraving in his spare time. His next employment was as a teacher at WITTON-LE-WEAR, near BISHOP AUCKLAND, but following his marriage to a local landowner's daughter he obtained a position as land agent to Lord Tankerville, at CHILLINGHAM, and here remained employed for most of his life. His interest in drawing led to his production of several topographical works, notable among which is his view of NEWCASTLE, for Brand's *History and Antiquities of Newcastle*, 1789,# and the various views in Northumbria which he drew and engraved for Hutchinson's histories of the counties of Northumberland and Durham.

In his later life Bailey became increasingly interested in agricultural matters, and published several works on this subject with George Culley, of Fowberry Tower, near BELFORD. Among these joint works was their *General View of the Agriculture of the County of Northumberland*, 1794, which contained several drawings of animals by Bailey, engraved by another hand. His most ambitious of these drawings portrayed the wild cattle of CHILLINGHAM, in a woodland setting. Other drawings were of agricultural implements, possibly engraved by Bailey. He also illustrated and published several works independently. Bailey, George Culley, and his brother Matthew Culley, were friends of Thomas Bewick (q.v.), and Bewick refers to all three in his autobiographical *Memoir*, published posthumously in 1862. In addition to acting as land agent to Lord Tankerville, Bailey also farmed on his own account, and was for some years connected with a bank at BERWICK-UPON-TWEED. He died at GREAT BAVINGTON, near CAMBO. The Bowes Museum, BARNARD CASTLE, has his watercolour study of Egglestone Abbey.

BAILLIE, Edward (d.1856)

Stained glass designer; draughtsman. He was born at GATESHEAD, but appears to have spent most of his life living and working in the South of England. He exhibited at the International Exhibition of 1851 his *Shakespeare reading a play to Queen Elizabeth*. Nothing more is known of him except that he died in London in 1856.

*BAKER, William (1863-1937)

Landscape painter in oil and watercolour; draughtsman; illustrator. Baker was born at SOUTH SHIELDS, and worked in his father's clothing shop before deciding at the age of twenty to become a professional artist. Within a short time he had established a ready market for his work and was giving lessons in his studio. He travelled widely throughout Scotland and the English Lake District for his landscape subjects, but the bulk of his work portrayed scenes around SOUTH SHIELDS, in particular the nearby village of CLEADON, at which he died in 1937. His snow scenes of this village are especially admired for their delicacy and luminosity.# He occasionally produced illustrations for local publications, an example being the 1895 edition of *The Banks O' Tyne: A Christmas Annual*, published by the *South Shields Daily Gazette*. Several of his relatives were also artistically gifted.

*BALMER, George (1805-1846)

Landscape and coastal painter in oil and watercolour. Balmer was born at NORTH SHIELDS the son of a house painter, and deciding to follow his father's trade, had himself bound as an apprentice to Thomas Coulson (q.v.), who had established a thriving decorating business at Edinburgh. Once settled in the Scottish capital he soon became acquainted with the work of fellow Northumbrian, and Coulson apprentice, John Wilson Ewbank (q.v.), and inspired to try his own hand as a professional artist, returned to NORTH SHIELDS. In 1826 he sent his first work for exhibition from his home town; a *View of North Shields*, to the Northumberland Institution for the Promotion of the Fine Arts, NEWCASTLE. He again exhibited at the Institution in the following

William Baker: Winter at Cleadon. Watercolour 18×24. *Dean Gallery.*

year, and showed no fewer than seven works at the first exhibition of the town's newly opened Northern Academy, in 1828. He continued to exhibit at NEWCASTLE for several years, and in the same period sent his first work for exhibition to the British Institution (1830): *Fishing Lodge near Inch Islay on the Tay – moonlight*, and several works to the Carlisle Academy. In 1831 he moved to NEWCASTLE, and in this year showed in the town one of his best known works: *The Juicy Tree Bit*, and collaborated in the production of another: *The Heroic Exploit of Lord Collingwood, when Captain of the Excellent at the Battle of Trafalgar*, with his close friend John Wilson Carmichael (q.v.).

As far as can be determined Balmer remained at NEWCASTLE until late in 1833, when he decided to move to London. In 1834 he sent his first work for exhibition at the Suffolk Street Gallery, and also exhibited at NEWCASTLE. He then set off on a tour of Holland, thereafter proceeding up the Rhine, and travelling through Switzerland, making several studies of the Alps en route. Next he went to Paris, where he spent several months studying at the Louvre, and copied the works of Cuyp, Claude Lorraine, Paul Potter and Ruisdael. Back in London by 1835 he sought out his friend and fellow Northumbrian artist, John Wykeham Archer (q.v.), and announced his intention of practising in the capital. He remained in London until 1842, during which period he continued to exhibit at the British Institution and the Suffolk Street Gallery, showing continental and Northumbrian scenes; among the former: *Scene near Dortrecht*, and *The Haarlem Mere – moonlight*, and the latter: *Entrance to the Port of Sunderland*, and *The Salmon Leap at Bywell*. Several of these works were bought by wealthy collectors, notably Harrison of Liverpool. In 1836 Balmer suggested to the engraver and publisher brothers Finden, a book on the *Ports and Harbours of Great Britain*. They accepted his proposal, and many of his views of such places along the Northumbrian coastline appeared in a volume published in 1842. A short while after its publication Balmer inherited some property near GATESHEAD, and retired there without, it seems, exhibiting his work again. He died at BENSHAM (now part of GATESHEAD), and was buried in the old cemetery, Jesmond, NEWCASTLE. Represented: Victoria and Albert Museum; Grace Darling Museum, Bamburgh; Laing A.G., Newcastle; North Tyneside Public Libraries; Shipley A.G., Gateshead; Sunderland A.G.

BARBER, Joseph, Senior (1706-1781)
Engraver. He was born near Dublin, but by 1738 had moved to NEWCASTLE, where in 1740 he was advertising the first copperplate print "ever performed" in the town. He opened the first known circulating library at NEWCASTLE, before 1746, and his business according to local directories eventually grew to embrace not only engraving, and running a circulating library, but book, stationery, print, drug, and optical instrument selling. He was in partnership with his son Martin *c.* 1778, until his death, but the latter does not appear to have been interested in engraving. Barber died at NEWCASTLE, and was buried at the North East corner of the churchyard of St. Nicholas Cathedral, where his tombstone still

George Balmer: Grey Horse Inn, Quayside, Newcastle. Oil 33½×24½. *Tyne & Wear County Council Museums, Laing Art Gallery.*

rests today within a short distance of his workshop site from 1754-1781, Amen Corner. The proximity of this workshop to that of Ralph Beilby (q.v.), William Beilby (q.v.), and later Thomas Bewick (q.v.), led to some familiarity between Barber and these men, Bewick engraving a bookplate for him which has been described as "of great artistic beauty not exceeded as a work of art by anything he (Bewick) afterwards produced of the same kind." Barber's eldest son, Joseph Barber, Junior (q.v.), was a talented landscape painter in watercolour, and drawing master, and his grandson, Stephen Humble, 1793-1853 (q.v.), was an artist of considerable ability.

BARBER, Joseph, Junior (1757-1811)
Landscape painter in watercolour; drawing master. He was born at NEWCASTLE, the son of Joseph Barber, Senior (q.v.), engraver, bookseller, etc. After receiving some tuition in drawing at NEWCASTLE, possibly from William Beilby (q.v.), whose place of work was close to that of his father when Barber was a youth, he settled as a drawing master at Birmingham. Here he taught at the Grammar School, and achieved a considerable reputation for his instructive capabilities, his best known pupil being David Cox. Barber's work was little known until a group of twenty of his watercolours appeared at Sotheby's in February, 1934. Martin Hardie made a study of these works, and says of them in his *Water Colour Painting in Britain*, Vol. III p. 242: "He has a kinship with John Laporte in colour, and William Payne

in his handling of trees and foreground". He also describes him as a "studied and versatile painter". He died at Birmingham. His sons CHARLES VINCENT BARBER (1784-1854), and JOSEPH VINCENT BARBER (1788-1838), were talented painters in watercolour. Represented: British Museum; Victoria and Albert Museum; Birmingham City A.G.; Dudley A.G.; Newport A.G.; Ulster Museum, Belfast.

BARKAS, Charles Edward (c.1856-1906)

Amateur draughtsman. He was the son of Thomas Pallister Barkas, bookseller, and later proprietor with Thomas Hall Tweedy (q.v.), of the Central Exchange News Room, NEWCASTLE. In his early years Charles Edward was associated with the art gallery which his father and Tweedy developed from their establishment, eventually becoming lessee of the gallery, and taking a keen spare-time interest in sketching. Many of his sketches of this period were later worked-up into illustrations for the *Newcastle Weekly Chronicle*, by George Hall (q.v.), with the credit "From a sketch by C. E. Barkas". He later went into the cycle business, then became an estate agent. He died at NEWCASTLE.

BARKAS, Henry Dawson, A.R.C.A. (1858-1924)

Landscape and architectural painter in watercolour; art teacher. Barkas was born at GATESHEAD, his family shortly after removing to St. Helier in the Channel Islands. He was educated at Jersey, and later at Granville, France, following which he entered Bath School of Art. At Bath he obtained a scholarship to the Royal College of Art, and on leaving the College he taught at Warrington and Bradford Schools of Art. He later settled at Reading, Berkshire, where he served as Headmaster of the School of Art & Science, before founding another school of art in the town about 1894. This school functioned until his death. Barkas is said to have spent all his summer vacations sketching, and while most of the resultant watercolours show a marked preoccupation with natural atmospheric effects he also produced many detailed architectural studies. He exhibited his work at the Royal Academy, the Fine Art Society, London (enjoying a special one-man exhibition in 1912 entitled: "English Pleasure Resorts"), the Royal Institute of Painters in Water Colours, and at various London and provincial art galleries. In 1892 he published: *Art Students' Pocket Manual*. He was an associate of the Royal College of Art. His brother HERBERT ATKINSON BARKAS (1870-1939), was also a professional artist and art teacher. Represented: Reading A.G.

BATY, Eleanor (c.1900 – after 1938)

Miniature painter. This artist practised at NEWCASTLE in the early 20th century. She first exhibited her work publicly when she sent *Joan* and *Winsome*, to the Royal Academy in 1919, also showing these two works, and a third, *Baby Belle*, at the Artists of the Northern Counties exhibition at the Laing Art Gallery, NEWCASTLE, in that year. She continued to exhibit at the Royal Academy and the Artists of the Northern Counties exhibitions until 1924. Between 1919 and 1938 she also showed

work at the Royal Miniature Society, and the Walker Art Gallery, Liverpool. Several of her exhibits portrayed members of the Royal Family, and other prominent public figures.

BEILBY, Mary (1750-1798)

Enamel painter on glass. She was born at DURHAM, the daughter of William Beilby, the silversmith and jeweller. Following the failure of her father's business at DURHAM she moved with her family first to GATESHEAD, later to NEWCASTLE, where she was instructed in enamel painting on glass by her brother William Beilby (q.v.). She later assisted her brother in much of his work in enamel painting on glass, principally handling the simpler styles of decoration. Thomas Bewick (q.v.), during his apprenticeship to another of her brothers, Ralph Beilby (q.v.), formed a strong emotional attachment to Mary, and would have married her had her family not discouraged his interest in the girl. Some time following her departure from NEWCASTLE for London with William in 1778, she suffered a paralytic stroke. About 1789 she moved with William and his wife to East Ceres, Fife, Scotland, to live on the estate owned by the uncle of her sister-in-law, dying there in 1798. The work of William and Mary Beilby in glass enamelling has been superbly documented and illustrated by James Rush, in his *The Ingenious Beilbys*, 1973.

BEILBY, Ralph (1743-1817)

Engraver; draughtsman. He was born at DURHAM, the son of William Beilby the silversmith and jeweller, and joined his father's business on leaving school. When the business failed he moved with his family to GATESHEAD, where he learnt seal-cutting under his brother Richard before following this trade himself at NEWCASTLE by 1760, in premises shared with his elder brother William Beilby (q.v.), and sister Mary Beilby (q.v.). In addition to seal-cutting he was soon handling many other tasks of the jobbing engraver, including engraving for reproduction. Indeed, as Beilby's apprentice from 1767, Thomas Bewick (q.v.), records in his *Memoir*, published posthumously in 1862: "At this time a fortunate circumstance, for my future master, happened which made an opening for him to get forward in his business unopposed by anyone in Newcastle – An Engraver of the name of Jameson, who had the whole stroke of the business in Newcastle to himself, having been detected in committing a Forgery upon the old Bank, was tried for the crime, but his life was saved by the perjury of a Mrs. Gray . . . and Jameson left the town". According to Bewick, Beilby's engraving in the reproductive field included "writing engraving of Bills, bank notes, Bills of Parcels, shop bills & cards – these last with Gent[s] Arms for their books . . ." and this ". . . he executed as well as most of the Engravers of the time . . ."

Towards the close of Bewick's apprenticeship, however, Beilby began to aspire to more ambitious work in reproductive engraving, and left for London "for the purpose of taking lessons in etching & engraving & practising upon large copperplates". Beilby found little demand for his new found skills immediately upon his return to NEWCASTLE, but this situation evidently changed in the late 1780's when the Rev. John Brand (for whom, as early as *c*.1770, he had engraved a vignette bookplate), commissioned him to engrave plates for *History and Antiquities of Newcastle*, published in 1789. Notable among Beilby's work for this book by Brand is his *Thornton's Monument, All Saints' Church, Newcastle*, in which his ability as an heraldic draughtsman and engraver are seen to perfection. He later handled other engraving for reproduction, but this mainly related to maps and plans. In 1798 he retired from the business in which he had been partner with Bewick from 1777, and joined Langlands & Robertson in establishing a watch-glass manufactory in the town. He retired from this business some time after 1806, and died at NEWCASTLE in 1817. Bewick's *Memoir* contains much interesting information about Beilby as artist and man, which despite the acrimony in which they eventually ended their partnership in 1798, may be taken to be largely objective and fair.

BEILBY, Thomas (d.1826)

Drawing master. He was born at DURHAM, the son of William Beilby, the silversmith and jeweller, and joined the family in their move to GATESHEAD, and thence to NEWCASTLE, following the failure of his father's business at DURHAM. At NEWCASTLE he received tuition from his brother William Beilby (q.v.) in glass enamelling and painting in the premises shared by William, his brother Ralph Beilby (q.v.), and sister Mary Beilby (q.v.). Although evidently trained in the skills which were later to make William and Mary famous, Thomas appears to have preferred giving instruction in drawing, to enamelling glass, and later obtained a position as drawing master at Grimshaw's Academy, Leeds. He died at Leeds in 1826.

*BEILBY, William (1740-1819)

Enamel painter on glass; landscape painter in watercolour; draughtsman; drawing master. He was born at DURHAM, the eldest son of William Beilby, the silversmith and jeweller. As a young man he was apprenticed at Bilston, Birmingham, where he learnt the art of enamelling on snuff box lids. When his father's business failed at DURHAM, the family moved first to GATESHEAD, later to NEWCASTLE, where William and his younger brother Ralph Beilby (q.v.), set up in business as engravers, etc., about 1760. Here, within a short period, William cultivated a demand for his skills as an enamel painter on glass, also involving his sister Mary Beilby (q.v.), in this type of work. The work of William and Mary Beilby in glass enamelling has been superbly documented and illustrated by James Rush, in his *The Ingenious Beilbys*, 1973. Less well known, however, are William's capabilities as a landscape painter in watercolour, draughtsman and drawing master. He would appear to have been one of the first drawing masters to advertise his services at NEWCASTLE, *Whitehead's First Newcastle Directory*, 1778, showing him with an address at Northumberland Street. This skill as a draughtsman also found expression in the production of several topographical and other drawings, amongst these the drawing of wagonways at NEWCASTLE, which he executed for Jean Morand's *L'Art d'exploiter les Mines de Charbon de Terre* (1768-79), and possibly his best known work: *The Assembly House*, which was reproduced in Brand's *History and Antiquities of Newcastle*, 1789.

Beilby's skill in drawing undoubtedly contributed greatly to his singular achievements as an enamel painter on glass, but of equal significance is the fact that he was also an able watercolourist, who when he later moved to London, exhibited his work at both the Royal

William Beilby: Landscape with classical ruins and shepherds, 1774. Watercolour 8¾×12¼. *Victoria and Albert Museum.*

14

Stuart Henry Bell: Sunderland Harbour. Oil 16×30. *Tyne & Wear County Council Museums, Sunderland Art Gallery & Museum.*

Academy, and the Society of Artists, though at the former he was treated as an Honorary Exhibitor, and at the latter appears to have shown mainly drawings. Beilby decided to leave NEWCASTLE about 1778, and settling in London established a school called "Battersea Academy". About five or six years after marrying a London girl called Ellen Turton, however, he moved from London with his wife, and sister Mary, to his wife's uncle's estate at East Ceres, Fife, Scotland. Here Beilby occupied himself with agricultural improvements to the estate until his wife inherited a fortune from an aunt, and he moved with his family to Hull. He spent his final years at Hull, dying there in 1819. Many examples of his work in watercolour were included in a special commemorative exhibition at the Laing Art Gallery, NEWCASTLE, in 1980: "The Decorated Glasses of William and Mary Beilby". His watercolour: *Italian Landscape with Classical Ruins and Shepherds*, 1774, is in the collection of the Victoria and Albert Museum.# His brother, Thomas Beilby (q.v.), was also a talented artist.

BELL, John (fl. late 18th, early 19th cent.)
Portrait painter in oil. Born on Tyneside, the son of Joseph Bell (q.v.), he was possibly taught by his father before practising as a portrait painter in NEWCASTLE. He was a playmate in his youth of the children of Thomas Bewick (q.v.): Jane Bewick (q.v.), Robert Elliot Bewick (q.v.), Elizabeth Bewick, and Isabella Bewick, his portrait of Bewick's son as a boy being one of the few examples of his work which have survived. This portrait is in the possession of the Natural History Society of Northumbria, NEWCASTLE, and shows Robert Elliot playing the Northumbrian pipes. Commenting on this work, Bewick's daughter Jane wrote: "John Bell . . . painted a portrait of my Brother when a boy – playing on the North^d. pipes, the likeness very good". She also wrote that Bell was "– Very dissipated – died in his prime". A "John Bell" is listed in the *Newcastle*

Directory, for 1811, under portrait and landscape painters, who may have been this artist.

BELL, Joseph (1746-1806)
Portrait painter in oil. Bell was born on Tyneside, and became a close friend of Thomas Bewick (q.v.), in consequence of their mutual interest in art. Bewick refers to Bell in his autobiographical *Memoir*, as "Joseph Bell, Painter, he also displayed considerable abilities as a painter, poet, & a Man of talents in other respects – but with keeping much company he became also much dissipated – he died 26 April 1806 aged 60 & was buried at St. Andrews".‡ Bewick's daughter, Jane Bewick (q.v.), wrote of Bell: ". . . painter & decorator – He painted portraits occasionally – & was a talented but somewhat dissipated man . . . He painted a portrait of my Father – he could not please himself with it and threw down the brush with an oath saying: 'nobody can paint you' ". He was the father of John Bell (q.v.), and is described by Robert Robinson in his *Thomas Bewick – his life and times*, 1887, as a "portrait painter of some ability" who lived in the town's "High Bridge", in a house "decorated with great taste". It is evident from directories of NEWCASTLE that Bell was a dealer in colours, in addition to practising as a "painter in general". He died at NEWCASTLE.

‡ *See p. 113, "A Memoir of Thomas Bewick, Written by Himself", edited and with an introduction by Iain Bain, Oxford University Press, 1975.*

*BELL, Stuart Henry (1823-1896)
Marine and scenic painter in oil. Born at NEWCASTLE of a family which could trace its descent from the Royal Stuarts of Scotland, Bell became connected with Tyneside theatres in his boyhood, and is said to have become a scene painter at an early age. His first commission was to paint scenery for the Theatre Royal, NEWCASTLE, following which he was engaged in this line by almost every metropolitan and provincial theatre, from 1850 achieving special recognition for his marine back-drops. In 1855 he moved to SUNDERLAND to decorate the

15

town's Theatre Royal, subsequently becoming lessee of this theatre, and of the nearby Drury Lane Theatre, which he later developed into a music hall. He remained associated with theatres at SUNDERLAND for many years, and at one time could boast of considerable affluence because of his flair for sensational scenic effects, and general management ability. Eventually, however, he was obliged to give up his theatre interests, and to devote himself increasingly to painting marine subjects, achieving such accomplishment that it is said that Queen Victoria regarded him as the best painter of these subjects since Clarkson Stanfield (q.v.).

It is commonly supposed that Bell never exhibited his work, but a scrutiny of fine art exhibition records relating to Tyneside shows that this was not the case. From 1870, until his death just over a quarter of a century later, he exhibited several times at NEWCASTLE, and on at least one occasion at GATESHEAD. In 1870, at the "Central Exchange News Room, Art Gallery, and Polytechnic Exhibition", NEWCASTLE, he showed: *Tynemouth, Flood Tide during a North East Gale*, and *Entrance to Sunderland Harbour* (his favourite subject); in 1878, at the town's exhibition of works by local painters at the Central Exchange Art Gallery, he showed three marine works and one genre painting, and he was an exhibitor at the Bewick Club, NEWCASTLE, in 1885, and the year before his death, on which latter occasion he showed: *Fisher Life in the North Sea – A Sudden Gale*, and *Saved by the Whitburn Fisherman – The Rocket Apparatus in 1860*. Bell remained at SUNDERLAND until close to his death, his painting activities in later years severely hampered by failing eyesight. He died at GATESHEAD. Sunderland Art Gallery has an excellent collection of his marine paintings, dated 1857-1896.

BELL, William (1740- *c.*1804)

Portrait and landscape painter in oil; drawing master. Bell was born at NEWCASTLE, the son of a bookbinder, and was one of the first students to be enrolled in the Royal Academy Schools. In 1770 the Council of the Academy offered a gold medal to the student who painted the best historical picture. Bell's entry was not successful, but in the following year he received a gold medal from Sir Joshua Reynolds for his *Venus Soliciting Vulcan to forge armour for her son Aeneas*. Several Northumbrian characters sat for Bell's huge canvas of this historical subject, amongst these Willie Carr, a blacksmith, who sat for the portrait of Vulcan. By the time that Bell painted his medal-winning work he had already come to the notice of Lord Delaval, and was giving lessons in drawing to the young ladies at Seaton Delaval Hall, near BLYTH. He had also started to paint full-length portraits of various members of the family, including Lord and Lady Delaval, their son John, and several of their six daughters. In 1775 he exhibited two landscapes at the Royal Academy, describing them as north and south views of *Seaton Delaval, built by Sir John Vanbrugh, the seat of Sir J. H. Delaval, Bart*, and giving as his address: "At Sir John Delaval's" – his patron's London home at Grosvenor House.

The last work which he painted, and exhibited while in London, was his *Susannah and the Two Elders*, shown at the Free Society of Artists, in 1776. This was another large historical painting. Bell then returned to NEWCASTLE, where he opened a drawing school, and resumed portrait painting. His portraits of this period have been described as "all extremely accurate and beautifully finished". One of these works portrayed his friend Thomas Bewick (q.v.), and came into the possession of William Bewick (q.v.), who wrote of it in 1864: "The portrait of Thomas Bewick that I possess was painted by Bell, in the style of Rembrandt . . . it is artistical, but not a domestic picture by any means, and no one would like a family likeness to be so treated. But it is well painted and I am often asked if it is by Rembrandt". Also in this period he painted a self portrait, a work entitled: *Two Children with a Lamb*, and portraits of stage performers Joseph Austin and his wife, who frequently appeared in NEWCASTLE between 1774 and 1778. His portrait painting did not, however, earn him much of a living, and he was obliged to continue giving drawing lessons, and later restored pictures, including those damaged by a fire at the Guildhall, NEWCASTLE, in 1791. His final years were spent in obscurity at NEWCASTLE, where he died about 1804. An excellent account of Bell's life and work appears in: *Eighteenth Century Newcastle*, by P. M. Horsley, Oriel Press, 1971. Several examples of his work may be seen at Seaton Delaval Hall.

BENNET, George Montagu, 7th Earl of Tankerville (1852-1931)

Amateur miniature painter. He was born in London, the son of Charles Bennet, 6th Earl of Tankerville, and Olivia Montagu, daughter of the 6th Duke of Manchester. He enlisted in the Navy in 1865, and served as a midshipman 1867-9, before resuming his education by attending Radley public school. He was commissioned a Lieutenant in The Rifle Brigade in 1872, and later served as aide-de-camp to the Lord Lieutenant of Ireland 1876-80. He was styled Lord Bennet 1879-99, succeeding his father as Earl of Tankerville, in 1899, and taking up permanent residence at the family home of Chillingham Castle, CHILLINGHAM, in that year. He was a talented artist from his youth, and in 1885 commenced exhibiting his work at the Royal Academy, contributing some thirty portrait miniatures between that date and 1900. Most of his exhibits portrayed members of the nobility. He died at Chillingham Castle. His wife, LEONORA SOPHIA, COUNTESS OF TANKERVILLE (née Van Marter), was also a talented artist, and exhibited her work.

BENNET, Lady Mary Elizabeth – see MONCK, Lady Mary Elizabeth.

*BERTRAM, Robert John Scott (1871-1953)

Landscape and historical painter in oil and watercolour; muralist; draughtsman; illustrator. Bertram was born at NEWCASTLE, the son of a ship's chandler, and began to show promise as an artist at an early age. At the end of his general education his parents decided that he should enter the coal trade, but after a short while in this

16

occupation he won a scholarship to the School of Art at NEWCASTLE, proving so successful here that he later became a part-time assistant teacher. In 1902 he was appointed full-time assistant, and in 1920 he became Master of Design at Armstrong College (later King's College; now Newcastle University), retaining this position until his retirement in 1937. Bertram is said to have been an artist of immense vitality who travelled widely throughout the North of England in search of subjects for landscape work in oil, watercolour, pen and ink, and pencil. Much of his pen and ink work became in demand from publishers, and in 1893 his drawings were used for the first volume of the *Northumberland County History*. He was passionately interested in the history of his native city, and produced many watercolours of the town as it probably looked in the past. This interest led to his involvement in painting a large lunette for the Laing Art Gallery, NEWCASTLE, depicting *The River Tyne during the great flood of 1771*.

Among Bertram's own published work were his pencil sketch books of NEWCASTLE and DURHAM, and a portfolio of lithographs of his native city. Apart from his contributions to various volumes of the *Northumberland County History*,# he executed illustrations for A *Fisher's Garland*, by John Harbottle, 1905, among many works published by others. In addition to teaching art, and practising actively as an artist, Bertram was extremely interested in matters relating to the preservation of old buildings at NEWCASTLE, and the creation of civic amenities. He exhibited sparingly outside Northumbria, showing one work at the Royal Academy in 1908, entitled: *Warkworth*, but he was an occasional exhibitor at the Bewick Club, NEWCASTLE, from its foundation, and also showed work at the Artists of the

Northern Counties exhibitions at the city's Laing Art Gallery, from their inception in 1905. Following his retirement he left Tyneside and settled at Whitby, North Yorkshire, where he continued to interest himself in art until his death. Represented: Laing A.G., Newcastle.

*BEVERLEY, William Roxby (1811-1889)
Marine, coastal and landscape painter in watercolour; scenic painter. He was born at Richmond, Surrey, the son of actor and theatrical manager William Roxby Beverley. It is popularly believed that he received his early training in art from Clarkson Stanfield (q.v.), but this is not the case. Indeed, on eventually moving to London to practise as a scenic painter he was, in his own words, "somewhat cold-shouldered by Clarkson Stanfield and other brothers of the brush". His first association with Northumbria came in 1831, when his family took over the management of the Northern Theatrical Circuit, including theatres at STOCKTON ON TEES, DURHAM, SUNDERLAND, NORTH SHIELDS and SOUTH SHIELDS. At the opening of the Drury Lane Theatre, SUNDERLAND, on 31st October of that year, one of the principal announcements on the bill referred to a new act-drop by "William Beverley, jun.". He remained based at SUNDERLAND for several years from 1831, combining his duties as scenic painter to the family circuit with those of actor, and in his leisure moments painting a number of local views. Notable among these views are his *Shipping*, 1831; *North Shields*, 1833, and *Tynemouth*, 1834, all three of which are in

Robert John Scott Bertram: Cowpen Hall, near Blyth, Northumberland. Pen and ink 3¾×5½, from "Northumberland County History".

Northumbrian public collections, and represent some of his earliest and least known work.

On leaving SUNDERLAND, Beverley worked as a scenic painter at Edinburgh, and later London, at which latter he established a reputation in his profession second only to that of Stanfield. Throughout his hectic life as a scenic painter, however, he never lost his interest in watercolour painting, though not until 1865 did he evidently think enough of his work to exhibit it publicly. From that date until 1880 he exhibited at the Royal Academy, the Dudley, and various other London galleries, the Glasgow Institute of Fine Arts, and the Arts Association, NEWCASTLE, many of his exhibits reflecting his involvement in this period in managing the family theatrical interests in Northumbria, by portraying North East coastal views.# Towards the end of his life Beverley's eyesight failed and he was obliged to give up scenic painting, and his spare-time relaxation of watercolour painting. He died at Hampstead. Represented: British Museum; National Gallery of Scotland; Victoria and Albert Museum; National Maritime Museum; Bridport A.G.; Fitzwilliam Museum, Cambridge; Laing A.G., Newcastle; Leeds A.G.; Leicester A.G.; Newport A.G.; Portsmouth City Museum & A.G.; Sunderland A.G; Ulster Museum, Belfast.

BEWICK, Jane (1787-1881)
Amateur landscape painter in watercolour. The eldest daughter of Thomas Bewick (q.v.), she was born at NEWCASTLE, and later assisted her father with much of the administrative work associated with the various publications which he illustrated. She occasionally painted in her spare time, and executed two views of the Ouseburn, NEWCASTLE, which were later reproduced in monochrome in *An Account of Jesmond*, by F. W. Dendy, 1904. The originals are in the possession of the Society of Antiquaries, NEWCASTLE, and show her to have been a capable amateur watercolourist,

though by no means as accomplished as her father, her brother Robert Elliot Bewick (q.v.), or uncle, John Bewick, The First (q.v.) She died at GATESHEAD.

BEWICK, John, The First (1760-1795)
Wood engraver; landscape painter in watercolour; draughtsman; illustrator; drawing master. He was born at CHERRYBURN, near OVINGHAM, the younger brother of Thomas Bewick (q.v.). In 1777 he joined Bewick at NEWCASTLE, lodging with his brother and soon making a favourable impression in the workshop run by the latter, and partner Ralph Beilby (q.v.), for his industry and cheerfulness. After five years in the workshop he expressed a wish to try out his skills as an engraver in London and Bewick released him two years short of his time for this purpose. He soon found a demand for his skills from the city's leading publishers and booksellers, and by 1787 was well established in the capital. His health eventually deteriorated, however, and he was forced to return to Tyneside to recover. As soon as he felt well enough he returned to London, but quickly found himself in the same state of ill-health as before. A second visit to Tyneside followed, during which he again made a good recovery, but although when he returned to London he sought to avoid the strain of previous years by taking a post as drawing master at Hornsey Academy, he was forced to return to his birthplace in the early summer of 1795. He died later in that year at his sister's home at OVINGHAM, and was buried in the graveyard of the Parish Church. Bewick's work as a wood engraver included many cuts for publishers of children's books, such as Newbery and Dr. Trusler, but he was also an able watercolourist, draughtsman and illustrator many of whose original works in these fields survive in public and private collections. His work as a wood engraver has been exhaustively studied, and reveals that although not as

talented as his elder brother he was capable of cutting blocks with considerable accomplishment. His work as designer of illustrations is probably best seen in the series of watercolour vignettes which he prepared for the *Poems of Goldsmith and Parnell*, 1795, though *The Chase*, by William Somervile, 1796, for which Thomas Bewick cuts his designs, contains many fine examples of his imaginative design work. Represented: British Museum; Laing A.G., Newcastle; Natural History Society of Northumbria, Newcastle.

BEWICK, John, The Second (1790-1809)
Draughtsman; engraver. The nephew of Thomas Bewick (q.v.), and John Bewick, The First (q.v.), he was born at CHERRYBURN, near OVINGHAM, the son of William Bewick. He was apprenticed to his uncle Thomas at NEWCASTLE, as a copperplate printer, but showed considerable promise as a draughtsman in a series of drawings which survived for many years at his birthplace. He died at nineteen, before completing his apprenticeship.

*BEWICK, Robert Elliot (1778-1849)
Architectural and natural history painter in watercolour; draughtsman; engraver; etcher. The only son of Thomas Bewick (q.v.), he was born at NEWCASTLE, and after serving an apprenticeship (1804-1810) with his father, was partner in the Bewick engraving business from 1812 until the latter's death in 1828. Later, he continued the business on his own account. Skilful as a watercolourist, copperplate engraver and etcher, but only moderately accomplished as a wood engraver, Robert Elliot never quite fulfilled his father's hopes for him, confessing to a friend that he felt unable to follow in Bewick senior's footsteps with credit. He is best known for his watercolour preparatory drawings for the *History of British Fishes*, which his father and he proposed to publish, but he shows in several drawings of an Elizabethan house at NEWCASTLE,# which he

prepared in the early years of the nineteenth century, and a drawing of Ovingham Church produced six years before his death, that he was a sensitive and capable handler of architectural perspective. *The History of British Fishes* was never published, but he exhibited a number of his drawings for the work at the First Exhibition of the Northumberland Institution for the Promotion of the Fine Arts, NEWCASTLE, in 1822, and several of them were reproduced in the form of wood engravings in a supplementary section of his father's autobiographical *Memoir*, published posthumously in 1862. Robert Elliot was, of course, together with his father, and several other well known Northumbrian artists, on the committee of the Northumberland Institution, having taken an active part in its foundation. He died at GATESHEAD, and was buried in the graveyard of the Parish Church at OVINGHAM. The British Museum has about 150 of his drawings, three of which were included in the "Thomas Bewick" exhibition, Laing Art Gallery, NEWCASTLE, Summer, 1978. Represented: British Museum; Laing A.G., Newcastle; Natural History Society of Northumbria, Newcastle.

*BEWICK, Thomas (1753-1828)
Wood engraver; bird, animal, landscape and genre painter in watercolour; illustrator; draughtsman. The most celebrated artist ever produced by Northumbria, Thomas Bewick was born at CHERRYBURN, near OVINGHAM, the son of a farmer and colliery lessee. He was educated at the Vicarage school at OVINGHAM, under the Rev. Gregson, and after displaying a marked interest in drawing throughout his childhood, was placed as an apprentice of Ralph Beilby (q.v.), at NEWCASTLE, at the age of fourteen. Here he was first put to copying *Copelands Ornaments*, later being introduced to all sorts of metal engraving, and at the instigation of local mathematician Dr. Hutton, wood engraving. His first work of note on wood was for Hutton's *Treatise on Mensuration*, which began publication in parts in 1768.

Robert Elliot Bewick: Elizabethan House in the Forth, Newcastle. Pen & ink 5¾×8¾. *Tyne & Wear County Council Museums, Laing Art Gallery.*

Hutton obtained the blocks of box-wood and tools necessary for his commission, and showed Beilby and Bewick how to handle the work which he required. Thus, by chance, Bewick – though later to excel in metal engraving – happened early in his career on a type of work for which he had a natural liking and ability, and through which his name was to become first nationally, then internationally famous. The Beilby workshop's commission from Hutton was followed by many other commissions to execute wood engravings, mainly from local printers, and Bewick, having by now displayed something of his talents in this direction, found himself cutting everything from bill heads, to illustrations for childrens' books. Some of his cuts for the latter were submitted by Beilby in Bewick's name, to the Society of Arts, and just before completing his apprenticeship in 1774 he received an award for seven guineas which he promptly presented to his mother.

Bewick remained with Beilby for a few weeks after the termination of his apprenticeship, then went to CHERRYBURN, where he did work for his friend Thomas Angus, printer at NEWCASTLE, Beilby, and others, until the summer of 1776. He then went on a long walking tour of Scotland, and on returning to NEWCASTLE, stayed there only long enough to earn his passage to London. The capital had little attraction for him, however, and although he could easily have obtained work there, he was back on Tyneside by June, 1777. After some months working on commissions which he had brought back with him, he rejoined his former master as partner, taking as his first apprentice his younger brother John Bewick, The First (q.v.). For the next seven years the partners concentrated mainly on the large volume of metal and wood engraving which their skills attracted, then Bewick one day proposed to Beilby that they should go into publication with a book illustrating and describing various types of four-legged animals, as most other works of this kind which he, Bewick, had studied, were poorly presented in these respects. After consultation with local bookseller, and editor of the *Newcastle Chronicle*, Solomon Hodgson, who thought it a good idea, Bewick began on the 15th of November, 1785, to cut the figure of a Dromedary. The work eventually published in 1790, as *A General History of Quadrupeds*, with illustrations by Bewick, and the text largely by Beilby, was an immediate success, encouraging the partners to produce several successive editions, and almost immediately to commence work on yet another natural history publication, the first volume of a book on British Birds. This work appeared in 1797, and was devoted to land birds of the British Isles. Like the *Quadrupeds*, it also was well received, but unfortunately the partners disagreed over the authorship of the book (Bewick feeling it should be regarded as joint; Beilby, his alone), and the partnership was ended in the following year. Bewick then set about illustrating and writing the second volume entirely on his own, and spent some time correcting and adding illustrations to the earlier volume, most of this work being done in the evenings after the workshop closed, much as he had worked on the *Quadrupeds*. Published in 1804, it set the seal on his reputation as a wood engraver, and together with the first volume, became the most popular of his illustrated books. His accurate and lifelike representations of birds contributed much to this popularity, but it was the tailpieces which excited particular delight by encompassing within the smallest spaces, nevertheless telling observations on contemporary rustic life and attitudes. Almost all of his illustrations for the *Birds* – both figure and tailpiece – were first prepared as watercolours, and in them it has been said, can be seen the true source of his genius as an engraver; his painter's eye, and dexterity as an engraver on wood, enabled him to produce unique work as an illustrator, and to exercise a lasting influence on all subsequent book illustration.

His last published work of note was *The Fables of Aesop*, which was embarked upon following a serious illness in 1812. He had by then taken his only son, Robert Elliot Bewick (q.v.), into the business as partner, and now settled at GATESHEAD, he began to draw his Fables' designs direct on to the wood, leaving their cutting to apprentices. This work duly appeared in 1818, and hardly had it been published when he set about producing with his son a history of British Fishes. Prospectuses were issued stating that it would be "put to the press" in 1826, but Bewick was by then beginning to feel the effects of old age, and this circumstance, coupled with the difficulty of obtaining suitable specimens for illustration, and his son's diffidence in proceeding with the work, led to its abandonment. In his final years Bewick spent much time writing his autobiographical *Memoir*, which has remained a prime source of information about his life and his work as an artist since it was published in an abridged form some thirty-four years following his death.‡ It was started at TYNEMOUTH in November, 1822, and occupied him until close to his death. He died at GATESHEAD, and was interred in the graveyard of the Parish Church at OVINGHAM. Bewick has been the subject of more portraits, biographical studies and articles, than any other artist of Northumbria, and deservedly enjoys a truly international reputation as one of the world's greatest wood engravers and book illustrators.

Bewick's work as a watercolourist has until recently remained little known. With the publication in 1981 of *The Watercolours & Drawings of Thomas Bewick and his Workshop Apprentices*, by Iain Bain, however, widespread recognition for his abilities in this field should now be possible. His work has been the subject of several important exhibitions since his death (he only exhibited once while alive, and this at the Northumberland Institution for the Promotion of the Fine Arts, NEWCASTLE, in 1822), notably at the Laing Art Gallery, NEWCASTLE, on the 100th and 150th anniversaries of his death. Represented: British Museum; Victoria and Albert Museum; Laing A.G., Newcastle; Natural History Society of Northumbria, Newcastle; Newcastle Central Library.

‡ *The first edition of Bewick's "Memoir" to give the complete text was not published until 1975, all its predecessors being based on the version published in 1862 by his daughter, Jane Bewick (q.v.). Edited and with an introduction by Iain Bain, it was published by Oxford University Press.*

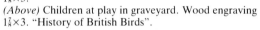

Thomas Bewick *(top)*: The Cheviot Ram. Wood engraving
1⅞×3.
(Above) Children at play in graveyard. Wood engraving
1⅞×3. "History of British Birds".

(Above) The Sparrow Hawk. Watercolour 11¾×10. *Natural
History Society of Northumbria.*
(Below) The Ox. Pencil 5½×7½. *Natural History Society of
Northumbria.*

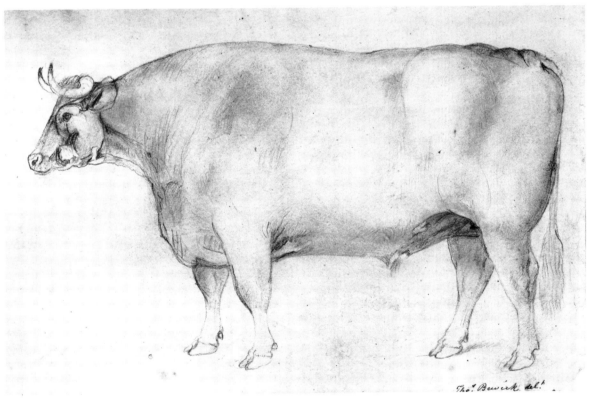

BEWICK, William (1795-1866)

Portrait, historical, biblical, genre and landscape painter in oil; draughtsman. Bewick was born at DARLINGTON, the son of an upholsterer, and served an apprenticeship with his father before deciding on a career in art. While still an apprentice he began experimenting with drawing and painting, receiving his first lessons from itinerant artists, later from George Marks (q.v.), in the latter's studio in the town. By the age of nineteen he had accumulated a portfolio of his drawings, and with £20 raised by the sale of these works he left for London in 1815. Here he met by chance the rapidly rising historical and genre painter Haydon, who accepted Bewick as a pupil, and with whom he remained for about three years. At Haydon's studio he met many famous men of the day, including Wordsworth, Hazlitt, Keats and Scott. Bewick worked hard under Haydon's influence, and besides working in his master's studio, attended the Royal Academy Schools, and the dissecting rooms of Sir Charles Bell. His health suffered from overwork, however, and he returned briefly to DARLINGTON to recuperate before resuming work in London by completing a series of drawings of the Elgin marbles for the poet Goethe.

He first began exhibiting his work in 1820, at the Old Water Colour Society (later the Royal Society of Painters in Water Colours). His first exhibit of note, however, was his *Jacob meeting Rachel*, which he sent to the British Institution in 1822, and later showed at DARLINGTON. In that year also he showed four examples of his work at the First Exhibition of the Northumberland Institution for the Promotion of the Fine Arts, NEWCASTLE. For the next seventeen years he confined his exhibiting activities to the provinces, where he showed work at NEWCASTLE, Glasgow and Carlisle. During the early part of this period he returned briefly to DARLINGTON to paint portraits, then borrowing some money he visited Edinburgh, where he was warmly received by the city's leading artists and citizens. He formed an anatomical drawing class in the Scottish capital, and spent much time producing life-sized likenesses of the celebrities he met, including Sir William Allan, Sir John Malcolm, and Lord Jeffrey. He next went to Glasgow, where he held an exhibition of his works, and again attracted portrait commissions. The same success attended his subsequent visit to Dublin, and returning to Scotland shortly afterwards he stayed with Sir Walter Scott, whose portrait he painted while the great author sat for Wilkie. On leaving Scotland Bewick returned to DARLINGTON, where he married and is said to have "painted several landscapes for different parties, to enable him to see the works of the Italian Schools". Sir Thomas Lawrence, the Royal Academician, became aware of Bewick's interest, and offered him 100 guineas for a large copy of Michelangelo's *Delphic Sybil*, in the Sistine Chapel. This commission was later extended to encompass other works in the Chapel, which Bewick was in the course of completing when Sir Thomas suddenly died. He was recompensed for his work by Sir Thomas's executors on his return to London after his four year stay in Rome, and here resumed portrait painting before once again returning to DARLINGTON, where he stayed until the late 1830's.

Back in London by 1839, he resumed exhibiting at the British Institution, and sent his first work to the Royal Academy, and the Suffolk Street Gallery. He continued to exhibit at the major institutions in London throughout this, his final stay in London, and also exhibited his work for Sir Thomas, at his London home in 1840. After returning to DARLINGTON in 1842 he exhibited in the capital on only one further occasion, this being when he sent his *The Historian Platina in Prison*, to the British Institution in 1848. He spent the last twenty-odd years of his life at his home at HAUGHTON-LE-SKERNE, near DARLINGTON, his efforts in the early part of this period being confined to the production of a cartoon of the *Triumph of David* as a competition entry for the decoration of Westminster Hall, and the painting of portraits and "fancy pictures". He died at HAUGHTON-LE-SKERNE, and is buried in the churchyard there. Much interesting information about Bewick, and several of his acquaintances among Northumbrian artists, including William Davison (q.v.), is contained in *The Life and Letters of William Bewick (Artist)*, edited by Thomas Landseer, 1871. Represented: British Museum; Scottish National Portrait Gallery; Darlington A.G.; Laing A.G., Newcastle.

BICKNELL, Phyllis Ellen (Mrs. Lovibond) (b. 1877)

Landscape and flower painter in watercolour. This artist practised at NEWCASTLE in the early 20th century, following study under Arthur G. Bell, and at Armstrong College (later King's College; now Newcastle University). In 1900 she sent one work to the Royal Institute of Painters in Water Colours, and four works to the Alpine Club, London, following this by becoming a regular exhibitor at the Artists of the Northern Counties exhibitions at the Laing Art Gallery, NEWCASTLE. Her first contributions in 1905, were entitled: *Corner at Hesleyside*, and *New Christ Church*. She lived mainly at NEWCASTLE, but spent some years at nearby ROWLANDS GILL. She continued to exhibit as Phyllis Ellen Bicknell after becoming Mrs. Lovibond.

BIGGE, Charles John (1803-1846)

Amateur landscape painter in watercolour; draughtsman. He was born at NEWCASTLE, the son of Charles William Bigge. He later took a prominent part in local council affairs, painting and drawing in his spare time. He was an Alderman of NEWCASTLE, and in 1835 became the first Mayor to be elected under the Municipal Corporation Reform Act. In 1836 he was made a Freeman of the town. He occasionally exhibited his work at NEWCASTLE commencing in 1831, when he showed four Italian views at the Northern Academy. Among his later exhibits were the *Bamborough Castle from the North . . .*, and *Pass in the Maritime Alps*, which he showed at the First Water Colour Exhibition of the Newcastle Society of Artists, 1836, after serving as Mayor. An example of his draughtsmanship is his drawing of Brinkburn Priory, 1833, reproduced as an engraving by William Collard (q.v.), in Hodgson's *History of Northumberland*, Vol. III, part III. He died in London.

BIGLAND, Mary Backhouse (b.1844)
Amateur landscape and flower painter in oil and water-colour. She was born at DARLINGTON, the daughter of Jane Backhouse, and Hodgson Bigland. Nothing is known of her early artistic training, but by 1869 she was exhibiting in London, from Birkenhead in Cheshire, showing one work at the New Water Colour Society (later the Royal Institute of Painters in Water Colours). She later became a regular exhibitor in London and the provinces, showing works at Liverpool and NEWCASTLE. Amongst her earliest exhibits at NEWCASTLE were the three works which she showed at the Arts Association in 1878, following her return to DARLINGTON. She showed other works at the Arts Association in the next three years, and later became a regular exhibitor at the Bewick Club, NEWCASTLE, showing landscapes and flower studies. Typical of the former was her *Harvest Time*, shown at the Club's exhibition in 1893. In her later years she was an occasional exhibitor at the Society of Women Artists' exhibitions.

BLACK, Albert Ernest (1882-1963)
Landscape, portrait, flower and street scene painter in oil and watercolour. He was born at NORTH SHIELDS, the second eldest son of Alderman Isaac Black, J.P. He sketched from his boyhood, taking special pleasure in visits to ROTHBURY for this purpose, with his mother who was also interested in art. He attended boarding school at NEWCASTLE, subsequently joining the staff of a shipowner in the city. At twenty-four he left his job at NEWCASTLE, and following his marriage in 1907, became bookkeeper to his father, who owned several tailoring and outfitting shops on Tyneside. About 1933 he retired from business to devote his life to painting, having throughout his bookkeeping employment exhibited his work frequently at SOUTH SHIELDS, and at the Artists of the Northern Counties exhibitions at the Laing Art Gallery, NEWCASTLE, in an amateur capacity. Many of the works which he exhibited at South Shields Art Club were later purchased by South Shields Museum & Art Gallery, and an exhibition of thirty-nine of his works was held by this establishment in 1956, proving so popular that it was extended. Most of his work featured local landscape, street and river scenes, some of these based on photographs. He died at SOUTH SHIELDS. He was the elder brother of Joseph Wallace Black (q.v.). Represented: South Shields Museum & A.G.

BLACK, Joseph Wallace (1884-1945)
Coastal painter in watercolour; illustrator. He was born at NORTH SHIELDS, the son of Alderman Isaac Black, J.P., and younger brother of Albert Ernest Black (q.v.). He followed a variety of occupations from his youth, principally connected with the publication of periodicals, some of which he illustrated himself. His best known publication was the *Shields Hustler*, an advertising freesheet which he published and edited from 1905-1937. In his later life he took an increasing interest in the tailoring and outfitting shops owned by his father. He died at NORTH SHIELDS. Represented: North Tyneside Public Libraries.

*BLACKLOCK, William Kay, A.R.C.A. (b.1872)
Landscape and genre painter in oil and watercolour; art teacher. Born at SUNDERLAND, Blacklock studied at the Royal College of Art before practising as a professional artist and art teacher. On leaving the College he returned to SUNDERLAND where he established a studio in the town, and began sending his work for exhibition to the Bewick Club, NEWCASTLE, by 1893. He continued to exhibit at the Club, then in 1897 sent his first work for exhibition at the Royal Academy: *The home of the fisherman – Whitby*, and *A Study*. In the following year he moved back to London to further his career, remaining there until he was appointed teacher at the School of Art, Edinburgh, in 1902. He remained at Edinburgh

William Kay Blacklock:
The Shepherd's Daughter.
Oil 20×30. *Private
collection.*

for some seven years, then went back to London, where he painted and taught art for many years. In addition to exhibiting frequently at the Royal Academy, Blacklock also exhibited many works at the Royal Scottish Academy, the Royal Institute of Painters in Water Colours, and sent some six works to the Royal Institute of Oil Painters. He also exhibited widely in the provinces, including the Artists of the Northern Counties exhibitions at the Laing Art Gallery, NEWCASTLE, to which he contributed from their inception in 1905, until the First World War years. He was an associate of the Royal College of Art. His wife, NELLIE BLACKLOCK (b. 1889), was also a talented artist, and exhibited her work.

BLAKELOCK, Clive Vernon (1880-1955)
Amateur landscape and coastal painter in watercolour. Born at SUNDERLAND, Blakelock studied at the town's Technical College, and later became assistant park superintendent at nearby SOUTHWICK. He became the first park superintendent at WHITLEY BAY, in 1914, and during his thirty-one years in this capacity was responsible for the planning of many of the town's beauty spots. He was a pupil and friend of John Atkinson (q.v.), and a lifelong acquaintance of David T. Robertson (q.v.), and showed his work at Sunderland Art Gallery, and the Artists of the Northern Counties exhibitions at the Laing Art Gallery, NEWCASTLE. Blakelock was one of Atkinson's most accomplished pupils, his work in watercolour the equal of much that was produced by the latter artist. Following his retirement in 1946 Blakelock spent five years at HEXHAM, then returned to WHITLEY BAY, where he died in 1955.

BOAG, George (fl. 1884-1902)
Animal painter in oil. This artist practised at NEWCASTLE in the late 19th century, where he was a regular exhibitor at the Bewick Club from 1884, until his death. Typical subjects of his work were horses and dogs. His studio was for many years in the city's Scotswood Road.

*BOUET, Joseph Sébastien Victor Francois (Nicolas) (1791-1856)
Genre, portrait and landscape painter in oil; draughtsman; caricaturist; lithographer. He was born in Paris, and following artistic training in the French capital, settled at DURHAM to practise as a professional artist, art teacher, and later teacher of French. He soon became well known for his artistic abilities at DURHAM, and later NEWCASTLE, at which latter he exhibited at the Northumberland Institution for the Promotion of the Fine Arts, from 1823, and the town's Northern Academy, from its inaugural exhibition in 1828, His exhibit at the Northern Academy in 1829: *The Bird's Nest*, earned from W. A. Mitchell in the *Tyne Mercury*, the remark: "As a pencil drawing this is in Bouet's usual excellent style". Bouet exhibited little in his later life, apart from showing a few works in pencil, chalk, etc., at the Polytechnic Exhibition held at the Durham Mechanics' Institute in 1843. He was, however, very active artistically, producing many pencil drawings of local landscape and architectural subjects, and works in lithography.# One of his major works in pencil was his series of drawings of the tapestries at Durham Castle, which were later drawn on the stone by James Dickson, and published as a volume of lithographic illustrations. Among his own work in lithography were his: *Gateway*

Joseph Sébastien Victor Francois (Nicholas) Bouet: Laughter and surprise, 1822. Lithograph 6½×8⅝. *Private collection.*

24

to the *Old Gaol at Durham* (taken down in 1821), printed by W. Day, and a *View of Durham from the lower Gilesgate area, with figures*, printed by G. Hull-mandel. In his later years Bouet increasingly relied on teaching French and drawing for his living, in the former activity having some connection with the University at DURHAM, and later the city's Grammar School. In his final years he preferred to be called "Nicolas Sébastien Bouet". He died at DURHAM. Represented : Sunderland A.G.

BOWLT, William (b. 1822)

Marine and coastal painter in oil. Born at GATESHEAD, Bowlt exhibited his work at NEWCASTLE at the North of England Society for the Promotion of the Fine Arts, in 1839, and 1841. In 1839 he showed: *The Mouth of the Tyne, Morning*, and in 1841: *The Herd Sands from the Mouth of the Tyne*, and *Rocks near Cullercoats*. Nothing more is known of this artist except that he was a member of a well known family at GATESHEAD, of which several members were tradesmen in the town.

BOWMAN, George G. (fl. 1890-1920)

Landscape and genre painter in oil and watercolour; illustrator; engraver. This artist practised at NEWCASTLE in the early 20th century, and first exhibited his work publicly when he sent a coloured print: *On the Tyne*, and a drawing: *Death of an Old Man*, to the Artists of the Northern Counties exhibition at the Laing Art Gallery, NEWCASTLE, in 1910. In 1913 he exhibited work at the Royal Scottish Academy, and the Artists of the Northern Counties exhibition, at the latter showing an oil: *Tootie after the bath*, and two drawings. He exhibited three further works at the Royal Scottish Academy in the next four years, and also exhibited at NEWCASTLE, but he appears to have ceased exhibiting entirely, shortly after the conclusion of the First World War.

BOWMAN, Thomas Stanton (c. 1840 -after 1886)

Landscape painter in oil. This artist practised at NEW-CASTLE in the second half of the nineteenth century, following a period in London during which he sent one work to the British Institution, and four works to various other exhibitions in London, 1866-67. His British Institution exhibit, contributed in 1867, was entitled: *A Revolt in the Kitchen*. He occasionally exhibited at NEWCASTLE, notably at the exhibitions of the Arts Association. He may have been related to George G. Bowman (q.v.).

BOYCE, Albert Ernest (1886-1956)

Amateur landscape painter in watercolour. Born at SOUTH SHIELDS, one of the nine sons of William Thomas Nichols Boyce (q.v.), Albert Ernest Boyce was a keen amateur artist in his early manhood, but is believed to have virtually abandoned painting about 1920. Prior to this he painted a number of local landscapes, such as his *Near Hartley*, shown at the Artists of the Northern Counties exhibition at the Laing Art Gallery, NEW-CASTLE, in 1913. He died at SOUTH SHIELDS. He was the brother of Herbert Walter Boyce (q.v.), and Norman Septimus Boyce (q.v.).

BOYCE, Herbert Walter (1883-1946)

Amateur seascape and landscape painter in watercolour. Born at SOUTH SHIELDS, one of the nine sons of William Thomas Nichols Boyce (q.v.), Herbert Walter Boyce was a keen amateur artist, throughout his life. Like his father, and brothers Albert Ernest Boyce (q.v.), and Norman Septimus Boyce (q.v.), he exhibited almost exclusively at SOUTH SHIELDS, and at the Artists of the Northern Counties exhibitions at the Laing Art Gallery, NEWCASTLE. He worked predominantly on a small scale, and exhibited at NEWCASTLE such titles as: *A Mill Stream* (1906); *By the Harbour Cliffs of Tyne-mouth* (1911), and *To the Rescue* (1912). He died at SOUTH SHIELDS. Represented: South Shields Museum & A.G.

BOYCE, Norman Septimus (1895-1962)

Amateur seascape, landscape and miniature painter in watercolour. One of the nine sons of William Thomas Nichols Boyce (q.v.), he was born at SOUTH SHIELDS, and began his working life as an engineering apprentice, but left his employer for the drapery trade. After service with the Royal Artillery in the First World War he took up the profession of artist for some twenty years, only abandoning it at the outbreak of the Second World War, when he went to Swindon, to work once more in engineering. After the war he settled at Derby, remain-ing there until he retired, when he returned to SOUTH SHIELDS. Like his father, and brothers Albert Ernest Boyce (q.v.), and Herbert Walter Boyce (q.v.), he exhibited almost exclusively at SOUTH SHIELDS, and at the Artists of the Northern Counties exhibitions at the Laing Art Gallery, NEWCASTLE, showing his first work at the latter in 1913: *Seascape*. His work is very similar to that of his father, and was painted mainly in water-colour, though a few oils are known. In later years he worked increasingly in monochrome. Represented: South Shields Museum & A.G.

*BOYCE, William Thomas Nichols (1857-1911)

Marine and landscape painter in oil and watercolour. Boyce was born in Norfolk, the son of a master mariner, but moved to SOUTH SHIELDS in 1872 with his parents. Here he became first an apprentice joiner, and later an employee in a draper's shop in the town, before becoming a full-time professional artist. His work from this point forward consisted mainly of watercolours of steam tugs, brigs, schooners and steam colliers, por-trayed in a wide range of climatic conditions, and providing a valuable, and artistically accomplished record of the transition from sail to steam before the First World War. He also painted these subjects in oil, showing an equal degree of accomplishment in the use of this medium, but examples are quite rare. Boyce is not known to have exhibited his work outside Northum-bria. He exhibited at South Shields Art Club, the Bewick Club, NEWCASTLE, and from 1905 until his death at SOUTH SHIELDS, the Artists of the Northern Counties exhibitions at the Laing Art Gallery, NEWCASTLE. Three examples of his work were included in the "Wearmouth 1300th Festival -19th Century Artists" exhibition at Sunderland Art Gallery, in 1974. These comprised:

William Thomas Nichols Boyce: Evening at the mouth of the Tyne, 1900. Watercolour 14×20. *Dean Gallery.*

Brig off the Tyne; Homeward Bound, and *Sunderland Harbour 1905*. His sons Albert Ernest Boyce (q.v.), Herbert Walter Boyce (q.v.), and Norman Septimus Boyce (q.v.), were all artistically gifted. Represented: Laing A.G., Newcastle; South Shields Museum & A.G.; Sunderland A.G.

*BOYD, Alice (1825-1897)

Amateur landscape and figure painter in oil and watercolour. She was born at Penkill Castle, Ayrshire, of an ancient Scottish family. Following the death of her father, her mother married a Mr. Mayhew, and she and her brother Spencer went to live in Wharfedale, Yorkshire, near the village of Arncliffe. Alice and her brother later moved to Tyneside, where she began to take a keen interest in painting after meeting William Bell Scott (q.v.), in 1859, while he was working on his murals for Wallington Hall, near CAMBO. He was then painting his Bernard Gilpin subject, and in addition to encouraging her interest in art, asked her to pose for the main figure of his Grace Darling mural. She later settled at NEWCASTLE, and became a pupil of Scott. Scott and his wife asked her to join them when they moved to London late in 1864, but she was detained by the illness of her brother at their home at TYNEMOUTH, and did not join the Scotts until 1865. From then on she spent every winter with the Scotts in London, while they spent their summers and autumns with her at Penkill Castle. While on one of her stays in London she showed her only work at the Royal Academy: *A Scottish Glen*. This work was shown in 1880, and was followed by the exhibition of several works at the Royal Scottish Academy, including her *The Incantation of Hervor*, and *The Wild Huntsman*. She was also an exhibitor at NEWCASTLE for several years, showing examples of her work at the Arts Association from 1878, and the Bewick Club from 1884. Scott continued to visit Penkill until his final years, dying there after a long illness throughout

which he was nursed by Alice. She also died at Penkill, and was buried in the same grave there as Scott. Much interesting information on their relationship, together with Scott's etching of her portrait after Dante Gabriel Rossetti, is contained in his *Autobiographical Notes etc.* 1892. She was not related to the family of Edward Fenwick Boyd (q.v.). Represented: Kyle & Carrick District Libraries, Ayr; Penkill Castle, Girvan, Ayrshire.

BOYD, Edward Fenwick (1810-1889)

Amateur landscape painter in watercolour; draughtsman. Boyd was born at NEWCASTLE, the son of a banker, and was educated at WITTON-LE-WEAR, near BISHOP AUCKLAND, and later Edinburgh University. He subsequently became a professional mining engineer, and for many years served several bodies in Northumbria as mine agent and supervisor. He was an acquaintance in his youth of Thomas Bewick (q.v.), and while at WITTON-LE-WEAR produced some sketches which came to the attention of Edward Swinburne (q.v.). Swinburne persuaded Boyd's father to place his son as a pupil of Thomas Miles Richardson, Senior (q.v.), at NEWCASTLE, and Boyd remained throughout his career in mining a keen spare-time painter and sketcher of local scenery, amassing over the years several portfolios of his work. He died at his home for many years, Moor House, LEAMSIDE, near DURHAM. He was the father-in-law of Janet Augusta Boyd (q.v.). His daughter was the well-known Bewick collector, Julia Boyd, author of *Bewick Gleanings*, 1886, which work she dedicated to her father.

BOYD, Mrs. Janet Augusta (1850-1928)

Amateur miniature painter. The daughter-in-law of Edward Fenwick Boyd (q.v.), she first exhibited her work while living with her husband George Fenwick Boyd, at WHITLEY BAY, showing portraits at the Bewick

Club, NEWCASTLE, in 1886. She continued to exhibit at the Bewick Club for some years subsequently, and in 1895 sent her first works to the Royal Academy. Some years after her father-in-law's death at Moor House, LEAMSIDE, near DURHAM, she moved with her husband to his father's former home, and from this address exhibited at the Royal Academy, the Royal Miniature Society, the Society of Women Artists, and the Walker Art Gallery, Liverpool, from 1896. Most of her exhibits were portraits of friends in Northumbria. She died at the home of her daughter, near Cheltenham, Gloucestershire.

BROWN, Forster (d. 1878)

Drawing master. He was born at DURHAM, the son of William Brown (q.v.), drawing master. He was apprenticed as a bookbinder and followed this trade at DURHAM for most of his later life, also serving for some years as drawing master at the Mechanics' Institute. He retired from business about 1871, and later moved to SUNDERLAND, where he died at the home of his son in 1878. It is said that he excelled as an "artistic penman". One of his pupils at the Mechanics' Institute was Clement Burlison (q.v.).

BROWN, James (c. 1870- after 1922)

Landscape painter in oil and watercolour; lithographer. This artist practised at GATESHEAD in the late 19th and early 20th centuries, from which he regularly sent work for exhibition to the Bewick Club, NEWCASTLE, and later the city's Laing Art Gallery, whose Artist of the Northern Counties exhibitions he contributed to from their inception in 1905, until the 1920's. Three of his Bewick Club exhibits of 1893 were described in the local press as: "a drawing of the Tyne at Stella, with quaint buildings and old coal staithes; a picture of Whittle Dene, and a sketch on the Derwent. They are all excellent". Brown painted widely throughout Britain,

but the majority of his works featured Northumbrian coastal, river and village scenes. The Shipley Art Gallery, GATESHEAD, has his oil: *Windsor Castle*, and his watercolours: *Street Scene*, 1899, and *Stalls in Bigg Market*, 1894. He may have been related to engraver JAMES BROWN (fl. late 19th cent.), who practised at NEWCASTLE until *c.* 1880.

BROWN, J. Gillis (fl. late 19th, early 20th cent.)

Genre and landscape painter in oil and watercolour; caricaturist; illustrator. He was born at SUNDERLAND, and worked much of his life as a baths superintendent in the town, painting and drawing in his spare time. He exhibited his work at the Bewick Club, NEWCASTLE, from its foundation, and later at the Artists of the Northern Counties exhibitions at the city's Laing Art Gallery. He was an acquaintance of John Atkinson (q.v.), and David Thomas Robertson (q.v.), and sometimes accompanied these artists on sketching trips. His best known work was in caricature, and he supplied many illustrations in this field to local publications, including the *Newcastle Weekly Chronicle*. Represented: Sunderland A.G.

BROWN, James Miller (fl. late 19th, early 20th cent.)

Landscape and coastal painter in oil and watercolour. This artist practised at SOUTH SHIELDS, and briefly at NEWCASTLE, in the late 19th and early 20th centuries. He was an exhibitor at the "Gateshead Fine Art & Industrial Exhibition", in 1883, contributing: *View on the Tees*, and later became a regular exhibitor at the Bewick Club, NEWCASTLE, showing a variety of Northumbrian landscapes in oil and watercolour. South Shields Museum & Art Gallery has two of his oils, a number of his local watercolours painted 1877-92, and a book of sketches.

Alice Boyd: From the window of Balcony House, Tynemouth, 1864. Oil 9¾×13¾. *Stone Gallery.*

John Brown: Old Kepier
Hospital, Durham, 1881.
Oil 14×23. *D. Kirkup.*

*BROWN, John (*c.*1812- *c.*1895)

Landscape painter in oil and watercolour; decorative painter. Brown was born on Tyneside, and as a young man became a member of an art society at NEWCASTLE, comprising John Henry Mole (q.v.), Thomas Henry Tweedy (q.v.), and other artists then seeking to develop their talents. This society flourished about 1830-35, and held its first exhibition at T. Bamford's Long Room at Amen Corner in the town. It later moved its meeting place and exhibition venue to the Old Tower, Pink Lane, where Mole began to assume a leading role in encouraging his fellow members in their progress. Brown's first attempt to seek wider exposure for his work occurred in 1834, when he sent two works: *Scene near Askew's Quay*, and *View near Winlaton Mills*, to the Newcastle upon Tyne Institution for the General Promotion of the Fine Arts, NEWCASTLE. From 1834 until 1878 he remained a regular exhibitor in the town, showing a large number of landscapes painted in the North East of England. He exhibited outside Northumbria on only one occasion in this period, showing two works at the 1850 exhibition of Carlisle Athenaeum. Soon after he first began exhibiting at NEWCASTLE, he moved to neighbouring GATESHEAD. In 1838 he exhibited at NEWCASTLE from a London address, but by 1841 he was back at GATESHEAD, and after returning to NEWCASTLE a few years later, he practised in the town until his death, in his later years also working as a decorative painter for J. Richardson & Co., of 42, Dean Street. He died at NEWCASTLE. His watercolour: *The Ouseburn at Heaton*, 1860, appears opposite page 288 in Volume XIII, of *The Northumberland County History*. St. Andrew's Church, NEWCASTLE has his oil showing the interior of the building in 1861.

BROWN, John (*c.*1829- *c.*1894)

Wood carver. Brown was born in Scotland, but moved to ALNWICK to take up employment as a wood carver with a cabinet maker in the town following his marriage in 1849. In 1854, the Fourth Duke, Algernon decided on a scheme of alteration for Alnwick Castle, which he placed in the hands of the Italian architect Canina, with the intention of remodelling it along the lines of an Italian castle. Wood carvers were engaged from Italy, under the superintendence of Bulletti, of Florence, in the belief that only they could execute the carving satisfactorily, but when Brown was observed one day carving a capital in his workshop he was asked to join the team as foreman. The main alteration work to the castle was completed in ten years, at a cost of £¼m., but at the end of it Brown was retained by the Duke, eventually serving him for some forty years. During this period Brown became the central figure of what has since become known as the "Alnwick School of Wood Carvers". His studio in the Abbot's Tower of the castle was frequently visited by the Duke's guests, one of whom, Lord Beaconsfield, was so impressed by Brown's work that he remarked: "If I were a wood carver and could do work like that, I should be as proud of it as I am to be Prime Minister of England". Examples of his work outside Alnwick Castle may be seen in the town's St. Michael's Church, which contains several fine pieces of his foliage carving. Brown was also something of a writer, and wrote a handbook to Alnwick Castle, which was published by Davison, the town printer. He died at ALNWICK. He was the father of J. R. Brown (q.v.), and grandfather of Paul J. Brown (q.v.). An account of his life and work, written by the latter, appeared in the *Newcastle Journal*, 8th July, 1938, under the title: "The Abbot's Tower, and the carver's shop in Alnwick Castle".

BROWN, John George (1831-1913)

Genre and portrait painter in oil and watercolour. Brown was born at GATESHEAD, but spent his boyhood at NEWCASTLE, where his father practised law. At the age of fourteen he became an apprentice in the glass trade on Tyneside, attending art classes in his spare time. On concluding his apprenticeship he moved to Edinburgh, where he worked for the Holyrood Glass

28

Company. Determined to become an artist, however, he studied whenever possible at the Royal Scottish Academy, making such good progress that he won a prize for his drawings of the Antique. In 1853 he decided to leave the Scottish capital for London to take up the profession of portrait painter. But he did not remain long in London, for after scarcely three months he fell under the spell of the emigrant songs of America then being sung by Henry Russell, and resolved to try his fortunes there. On arriving at New York he thought it wise to work in his old trade while looking for commissions to paint. He obtained a position with William Owen, the leading glass maker in Brooklyn, meanwhile studying at the National Academy of Design. In 1855 he married his employer's daughter, and encouraged by Owen, he once more became a professional painter. His father-in-law died in 1856, however, and when the glass firm collapsed in the financial panic of the following year he was obliged to depend entirely on his income as a painter to support his family.

Brown's first success in portraiture was a commission from a business associate of his late father-in-law, and several other commissions soon followed. But it was his early love of painting street urchins which eventually earned him fame, and following his move to New York City to practise his progress was rapid. In 1862 he was elected an associate of the National Academy, and in the following year he became a full member. His street urchin pictures – bootblacks and newsboys – sold well throughout his career, and he became one of the best known and loved artists on the West Atlantic Coast. Other honours followed his election as member of the Academy, including the Presidency of the Water Colour Society, the Presidency of the Arts Fund, and the Vice-Presidency of the Academy. Brown exhibited frequently throughout his career in America, showing his work at the National Academy, the Boston Athenaeum, and the Pennsylvania Academy. He also exhibited at the Royal Academy, London, in 1880, and 1885 showing genre works. He died at New York City. Represented: Metropolitan Museum, New York; Concoran A.G., Washington, D.C.

*BROWN, J. R. (d.1918)

Illustrator. He was born at ALNWICK, the son of John Brown (q.v.), and following his education in the town was apprenticed to a local architect. On completing his apprenticeship he studied at South Kensington School of Art, and began contributing illustrations to *The Builder*, and other technical papers. He worked for a period as an art master at a boys' school in Yorkshire, then was commissioned by *The Graphic* to go as a special artist to America, and to Ireland during the Fenian rising. Together with his brother JAMES BROWN, he originated the humorous character of *Wild Scotchman, McNab*, the first of a series of comic drawings featuring their creation appearing in *The Graphic*. Later on Brown's sketches appeared in *Judy*, and *Ally Sloper*. In partnership with his brother he did a considerable amount of decorative work in London, and designed the greater part of the popular shows *Venice*, and *Constantinople*. On the death of his brother he joined the firm of Goodall's, of Manchester, to supervise their restoration of large houses, hotels, castles, etc., meanwhile continuing to contribute illus-

J. R. Brown: Grey Street, Newcastle. Engraving after sketch by the artist, in the "Illustrated London News".

29

trations and humorous articles to various periodicals, including the *Newcastle Weekly Chronicle*. His work for *The Graphic* spanned the years 1874-77, and 1885-88. He also exhibited his work during these years, notably at Liverpool and Manchester. Probably his best known illustration was his *Common Lodging House*, 1888. His son, Paul J. Brown (q.v.), was also a talented illustrator.

BROWN, J. W. (1842-1928)
Portrait, genre and landscape painter in oil and watercolour; stained glass designer. Brown was born at NEWCASTLE, and received his early training in art at the Government School of Design in the town, under William Bell Scott (q.v.), later serving as assistant master at the School. In 1866 he sent a landscape work entitled: *Newburn from the East*, to the "Exhibition of Paintings and other Works of Art", at the Town Hall, NEWCASTLE, while still at the School, following which he left the town for London. In the immediately following years he formed a close association with William Morris, later taking up a position with the stained glass firm of James Powell of London, where his work was greatly admired by John Ruskin. He later left Powell and set up a studio at Stoke Newington. However, ill-health eventually obliged him to leave the country for Australia. During his career as a stained glass designer windows by him were placed in Salisbury Cathedral, Liverpool Cathedral, St. George's Church, in the Jesmond area of NEWCASTLE, as well as in many cathedrals in Australia and America. He never abandoned his love of painting, however, exhibiting three genre works in London between 1876 and 1878, and sometimes painting portraits. He died at Salisbury. Represented: Laing A.G., Newcastle.

BROWN, Paul J. (d. 1950)
Illustrator. He was the son of J. R. Brown (q.v.), and grandson of John Brown (q.v.), and practised as an artist and author in NEWCASTLE in the first half of the

20th century. He first worked as a reporter for the *Newcastle Daily Leader*, but became increasingly involved in commercial art and writing for newspapers in his spare time. He was a regular contributor of articles on local history to the *Newcastle Journal*, many of these articles, and his accompanying illustrations, later appearing in a series of publications called the *Friday Books*. He also took a lifelong interest in the Roman Wall, and published a work *The Great Wall of Hadrian in Roman Times*. He was a member of the Society of Antiquaries, NEWCASTLE, among several bodies concerned with the study and preservation of old buildings. He died at NEWCASTLE.

BROWN, William (fl. early 19th cent.)
Drawing master. This artist practised as a drawing master at DURHAM in the early 19th century. It was said in the obituary of his son, Forster Brown (q.v.), that he was well known in his day for his works of art.

*BROWNLOW, George Washington (1835-1876)
Genre, portrait, landscape and religious painter in oil; modeller. He was born at NEWCASTLE the son of a cordwainer, and received his first tuition in art at the Government School of Design in the town under William Bell Scott (q.v.). At the age of twenty he was awarded a gold medal for his work as a student, and as a result of this achievement came to the notice of his future principal patron, the Rev. J. St. Clere Raymond, of Belchamp Hall, Belchamp Walter, in Essex. The first portrait painted by Brownlow was of Raymond, and when his patron some time later succeeded to the Belchamp estate he induced his protégé to settle in a cottage at Belchamp Walter. Brownlow meanwhile had enrolled as a student at the Royal Academy Schools, and made such good progress that by 1858 he was exhibiting at both the British Institution and the Suffolk Street Gallery. By 1860 he had commenced exhibiting at the Royal Academy, remaining a regular exhibitor

George Washington Brownlow: A Fisherman's Cottage, Ireland. Oil 11½×18½. *Christopher Wood Ltd.*

30

there and at the Suffolk Street Gallery until a year before his death. His exhibited work included many genre subjects, with such titles as: *Daddy's Coming, The Mother's Lesson*, and *The First Tiff*, but he also exhibited many homely Scottish and Irish cottage scenes,# and occasionally showed portraits and pure landscapes.

As a relaxation Brownlow was especially fond of painting the portraits of children at Belchamp Walter engaged in play, and other activities, and frequently modelled in clay. Among his less typical work in painting was the series of panels for the pulpit and the front of the altar of the local church. His work was also in some demand for reproduction, examples being used for works published by his patron, and Fulcher's *Pocket Book and Miscellany*; the latter publication used as its frontispiece an engraving of Brownlow's last, and largest work: *The Moorhen's Nest*, which now hangs in Sudbury Old Town Hall. One of his best known works was his *Early Days of the Ettrick Shepherd*, which was exhibited at NEWCASTLE in 1866, at the "Exhibition of Paintings and other Works of Art", at the Town Hall, and again, in 1878, at the exhibition of works by local painters, at the town's Central Exchange Art Gallery. Brownlow died at Sudbury, in Suffolk, but was buried in the village of Belchamp Walter, Essex, where he had spent much of his time from the middle 1860's. A window was later erected to his memory in the church there, its execution entrusted to the stained glass manufactory of William Wailes (q.v.). Brownlow's work has become increasingly appreciated in recent years; his *Cadogan Pier, Chelsea*, was singled out for comment and illustration in Satcheverell Sitwell's *Victorian Narrative Pictures*, 1969, and in 1981 his *The Village Schoolroom* established a record price for his work of £14,500. He was the younger brother of Stephen Brownlow (q.v.).

BROWNLOW, Stephen (1828-1896)
Landscape, genre and portrait painter in oil and watercolour. Brownlow was born at NEWCASTLE, the son of a cordwainer, and showed a talent for painting from an early age. He followed his general education by receiving some tuition from William Bell Scott (q.v.), at the Government School of Design at NEWCASTLE, and soon after became a full-time professional artist. He made his first major appearance at an exhibition in 1878, when he showed several works at the exhibition of works by local painters, at the Central Exchange Art Gallery, NEWCASTLE, including: *The Shrimp Girl*, a marine work and two landscapes, also showing one work: *Sunset on the Tyne*, at the Arts Association exhibition in that year. From 1878 he was a regular exhibitor in the city, notably at the Bewick Club, of which he was a member from its foundation until his death. Works shown at the Bewick Club included: *The Poacher* (1884), and *The Busy Tyne* (1893), amongst a wide range of local genre and landscape subjects. Brownlow was a friend, and portrait subject of Ralph Hedley (q.v.), the latter's portrait of Brownlow showing the artist in his studio close to Hedley's in the city's New Bridge Street. His greatest friend, however, was Robert Jobling (q.v.), with whom he travelled widely to paint. He was the elder brother of George Washing-

ton Brownlow (q.v.). His son, GEORGE BROWN-LOW, was a capable amateur artist, and also exhibited his work at the Bewick Club, NEWCASTLE. Represented: Laing A.G., Newcastle; North Tyneside Public Libraries.

BUCHANAN, Evelyne Oughtred, M.S.S.A., M.S.S.W.A., M. Council S.S.W.A. (b.1883)
Landscape painter in oil and watercolour. She was born at STOCKTON ON TEES, but later moved to Edinburgh, where she practised as an artist until after the middle of the present century. She exhibited her work at the Royal Academy, the Royal Scottish Academy, the Royal Institute of Oil Painters, and the Society of Women Artists, and widely in the provinces. Three of her works were included in the "Contemporary Artists of Durham County" exhibition staged at the Shipley Art Gallery, GATESHEAD, in 1951, in connection with the Festival of Britain. She was a member of the Society of Scottish Artists, and a member of the Scottish Society of Women Artists, also serving on the Council of the latter. Her daughter ELSPETH BUCHANAN (b. 1915), has also practised as an artist, and exhibited her work.

BULLOCK, Ralph, M.A. (1867-1949)
Portrait, landscape, animal and flower painter in oil and watercolour. Bullock was born at MORPETH, the son of a well known local sportsman and greyhound breeder, and subsequently moved to nearby KILLINGWORTH, before attending the School of Art, NEWCASTLE. Here he soon became recognised as an outstanding pupil, and on completing his studies was asked to remain as a member of staff, eventually receiving the designation Master of Painting when the School became absorbed into Armstrong College (later King's College; now Newcastle University). During his period of teaching at the College, Bullock established a reputation as one of Northumbria's most respected artists and teachers. Among his pupils were Byron Eric Dawson (q.v.), and John Thomas Young Gilroy (q.v.), as well as dozens of amateurs who attended evening classes under his tutelage. He first began exhibiting his work at the Bewick Club, NEWCASTLE, later becoming a regular exhibitor at the city's Laing Art Gallery, whose Artists of the Northern Counties exhibitions he contributed to for many years. In 1927 and 1928 he exhibited at the Royal Academy; in the first year contributing: *Northumberland*, and in the second: *Portrait of the Rev. J. Mackenzie*. In 1930 he was one of several leading local artists commissioned to paint a lunette for the Laing Art Gallery, his subject being: *The Entry of Princess Margaret into Newcastle upon Tyne c. 1503*. Bullock was a friend of Arthur Heslop (q.v.), John Atkinson (q.v.), and many other local artists, and frequently shared exhibitions with them. He also took a keen interest in artistic activities outside the College, and in 1923 received an honorary Master of Arts Degree from Durham University in recognition of his contribution to art in Northumbria. He was a member of the Pen & Palette Club, NEWCASTLE, and a founder member of the Newcastle Society of Artists. He died at his home for many years, FOREST HALL, near NEWCASTLE. Represented: Laing A.G., Newcastle.

BURLISON, Clement (1815-1899)
Portrait, landscape and allegorical painter in oil; copyist. He was born at EGGLESTON, near MIDDLETON-IN-TEESDALE, the son of William Burlison, joiner and later clerk of works to leading architect at DURHAM, Ignatius Bonomi. Early in his boyhood he was encouraged by the example of his elder brother John Burlison (q.v.), to draw and paint, and when his family later moved to DURHAM, he was allowed to attend the art classes at the Mechanics' Institute one evening a week. His first employment as an artist was as an heraldic painter to a coach builder at DARLINGTON, with whom he served an apprenticeship c.1828- c.1835. On completing this apprenticeship, however, he turned to portrait painting, and with money saved from commissions obtained at STOCKTON ON TEES and HARTLEPOOL, paid for his first visit to London, about 1836. Here he made copies of works in the National Gallery, shortly afterwards returning to Northumbria, where he remained for the next six years. In 1843 he sent his first work for exhibition, showing several portraits, and copies of works in the National Gallery, at the Polytechnic Exhibition at the Mechanics' Institute, DURHAM. Shortly after this he went to London, staying there briefly to make further copies of works in the National Gallery before visiting Paris, Rome, and Venice, where he also made copies, and painted several original works.

It would appear that on all or part of this tour he was accompanied by his brother John, as on returning to London in 1846 both men exhibited at the Royal Academy, showing Italian subjects; Clement showed his *Portrait of an Italian Girl*; his brother, two landscapes. In the following year he again visited Italy to paint copies of works in public and private collections, then settling at DURHAM, he remained based there for the rest of his life. He exhibited at the Royal Academy and the British Institution until 1863, and also showed his work at NEWCASTLE, notably at the exhibitions staged by the North of England Society for the Promotion of the Fine Arts and the Government School of Design, in 1850, and 1852; the "Exhibition of Paintings and other Works of Art", at the Town Hall, in 1866, and at the exhibitions of the Arts Association, and the Bewick Club, later in the century. On his death at DURHAM in 1899 Burlison bequeathed many of his copies of works in famous public collections, and a number of his own compositions, to the Corporation at DURHAM, and these were later housed in part of the Old Town Hall which became known as the "Burlison Art Gallery". His widow and daughter also set aside a sum of money to provide "Clement Burlison Art Prizes", to be competed for annually by pupils at Durham High School. Represented: Darlington A.G.; Gray A.G. & Museum, Hartlepool; Old Town Hall, Durham.

BURLISON, John (c.1812- after 1846)
Landscape, figure and animal painter in watercolour; draughtsman. He was the son of William Burlison, joiner and later clerk of works to leading architect at DURHAM, Ignatius Bonomi, and was possibly born at EGGLESTON, near MIDDLETON-IN-TEESDALE. He was a talented artist from his youth, his younger brother Clement Burlison (q.v.), clearly recalling in later years

watercolours of sawyers in a saw pit, and a horse, painted by him as early as c.1822. Indeed, it was these same watercolours which provided Clement's first attraction to drawing. John later assisted his father in the supervision of building work for Bonomi, one of the last works in which they were involved together being the construction of St. Paul's, WINLATON, near GATESHEAD, when John was about sixteen. He later worked for a builder at DARLINGTON, after which nothing is known of him except that he appears to have accompanied Clement on part of the latter's first tour of the continent, for at the Royal Academy in 1846, he exhibited two Italian views: *Sorrento, Bay of Naples*, and *Grand Canal, Venice*.

BURRELL, Mrs. H. Théonie (c.1870- after 1920)
Portrait painter in oil and watercolour. This artist practised at NEWCASTLE in the late 19th and early 20th centuries. She first exhibited her work at the Bewick Club, NEWCASTLE, later showing examples at the Royal Academy, the Royal Society of British Artists and the Society of Women Artists, of which last named body she was elected an associate in 1905. She also exhibited her work at the Artists of the Northern Counties exhibitions at the Laing Art Gallery, NEWCASTLE, from their inception in 1905. She last exhibited at the Royal Academy in 1920.

BUTCHART, Theresa Norah – see COPNALL, Mrs. Theresa Norah.

BYNON, Herbert Stanley (1898-1982)
Landscape and portrait painter in oil and watercolour; etcher. He was born at Macclesfield, Cheshire, but moved in his infancy to Tyneside. Here he trained as an artist following service in the First World War, attending Armstrong College (later King's College; now Newcastle University), under Richard George Hatton (q.v.). He later worked in the art department of Mawson Swan & Morgan, NEWCASTLE, but after service in the Second World War he turned to picture restoration on his own account, and eventually established a reputation as one of the leading practitioners in his field. Throughout his life he took a keen spare-time interest in painting and etching, showing his first work in the latter medium at the Artists of the Northern Counties exhibition at the Laing Art Gallery, NEWCASTLE, in 1916. He later exhibited his work on many occasions locally, and produced several limited edition etchings of Northumbrian subjects, some of them with the addition of colour. He died at NEWCASTLE.

CALDECOTT, H. S. (1870-1942)
Landscape painter in oil. Born at SUNDERLAND, this artist practised in the town in the late 19th and early 20th centuries. Sunderland Art Gallery has his oil: *Tree Study*.

CALVERT, John Smales (1836-1926)
Amateur landscape and architectural painter in water-colour. He was born at Staithes in North Yorkshire, but moved to MIDDLESBROUGH with his parents while still a child. He later spent a short period of time with his family in France, where his father was employed on the construction of the first French railway, then returning to MIDDLESBROUGH he attended the only school then in the town, later becoming a pupil teacher there. On qualifying as a teacher he taught for some twenty years, later becoming secretary to the School Board at MID-DLESBROUGH, and ultimately Director of Education. He was a keen spare-time painter throughout his life, and painted many views in North Yorkshire, France, Belgium, Norway and Germany. He was a member of the town's Literary and Philosophical Society, and a foundation member of the Cleveland Field Club, and the Cleveland Sketching Club. He died at MIDDLESBROUGH. Middlesbrough Art Gallery has several of his works, together with his life-size portrait by Frank Stanley Ogilvie (q.v.).

CALVERT, Samuel (fl.19th cent.)
Marine and coastal painter in oil. This artist practised in Northumbria in the middle of the 19th century, where a strong connection with SUNDERLAND is claimed. Two of his seascapes were included in the exhibition of works by local painters, at the Central Exchange Art Gallery, NEWCASTLE, in 1878, the catalogue notes of which describe him as: "Calvert, a clear but little known artist who excelled at seascapes". He was also described in the notes as deceased. The Laing Art Gallery, NEW-CASTLE, has a view of *Tynemouth Bar* attributed to this artist, and a view of the High and Low Lights at NORTH SHIELDS is known.

*CAMPBELL, John Hodgson (1855-1927)
Portrait and genre painter in oil; landscape painter in watercolour; illustrator. The eldest son of John Thompson Campbell (q.v.), he was born at NEWCASTLE and received his early training in art from William Cosens Way (q.v.), at the town's School of Art. At the age of fourteen he was apprenticed to William Wailes (q.v.), in the Wailes stained glass manufactory at NEWCASTLE, meanwhile continuing his studies at the School of Art. He remained with Wailes for a year after completing his apprenticeship, but deciding that he did not like being a stained glass designer, left his trade with the intention of becoming a professional artist. With this object in mind he went to Edinburgh, and entered himself as a student at the Statue Gallery in the city. On the death of his father about 1880, however, he felt obliged to return to NEWCASTLE, and was only able to continue his studies at Edinburgh sporadically over the next few years by visiting the city for a month or two at a time.

By 1878 he was exhibiting at the Arts Association, NEWCASTLE, and six years later he began exhibiting at the Royal Academy, showing: *Ovingham, the burial place of Thomas Bewick*. In 1884 he also began exhibiting at the New Water Colour Society (later the Royal Institute of Painters in Water Colours), and at the

Bewick Club, NEWCASTLE, remaining a regular exhibitor at the latter for the rest of his life. He also exhibited at the Royal Scottish Academy, and several provincial exhibitions, including the Artists of the Northern Counties exhibitions at the Laing Art Gallery, NEWCASTLE. Although Campbell's main profession was that of portrait painter, he was by preference a painter of landscapes in watercolour, and in recognition of this a major exhibition of his work in this medium was held at NEWCASTLE in 1924. He was a lifelong member of the Pen & Palette Club, NEWCASTLE, and frequently exhibited with the Club. He died at WHICKHAM, near GATES-HEAD, where he had lived for some years prior to his decease. Represented: British Museum; Laing A.G., Newcastle; Shipley A.G., Gateshead; South Shields Museum & A.G.

CAMPBELL, John Thompson (1822- c.1880)
Stained glass designer; genre, portrait and landscape painter in oil, watercolour and crayon. He was born at Edinburgh, and studied under Sir William Allan, later president of the Royal Scottish Academy, and at the Royal Institution in the city, where he was a successful student. About 1840 he joined the design staff of William Wailes (q.v.), in the Wailes stained glass manufactory at NEWCASTLE, with fellow Scotsmen James Sticks (q.v.), and Francis Wilson Oliphant (q.v.).

John Hodgson Campbell: Winlaton Mill, near Gateshead, from the South. Watercolour 22×15. *Dean Gallery.*

33

Together with these two artists he visited the continent to study the best examples of stained glass in cathedrals and other buildings, subsequently becoming one of Wailes' most distinguished designers. He occasionally painted in his spare time, exhibiting this work at NEWCASTLE, where in 1848 he showed his *Academy Study of the Laacoon*, and *Portrait in Crayons*, at the "Exhibition of Arts & Manufactures & Practical Science". He followed this by exhibiting his *Gossips at the Well; The Letter; Asleep in the Wood; An Anxious Moment*, and a stained glass study, at the "Exhibition of Paintings and other Works of Art", in 1866, and showed two Scottish landscapes at the "Central Exchange News Room, Art Gallery, and Polytechnic Exhibition", in 1870. He last exhibited when he sent two landscapes to the Arts Association exhibition at NEWCASTLE, in 1878: *Glenlochy, Killen, Perthshire*, and *Swalwell from Whickham Bank*. He was the father of John Hodgson Campbell (q.v.).

CANNON, William (b. 1840)

Marine painter in watercolour. Cannon is said to have been born at NEWCASTLE, and to have studied under Thomas Bush Hardy before practising as a marine painter. He lived and worked for some time in France and Italy, but is said to have returned to England in his

Herbert Carmichael: Summer Blooms, 1900. Oil 30×18. *Anderson & Garland.*

34

later years, dying at NEWCASTLE. He exhibited his work at the Royal Institute of Painters in Water Colours, and the Royal Water Colour Society, and in 1877 received a gold medal in Paris. He appears to have produced little work in Northumbria, although a watercolour: *Off Whitley Bay*, is known.

*CARMICHAEL, Herbert (née Schmalz, Herbert Gustave) (Angelico) (1856-1935)

Portrait, landscape, religious, classical and flower painter in oil. He was born at RYTON, the son of merchant, and later Prussian Consul at NEWCASTLE, Gustave Schmalz, and Margaret Carmichael, eldest daughter of John Wilson Carmichael (q.v.). He first began painting as a child of eight during an illness caused by a burn sustained at his boarding school at NEWCASTLE, and is believed to have been encouraged in this respect by the sight of his grandfather's paintings in the drawing room of his home, The Tower, at RYTON. He subsequently spent two years at school at DURHAM, then was sent to Gothic House College, London, where he won every drawing prize available. Following his education he returned to Tyneside to study at the School of Art at NEWCASTLE, under William Cosens Way (q.v.), but at seventeen he went back to London, first to attend South Kensington Art School, later the Royal Academy Schools. He then spent the remainder of his life in the South of England, though visiting Northumbria frequently while his parents were still alive.

He first began exhibiting his work in 1879, as Herbert Gustave Schmalz, showing two works at the Royal Academy: *Light and Shade*, and *I cannot mind my wheel mother* . . . He retained this name while exhibiting at the Royal Academy, the Royal Hibernian Academy, the Fine Art Society, the Leicester Gallery, and widely in the provinces, until 1918, whereafter he contributed his work as "Herbert Carmichael", having adopted his mother's maiden name because, it is said, of prevailing anti-German feeling in Britain. Schmalz's work was well appreciated in his lifetime and in 1911 encouraged Trevor Blakemore to publish: *The Art of Herbert Schmalz*, illustrating many of his works. His *Zenobia's Last Look at Smyrna* was acquired for The Art Gallery of South Australia, Adelaide, and his *Too Late*, for the Bendigo Art Gallery, Victoria, while his *Rabboni* is in a chapel at Stockport. He retained an interest in the artistic activities of his native Tyneside throughout his professional career, exhibiting many works at the Bewick Club, NEWCASTLE, and later the city's Laing Art Gallery, NEWCASTLE, whose Artists of the Northern Counties exhibitions he contributed to, from their inception in 1905, until several years after he changed his name to Carmichael. A major exhibition of his work was held in the year following his death, at Robertson's Gallery, London, comprising some thirty-two paintings. Among these were examples of his flower works signed "Angelico". Represented: Middlesbrough A.G., and various provincial and overseas art galleries.

*CARMICHAEL, John Wilson (1799‡-1868)

Marine, landscape and figure painter in oil and watercolour; draughtsman; illustrator; drawing master. He was born at NEWCASTLE, the son of a shipwright, and after some years at sea as a boy, was himself apprenticed to this trade with Tyneside shipbuilders Richard Farrington and Brothers. Here he soon began to display a talent for drawing, and was occasionally allowed to work in the drawing office of the firm. Later one of his employers, amateur artist JOSEPH FARRINGTON, gave him his first box of watercolours, and from then on he both drew and painted his compositions. On concluding his apprenticeship he was at first undecided whether to become a professional artist, but encouraged by his employers, and later mining engineer Nicholas Wood, he established a studio at NEWCASTLE by his early twenties, and in 1825 began exhibiting his work, showing at the Northumberland Institution for the Promotion of the Fine Arts, in the town: *A Seventy-four in a heavy sea*, and *Outward and homeward-bound Indiamen passing the Downs*. In the following year (20th March, 1826), he married at Holy Cross Church, RYTON, a girl from his own background, Mary Sweet, and living at various places on Tyneside over the next twenty years, remained a regular exhibitor at NEWCASTLE, also sending work to the Carlisle Academy from 1828, the Royal Academy from 1835, the Suffolk Street Gallery from 1838, and the British Institution from 1846.

Carmichael's twenty-odd year period at NEWCASTLE as a professional artist saw him develop from a painter of miniatures and drawing master, into one of the best liked and respected landscape and marine artists of Northumbria. It saw him take an active interest in the promotion of art in his native town, and the development of a style in marine painting considerably influenced by the work of the many famous artists whose work was thereby exhibited. He received his first major commission in the year of his marriage, *The Bombardment of Algiers, 1816*, for Trinity House, NEWCASTLE. Three years later, and exhibiting some nine works at the Northern Academy, NEWCASTLE, he began attracting praise from local critics, and in 1831, working from sketches provided by his friend and fellow artist George Balmer (q.v.), he consolidated his position as one of the area's most promising marine painters by executing *The Heroic Exploit of Lord Collingwood . . .*, for Trinity House. Much work followed the production of this popular painting; a series of drawings of the construction of the Newcastle and Carlisle Railway, commenced in 1835, and issued as engravings 1836-38, before their collective presentation as a volume in 1839; colouring and figure drawing for the compositions of local architects, including John Dobson (q.v.); tuition in drawing

John Wilson Carmichael: The Newcastle Whaling Fleet in the Arctic, *c.* 1835. Oil 42×63. *N. R. Omell Ltd.*

35

and painting for a number of pupils, such as John Scott (q.v.), and the production of a number of views of towns and buildings, including towards the end of his period at NEWCASTLE, his well known view of the town from GATESHEAD, incorporating the then as yet unbuilt High Level Bridge, later issued as an engraving.

At the age of almost forty-seven Carmichael felt the need to test his abilities more fully, and moving to London in 1846, he practised there with considerable success until 1862. His work there soon became popular with influential patrons, and at times he was completing a picture a day while advancing more elaborate work. By 1852 he was able to record: "Hard at work as usual, with better results this year . . .", and three years later the *Illustrated London News* was proudly announcing to its readers that it had secured the services of "Mr. J. W. Carmichael, the celebrated marine painter" to sketch the events of the "coming campaign in the Baltic". During his stay in London he came increasingly to regard himself as a marine painter, and apart from his trip with the Baltic Fleet for the latter assignment, made trips to Portsmouth, the Isle of Wight, Calais and Dunkerque, to handle commissions in this field. Others also viewed him in this light, Winsor & Newton engaging him to write *Marine Painting in Water Colours* 1859, and four years later, *Marine Painting in Oils*. By the time that the second book appeared, however, ill-health had driven him to Scarborough, and here he remained until his death on 2nd May, 1868. Carmichael is popularly supposed to have given up painting when he moved to Scarborough, but recent research ("John Wilson Carmichael – the missing years at Scarborough", Marshall Hall, *Art & Antiques Weekly*, 15th, October, 1977) has revealed that he painted until close to his death. He was the grandfather of Herbert Carmichael (q.v.). A major exhibition of Carmichael's work was held at the Laing Art Gallery, NEWCASTLE, in 1968, to mark the centenary of his death. Represented: British Museum; National Maritime Museum; Victoria and Albert Museum; Carlisle A.G.; Grace Darling Museum, Bamburgh; Gray A.G. & Museum, Hartlepool;

Laing A.G., Newcastle; North Tyneside Public Libraries; South Shields Museum & A.G.; Sunderland A.G.

‡ *Carmichael was born 9th June, 1799, and baptized at All Saints' Church, NEWCASTLE, on 31st July of that year, according to the baptismal records of the church, now in the Northumberland County Record Office.*

CARTER, Mrs. Eva (née Lawson) (1885-1963)
Landscape, flower, fruit and portrait painter in oil and watercolour. She was born at NEWCASTLE, and appears to have become a largely self-taught artist before setting up a studio in the city alongside other professionals such as Byron Eric Dawson (q.v.), and Thomas William Pattinson (q.v.). She first began exhibiting her work shortly after her marriage to schoolmaster John Carter, sending a work entitled: *A Study in Colour*, to the Artists of the Northern Counties exhibition at the Laing Art Gallery, NEWCASTLE, in 1908. Three years later she commenced exhibiting outside Northumbria, sending five works to the Royal Academy between 1911-16. She later exhibited almost exclusively on Tyneside, sending work regularly to the exhibitions of the Artists of the Northern Counties, the Federation of Northern Art Societies exhibitions at the Laing Art Gallery, and those of Gateshead Art Club, at the Shipley Art Gallery, GATESHEAD. She was a talented writer, and in addition to contributing articles to the *Evening Chronicle*, NEWCASTLE, 1935-51, wrote and illustrated a book: *Tales of the North Country*, 1947. Two of her more important works as an artist were her memorial to the 43rd and 49th Tank Regiments, entitled: *Rhine Crossing*, unveiled at the Territorial Army Centre, NEWCASTLE, in 1948, and her portrait of Captain E. G. Swan, Honorary Curator of the Museum of Science & Engineering, NEWCASTLE. Represented: Laing A.G., Newcastle; Shipley A.G., Gateshead.

*CARTER, Francis Thomas (1853-1934)
Landscape painter in oil. Carter was born at WARKWORTH, the son of the local stationmaster. He later moved to NEWCASTLE, where he began a career in

Francis Thomas Carter: Eighton Banks, Gateshead. Oil 17×30. *Dean Gallery.*

John Chambers: The
burning of the
"Wellesley". Watercolour
24×32. *J. C. Featonby.*

business with station newsagents W. H. Smith, abandoning this employment some years subsequently to join his father, who had become lessee of the Pineapple Grill & Restaurant in the city's Nun Street. Later his father, his brother Charles and himself, took over the Nag's Head in the same street, this public house soon becoming widely known throughout Tyneside, as "Carter's". His first introduction to painting came about by accident, he once claimed. A friend had asked him to dispose of "a painter's outfit", and experimenting with it he found he could paint passably well. Following this experiment he spent an increasing amount of time on his new hobby, and became so accomplished an artist that he was soon selling his work.

He first began exhibiting his work at the Bewick Club, NEWCASTLE, and by 1898 had sent his first work to the Royal Academy: *Vale of Aln*. He later became a regular exhibitor at the Academy, also sending his work to the Royal Scottish Academy, the Royal Hibernian Academy, the Royal Cambrian Academy, the Suffolk Street Gallery, the Royal Institute of Oil Painters, and to various London and provincial galleries, including among the latter the Laing Art Gallery, NEWCASTLE, whose Artists of the Northern Counties exhibitions he contributed to from their inception in 1905. In 1934 he shared a loan exhibition at the last named establishment with Thomas Bowman Garvie (q.v.), George Edward Horton (q.v.), and John Falconar Slater (q.v.). It is said that for six days a week Carter conducted his business as an inn-keeper, while on Sundays he took out his palette and brushes at his studio at GATESHEAD, and painted pictures from his sketches made during the summer months. His establishment in Nun Street, NEWCASTLE, from its early days was a resort of the "intelligentsia" of the city, fellow artists, writers, and professional men crowding its picture hung rooms to discuss their mutual interests. When asked for a price for one of his works he quickly fixed a sum, and if that figure were not accepted no further negotiations would

be entertained. His accomplishment as an artist was considerable, and all the more remarkable because it was entirely self-developed. His favourite subject matter was the hills, lakes and streams of the English Lake District, but he also painted many Northumbrian landscapes and was no stranger to Scotland. He died at GATESHEAD. Represented: Laing A.G., Newcastle; Shipley A.G., Gateshead; South Shields Museum & A.G.

*CHAMBERS, John (1852-1928)

Landscape, seascape and portrait painter in oil and watercolour; illustrator. Chambers was born at SOUTH SHIELDS, and educated at the Union British Schools in the town. Drawing was taught at the Schools, and pupils were particularly encouraged to draw ships and other nautical subjects. Chambers found that he liked drawing, and although he entered the Tyne Pilot Service soon after leaving school he had even then decided that he would one day become an artist. Before reaching manhood he left the Pilot Service, and enrolled in the Government School of Design at NEWCASTLE, under William Cosens Way (q.v.), later studying in Paris in the ateliers of Professors Boulanger and Fevre, before settling at NORTH SHIELDS as a professional artist. He first began exhibiting his work by showing his *Parton Hall, and Harbour*, at the exhibition of works by local painters, at the Central Exchange Art Gallery, NEWCASTLE, in 1878. He followed this by exhibiting at the Arts Association, NEWCASTLE, in 1879, and was an exhibitor at the "Gateshead Fine Art & Industrial Exhibition", in 1883. In the following year he began an association with the exhibitions of the Bewick Club, NEWCASTLE, which lasted throughout his life, and in 1886 he sent his first work to the Royal Institute of Painters in Water Colours. From 1905 he also exhibited at the Artists of the Northern Counties exhibitions at the Laing Art Gallery, NEWCASTLE, showing as his first exhibits: *Lost 'Fame' Tynemouth*, and *Redheugh*

Salmon Fishing Station, near Fast Castle Point, N.B.
Most of his work was executed in watercolour and
predominantly portrayed local landscape and nautical
subjects, some of which were etched for sale locally, or
were interpreted by himself as line drawings for reproduction. Among his less typical works are a number of
portraits in watercolour, among these one of Henry
Hetherington Emmerson (q.v.), now in the possession
of the Laing Art Gallery, NEWCASTLE. Represented:
Laing A.G., Newcastle; North Tyneside Public Libraries; South Shields Museum & A.G.

CHANCER, Thomas (1761-1819)
Sculptor; stonemason. Chancer was a well known
stonemason and occasional sculptor at RYTON in the late
18th century. He was responsible for the production of
the Village Cross erected in 1795. He is buried in the
churchyard of Holy Cross Church, RYTON.

CHAPMAN, Abel, M.A. (1851-1929)
Amateur bird and animal painter in watercolour; illustrator. He was born at Silksworth Hall, SUNDERLAND,
the son of a brewery owner, and following his general
education joined the family business as a director. Part
of his responsibility as a director was to travel abroad,
and many of these trips he combined with hunting and
natural history expeditions which eventually took him
throughout Europe, and into North, South, and East
Africa. He wrote prodigiously of his experiences and
observations on these expeditions, illustrating some of
his books with his own watercolours, or drawings.
Notable amongst these were *Bird Life of the Borders*,
1907, and *The Borders & Beyond*, 1924, which latter he
illustrated with W. H. Riddell, providing 170 sketches
himself. Chapman remained director of the brewery for
some thirty years, at the end of this period retiring to
WARK, on the North Tyne. Here he stayed for the rest
of his life, occupying much of his time writing his
autobiographical: *Retrospect: Reminiscences 1851-1928*,
and the two books mentioned earlier. In 1922 his
contributions to literature were recognised by Durham
University, and an honorary Master of Arts Degree was
conferred upon him. Many of his drawings, big game
trophies and natural history specimens now form part
of the collection of the Hancock Museum, NEWCASTLE.
He was a cousin of Joseph Crawhall, The Third (q.v.).

*CHAPMAN, William (1817-1879)
Engraver; landscape and architectural painter in watercolour. He was born at SUNDERLAND, and became a
pupil of William Miller, a well known Edinburgh
engraver, before setting up himself in that city as an
engraver. He later moved to London, where in 1866 he
sent to the Royal Academy an engraving of Henry
Dawson's: *Westminster Palace and Abbey*. By 1869 he
had moved to York, from which in that year he sent to
the Academy a second engraving: *Tynemouth Pier*,
after A. W. Hunt. After settling at York he mainly
concentrated on producing views of the city, and its
various architectural landmarks. He died at York. He
was related to the family of Joseph Crawhall, The

William Chapman: Sunderland Harbour. Watercolour
10⅜×6¼. *Tyne & Wear County Council Museums, Sunderland
Art Gallery & Museum.*

Second (q.v.) and received considerable help from this
artist at one stage in his career. He also contributed
work in the form of etchings to some of Crawhall's
publications. Represented: British Museum; Laing
A.G., Newcastle; Leeds A.G.; Sunderland A.G.; York
City A.G.

CHARLETON, Robert John (1849-1925)
Amateur landscape and architectural painter in watercolour. He was born at HEXHAM, but at the age of five
moved with his parents to NEWCASTLE. Here he later
worked for a hardwareman before branching out on his
own account in this line, but adding electrical lighting
to his business. Charleton lived at NEWCASTLE throughout his career in business, from his earliest years taking
a keen interest in writing. He published three historical
novels as well as several books on local history, of which
latter the best known is his *Newcastle Town*, 1885,* with
illustrations by Robert Jobling (q.v.). He was also
interested in painting and drawing and was friendly with
many leading Northumbrian artists of his day, among
these Jobling, and Ralph Hedley (q.v.). His *Newcastle
Town* devotes several pages to artists of the area.
Charleton occasionally exhibited his work at NEW-
CASTLE, notably at the exhibitions of the Arts Association. His first exhibit at the Association was his *On the
Derwent*, shown in 1878. He died at NEWCASTLE.

Reprinted by Frank Graham, 1978.

*CHARLTON, John, R.B.A., R.O.I. (1849-1917)

Animal, sporting, battle scene and figure painter in oil and watercolour; illustrator. Charlton was born at BAMBURGH, and received his first drawing lessons from his father. At an early age he obtained employment in the bookshop at NEWCASTLE, of Robert Robinson, later biographer of Thomas Bewick (q.v.). Here he displayed a keen interest in painting and drawing, and when he subsequently took up an engineering apprenticeship with Sir Isaac Lowthian Bell, his master gave him one day off a week to attend the Government School of Design under William Cosens Way (q.v.). He decided after some time that he would prefer a career in art to that of engineering, and after studying at South Kensington for some weeks he returned to NEWCASTLE to establish himself as a full-time professional artist. In 1870 he confirmed the wisdom of his choice by having a work accepted for showing at the Royal Academy: *Harrowing*, and also exhibited at the "Central Exchange News Room, Art Gallery, and Polytechnic Exhibition" at NEWCASTLE, in that year. In the following year he showed his first of many works at the Suffolk Street Gallery: *Head of a Fox Terrier*, and by 1875 he had decided to establish himself in London. Here he first shared a studio with John Dawson Watson, from whom he is said to have received much valuable instruction, and the encouragement to concentrate on figure painting. The two artists collaborated in the painting of a work shown at the Suffolk Street Gallery in 1876/7: *A Check*, and remained friendly for many years.

Following the showing of *A Check*, Charlton set up his own studio in the capital, and with his Royal Academy exhibit of 1878: *Gone Away*, established himself as one of the foremost sporting painters of his day. He continued to exhibit at the Royal Academy, and the Suffolk Street Gallery over the next three years, and also sent work to the Arts Association exhibitions at NEWCASTLE. He next attracted attention with his 1883 exhibit at the Academy: *The British Artillery entering the enemy's lines at Tel-el-Kebir*, this impressive work possibly paving the way to his commission to paint for Queen Victoria four years later the Royal Procession in connection with her Jubilee, and a similar commission in connection with her 1897 Jubilee. Interestingly, he received news of the first commission while holidaying at CULLERCOATS, a village which he had visited regularly from his childhood. Charlton continued to exhibit at the Royal Academy until the year of his death, and at the Suffolk Street Gallery until 1891. He also exhibited his work at the Royal Society of Portrait Painters, and at various other London and provincial establishments, including the Bewick Club, NEWCASTLE, and later the city's Laing Art Gallery, whose Artists of the Northern Counties exhibitions he contributed to from their inception in 1905. In addition to practising as a highly successful painter, Charlton was a popular illustrator, working for *The Graphic* 1876-95, and illustrating at least two books: *Twelve Packs of Hounds*, 1891, and *Red Deer*, 1896. He was elected a member of the Royal Society of British Artists in 1882, and a member of the Royal Institute of Oil Painters in 1887. Following his death at Lanercost, Cumberland, in 1917, the Laing Art

John Charlton: The Women, 1910. Oil 60×95. *Tyne & Wear County Council Museums, Laing Art Gallery.*

Gallery held a major memorial exhibition of his work. One of his two sons, HUGH V. CHARLTON (d. 1916), was a talented landscape and bird painter, and exhibited his work. Represented: Victoria and Albert Museum; Gray A.G. & Museum, Hartlepool; Laing A.G., Newcastle; Shipley A.G., Gateshead; South Shields Museum & A.G.

CHARLTON, William Henry (1846-1918)
Landscape and coastal painter in oil and watercolour; lithographer. He was born at NEWCASTLE, and began his studies in art at the town's Percy Street Academy, under Charles Richardson (q.v.). He later studied at the Academie Julian, in Paris, and on his return to NEWCASTLE commenced exhibiting widely throughout Britain, showing examples of his work at the Royal Academy, the Royal Scottish Academy, the Glasgow Institute of Fine Arts, the Walker Art Gallery, Liverpool, the Bewick Club, NEWCASTLE, and later the city's Laing Art Gallery, whose Artists of the Northern Counties exhibitions he contributed to from their inception in 1905, until his death at nearby GOSFORTH, in 1918. Charlton painted and exhibited several continental subjects, in addition to his many Northumbrian subjects, and frequently worked on a small scale. He sometimes worked in chalk, and experimented with lithography. Represented: British Museum; Laing A.G., Newcastle; North Tyneside Public Libraries.

CHISHOLM, Peter, A.R.C.A. (1875-1962)
Landscape painter in oil and watercolour; draughtsman; art teacher. Chisholm was born at Selkirk, in Scotland, but in his youth moved to NEWCASTLE, where he attended the city's Rutherford College. On completing his studies at the College he practised as an artist for some time at NORTH SHIELDS, from which in 1897 he sent his only work to the Royal Academy: *November*. Following this he enrolled as a student of the Royal College of Art, but remained a regular exhibitor at the Rutherford College Art Club for a number of years, until his appointment as Senior Art Master at the Douglas School of Art, Isle of Man. After this appointment he exhibited only at the Royal Scottish Academy, and at Liverpool. He later retired from the School of Art and taught art at Douglas High School. He died at Douglas. He was an associate of the Royal College of Art. The Manx Museum, Douglas, has examples of his work in oil, watercolour and pen and ink.

CHURNSIDE, Thomas Edward (fl. late 19th, early 20th cent.)
Amateur landscape painter in watercolour. Churnside worked as a hairdresser at SOUTH SHIELDS for much of his life, painting in his spare time. He exhibited his work from 1901, showing one work at the Royal Cambrian Academy, one work at the Royal Hibernian Academy, and one work at the Glasgow Institute of Fine Arts. He also exhibited at the Artists of the Northern Counties exhibitions at the Laing Art Gallery, NEWCASTLE, in 1908, showing: *On Bellingham Moors*. He later moved to NEWCASTLE, where in trade directories published just before the First World War, he was

listing himself as a professional artist. Represented: Shipley A.G., Gateshead.

*CLARK, James, R.I., R.O.I., N.E.A.C. (1858-1943)
Portrait, figure, genre, biblical, landscape and flower painter in oil, watercolour and pastel; muralist; illustrator; stained glass designer. Clark was born at WEST HARTLEPOOL (now HARTLEPOOL), and after studying at the local School of Art, went on to study at South Kensington, where he gained the Gold Medal for Watercolour Studies. Later he went to Paris, where he worked in the studio of Bonnat, and afterwards at the Ecole des Beaux Arts, under Gérôme. On leaving Paris he returned to his native town, where he practised as an artist until settling in Chelsea in 1877. In 1881 he sent his first work to the Royal Academy: *Hagar and Ishmail*. He returned to WEST HARTLEPOOL in the following year and while working here for some three years continued to exhibit at the Royal Academy, and also sent work for exhibition widely in the provinces, including the Bewick Club, NEWCASTLE, at which in 1884 he showed an oil: *A Fisherman's Cottage*.

On moving back to London by 1885, Clark began exhibiting at the Suffolk Street Gallery, the Royal Institute of Painters in Water Colours, the Royal Institute of Oil Painters, the Royal Society of Portrait Painters, and several London galleries, including the Fine Art Society. He was elected a member of the New English Art Club in 1886, the Royal Institute of Oil Painters in 1893, and the Royal Institute of Painters in Water Colours in 1903, and apart from occasional professional visits to Northumbria, appears to have spent most of his later life in London. Here, in addition to practising as a highly succesful artist patronised by the Royal Family, he also served as Examiner and Inspector of Art for the Board of Education, and an Examiner in Art for the University of Cambridge. He continued to exhibit his work widely until late in life, from 1908 regularly sending works to the Artists of the Northern Counties exhibitions at the Laing Art Gallery, NEWCASTLE, and in 1926 enjoying a one-man show of his work at the Gray Art Gallery, WEST HARTLEPOOL, at which some eighty-eight examples of his work were shown. He died at Reigate, Surrey. His son JOHN COSMO CLARK (1897-1967), was also a distinguished artist. The Gray Art Gallery & Museum, HARTLEPOOL, has a fine collection of his work, including a self portrait. Represented: Gray A.G. & Museum, Hartlepool; Laing A.G., Newcastle; Pannett A.G., Whitby; Shipley A.G., Gateshead; Sunderland A.G.

CLARK, James Waite (fl. late 19th, early 20th cent.)
Landscape and coastal painter in oil and watercolour. This artist practised at NORTH SHIELDS in the 1880's, from which he regularly sent work for exhibition to the Bewick Club, NEWCASTLE, and to the Art Club at TYNEMOUTH, of which he was for some time treasurer. By 1899 he had moved to SOUTH SHIELDS, from which in the following eight years he sent work to the Royal Academy, the Royal Institute of Painters in Water Colours, and to various London and provincial galleries, including the Laing Art Gallery, NEWCASTLE, whose

James Clark: The Bombardment of Hartlepool. Pencil and watercolour 9×14¾. Gray Art Gallery & Museum.

Artists of the Northern Counties exhibitions he contributed to in 1905, and 1908. His Royal Academy contribution of 1900, was entitled: *On Whitley Sands*. Clark's name was sometimes misprinted in catalogues of his period as "Waiteclark"; trade directories, however, confirm his correct name as shown above.

CLARK, John Stewart (STEWART, Ian) (1883-1956)
Portrait, landscape and fruit painter in oil and watercolour; miniaturist; etcher. The second son of Joseph Dixon Clark, Senior (q.v.), and younger brother of Joseph Dixon Clark, Junior (q.v.), he was born at BLAYDON, near GATESHEAD, and began exhibiting at the Royal Academy at the age of eighteen, showing a portrait miniature entitled: *Miss Brown*. Following this early success he became a frequent exhibitor at the Academy, mainly showing portraits in miniature of Northumbrian clients, and acquaintances, but also in a freelance capacity portraying many famous personalities, among these, members of the Royal Family, Sir Winston Churchill, and Queen Salote of Tonga. For much of his early professional life he ran a photographic studio at GATESHEAD, where he also tinted photographs in colour; this work led to commissions from many other photographic houses, for which he both coloured photographs, and interpreted them in a variety of media including crayon and etching. He exhibited at the Royal Academy until 1937, one of his exhibits in 1918: *Miss Katherine Vincent*, earning from *The Studio*, the comment: "John Stewart Clark has a shrewd perception of present day necessities. In his examples of miniatures

which are reproduced it can be clearly seen that there is no necessity to impose the snapshot manner for the sake of securing a definitely characteristic likeness."

Clark spent most of his life on Tyneside, and formed several friendships among brother artists, including Harry James Sticks (q.v.), a portrait of whose son Harry, he exhibited at the Artists of the Northern Counties exhibition, at the Laing Art Gallery, NEWCASTLE, in 1914. Most of the works which he sent to the Artists of the Northern Counties exhibitions at NEWCASTLE, and to the Walker Art Gallery, Liverpool, were portrait miniatures, but he occasionally showed full-size portraits in oil. As relaxations from his portrait work he also painted, but rarely showed publicly, watercolour studies of gardens, fruit, etc. In his later years Clark lived and worked in the Midlands and South of England, dying in London in 1956. He sometimes sent work to exhibitions signed: "Ian Stewart", several of these works being accepted for showing at the Royal Academy, the Royal Scottish Academy, and in London galleries. His sister, Laura Annie Clark (q.v.), was also a talented painter of portrait miniatures.

*CLARK, Joseph Dixon, Senior (1849-1944)
Animal, landscape and portrait painter in oil and watercolour; sculptor; wood carver; furniture designer. One of Northumbria's best known animal painters of this century, "Dixon Clark", as he preferred to sign himself for the greater part of his long career as a professional artist, was born at NORTH SHIELDS. Details of his early artistic training are not known, but by 1884,

41

and exhibiting at the first exhibition of the Bewick Club, NEWCASTLE, two works: *O Ye Dales*, and *The Turnip Field*, he had taken a studio in the city, and was living at nearby BLAYDON, and supporting a family of four children, three of whom: Joseph Dixon Clark, Junior (q.v.), John Stewart Clark (q.v.), and Laura Annie Clark (q.v.), were also to become artists. Clark continued to live at BLAYDON until the turn of the century, meanwhile consolidating his reputation as an artist by exhibiting at the Royal Academy, the Royal Scottish Academy, and at various London and provincial exhibitions, mainly showing cattle pictures. He also continued to exhibit at the Bewick Club, of which he remained a member throughout its existence.

By 1900 Clark's success as an artist was such that he was able to purchase a large house at WHICKHAM, near GATESHEAD, and build a studio at the bottom of his two and a half acre garden. He thereafter confined his exhibiting activity to Tyneside, however, where his works were often the centre of attraction at the Bewick Club exhibitions, and later the Artists of the Northern Counties exhibitions at the Laing Art Gallery, NEWCASTLE. Clark lived at WHICKHAM for many years before settling finally at WHITLEY BAY, where he died at the age of ninety-five. In addition to being an accomplished animal painter, Clark was an able landscape and portrait painter, a sculptor and wood carver of considerable ability, and designed and made his own furniture. He painted until close to his death, his last exhibits being the two works which he sent to the Artists of the Northern Counties exhibition in 1944: *Incoming Tide, Whitley Bay*, and *Pilot's Lover*. Represented: Shipley A.G., Gateshead; Sunderland A.G.

CLARK, Joseph Dixon, Junior (1878-1966)
Landscape painter in oil and watercolour. The first son of Joseph Dixon Clark, Senior (q.v.), and brother of John Stewart Clark (q.v.), and Laura Annie Clark

(q.v.), he was born at BLAYDON, near GATESHEAD, and later qualified as an architect. While studying architecture he became a keen amateur painter, and evidently travelled to the Middle East, for by 1911 he was exhibiting Egyptian scenes at the Artists of the Northern Counties exhibitions at the Laing Art Gallery, NEWCASTLE. He continued to exhibit at NEWCASTLE until the outbreak of the First World War, when he enlisted in the Royal Flying Corps. At the end of the war he returned to NEWCASTLE, sending one work to the Royal Academy as "Dixon Clark Jun.", in 1919, entitled: *In Fancy Dress*, and resuming exhibiting at the Artists of the Northern Counties exhibitions by sending two oils: *Bamborough Castle*, and *Barnard Castle*. Clark spent his later years in the South of England, dying in London in 1966.

CLARK, Laura Annie – see ADAMS, Mrs. Laura Gladstone

CLARKSON, George Henry (fl. early 20th cent.)
Landscape painter in watercolour; enamel painter; sculptor. This artist practised at SUNDERLAND in the early 20th century. He exhibited his work at the Royal Academy, and at the Artists of the Northern Counties exhibitions at the Laing Art Gallery, NEWCASTLE, at the former mainly showing enamels; at the latter enamels and occasional works in watercolour.

CLEET, James Henry (1877-1959)
Amateur marine painter. Cleet was born at SOUTH SHIELDS, the son of a sea captain, and later practised as a photographer in the town, painting marine and coastal subjects in his spare time. He died at SOUTH SHIELDS. His work as a photographer, particularly that relating to buildings at SOUTH SHIELDS in the 1930's, has recently been the subject of a number of exhibitions. Represented: South Shields Museum & A.G.

*CLENNELL, Luke (1781-1840)

Landscape, portrait and genre painter in oil and water-colour; wood engraver. Clennell was born at ULGHAM, near MORPETH, and worked in his uncle's grocery and leather tanning business at the latter before becoming and apprentice of Thomas Bewick (q.v.), at NEWCASTLE, in 1797. He joined Bewick in the year in which his master published the first volume of the "Birds", and soon became involved in cutting many tailpieces for the second volume, which appeared in the last year of his apprenticeship, 1804. While working with Bewick, Clennell appears to have received instruction in water-colour painting from his master, and followed Bewick's practice of producing studies in this medium for his subsequent engravings. Many of his watercolours were, however, completely unrelated to known engravings, suggesting that at this early stage he was already attracted to their painting for purely personal reasons. Bewick was obviously impressed by Clennell's abilities as an illustrator and wood engraver, and worked with him in the last two years of his apprenticeship on *The Hive of Ancient and Modern Literature*, published by Solomon Hodgson in 1806. The two also worked together after the expiry of Clennell's apprenticeship, on Hume's *History of England*, Clennell later being invited by the publisher to continue the commission in London.

Settled in the capital by the end of 1804, Clennell soon began to receive many other commissions as wood engraver, reproducing his own, or other artists' designs. In 1806 he was awarded the gold palette of the Society of Arts, and in 1809 a gold medal for his large engraving from a design by Benjamin West, for the diploma of the Highland Society. The turning point in his career came in 1810, with the publication in that year of his most successful commission to date; engravings for Samuel Roger's *Pleasures of Memory*. At this time he began to forsake engraving for watercolour painting, and became a member of the Associated Artists, exhibiting his work at their Bond Street Gallery. In 1811 he showed his first

work at the British Institution, and was commissioned to produce the bulk of the illustrations for *The Border Antiquities of England & Scotland*, by Scott; in the following year he consolidated his success by sending his first work to the Royal Academy, and becoming an associate of the Old Water Colour Society. By this time he was experimenting with compositions for oil paintings, his cartoon for *The Charge of the Life Guards at Waterloo*, gaining a premium of 150 guineas from the British Institution. In 1813 he showed his first major oil painting, *Sportsmen taking refreshment at the door of a country ale house*, at the British Institution, and in 1814 received his first important commission for an oil—a group portrait of the allied sovereigns and their generals at the Guildhall, London, for the Earl of Bridgewater. Unfortunately, this work proved so difficult to complete that in 1817 Clennell lost his reason, and was never wholly himself again. A compositional sketch for this work in the Laing Art Gallery, NEWCASTLE, shows that he was able to cope with its basic artistic requirements, and he is known to have completed portrait sketches of the almost 400 personages present, but the total work involved so taxed his capacities that he fell into a state of complete dejection and was admitted to an asylum in London. His wife died shortly afterwards, and in an effort to provide for Clennell and his three young children the Earl purchased the picture in its unfinished state (commissioning Edward Bird, the Royal Acade-mician, to finish it), and a print of his *Life Guards* picture, engraved by William Bromley, was sold for their benefit.

Clennell last exhibited in London in 1818, showing *The Day after the Fair*, at the British Institution. This painting was purchased by Mark Lambert (q.v.), and was included in the First Exhibition of the Northum-berland Institution for the Promotion of the Fine Arts, NEWCASTLE, in 1822. In the following year Clennell, still living in London, it seems, exhibited two works at the Northumberland Institution: *Dover Pier*, and *The House in which Robert Burns was born*, and one work

Luke Clennell: Bill Point on the Tyne. Watercolour 5×7⅞. Tyne & Wear County Council Museums, Laing Art Gallery.

at the Carlisle Academy in 1826, and in the following year moved to TRITLINGTON, near MORPETH, where it was thought he had made a good recovery from his illness until in 1831 he suddenly became violent, and he was placed in the asylum at NEWCASTLE. He spent the remainder of his days at NEWCASTLE, sometimes in the asylum, sometimes at relatives in the town. He exhibited his last work at NEWCASTLE in 1836, showing his watercolour: *Turnpike Gate*, at the First Water Colour Exhibition of the Newcastle Society of Artists. His *The Day after the Fair* was also shown in that year, at the Second Annual Exhibition of the Society, courtesy of Lambert, whereafter Clennell lived several years with a relative at St. Peter's Quay, NEWCASTLE, "beguiling the weary days in drawing, music, and writing poetry", but ended his days in the town asylum. Four years after his death a handsome monument to his memory, by Richard George Davies (q.v.), was placed in St. Andrew's Church, NEWCASTLE. Clennell is today regarded as Bewick's most gifted pupil, and might have emerged as a major figure in British watercolour painting had his career as a painter not been cut short by mental illness. A large exhibition of Clennell's work was held at the Laing Art Gallery in 1981, accompanied by an excellent catalogue detailing his life and work. Represented: British Museum; Victoria and Albert Museum; Carlisle A.G.; Dundee A.G.; Laing A.G., Newcastle; Natural History Society of Northumbria, Newcastle; Newcastle Central Library; Newport A.G.; Ulster Museum, Belfast.

COLE, Lillian (born *c*.1875)
Landscape, coastal and genre painter in oil. The daughter of William Cole (q.v.), she received tuition in painting from her father before joining him in his studio at GATESHEAD at an early age. She first exhibited her work at the Bewick Club, NEWCASTLE, later exhibiting at the Royal Academy, and widely in the provinces, including the Artists of the Northern Counties exhibitions of the Laing Art Gallery, NEWCASTLE, from their inception in 1905. She practised successively at GATESHEAD, WHITLEY BAY, and Hinderwell, North Yorkshire. She was practising at the last-named place when she exhibited at the Royal Academy in 1911: *A Rugged Pasture*, and in 1913: *April at Runswick*, and was exhibiting at NEWCASTLE from Hinderwell in the First World War years.

COLE, Sir Ralph (1625-1704)
Amateur portrait painter in oil; engraver. He was the son of Sir Nicholas Cole, of Brancepeth Castle, near DURHAM, who was created a baronet in 1640. On his father's death Sir Ralph inherited a considerable fortune, and spent the greater part of it on art, and the patronage of artists. He took lessons from Van Dyck, and painted several portraits, among these a portrait of Thomas Wyndham, which was later mezzotint engraved by R. Tompson. He also produced a portrait of Charles II, which he engraved himself. His own portrait was painted by Lely, and mezzotint engraved by Francis Place (q.v.), a friend and brother dilettante of Cole. He is said to have retained several Italian painters in his employment, but his extravagant expenditure in this,

and other directions, later obliged him to sell the family castle. He died three years later and was buried close to the castle.

COLE, William (born *c*.1852)
Landscape and genre painter in oil. This artist practised at GATESHEAD in the 1880's, later practising at WHITLEY BAY, MONKSEATON, and at Hinderwell, North Yorkshire, with his daughter Lillian Cole (q.v.). Cole exhibited his work at the Bewick Club, NEWCASTLE, and at the Artists of the Northern Counties exhibitions at the city's Laing Art Gallery, from their inception in 1905, until 1918.

COLLARD, William (1792-1847)
Engraver; etcher; lithographer; draughtsman. Collard was one of the most prolific engravers at NEWCASTLE in the early 19th century, and was also an accomplished draughtsman. His work embraced the engraving or etching of many illustrations for publications associated with Northumbria, including Hodgson's *History of Northumberland*, and *Architectural and Picturesque Views in Newcastle*, for both of which publications he also provided drawings. He also occasionally exhibited his drawings, his exhibits at the Northern Academy, NEWCASTLE, in 1829, earning from W. A. Mitchell, in the *Tyne Mercury*, several favourable comments; of his *View in Ouseburn; near West Jesmond*: ". . . a clear, fresh spirited drawing; carefully done, and highly creditable to Mr Collard, who has seldom come before the public except as an engraver . . .", and of his *Rocks at Cullercoats*: ". . . a beautiful drawing . . .". Collard collaborated in some of his engraving work with Mark Lambert (q.v.), and taught his skills to George Finlay Robinson (q.v.). His work outside pictorial engraving for reproduction consisted of the usual work of the jobbing engraver, plus the engraving of a number of railway plans. He died at GATESHEAD, where he had lived for some years prior to his decease.

COLLEY, Andrew (*c*.1868- after 1910)
Genre, landscape and industrial painter in oil. He was born on Tyneside, the son of a local twine merchant, and is believed to have studied art in the town while working in his father's business at NEWCASTLE. He remained in this business throughout his stay in the city, during which period he began exhibiting at the Bewick Club, NEWCASTLE, in 1891, showing two genre works in oil: *Morning Studies*, and *Waiting for Dad*. Two years later he commenced exhibiting at the Royal Academy, showing an industrial scene: *Glass Blowing: lamp chimney making*, and in this year (1893) became a member of the Bewick Club committee, describing himself as "a merchant". He remained at NEWCASTLE until the turn of the century, continuing to exhibit at the Royal Academy, and at the Bewick Club, as well as at various London and provincial galleries. Working in London from 1904, he exhibited at the Royal Academy in 1905, 1907, and 1909, and at the New English Art Club in 1909, at both of these institutions showing continental subjects among his several genre and landscape works. He last exhibited in 1910, when living at Chelsea, London, after which nothing is known of him. The Laing Art Gallery, NEWCASTLE, has his Royal Academy exhibit of 1905: *Venetian Embroidery Makers*.

CONNELL, William (fl. late 19th, early 20th cent.)
Landscape and coastal painter in oil and watercolour; stained glass designer. This artist practised at GATES-HEAD in the late 19th and early 20th centuries, from which he regularly sent work for exhibition to the Bewick Club, NEWCASTLE, and later the city's Laing Art Gallery, whose Artists of the Northern Counties exhibitions he contributed to from their inception in 1905, until the 1920's. He mainly exhibited local landscape and coastal views, but his Laing Art Gallery exhibits included several examples of his skill as a stained glass designer. Represented: Laing A.G., Newcastle; Shipley A.G., Gateshead; Sunderland A.G.

COPLAND, Elijah (1846-1916)
Wood carver; draughtsman. Copland was born at NEW-CASTLE, and received his education at the town's St. Andrew's Charity School, having early lost his father. He left school at the age of twelve to become a milk delivery boy, but showed such promise as an artist that he was taken on as an apprentice by Thomas Hall Tweedy (q.v.), the Tyneside wood carver. At the conclusion of his apprenticeship with Tweedy he went to London, where he obtained employment in a carver's shop at Bloomsbury. He remained there some four months, then returning to NEWCASTLE, he secured an engagement in the studio of Gerrard Robinson (q.v.). He worked for Robinson for two years, afterwards moving to ALNWICK, where he was employed by Robertson & Sons for four years. On leaving ALNWICK, he next worked for Whitty, of Princess Street, NEWCASTLE, then in 1875 decided to try his fortune again in London. He worked for various carving shops in the capital for three years. Then, after a serious accident, he returned to NEWCASTLE, where, after a long convalescence, he set-up his own carving shop. He quickly became successful as his own master, and attracted considerable praise for his work, which consisted of "solid figures, character pieces in alto relievo, friezes, finials, and designs for art furniture and ornaments". He died at NEWCASTLE. He was well known throughout his adult life for his interest in politics, and at one time was considered as a Labour candidate for NEWCASTLE.

COPNALL, Mrs. Theresa Norah (née Butchart) (b. 1882)
Flower and portrait painter in oil. She was born at HAUGHTON-LE-SKERNE, near DARLINGTON, and studied art at the Slade under Tonks, Brown, and Steer, at Bushey, Herts, at the School of Sir Hubert Von Herkomer, and in Brussels. Following her training she practised as an artist at Barrow-in-Furness, and Liverpool, before settling at Hoylake, Cheshire, with her artist husband Frank T. Copnall, where she spent the remainder of her life. She exhibited her work widely throughout Britain, showing examples at the Royal Academy, the Royal Scottish Academy, the Royal Cambrian Academy, and at various London and provincial galleries. She first exhibited at the Royal Academy in 1927, showing: *A mixed bowl*, and sent her final exhibit in 1954: *Flowers in a crystal bowl*.

CORNER, Frank W. (d. 1928)
Landscape and coastal painter in watercolour and pastel; etcher. Born at NORTH SHIELDS, Corner practised as an artist in the town throughout his career. He was particularly fond of working in pastel, and produced a substantial number of etchings. He exhibited his work at the Bewick Club, NEWCASTLE, and later at the city's Laing Art Gallery, whose Artists of the Northern Counties exhibitions he contributed to for the last eighteen years of his life. He lived for many years at WILLINGTON, near NORTH SHIELDS, but returned to his birthplace shortly before his death in 1928. The Laing Art Gallery has his pastel: *A Northumbrian Village*. Represented: Laing A.G., Newcastle; North Tyneside Public Libraries; Sunderland A.G.

COULSON, Henry Major (b. 1880)
Landscape painter in oil and watercolour; etcher. He was born at SOUTH SHIELDS, and later practised as a painter and etcher, mainly in the Midlands. He exhibited eight works at the Royal Scottish Academy, and nine works at the Walker Art Gallery, Liverpool, between 1921 and 1937. He also exhibited at the Artists of the Northern Counties exhibition at the Laing Art Gallery, NEWCASTLE, in 1927, showing three etchings.

COULSON, Thomas (fl. late 18th, early 19th cent.)
Landscape and decorative painter in oil. He was born at NEWCASTLE, and served an apprenticeship as a watchmaker before placing himself as a pupil under Thomas Miles Richardson, Senior (q.v.), in the hope of becoming a landscape painter. He later became interested in decorative and house painting, however, and was soon receiving commissions from as far afield as Edinburgh. By 1814 he had become recognised as one of the leading practitioners in decorating in his native town, with a special skill in imitating the effects of wood, marble etc., and decided to move to Edinburgh, taking with him apprentice John Wilson Ewbank (q.v.), and possibly Thomas Fenwick (q.v.). Coulson is said to have revolutionised the art of house painting in Scotland, and to have attracted apprentices from all over the North of England, and Southern Scotland. One of the apprentices whom he engaged shortly after setting-up in Edinburgh was George Balmer (q.v.). Thomas Bewick (q.v.), called on Coulson when visiting Edinburgh in August, 1823, after which little is known of his activities, except that he advertised his services at Edinburgh for several years after this date, sometimes under the heading of landscape painter, etc. Bewick was, of course, familiar with Coulson from the latter's days at NEWCASTLE, and cut a business card for him featuring a view of the Tyne, and the castle in the town, together with cherubs and a shield bearing particulars of his name and trade.

*CRAWHALL, Joseph, The First (1793-1853)
Amateur landscape, figure and animal painter in oil and watercolour; caricaturist; lithographer; etcher; wood engraver. The first member of the old Northumbrian family of Crawhall to distinguish himself artistically, he was born at NEWCASTLE, where he was apprenticed to

Joseph Crawhall, The First: On 'Change. Watercolour 17½×21½. *Literary and Philosophical Society, Newcastle upon Tyne.*

a ropemaker at sixteen. Eventually he bought his employer's ropery, and by 1830 had become one of the town's more prosperous businessmen. Before becoming deeply involved in his business affairs Crawhall had taken a considerable interest in painting and drawing, indeed his friend Thomas Bewick (q.v.), remarked: "Joseph . . . excelled as a painter, for which nature had furnished him with the requisite innate powers – but in this he was taken off by his business of a Rope maker."‡ Little of Crawhall's work up to the time of Bewick's death has survived; his *On 'Change,* # is in the collection of the Literary and Philosophical Society, NEWCASTLE, and a landscape with cattle and figures is owned by Charles S. Felver, U.S.A., author of a book on Joseph Crawhall, The Second (q.v.).

We know that Crawhall exhibited alongside fellow committee member Bewick, at the First Exhibition of the Northumberland Institution for the Promotion of the Fine Arts, NEWCASTLE, showing a watercolour copy of *The marriage of St. Catherine*, by Parmigianino, and two dog portraits, and showed work at later exhibitions at NEWCASTLE, but what has become of these works is uncertain. His best known work of his pre-1830 period is, however, easily accessible: the lithographic portrait of himself, and the several drawings wittily portraying sporting incidents, contained in his *Grouse Shooting made Quite Easy to Every Capacity*, published in 1827 under the pseudonym "Jeffrey Gorcock". Although hard pressed in later years by his business and civic commitments (he was elected Sheriff of NEWCASTLE in 1846, and served as Mayor 1848-50), he never, indeed, lost his love for drawing, often filling his account books with sketches, and frequently dashing off satirical drawings and etchings for the amusement of his friends and

family. He died at STAGSHAW, near CORBRIDGE. His sons Joseph Crawhall, The Second (q.v.), GEORGE ED-WARD CRAWHALL, and THOMAS CRAWHALL, and daughter MARY ELIZABETH CRAWHALL, were also artistically gifted, only the first named, however, developing skill as an artist to a marked degree. His family had connections with that of William Chapman (q.v.). Represented: Literary and Philosophical Society, Newcastle.

‡ *See p. 180, "A Memoir of Thomas Bewick, Written by Himself ", edited and with an introduction by Iain Bain, Oxford University Press, 1975.*

CRAWHALL, Joseph, The Second (1821-1896)

Wood engraver; figure and genre painter in watercolour; caricaturist; commercial artist; book designer. The eldest son of Joseph Crawhall, The First (q.v.), he was born at West House, NEWCASTLE, and joined his father's ropery business as soon as he left school. Like his father he became keenly interested in art and probably received some guidance in painting and drawing from Crawhall, Senior, before embarking on his own activities in these fields. Early in life he became fascinated by wood engraving, later producing many books to which he contributed his own illustrations in this medium. His first such publication of note was *The Compleatest Angling Booke That Ever was Writ*, published in 1859, and both illustrated and printed by him entirely independently. This was followed by a succession of books until 1889, when his *Impresses Quaint* was published at NEWCASTLE containing a collection of his choicest wood engravings, including some of his earliest and latest work. According to his biographer Charles S. Felver

(p. 115, *Joseph Crawhall, The Newcastle Wood Engraver*, Frank Graham 1972), his "most brilliant and best known book" was his *Chapbook Chaplets*, published under the imprint of Field & Tuer, in 1883.

Crawhall was a close friend of Charles Keene, the famous illustrator of *Punch*, and sent sketches to Keene which Keene re-drew for this publication. Glasgow Art Gallery has twenty-one albums of these drawings, and Adrian Bury, who studied them in connection with his book on Crawhall's son, Joseph Crawhall, The Third (q.v.), describes them as showing "an inexhaustible sense of fun, characterisation of human types of all classes, and adequate feeling for composition. As a whole, they make an amusing social document of the time. For one who had no formal training in figure-drawing they are surprisingly good". Although Crawhall's wood engraving was treated with some amusement by his contemporaries, for its crudity compared with that of the highly skilled reproductive engraving of such engravers as the Dalziels,* it has since been recognised that his influence on the work of later engravers was considerable, and that it was boldly original. His interest in art outside his own self-expression was considerable, and he was one of the founders of the Arts Association, NEWCASTLE, formed in 1878, serving as joint secretary, and later secretary. He is also said to have offered much encouragement to his relative William Chapman (q.v.), when Chapman was still struggling to succeed as a professional artist. He was a close friend of the descendants of Thomas Bewick (q.v.), and as one of the executors of the will of Isabella Bewick, last surviving daughter of Bewick, was responsible for the presentation of hundreds of the artist's original watercolours, and drawings to what is now the Natural History Society of Northumbria. He died in London. His brothers GEORGE EDWARD CRAWHALL and THOMAS CRAWHALL, and sister MARY ELIZABETH CRAWHALL, were also artistically talented. Another sister, Jane Ann Crawhall, became the mother of Abel Chapman (q.v.). Represented: British Museum; Glasgow A.G.; Newcastle Central Library.

* See George Dalziel (q.v.), and Edward Dalziel (q.v.): "The Brothers Dalziel".

*CRAWHALL, Joseph, The Third, R.S.W. (1861-1913)
Amateur animal, bird and sporting painter in oil and watercolour; illustrator. Born at MORPETH, the son of Joseph Crawhall, The Second (q.v.), Crawhall received his first artistic instruction from his father. His father introduced him to the practice of always drawing from memory, and never correcting or erasing his work, a practice which remained with the artist all his life and contributed greatly to the distinctiveness of his later work. Early in his boyhood the Crawhall family moved to NEWCASTLE, where Joseph was sent to school. Later he attended King's College, London, then went to Paris to study under Aimeé Morot. His stay with Morot was brief and had little influence on his subsequent artistic development, and returning to Britain he rejoined his family at NEWCASTLE, where at seventeen he exhibited for the first time, showing two works at the 1878 exhibition of the Arts Association: *Fox Hounds – Morpeth*, and *A Collie Dog*. In the following year an event occurred which was to have a lasting effect on his career in art; his sister had married the brother of Scottish artist Edward Arthur Walton, and this resulted in Joseph's first visit to Scotland, where he was soon painting in the countryside around Glasgow with Walton, and fellow artist James Guthrie. In the 1880 Spring Loan & Sale Exhibition of the Arts Association, NEWCASTLE, Joseph and the latter artist exhibited a joint work: *Bolted*, and in 1882, in the company of Guthrie, he painted what was to become his only Royal Academy exhibit: *A Lincolnshire Pasture*, shown in 1883.

Crawhall's later artistic associations were almost exclusively with Glasgow, where he became a leading member of the Glasgow School, and regularly exhibited his work at the Royal Scottish Academy, the Royal Scottish Society of Painters in Water Colours (of which he was elected a member), the New English Art Club, and at various international, London and provincial exhibitions. Despite his attachment to Glasgow, however, he chose to spend much of his later life in Tangier and elsewhere abroad, finally settling at Brandsby, near York. His period in Yorkshire was one of intense artistic activity during which he would shut himself up in his studio and disregard sleep and food in his creative frenzy. Any work which did not please him was immediately destroyed. He died in London. In addition to his work in oil and watercolour, Crawhall was an

Joseph Crawhall, The Third: Tawny Owl. Watercolour 9¼×7. *Tyne & Wear County Council Museums, Laing Art Gallery.*

accomplished illustrator in line, his first productions being for his father's publications, such as *Border Notes & Mixty Maxty*, 1880; later for the *Pall Mall Gazette*. An excellent account of his life and work is contained in Adrian Bury's: *Joseph Crawhall, the Man and the Artist*, 1958. His brother HUGH CRAWHALL, and cousin Abel Chapman (q.v.), were also artistically gifted. His work has been the subject of several exhibitions since his death, notably at the Laing Art Gallery, NEWCASTLE. Represented: British Museum; Victoria and Albert Museum; Tate Gallery; Berwick A.G.; Dundee A.G.; Glasgow A.G.; Hatton Gallery, Newcastle; Laing A.G., Newcastle.

CRAWHALL, William (c.1825- after 1878)

Marine and landscape painter in oil. He was probably the son of William Crawhall, brother of Joseph Crawhall, The First (q.v.), and farmer, at STAGSHAW, near CORBRIDGE.* It is possible that he received some tuition in art from his uncle after moving to NEWCASTLE in the later 19th century, where he took a studio in the premises occupied by Thomas Hall Tweedy (q.v.), the wood carver and gilder, at 44, Grainger Street. He first exhibited his work publicly when he sent a *Sea View* to the Suffolk Street Gallery in 1860. In 1863, and 1864, he exhibited at the British Institution, showing a total of three works: *Wreck, Sunrise; Morning After the Storm*, and *A Calm Evening at Sea*. He was an exhibitor at NEWCASTLE from 1866 until 1878, at the first of these exhibitions: "The Exhibition of Paintings & Other Works of Art", at the Town Hall, in 1866, showing one of his British Institution exhibits of 1864; at the second exhibition: "The Central Exchange News Room, Art Gallery, and Polytechnic Exhibition", in 1870, showing his *Ship on Shore, South Shields*; and *Small Breeze at Sea*, and at the last of these exhibitions: the exhibition of works by local painters, at the Central Exchange Art Gallery, in 1878, showing two landscapes and a "seapiece". Nothing is known of him after 1878, in which year the catalogue of the last named exhibition indicated him as a living artist. The Laing Art Gallery, NEW-CASTLE, has his *Mouth of the Tyne*, and a *View of St. Nicholas with figures* is known.

* Before his retirement to become a farmer he was chief lead mining agent at ALLENHEADS, for many years.

CROSBY, Frederick Gordon (b.1885)

Illustrator. He was born at SUNDERLAND and practised as an illustrator in the town for various locally printed publications. He was possibly related to William Crosby (q.v.).

*CROSBY, William (1830-1910)

Portrait, genre, landscape and seascape painter in oil and watercolour. Crosby was born at SUNDERLAND, the son of Stephen Crosby, an inn-keeper in the town. At fourteen he was apprenticed to the same painter and glazier as James Stokeld (q.v.), and like his fellow apprentice he decided to abandon his trade soon after completing his indentures. An exhibition of paintings in the town about this time is said to have "fanned the flame of his artistic ambition", and after succeeding in selling several of his paintings he decided to use the money to stay in Antwerp for two or three years making copies of the Old Masters, in the company of John Reay (q.v.). On his return to SUNDERLAND he soon established himself as one of the town's leading artists, mainly concentrating on portraiture, and producing likenesses of many local celebrities, including Edward Backhouse (q.v.), whose wife was one of the artist's patrons. Crosby also painted many genre, landscape and seascape subjects, exhibiting eight such works at the Royal Academy, and five works at the Suffolk Street Gallery, between 1859 and 1873. Following this period he increasingly concentrated on exhibiting his work in Northumbria, where he showed work at several major exhibitions at NEWCASTLE, including the exhibition of works of local painters shown at the Central Exchange Art Gallery, in 1878, and subsequently at the annual exhibitions of the Bewick Club in the city. A landscape and a seascape were on show at the Stanfield Art Exhibition, SUNDERLAND, at the time of his death in the

William Crosby: Whitburn Bay. Oil 18×31. *Tyne & Wear County Council Museums, Sunderland Art Gallery & Museum.*

48

town in 1910. Sunderland Art Gallery has several examples of his work, including his portrait of Edward Backhouse (q.v.).

CUTHBERT, Alfred Edward (1898-1966)
Amateur landscape and seascape painter in watercolour. He was born at SOUTH SHIELDS, and worked as an insurance agent, painting in his spare time. He was a founder of South Shields Art Club, and a member of Sunderland Art Club, regularly exhibiting his work with both of these Clubs, and at the Artists of the Northern Counties exhibitions at the Laing Art Gallery, NEWCASTLE. Many of his works were offered as prizes in the National Savings Campaign conducted during the Second World War. Represented: South Shields Museum & A.G.; Sunderland A.G.

DALRYMPLE-SMITH, Edith Alexandra (1897-1958)
Amateur landscape painter in oil and watercolour. She was born at SUNDERLAND, and was a keen spare-time painter and calligrapher. She was a member of Sunderland Art Club. Sunderland Art Gallery has her oil: *Mowbray Park, Sunderland*, and several examples of her work in calligraphy.

DALZIEL, Alexander, Senior (1781-1832)
Portrait, still-life, animal, genre and fruit painter in oil. He was born at WOOLER, and was a horticulturist, and commissioned officer in the Northumbria Militia, before taking up art as a profession. While still living at WOOLER, Dalziel married, and fathered eleven of his twelve children. Just before the birth of his twelfth child, however, and in his forty-second year, he moved to NEWCASTLE to further his career as an artist, remaining there for the rest of his life. Dalziel exhibited his work at NEWCASTLE from 1824 until his death, and also exhibited at the Carlisle Academy in 1825 and 1826. Most of the works he exhibited were still-life subjects, typical of which were his fish paintings, shown at the Northumberland Institution for the Promotion of the Fine Arts, NEWCASTLE, in 1824, and *The Sideboard*, and *Group of Musical Instruments*, shown at the Carlisle Academy in 1826. He died at NEWCASTLE. He was the father of William Dalziel (q.v.), Robert Dalziel (q.v.), Alexander Dalziel, Junior (q.v.), George Dalziel (q.v.), Edward Dalziel (q.v.), Margaret Jane Dalziel (q.v.), John Dalziel (q.v.), and Thomas Bolton Gilchrist Septimus Dalziel (q.v.).

DALZIEL, Alexander, Junior (1814-1836)
Draughtsman. He was born at WOOLER, one of the eight sons of Alexander Dalziel, Senior (q.v.), and moved with his family to NEWCASTLE at an early age. It was said of him by his brothers George Dalziel (q.v.), and Edward Dalziel (q.v.), in their autobiographical: *The*

Brothers Dalziel, 1901, that had he lived he "must necessarily have made a great name for himself as a designer and draughtsman in black and white", but he caught a chill which terminated in consumption, and returning to NEWCASTLE to his mother's home, he died there in his twenty-third year. He was the brother of William Dalziel (q.v.), Robert Dalziel (q.v.), George Dalziel (q.v.), Edward Dalziel (q.v.), Margaret Jane Dalziel (q.v.), John Dalziel (q.v.), and Thomas Bolton Gilchrist Septimus Dalziel (q.v.).

*DALZIEL, George (1815-1902) and DALZIEL, Edward (1817-1905), "The Brothers Dalziel"
Wood engravers; draughtsmen. They were born at WOOLER, two of the eight sons of Alexander Dalziel, Senior (q.v.), and following a brief period with their family at NEWCASTLE, went to London. At the age of nineteen George became a pupil of Charles Gray, the wood engraver. He remained with Gray for four years, and on the completion of his engagement with his master commenced wood engraving on his own account. Within a few weeks, however, he joined his brother Edward Dalziel (q.v.), who was also working in London as an engraver, in founding their own wood engraving establishment, this eventually becoming the most famous and prolific such establishment in Great Britain in the 19th century. These two, "The Brothers Dalziel", not only engraved for the publications of others, but printed and published their own publications, acted as editors, and commissioned illustrations for books and magazines. Among the books which they illustrated – sometimes in association with their brother Thomas

"The Brothers Dalziel": Wood engraving after drawing by Myles Birket Foster (q.v.), for Thomas Pringle's "Come awa', Come awa'."

49

Bolton Gilchrist Septimus Dalziel (q.v.) – were some of the most popular publications of the Victorian era, such as Tenniel's *Alice*, and Houghton's *Arabian Nights*, while one of their typical trade assignments was the engraving of the prospectus for *Punch*, of which one of the original projectors and proprietors was fellow Northumbrian, Ebenezer Landells (q.v.).

The Brothers were distinctive among the reproductive wood engravers of their day in being able to actually improve on the original designs from which they worked, and which were frequently prepared by leading artists of the time. Tenniel's *Alice*, for instance, owes much to the artistry of "The Brothers Dalziel" for its attractiveness. Most of their work in wood engraving simply carried the name "Dalziel", as the brothers collaborated so much in the work of their establishment. All their contributions to the Royal Academy between 1861 and 1870 were entered as "Dalziel Brothers, Wood Engravers", and consisted of their interpretations on wood of paintings by leading contemporary artists such as Sir John Everett Millais, and Myles Birket Foster (q.v.). Edward is said to have been more seriously interested in illustration than his brothers George, and Thomas Bolton Gilchrist Septimus; he studied at the Clipstone Academy alongside Charles Keene, and Sir John Tenniel, and exhibited his paintings at the Royal Academy, and the British Institution, between 1841 and 1871. An excellent account of the work of the wood engraving establishment which George and Edward ran from 1840 until 1890, together with much interesting biographical information and many illustrations, is their joint work: *The Brothers Dalziel*, 1901, while a comprehensive listing of the various works to which they contributed illustrations throughout their entire careers may be found in *The Dictionary of British Book Illustrators and Caricaturists, 1800-1914*, by Simon Houfe, Antique Collectors' Club, 1978. Edward's sons, EDWARD GURDEN DALZIEL (1849-1888), and GILBERT DALZIEL (1853-1930), also practised as artists, and exhibited their work.

DALZIEL, John (1822-1869)
Wood engraver. He was born at WOOLER, one of the eight sons of Alexander Dalziel, Senior (q.v.), and following some years at NEWCASTLE, where he is believed to have received some tuition from the pupils of Thomas Bewick (q.v.), he joined his brothers George Dalziel (q.v.), Edward Dalziel (q.v.), and Thomas Bolton Gilchrist Septimus Dalziel (q.v.), in their wood engraving establishment in London. He worked with his brothers from 1852 until 1868, when ill-health forced him to retire to Drigg, in Cumberland, where he died in 1869. He was the brother of William Dalziel (q.v.), Robert Dalziel (q.v.), Alexander Dalziel, Junior (q.v.), George Dalziel (q.v.), Edward Dalziel (q.v.), Margaret Jane Dalziel (q.v.), and Thomas Bolton Gilchrist Septimus Dalziel (q.v.).

DALZIEL, Margaret Jane (1819-1894)
Painter; illustrator. She was born at WOOLER, one of the four daughters of Alexander Dalziel, Senior (q.v.), and moved with her family to NEWCASTLE at an early age. She received tuition in art from her father, and later moved to London to join her brothers George Dalziel (q.v.), and Edward Dalziel (q.v.), to assist them in their engraving establishment. She worked mainly as a painter, however, though she is not known to have exhibited her work. She died in London. She was the sister of William Dalziel (q.v.), Robert Dalziel (q.v.), Alexander Dalziel, Junior (q.v.), George Dalziel (q.v.), Edward Dalziel (q.v.), John Dalziel (q.v.), and Thomas Bolton Gilchrist Septimus Dalziel (q.v.).

DALZIEL, Robert (1810-1842)
Portrait and landscape painter in oil; modeller. He was born at WOOLER, one of the eight sons of Alexander Dalziel, Senior (q.v.). He received his first tuition in art from his father, and later under Thomson of Duddingston, and after practising successfully at Glasgow and Edinburgh, moved to London. He first began to exhibit his work publicly in 1831, while practising at NEWCASTLE, showing two works alongside those of his father at the town's Northern Academy. Leaving NEWCASTLE some time after 1834, however, he did not apparently exhibit again until 1840, when he sent work to both the British Institution and the Suffolk Street Gallery, showing landscapes and genre paintings. He continued to exhibit at both these venues until his death at London in 1842. A bust of his father which he modelled in the classical manner, together with portraits in oil of his mother Elizabeth, and brothers George Dalziel (q.v.), and Edward Dalziel (q.v.), are illustrated in *The Brothers Dalziel*, 1901, written and illustrated by the two last named artists. He was the brother of William Dalziel (q.v.), Alexander Dalziel, Junior (q.v), George Dalziel (q.v.), Edward Dalziel (q.v.), Margaret Jane Dalziel (q.v.), John Dalziel (q.v.), and Thomas Bolton Gilchrist Septimus Dalziel (q.v.).

DALZIEL, Thomas Bolton Gilchrist Septimus (1823-1906)
Landscape and figure painter; illustrator; copper engraver; wood engraver. He was born at WOOLER, one of the eight sons of Alexander Dalziel, Senior (q.v.). After some time at NEWCASTLE with his family, and possibly receiving some tuition there in copper engraving, he moved to London, where by 1846 he was exhibiting at the Suffolk Street Gallery, showing a genre work: *Thieves Alarmed*. In 1856 he began exhibiting at the Royal Academy, showing: *A Triton*, and in 1858 sent his only work to the British Institution: *On the Shore*. In 1860, and with an already impressive record of book illustrating behind him, he joined his brothers George Dalziel (q.v.), and Edward Dalziel (q.v.), in their wood engraving establishment in London, subsequently carrying out much fine illustrative work for various of their publications. Among the many widely popular works to which he contributed illustrations was: *Houghton's Arabian Nights*, 1865. He rarely exhibited his paintings after 1866, when he last showed at the Suffolk Street Gallery, though he did show two works at the Royal Hibernian Academy, and two works at Manchester, in 1881. He was the youngest of the brothers comprising the Dalziel wood engraving establishment, and remained associated with it until his death in 1906. He

was the brother of William Dalziel (q.v.), Robert Dalziel (q.v.), Alexander Dalziel, Junior (q.v.), George Dalziel (q.v.), Edward Dalziel (q.v.), Margaret Jane Dalziel (q.v.), and Thomas Bolton Gilchrist Septimus Dalziel (q.v.). His sons HERBERT DALZIEL (1853-1941), and OWEN DALZIEL (1861-1942), also practised as artists, and frequently exhibited their work.

DALZIEL, William (1805-1873)
Still-life painter in oil; heraldic and ornamental book decorator. He was born at WOOLER, one of the eight sons of Alexander Dalziel, Senior (q.v.). He moved with his family to NEWCASTLE in his teens, and following some tuition from his father practised as a painter of still-life subjects. He spent some time in London with his brothers George Dalziel (q.v.), and Edward Dalziel (q.v.), possibly assisting them in the preparation of book illustrations, but later moved to Penarth, Wales, where he died in 1873. He was the eldest brother of Robert Dalziel (q.v.), Alexander Dalziel, Junior (q.v.), George Dalziel (q.v.), Edward Dalziel (q.v.), Margaret Jane Dalziel (q.v.), John Dalziel (q.v.), and Thomas Bolton Gilchrist Septimus Dalziel (q.v.).

*DAVIES, Richard George (c.1790- after 1857)
Sculptor; marble mason. Davies practised as a sculptor and marble mason in Northumbria from the early years of the 19th century, until about 1860. Eneas Mackenzie, in his *History of Newcastle*, says that Davies' predecessor in his profession was "The late John Jopling . . . a good sculptor" who also had "a fine taste in miniature painting", but whether this implies that Davies took over the business of John Jopling (q.v.), or was merely taught by him, is not clear. Davies married at St. Andrew's Church, NEWCASTLE, in 1812, and was soon busy enough in his studio to take on Christopher Tate (q.v.). Among his early work are monuments to Phillis Craster (d. 1813) – a sarcophagus and obelisk; and Winefrid Haggerston (d. 1815) – a draped urn and obelisk, both at St. Maurice's Church, ELLINGHAM.

Most of his later work lay in the field of producing monuments, examples of which may be found in churches throughout Northumbria, but he did occasionally aspire to more demanding work, some of which he sent for exhibition. In 1844, at the Westminster Hall, London, he exhibited his *Actaeon Devoured by his Hounds*, but this work was scathingly remarked upon by the *Literary Gazette* (1844 – page 482), which said: "We wish the unfortunate hunter had been entirely devoured, so that we might have been spared the sight of so disgusting a group". The *Illustrated London News* of the same year implied a better appreciation of his work, however, when it published wood engravings of his newly erected monuments to Grace Darling, at St. Cuthbert's Chapel, FARNE ISLANDS, and Luke Clennell (q.v.), at St. Andrew's Church, NEWCASTLE. In 1846, Davies, then evidently working at Carlisle, sent eleven works to the exhibition in that year of Carlisle Athenaeum, but after returning to Northumbria some time after this event, he established himself at CHESTER-LE-STREET, after which nothing is known of him. His monument to Luke Clennell, consisting of a garlanded

palette, with maulstick, once occupied a prominent place at the entrance to the chancel of St. Andrew's, but has now been removed to a position high on the inside right hand wall. An example of his work in statuary is the figure of the Duke of Northumberland which he finished for his former pupil Tate, and which was later erected outside the Master Mariners' Asylum, TYNEMOUTH. #

DAVISON, John (born c.1896)
Portrait painter in oil. This artist practised at GATESHEAD in the early years of the present century, following five years' art training at Hospital Field House, Arbroath. He exhibited at the Royal Hibernian Academy in 1917, and at the Artists of the Northern Counties exhibitions at the Laing Art Gallery, NEWCASTLE, from 1918.

DAVISON, William (c.1805-c.1870)
Amateur marine, coastal and landscape painter in oil and watercolour. This artist lived at SUNDERLAND, and later HARTLEPOOL, in the 19th century, and first began exhibiting his work publicly from the former, sending his *Moonlight; Fishing Boat off Hartlepool*, and *A*

Richard George Davies: Statue of Duke of Northumberland, outside Master Mariners' Asylum, Tynemouth. Stone.

Calm, to the Northern Academy, NEWCASTLE, in 1829. In the following year he exhibited at both the Northern Academy, and the Carlisle Academy, and in this year also became a member of the Northern Society of Painters in Water Colours, NEWCASTLE, along with Thomas Miles Richardson, Senior (q.v.), and others. He thereafter exhibited little at NEWCASTLE, and on only one further occasion at Carlisle, following which he left SUNDERLAND for HARTLEPOOL, where he remained until his death. Davison was a close friend of William Bewick (q.v.), many of Bewick's letters to him *c.* 1845-1864 appearing in *The Life and Letters of William Bewick (Artist)*, by Thomas Landseer, 1871. Several of these letters discuss Davison's artistic activities, one such letter dated 7th December, 1850, stating that much rather than look at his friend's copies of Rembrandt's work "I cannot but long that you should be doing, what in your own peculiar line you do so well, those delightful bits of sea-side scenes". Two of Davison's coastal views were included in the exhibition of works by local painters, at the Central Exchange Art Gallery, NEWCASTLE, in 1878, the catalogue describing them as by "W. Davison of Hartlepool, an amateur whose paintings are full of truth of feeling, with marked truthfulness to nature". The catalogue also described him as deceased.

*DAWSON, Byron Eric (1896-1968)
Landscape, architectural and subject painter in oil, tempera and watercolour; draughtsman; illustrator; art teacher. Dawson was born at Banbury, Oxfordshire, but moved to NEWCASTLE following the death of his parents to serve an engineering apprenticeship. His skill at drawing was soon noticed by his employers, however, and he was encouraged to become an art student at the city's Armstrong College (later King's College; now Newcastle University). At the conclusion of his studies he was asked to remain at the College as assistant master in painting, working in this capacity until 1927, when he embarked on his career as a professional artist by preparing for submission to the Royal Academy a work entitled: *Panel for Morning Room*. This work was

exhibited at the Academy in 1928, and enabled him to attract several local commissions for his work, among these one to paint a large lunette for the Laing Art Gallery, NEWCASTLE, depicting *John Baliol paying homage to Edward the First at Newcastle, in 1292*. In 1928 he exhibited the first of three works at the Royal Scottish Academy, and in 1929 sent one work to the North East Coast Exhibition, Palace of Arts. He exhibited one further work at the Royal Academy in 1931: *Shepherd and Three Graces*, but by 1933 he had ceased exhibiting outside Northumbria altogether, contenting himself by exhibiting at the Artists of the Northern Counties exhibitions at the Laing Art Gallery, NEWCASTLE, and in the city's private galleries.

Two of the finest exhibitions of Dawson's work in his lifetime are said to have been those mounted by the Laing Art Gallery in 1932, and the Shipley Art Gallery, GATESHEAD, in 1954. Most of his later life was taken up with architectural painting and drawing, his work once being described by Sir David Y. Cameron, the Royal Scottish Academician, as possessing ". . . a delicate beauty . . . a sensitive architectural draughtsmanship". He painted and drew street scenes, historic buildings, landscapes, seascapes, and industrial scenes. Two of his favourite subjects were the cathedrals of DURHAM and NEWCASTLE, of which he probably produced more watercolours than any other artist in history. In oil he preferred to produce works of the imagination, and sometimes on a large scale. The lunette referred to earlier was his largest work in this medium, but he also produced several other canvasses of massive proportions. He was for several years a newspaper illustrator, many of his pen and ink drawings appearing in the *North Mail*, later amalgamated with *The Journal*, NEWCASTLE. His final years were spent in considerable poverty, with only a small income from the tuition of private pupils, and the sale of occasional watercolours of local scenes to enable him to survive. He died in a sanatorium in the Tyne Valley, following an operation. Represented: Victoria and Albert Museum; John George Joicey Museum, Newcastle; Laing A.G., Newcastle; Shipley A.G., Gateshead.

Byron Eric Dawson: Eldon Square, Newcastle. Watercolour 13×24. *Private collection.*

DEES, Herbert Bewick (1892-1965)

Amateur genre, landscape and cattle painter in oil and watercolour. He was born at GATESHEAD, a member of a family connected with that of John Graham Lough (q.v.), and younger brother of John Arthur Dees (q.v.). He studied art privately while training as a painter and decorator, deciding at the conclusion of this training that he would remain a tradesman rather than attempt to succeed as an artist. He later moved to SPENNYMOOR to carry on his trade as painter and decorator, and here became actively involved in the work of the Spennymoor Settlement, teaching art to miners, and helping with its administration. He first began to exhibit his work at the Artists of the Northern Counties exhibitions at the Laing Art Gallery, NEWCASTLE, in 1921, showing a landscape work: *Under the trees.* He remained attached to landscape painting all his life, but also painted many studies of miner's cottages, and miners at work and play, at SPENNYMOOR. He contributed one work to the North East Coast Exhibition, Palace of Arts, in 1929, and later had several examples of his studies of miners toured with the "Art of the People" travelling exhibition. He died at SPENNYMOOR.

*DEES, John Arthur (1875-1959)

Amateur landscape, cattle and portrait painter in oil and watercolour. Dees was born at NEWCASTLE, a member of a family connected with that of John Graham Lough (q.v.). He studied at the School of Art at GATESHEAD, winning gold medals in 1895, and 1896, but decided on a career in commerce, and thereafter painted mainly in his spare time. He first exhibited his work at the Bewick Club, NEWCASTLE, where he soon won a reputation for the quality of his landscapes and formed friendships with several local professional art-

ists, among these John Atkinson (q.v.). He was an exhibitor at the Artists of the Northern Counties exhibitions at the Laing Art Gallery, NEWCASTLE, from their inception in 1905, and as a member of the city's Pen & Palette Club, was associated with various of its exhibitions. He first exhibited outside Northumbria in 1911, when he sent one work to the Royal Institute of Painters in Water Colours. In 1913 he sent the first of two works to the Royal Academy: *A North Country Valley,* having by this time moved to GATESHEAD, where he lived until just short of his death. He was given his first one-man show by the town's Shipley Art Gallery in 1927, and was a contributor to its "Contemporary Artists of Durham County" exhibition, staged in 1951 in connection with the Festival of Britain. He exhibited at the Royal Academy on only one further occasion, contributing a work entitled: *An Autumn Afternoon,* in 1915, but remained a regular exhibitor on Tyneside all his life, sending two works to the North East Coast Exhibition, Palace of Arts, in 1929, and enjoying a special retrospective exhibition of his work at the Shipley Art Gallery, in 1954. Towards the close of his life he exhibited mainly with the Newcastle Society of Artists. He died at Scunthorpe, Lincolnshire, while staying with his daughter. He was the elder brother of Herbert Bewick Dees (q.v.). Represented: Laing A.G., Newcastle; Shipley A.G., Gateshead.

*DE LACY, Charles (c.1860-1936)

Landscape, coastal and marine painter in oil and watercolour; illustrator. He was born at SUNDERLAND, the son of Robert de Lacy, photographer and music teacher, and trained as an engineer and had some experience in the Army and Navy before deciding on a caree in art, and studying at Lambeth, and later South

Kensington Museum, and the National Portrait Gallery. Following his studies he settled in London, where he first began to exhibit his work publicly when he sent his *The Thames from Greenwich*, to the Suffolk Street Gallery in 1885. In 1889 he commenced exhibiting at the Royal Academy, showing: *Near the Commercial Docks: end of a Winter's Day*. He exhibited at the Suffolk Street Gallery until 1894, and the Royal Academy until 1918, and occasionally sent work to provincial exhibitions, including those of the Bewick Club, NEW-CASTLE, at which his exhibit in 1892: *Cony hole derrick at Bugsby's Hole, near Woolwich*, was described in the Tyneside press as an "extremely realistic and pictur-esque rendering of a busy scene". From 1890 De Lacy increasingly concentrated on illustrative work, contrib-uting to the *London Illustrated News*, and *The Graphic*, and also illustrating for the Admiralty and the Port of London Authority. He also produced illustrative work for: *A Book About Ships*, by A. O. Cook, 1914, and *Our Wonderful Navy*, by J. S. Margerison, 1919. He is believed to have died at Cheam. Represented: National Maritime Museum; Whitehaven Museum.

DENYER, Edwin Ely (*c.*1840- after 1905)

Landscape painter in watercolour; art teacher. Denyer practised as an artist and art teacher at WEST HARTLE-POOL (now HARTLEPOOL), in the second half of the 19th century, serving as Headmaster of the town's School of Art until 1905. He was succeeded as Headmaster by Alfred Josiah Rushton (q.v.). The Gray Art Gallery & Museum, HARTLEPOOL, has Denyer's sepia wash: *West Hartlepool at the time of granting of the Charter of Incorporation, 1887*.

54

DICKINSON, John (1852-1885)

Portrait painter in oil. Dickinson was born at Merthyr-Tidfil, South Wales, where his father, an engineer from ALLENDALE, was temporarily employed on the construc-tion of a railway. His father shortly afterwards fell ill, and the family moved back to ALLENDALE, and here Dickinson remained until the age of fourteen, when he left home to become an apprentice to an engraver at NEWCASTLE. He did not like the work, however, and in 1870 left for London, where he began studying at South Kensington Museum. In 1873 he entered the Royal Academy Schools, where he received the silver medal for the best painting of a portrait in oil. He began exhibiting at the Royal Academy in 1876, showing a portrait study: *Contemplation*, and remained a regular exhibitor at the Academy for the rest of his life, also showing one work at the Suffolk Street Gallery: *Study of a head*. Almost all of his Royal Academy exhibits were portraits, these including artists John Charlton (q.v.), and Dickinson's cousin, Thomas Dickinson (q.v.). Although he practised in London during this period he returned to NEWCASTLE each year to carry out portrait commissions, and was an occasional exhibitor in the town. One of his works: *The Sultana*, was shown at the exhibition of paintings by local artists, at the Central Exchange Art Gallery, in 1878, a catalogue note stating: "This, his last painting, is one of the most refined and exquisite female studies we have seen. The whole pose, tone, colour and feeling of the painting are admirable and we heartily congratulate Mr Dickinson on the lovely life-like and refined beauty of the subject". Dickinson last exhibited at a major exhibition in 1882, showing four works at the Royal Scottish Academy. He died of consumption at the early age of thirty-two.

DICKINSON, Thomas (1854- after 1902)
Amateur portrait and landscape painter in oil. He was born at ALLENDALE, and studied art at the Government School of Design, NEWCASTLE, and under his cousin, portrait painter John Dickinson (q.v.). He did well in his examinations at the School, but decided against a career as a professional artist because of the precarious state of his health. Dickinson is best remembered for his work in promoting and organising art in Northumbria, amongst his most notable achievements being his work in helping to found the Bewick Club, and the Pen & Palette Club, at NEWCASTLE, and his association with the organisation of several major exhibitions in the city.

DICKMAN, George (born c.1898)
Landscape and coastal painter in oil and watercolour. He was born at NEWCASTLE, and practised as an artist in the city throughout the first half of the present century. He exhibited his work at the Bewick Club, NEWCASTLE, and at the Artists of the Northern Counties exhibitions at the city's Laing Art Gallery, from 1919, until they were replaced by the Federation of Northern Art Societies' exhibitions many years later. He was for some time Honorary Secretary of the Benwell Art Club, in the West End of NEWCASTLE. He died at NEWCASTLE.

DIXON, Dudley (c.1900- after 1948)
Landscape and still-life painter in oil. He was born at GATESHEAD, the son of solicitor and clerk to the County Justices, Dr. J. A. Dixon. After completing his general education he studied at Armstrong College (later King's College; now Newcastle University), and later under Frank Spenelove-Spenelove, before practising as a professional artist, mainly in London. He first began exhibiting his work publicly in 1919, at the Artists of the Northern Counties exhibition at the Laing Art Gallery, NEWCASTLE, later sending work to the Royal Academy, the Royal Scottish Academy, the Royal Hibernian Academy, the Royal Institute of Oil Painters, and Walker's Gallery, London. The Shipley Art Gallery, GATESHEAD, has his oil: *Still-Life*, 1927. He was the brother of Joyce Deighton Dixon (q.v.).

DIXON, Elsie M., S.W.A. (1894-1972)
Landscape and flower painter in watercolour. She was born in India, but later settled in Northumbria, near DARLINGTON. She was a founder member of the Darlington Society of Arts, and in addition to serving on its committee was elected President in 1969. She is said to have exhibited her work at the Royal Institute of Painters in Water Colours, the Society of Women Artists (of which she was a member), the Royal Water Colour Society, and the annual exhibitions of the Darlington Society of Arts. Darlington Art Gallery has her watercolour: *Rhododendron Farges II.*

DIXON, George Pelham (1859-1898)
Seascape and landscape painter in oil and watercolour. The eldest son of George Dixon, first Librarian of TYNEMOUTH, Dixon was a self-taught artist who quickly became so proficient that he was able to offer instruction to brother artists no older than himself. He later, in

fact, devoted much of his life to teaching art, serving as Head Master of Turton Hall College, Leeds, Yorkshire, and the Collegiate School, Morley, Derbyshire, and issuing in a private capacity and advertising card reading: "Lessons given in sketching, oil and watercolours, practical geometry and pencil and chalk drawing". He practised as an artist both before and after his teaching appointments, producing many local seascapes and coastal views, usually in watercolour, and frequently in vignette form of small proportions. He was a member of both North Shields Art Club, and South Shields Art Club, and appears to have exhibited his work exclusively in Northumbria, mainly at the exhibitions of the aforementioned clubs, but also occasionally at the Bewick Club, NEWCASTLE. At South Shields Art Club in 1892, he exhibited an oil entitled: *Frenchman's Bay;* and at the Bewick Club in 1894, a watercolour: *Twixt Tyne and Wear.* South Shields Museum and Art Gallery has several of his works in watercolour, including: *Tynemouth; North Shields in the distance*, painted in the year of his death at SOUTH SHIELDS.

DIXON, John, M.A. (1835-1891)
Amateur marine painter in watercolour. He was born at NEWCASTLE, and following his education at Dr. Bruce's School in the town, served an engineering apprenticeship with Robert Stephenson & Co. On leaving Stephenson's he obtained an appointment as an engineer to the Derwent Iron Co., at CONSETT, leaving the company some time later to go into partnership with a Mr. Mounsey, at BEDLINGTON, in an attempt to revive the prestige of the iron works long associated with the town. Their attempt failed, and in 1867 Dixon moved to London to work as a civil engineer and contractor. His success in his chosen new profession was phenomenal, and in the next twenty-four years he was responsible for major civil engineering works in various parts of the world, including a bridge across the Nile at Cairo, piers in Mexico, and in 1874 the construction of the first railway in China, between Shanghai and Woosung. He also handled projects in Portugal, Gibraltar, and Britain, but perhaps his most famous undertaking was the transportation from Alexandria to London of Cleopatra's Needle.

Dixon was evidently a keen spare-time painter throughout his life, though not until he was working in London did he seriously begin to exhibit his work. In the period 1880-87, he sent four works to the Suffolk Street Gallery, one work to the Royal Institute of Painters in Water Colours, and three works to the Dudley Gallery. Most of these works were marine paintings, some of which were executed while he was working abroad on his civil engineering projects. Towards the end of his life failing health sent him to South Africa to recover. His health did not improve there, however, and returning to London, he died at East Croydon in 1891. Dixon received several honours in his lifetime; he was Deputy Lieutenant of the City of London, and received an honorary Master of Arts Degree from Durham University; his name appears on the bronze tablet at the foot of Cleopatra's Needle, in London.

DIXON, John (1869- after 1937)

Landscape, portrait and flower painter in oil and watercolour. Dixon was born at SEATON BURN, and received his tuition in art at NEWCASTLE, and later St. John's Wood, London, and the Royal Academy Schools. On returning to Northumbria he settled at MORPETH, and began exhibiting his work at the Bewick Club, NEWCASTLE. At the age of thirty he sent his first work to the Royal Academy: *Wild Roses*, and in 1905 contributed the first of his many works to the Artists of the Northern Counties exhibitions at the Laing Art Gallery, NEWCASTLE: *Autumn Gold*, and *Wind in the Valley*. He did not resume exhibiting at the Royal Academy until 1926, when he contributed a portrait of a *Mrs. Duncan*. He last exhibited at the Academy in 1937, when his contribution was entitled: *Mrs. Dorothy M. Osborne*. Dixon continued to contribute to the Artists of the Northern Counties exhibitions until close to his death, mainly showing landscapes. Represented: Laing A.G., Newcastle.

DIXON, John Turnbull (c.1846- after 1921)

Amateur landscape painter in oil and watercolour; illustrator. He was the son of William Dixon, village draper at WHITTINGHAM, near ALNWICK, and brother of David Dippie Dixon (1842-1929), author of *The Vale of Whittingham*, and *Upper Coquetdale*, published in NEWCASTLE. Both brothers worked for their father's business of Dixon & Sons, ROTHBURY, from its opening in 1862, David spending much of his spare time preparing the texts for his books; John, the illustrations, most of which were in line. John also painted considerably in his spare time, contributing work to several exhibitions at NEWCASTLE, notably the Bewick Club exhibition of 1891, at which he showed an oil entitled: *St. Mary's Isle, near Whitley; a storm in the offing*, and the Artists of the Northern Counties exhibition at the Laing Art Gallery in 1921, at which he showed a watercolour entitled: *An incoming tide*. Both works were contributed to these exhibitions from ROTHBURY, his home for most of his life. Several examples of his work may be seen at Cragside, the former home of the Armstrong family at ROTHBURY, courtesy of the National Trust.

DIXON, Joyce Deighton (c.1899- after 1950)

Landscape, portrait and flower painter in oil and watercolour. She was born at GATESHEAD, the daughter of solicitor and clerk to the County Justices, Dr. J. A. Dixon. After completing her general education she studied art at Armstrong College (later King's College; now Newcastle University), and later under Frank Spenelove-Spenelove, before practising as a professional artist, mainly in London. She first began exhibiting her work publicly in 1919, when she sent examples to the Artists of the Northern Counties exhibition at the Laing Art Gallery, NEWCASTLE, and to several other provincial exhibitions. She subsequently exhibited widely in Britain, showing her work at the Royal Scottish Academy, the Royal Hibernian Academy, the Royal Cambrian Academy, the Royal Institute of Oil Painters, the Society of Women Artists, and in 1950, at the Royal Academy, at which her *Snow in Chelsea*, was

shown. She also exhibited at the Paris Salon, in 1923. She shared a studio for some years in London with her brother, Dudley Dixon (q.v.). Represented: Shipley A.G., Gateshead; South Shields Museum & A.G.

DIXON, William (died c.1830)

Portrait and landscape painter in oil and watercolour. This artist first came to prominence in Northumbria about 1816, when jointly with Thomas Miles Richardson, Senior (q.v.), he embarked on the publication of a series of aquatint illustrations of places of interest in NEWCASTLE. He published further illustrations in this form in 1819 and 1820, covering Northumberland, and showing his address as London, but by 1822, and exhibiting at the First Exhibition of the Northumberland Institution for the Promotion of the Fine Arts, NEWCASTLE, he was describing himself as a resident of both NEWCASTLE, and London. His exhibit at the Institution was a portrait of Francis Humble, newspaper proprietor of DURHAM, Dixon not only contributing to the exhibition, but serving on its committee, along with Richardson, Senior, Thomas Bewick (q.v.), Henry Perlee Parker (q.v.), John Dobson (q.v.), and others. These circumstances, coupled with the type of work which he subsequently exhibited at NEWCASTLE, suggest that he may have been the William Dixon who commenced exhibiting at the Royal Academy in 1796, and the British Institution in 1808, while working in London.

Certainly Dixon established a considerable status as an artist very quickly after moving to NEWCASTLE, in 1817 receiving a visit from John Linnell (1792-1882), and introducing this former pupil of John Varley to Richardson, Senior. Dixon's involvement in the artistic activities of the area were not to last long, however. He continued to exhibit at the Institution at NEWCASTLE, for a number of years, and also exhibited at the town's Northern Academy in 1828, but must have died shortly after the latter exhibition, as he did not show his work again. Dixon lived successively at NEWCASTLE, DURHAM and SUNDERLAND, during his exhibiting period at NEWCASTLE, and showed mainly portraits and landscapes, among the former a portrait of Joseph Sébastien Victor Francois Bouet (q.v.), and the latter, the *Ruins of Finchdale Priory*, and *View on the River Wear*. He also in this period collaborated with John Dobson (q.v.), in producing a stage drop-scene for the old theatre at NEWCASTLE. His work was occasionally exhibited at NEWCASTLE after his death, notably at the exhibition of the Newcastle Society of Artists, in 1836, in the catalogue of which he was described as "Dixon, Wm., the late", and the exhibition of works by local painters, at the Central Exchange Art Gallery, in 1878, comprising a portrait of John Dobson, and a landscape.

*DOBBIN, John (1815-1888)

Landscape and architectural painter in oil and watercolour; mosaic artist. Dobbin was born at DARLINGTON, the son of a weaver employed at Pease's Mill in the town. Details of his early artistic training are not known, but he practised at DARLINGTON before moving to London in his mid-twenties, and sent work to NEWCASTLE, for exhibition at the Newcastle Society of Artists in 1836, while still living in his native town. In

John Dobbin: Opening of the Stockton & Darlington Railway, A.D. 1825. Watercolour 30×52. *Darlington Art Gallery.*

London by 1842, he commenced exhibiting at the Royal Academy, showing a landscape: *Loch Catrine, Scotland.* In the following year he sent his first work to the Suffolk Street Gallery; three watercolour studies of Northumbrian scenery, and in 1851 commenced exhibiting at the British Institution, showing: *On the Skerne, Darlington.* He remained a regular exhibitor at the Royal Academy until 1875, and showed work at the British Institution for four years. He mainly exhibited at the Suffolk Street Gallery, however, showing some 102 works between 1843 and the year of his death. Most of these works were in watercolour, and included subjects painted in Holland, France, Spain and Germany, as well as in Scotland, and in his native Northumbria.

Most of Dobbin's professional life was spent in London, but he made frequent visits to his home town, one of these resulting in a commission to paint probably his best known work: *Opening of the Stockton and Darlington Railway, A.D. 1825.#* This large watercolour, painted in 1871, was first exhibited in the Central Hall, DARLINGTON, in 1875. A mosaic reredos in St. Cuthbert's Church, DARLINGTON, is also Dobbin's work, having come into its possession after Westminster Abbey refused it as being ". . . too Byzantine in style and Unchristian". This mosaic was cut entirely by Dobbin himself with handshears and presented to the Church in 1875. In addition to being a prolific painter in watercolour, Dobbin also restored such work, notably that by Turner. Represented: Victoria and Albert Museum; Cartwright Hall, Bradford; Darlington A.G.; Shipley A.G., Gateshead; Sunderland A.G.

DOBSON, Alexander Ralph (1826-1854)
Architectural draughtsman. He was born at NEWCASTLE, the youngest son of John Dobson (q.v.), and received his first tuition in drawing from his father. He later decided to follow his father's profession as architect, and was placed as a pupil under Sydney Smirke (his brother-in-law, and later Royal Academician), in London. He worked diligently at his studies under Smirke, and gained the First Prize for Architecture (Fine Arts), and First Prize for Architecture (Construction), from University College, London. In 1852 he returned to NEWCASTLE and joined his father's practice. He died two years later in an explosion at GATESHEAD. It is said that he was "favourably known in his profession for some clever drawings".

DOBSON, Mrs. Isabella (née Rutherford) (1795-1846)
Amateur miniature painter. She was born at GATESHEAD, the eldest daughter of Alexander Rutherford of Warburton House, and in 1816 became the wife of John Dobson (q.v.). Details of her early artistic training are not known, but by 1828, and exhibiting portraits at the Northern Academy, NEWCASTLE, and the Carlisle Academy, she had obviously achieved some competence as an artist. She exhibited little after 1828, though a miniature of her sister, Anne Rutherford (shown at the Northern Academy, in 1828), was included in the exhibition of work by local painters, at the Central Exchange Art Gallery, NEWCASTLE, in 1878. Her daughter, Margaret Jane Dobson, in a Memoir of Dobson published in 1885, refers to her as "a lady of great

John Dobson: Seaton
Delaval Hall. Watercolour
23¾×35½. *Tyne & Wear
County Council Museums,
Laing Art Gallery.*

artistic talent, her miniature painting being far beyond ordinary amateur work". Her son, Alexander Ralph Dobson (q.v.), was also talented artistically. She died at NEWCASTLE.

*DOBSON, John (1787-1865)

Architectural and landscape painter in watercolour; draughtsman. Born at NORTH SHIELDS, the son of a gardener, Dobson is best known as one of Northumbria's most outstanding architects of the 19th century. He was, however, also a superb architectural draughtsman, and one who showed a talent for drawing from his earliest years. Indeed, at the age of eleven he was appointed "Honorary Draftsman" to a well known local damask weaver, and four years later we find him being welcomed as a pupil of architect and builder David Stephenson, at NEWCASTLE, and taking lessons in drawing from Boniface Muss (q.v.), along with John Martin (q.v.). He also had ambitions as a watercolourist, and on completing his studies with Stephenson by 1810, he went to London to study under no less a master of the art than John Varley. He remained with Varley for several months and developed a close friendship with his master, and several other leading artists of the day, including Robert Smirke, the painter Royal Academician, whose son was later to marry Dobson's eldest daughter. Back at NEWCASTLE no later than 1811, Dobson did not pursue his ambitions as watercolourist, but set-up in the town as an architect. That he remained attached to his early love of drawing and watercolour painting, however, is evidenced by the many works which he subsequently exhibited, albeit sometimes assisted in the latter respect by other artists.

His first exhibit of note was his *Perspective View of Seaton Delaval House*, sent to the Royal Academy in 1818, this work attracting considerable attention because of its novelty as a coloured perspective drawing.

He again chose Seaton Delaval Hall, when he next exhibited his work, this time as a founder and committee member of the Northumberland Institution for the Promotion of the Fine Arts, at its first exhibition at NEWCASTLE, in 1822. At the First Exhibition of the Northern Academy, NEWCASTLE, in 1828, he showed his design for one of his earliest important ecclesiastical commissions: *The Chapel of St. Thomas*, for the Haymarket area of the town, and at the Carlisle Academy, in the same year, two of his other designs for buildings. He continued to exhibit at NEWCASTLE throughout his rise to prominence as the town's best respected architect, and again in the Royal Academy in 1850, showing: *The Arcades and Portico, Central Station, Newcastle upon Tyne.* The most notable occasion on which he exhibited at NEWCASTLE was in 1838, when he showed no fewer than fifteen of his drawings, mainly of buildings which he had designed. In some of his exhibited work he collaborated with John Wilson Carmichael (q.v.), the latter providing the figures, and frequently the colouring. In another instance of artistic collaboration he worked with William Dixon (q.v.), in the production of a stage drop-scene for the old theatre, NEWCASTLE, which was so successful that a copy of it was used at Drury Lane, London, for many years.

Dobson took an active interest in art promoting activities at NEWCASTLE for much of his life, and as one of the area's most respected architects, and Fellow of the Royal Institute of British Architects, was the natural choice as first president of the Northern Architectural Association. He suffered a stroke in 1863, and retired to RYTON. He later returned to NEWCASTLE, where he died at his home in the town's New Bridge Street in 1865. His wife Isabella Dobson (q.v.), and son Alexander Ralph Dobson (q.v.), were also talented artistically. Represented: British Museum; Laing A.G., Newcastle.

58

DODD, Barrodail Robert (fl. early 19th cent.)
Amateur portrait painter; copyist. Dodd was born on
Tyneside, and practised as a civil engineer, engineer
and architect at NEWCASTLE in the early 19th century.
He was evidently a keen painter of portraits in his spare
time, at the First Exhibition of the Northumberland
Institution for the Promotion of the Fine Arts, NEW-
CASTLE, in 1822, showing two such works: *The Late
Henrietta A. Dodd*, and *Portrait of a Lady, after Sir
Thomas Lawrence*, and at the Institution's exhibition in
the following year: *The Misses Ella, Eliza and Mary
Ann Dodd*. Thomas Miles Richardson, Senior (q.v.),
was once occasioned to defend Dodd in a letter to the
Tyne Mercury (29th November, 1823), when Dodd's
visit to an exhibition of the Institution to make notes of
colours in the paintings on view was criticised in the
press as copying. He does not appear to have exhibited
his work after this criticism, concentrating instead on
his work as civil engineer, etc. He may have been the
son of Robert Dodds (q.v.), despite the different
spelling of this artist's name.

DODDS, Robert (fl. late 18th, early 19th cent.)
Amateur portrait painter. Mackenzie, in his *History of
Newcastle*, Volume II, p. 585, states that "a portrait of
Mr. Bewick, when in the prime of life, by the late
Robert Dodds, engineer, is now in the possession of his
son, R. B. Dodds, of Newcastle, civil engineer". The
"R. B. Dodds" referred to in connection with this
portrait of Thomas Bewick (q.v.), may have been
Barrodail Robert Dodd (q.v.).

James Doxford: Vera Gomez. Oil 30×20. *Tyne & Wear
County Council Museums, Shipley Art Gallery.*

*DOXFORD, James, A.R.W.A., A.T.D. (1899-1978)
Landscape, portrait and flower painter in oil and
watercolour; art teacher. Doxford was born at NORTH
SHIELDS and studied art at Armstrong College (later
King's College; now Newcastle University), under
Richard George Hatton (q.v.), and E. M. O'Rorke
Dickey, before practising as a professional artist in his
native town until the early 1930's. During this period he
was a regular exhibitor at the Artists of the Northern
Counties exhibitions at the Laing Art Gallery, NEW-
CASTLE, showing a wide variety of work in oil and
watercolour. He was later appointed Principal of Bridg-
water (and later) Barnstaple Art and Technical Schools,
and in 1945 took up the post of Head of the Art
Department of the Grammar School at GATESHEAD,
remaining there until his retirement in 1964. He exhibited his work at the Royal Academy on five occasions
from 1939, and also showed his work widely in the
provinces. Three of his works in oil: *Myself; Vera
Gomez,#* and *Asters*, were included in the "Contemporary Artists of Durham County" exhibition at the
Shipley Art Gallery, GATESHEAD, staged in 1951 in
connection with the Festival of Britain. He was an
associate of the Royal West of England Academy, and
was a holder of the Art Teachers' Diploma. Following
his retirement he moved to Canterbury. He died at
Canterbury. Represented: Shipley A.G., Gateshead.

DRESSER, Alfred B. (d.1939)
Landscape and architectural painter in watercolour;
draughtsman; art teacher. He was born at DARLINGTON,
the son of William Dresser, well known printer and
stationer in the town. He was a talented artist from his
youth, and after training at the Slade taught art at
Darlington Grammar School, and the town's Ladies'
Training, and Technical Colleges. Throughout much of
his life as a teacher he maintained a studio at Blackwellgate, DARLINGTON, and regularly showed his work
at the exhibitions of the Darlington Society of Arts. He
died at DARLINGTON. He was the elder brother of
George Cuthbert Dresser (q.v.). His grandfather WIL-
LIAM DRESSER was also artistically talented. Represented: Darlington Public Library.

DRESSER, George Cuthbert (1872-1951)
Amateur landscape painter in watercolour. He was
born at DARLINGTON, the son of William Dresser, well
known printer and stationer in the town. Although a
talented artist from an early age, Dresser preferred to
become a structural draughtsman with a local firm
rather than paint and draw for a living, and thereafter
pursued these activities only as a relaxation. He occasionally exhibited his work at the Royal Institute of
Painters in Water Colours, and was a regular exhibitor
at the exhibitions of the Darlington Society of Arts, of
which he was also a lifelong member. He died at
DARLINGTON. He was the younger brother of Alfred B.
Dresser (q.v.). Represented: Darlington A.G.

*DUNCAN, John (c.1846- after 1898)
Bird painter in oil and watercolour; illustrator; lithographer; glass painter. He was the son of Robert Duncan,
taxidermist, of NEWCASTLE, and at the age of fourteen

John Duncan: The Magpie. Watercolour 13×9.
G. R. McArdle.

was apprenticed to William Wailes (q.v.), at his stained glass manufactory in the town. Like many of Wailes' apprentices he attended the Government School of Design in the town under William Bell Scott (q.v.), later working for his master, and for the firm of Wailes & Strang, for more than forty years. Duncan was interested in making studies of birds in oil and watercolour from his teens, this leading to a commission from the *Newcastle Weekly Chronicle*, about 1888, to produce a series of pen and ink drawings of British Birds for reproduction in its pages. The series ran for almost ten years, proving so successful that his drawings and accompanying texts were published as a limited edition book entitled: *Birds of the British Isles*, in 1898 (many of these drawings and texts also appeared in the locally printed *Monthly Chronicle* of *North Country Lore and Legend*, 1887-1891). Duncan occasionally exhibited his work at NEWCASTLE, one of his earliest exhibits being the chalk study of a Greenland Falcon which he sent to the "Exhibition of Paintings and other Works of Art", at the Town Hall, in 1866. In addition to his illustrative work in pen and ink, he produced work in lithography. His work for Wailes was widely used in Britain, and the United States of America. The Natural History Society of Northumbria, NEWCASTLE, has examples of his work.

DUNNING, John Thomson, R.B.A. (1851-1931)
Landscape and figure painter in oil and watercolour. Dunning was born at MIDDLESBROUGH, and was educated at Ackworth Quaker School in Yorkshire, before studying art at Heatherley's School, and in Exeter. On completing his art training he settled in London, and commenced exhibiting his work at various London and provincial exhibitions, including among the latter those of the Bewick Club, NEWCASTLE. He later exhibited mainly at the Suffolk Street Gallery, also sending works to the Royal Academy, the Royal Scottish Academy, the Royal Hibernian Academy, the Royal Institute of Painters in Water Colours, and to a wide range of London and provincial galleries. He was elected a member of the Royal Society of British Artists in 1899, and appears to have spent most of his professional life based in London, while painting landscapes widely throughout South West England, and other parts of Britain. Dunning was an occasional illustrator in his early years, and published a work: "Middlesbrough in 1885", containing many of his drawings. Represented: Middlesbrough A.G.

DYSON, John William (1855-1916)
Landscape and figure painter in oil and watercolour; architectural draughtsman. Dyson was born at Addingham, in Wharfedale, and was trained as an architect under William Vickers Thompson, of BISHOP AUCKLAND. On completing his training he set up practice at NEWCASTLE, later becoming a founder member of the Bewick Club in the city, and serving in various capacities on its committees. He was a keen spare-time painter when not involved in his architectural design work for local public and private buildings, and exhibited his work regularly at the Bewick Club until his death at NEWCASTLE in 1916.

EAST, Mary Margaret – see ANDERTON, Mrs. Mary Margaret.

ECKHARDT, Oscar, R.B.A. (1872-1904)
Landscape painter in oil; illustrator. He was born at SUNDERLAND, but early in his life moved to London. Here he practised as a professional artist until his death at the early age of thirty-two, establishing considerable success in his brief career as painter and illustrator. He exhibited at the Royal Society of British Artists' exhibitions from the age of twenty-four, showing some eighteen works prior to his death. He also exhibited at the Royal Institute of Oil Painters, and at the Walker Art Gallery, Liverpool. He worked for numerous publications as a pen and ink illustrator between 1893-1900, including: *The Butterfly*, 1893; *The Daily Graphic*, 1895; *The St. James's Budget*, 1898, and *Illustrated Bits*, 1900. He was elected a member of the Royal Society of British Artists in 1896. Represented: Victoria and Albert Museum.

EDDOWES, W. K. (fl. early 19th cent.)
Amateur religious and landscape painter in oil. Eddowes practised in Northumbria in the early 19th century, and was evidently a man of some means who

60

painted in his spare time. He exhibited two examples of his work at the Northern Academy, NEWCASTLE, while living at SOUTH SHIELDS, these being *A Magdalen*, in 1828, and a *Landscape*, in 1829. He later moved to TYNEMOUTH, but does not appear to have continued exhibiting while there, although he remained keenly interested in the exhibitions at NEWCASTLE, buying from one of these the *Tynemouth* exhibited by George Balmer (q.v.). He was a collector of works of art, and owned examples by Dürer, and Van Huysum. It is said that he spent his later life at SOUTH SHIELDS.

EDEN, Sir Timothy Calvert, 8th Baronet, West Auckland (1893-1963)

Amateur flower and still-life painter in oil and watercolour. The son of Sir William Eden (q.v.), he was born at Windlestone Hall, near BISHOP AUCKLAND, and received his education at Eton, and later Christ's Church College, Oxford. In the period 1914-16 he was interned as a prisoner at Ruhleben, Germany, in the middle of this period succeeding to the Baronetcy, on the death of his father. On returning to England he enlisted in the Army, serving until the end of the First World War. He also served in the Second World War, 1939-43, as a Staff Captain. Like his father, Sir Timothy was a talented amateur artist and may, indeed, have received some tuition from Sir William, as a young man. He exhibited his work mainly at Arthur Tooth & Sons' Gallery, in London, also sending several works to the Alpine Club Gallery, and to the Artists of the Northern Counties exhibitions at the Laing Art Gallery, NEWCASTLE. He also wrote several books, among these: *Five Dogs and Two More*, 1928; *The Tribulations of a Baronet* (a biographical work concerning his father), 1933, and *Durham*, 1952. He was the elder brother of Sir Anthony Eden, later 1st Earl of Avon.

EDEN, Sir William, 5th Baronet Maryland, North America, 7th Baronet, West Auckland (1849-1915)

Amateur landscape painter in watercolour. He was born at Windlestone Hall, near BISHOP AUCKLAND, son of SIR WILLIAM EDEN (1803-1873), 4th BARONET OF MARYLAND, NORTH AMERICA, and 6th BARONET OF WEST AUCKLAND, a talented amateur artist. He was educated at Eton, where his early attempts to draw and paint were encouraged by Sam Evans. It was not, however, until some thirteen years after leaving Eton to prepare for the Army that he began to paint seriously, and then only because an ankle injury kept him from his duties as a Lieutenant in the 8th Hussars. He began taking lessons from Nathaniel Everett Green, later painting much in the company of this artist, David Green, Alfred East, and others. He also went to Paris, where he spent time in the studios of James Abbott McNeill Whistler, and Jacques Blanches. Sir William sketched widely around the world, touring Europe at the age of seventeen, and later visiting among many countries, Egypt, Algeria, India, China, Japan, and America. He exhibited his work in London and Paris, showing some 133 examples at the Goupil Gallery, more than 100 at the Dowdeswell Gallery, and twenty-two at the New English Art Club, apart from sending occasional works for exhibition at the Royal

Institute of Painters in Water Colours, the International Society, and the London Salon. On the conclusion of his service in the Army as Colonel in Command of the 2nd V.B. Durham Light Infantry 1889-96, he took an increasing interest in the sporting life of his County, adding to his already established reputation as a boxer, that of fox-hunter and field sportsman. His son, Sir Timothy Calvert Eden (q.v.), was also a talented amateur artist, and wrote a number of books, among these one about his father: *The Tribulations of a Baronet*, 1933, in which reference is made to Sir William's famous legal battle with Whistler, which became known as the "Baronet and the Butterfly" lawsuit. Represented: Laing A.G., Newcastle.

ELLIOT, George (fl. 19th cent.)

Portrait and imaginative painter in oil. Little is known of Elliot except that he spent many years in Bensham Asylum, GATESHEAD, and that he painted several pictures in which he portrayed himself grandiosely robed and bejewelled in regal surroundings. One of his pictures, dated 1856, hung for many years in the Davy Inn, WALLSEND, near NEWCASTLE, and portrays Elliot crowned and robed, in a fantastic architectural setting with dozens of surrounding figures in biblical clothing. In a lengthy inscription on this picture, written by Elliot, he tells us that it is "Dedicated to the World", and that it portrays "George Elliot, Emperor of the World and True Live God, George the Fifth of Great Britain". This picture was sold at Sotheby's Belgravia saleroom on February 1st, 1972, for £160. A self portrait in pen and wash is in the possession of Gateshead Central Library.

*ELLIOTT, Robinson (1814-1894)

Genre, portrait, figure and landscape painter in oil. The son of a prosperous hatter at SOUTH SHIELDS, Elliott showed an aptitude for drawing from an early age and was sent by his father to study at the school of Henry Sass, where one of his fellow pupils was Sir John Everett Millais, afterwards President of the Royal Academy. On returning to SOUTH SHIELDS after his training he established a studio in the town, and shortly afterwards sent his first work for exhibition, showing three works at the Newcastle upon Tyne Institution for the General Promotion of the Fine Arts, 1833. Two years later, and living briefly in London, he exhibited for the first time outside Northumbria, showing *Smuggler on the Watch*, at the Suffolk Street Gallery. He continued to exhibit at NEWCASTLE until late in his life, taking up residence in the town by 1841, and three years later sending his first work to the Royal Academy: *A morning call*, and *Children in the wood*; in the following year he sent his first work to the British Institution: *The Ascension; sketch for an altar-piece*. He continued to exhibit at the Suffolk Street Gallery until 1868; the British Institution until 1852, and the Royal Academy until 1881, also exhibiting his work at NEWCASTLE, and on two occasions at Carlisle Athenaeum: 1846 and 1850. Several of his later Academy works were coastal scenes near SOUTH SHIELDS, to which he returned to practise by the late 1850's. Elliott was a popular teacher of painting and attracted many pupils to his studios at SOUTH SHIELDS

Robinson Elliott: School-time. Oil 12×8¾. *Tyne & Wear County Council Museums, Sunderland Art Gallery & Museum.*

and NEWCASTLE. He was also a poet of considerable ability, whose work was collected and published in his lifetime. One of his less characteristic works was the designing of the Coat of Arms, and Seal, of his native town. Elliott continued to paint vigorously into his late life. He died at SOUTH SHIELDS. Represented: South Shields Museum & A.G.; Sunderland A.G.

ELTON, Edgar Averill (1859-1923)
Landscape painter in watercolour; art teacher. The son of Samuel Averill Elton (q.v.), he was probably born at DARLINGTON after his father had taken up residence in the town. He studied art at the schools of South Kensington Museum, and in 1886 succeeded his father as professor at the School of Art, at DARLINGTON. Elton appears to have exhibited exclusively in Northumbria, amongst his few known exhibits being the three works which he sent to the Bewick Club, NEWCASTLE, in 1893: *Still Life; Piercebridge, near Darlington*, and *Kate*. Soon after the First World War he was forced to retire from his teaching post due to ill-health. He died at DARLINGTON. Darlington Art Gallery has his watercolour: *Whitby*.

ELTON, Samuel Averill (1827-1886)
Landscape and coastal painter in oil and watercolour; art teacher. Elton was born at Newnham, Gloucestershire, but spent most of his life at DARLINGTON, where

he was for many years professor at the School of Art. While living at DARLINGTON he exhibited at the Royal Academy and at the Suffolk Street Gallery. He also sent work to various other London exhibitions, and was an exhibitor at the Arts Association, and Bewick Club exhibitions, at NEWCASTLE, from their foundation. His Royal Academy exhibits were entitled: *Mousehold Heath, Norwich* (1874), and *Purple Iris* (1884); those at the Suffolk Street Gallery: *A study near Rokeby* (1860), and *Whitby Sands* (1880). His exhibits at NEWCASTLE consisted of Northumbrian, South of England, and continental landscape and coastal views. He died in London. His son Edgar Averill Elton (q.v.), was also a talented landscape painter. Represented: Victoria and Albert Museum; Bowes Museum, Barnard Castle; Darlington A.G.

EMERY, John (1777-1822)
Coastal, landscape, animal and genre painter in oil. He was born at SUNDERLAND, the son of a country actor, and later followed his father in this profession, achieving considerable critical acclaim for his performances in comical roles. He was originally trained as a musician, however, following a rudimentary education at Ecclesfield, Yorkshire, by playing in an orchestra at Brighton at the age of twelve. He continued to play fiddle for several years, occasionally taking the part of country boys in provincial theatrical productions. His first important engagement as an actor came in 1798, when he was engaged to replace T. Knight at Covent Garden, London, as Frank Oakland, in Morton's "A Cure for the Headache". A number of other parts followed, then from 1801 until his death he acted almost exclusively at Covent Garden, and from that year until 1817 sent no fewer than nineteen works to the Royal Academy. Most of these works were coastal, landscape, animal or genre studies, among these: *View of part of the town of Liverpool after sunset* (1804); *Portrait of an Irish Mare* (1808), and *View of the North Pierhead and Lighthouse, Sunderland* (1817). From 1803 he was described as "An Honorary Exhibitor". Emery continued to act until a month before his death but is not known to have produced any work in painting after 1817. His masterly portrayal of comic figures on the stage, notably "Tyke", in Morton's "School of Reform", made him a popular portrait subject for other artists, and no less than seven portraits of him in various characters were painted, apart from an unknown number of conventional portraits, such as Samuel Raven's miniature in the National Portrait Gallery, London. He died in London.

EMMERSON, Henry Bewick (fl. late 19th, early 20th cent.)
Animal, sporting and landscape painter in oil and watercolour. He was one of the two artist sons of Henry Hetherington Emmerson (q.v.), and first began exhibiting his work after the family had settled at CULLERCOATS in the early 1880's. At the first exhibition of the Bewick Club, in 1884, he exhibited alongside his father, and brother Percy Emmerson (q.v.), showing: *Rams Head; Throwing off Hounds*, and *Return to the Meet*. He continued to exhibit at the Bewick Club after

moving to nearby WHITLEY BAY, in the following year, but appears to have abandoned painting in favour of some other profession or occupation, in later years.

*EMMERSON, Henry Hetherington (1831-1895)

Genre, portrait and landscape painter in oil and water-colour; muralist; illustrator. He was born at CHESTER-LE-STREET, and came to NEWCASTLE at the age of thirteen to study at the Government School of Design, under William Bell Scott (q.v.). Bell Scott is said to have taken a special interest in Emmerson, and had tutored him for some two years, when a clergyman who had heard of the boy's talent sent him to Paris for six months so that he could spend time copying works in the Louvre. At the end of his stay in Paris, Emmerson went to London, where he was successful in gaining entry to the Royal Academy Schools. While studying at the Schools he had to support himself entirely unaided, but found his special gift for painting children brought him more than enough commissions to meet this requirement. In 1851 his oil: *The Village Tailor* (portraying his father), was accepted for exhibition at the Royal Academy, and was honoured with a position on the line. Emmerson decided to leave London, however, and back in Northumbria by 1856, he lived briefly at WHICKHAM, near GATESHEAD, then marrying in 1857, he moved first to EBCHESTER, then to STOCKSFIELD, where he remained for some six years.

About 1865 he moved to CULLERCOATS, retaining a home there for the rest of his life, although he spent a number of years living mainly at ROTHBURY, under the patronage of Lord Armstrong. Emmerson continued to exhibit at the Royal Academy until two years short of his death, showing a total of fifty-eight works, and establishing a considerable reputation as an artist. He also exhibited his work at NEWCASTLE, notably at the exhibitions of the Arts Association, and later at the Bewick Club, at which latter his work was sometimes to be seen accompanied by that of his two artist sons:

Henry Bewick Emmerson (q.v.), and Percy Emmerson (q.v.). Emmerson frequently painted on a large scale, amongst his largest works being the four murals which he executed for the banqueting hall of the Crown Hotel, NEWCASTLE. These murals, each measuring about twenty feet in length, had as their subjects *Pastimes – Past and Present*, and are said to have earned him 400 guineas. In his later life Emmerson became increasingly interested in illustration. In 1878 he illustrated along with John George Sowerby (q.v.), Joseph Crawhall, The Third (q.v.), and Robert Jobling (q.v.), notes on the Arts Association exhibition at NEWCASTLE in that year, and two years later, with Sowerby alone, he produced illustrations for *Afternoon Tea*. This highly successful book was followed by a work dealing with the childhood of the Queen, which Emmerson illustrated entirely on his own. A major exhibition of his oils and watercolours was opened at NEWCASTLE shortly after his death at CULLERCOATS, in 1895. A large selection of his work may be seen at the one-time home of Lord Armstrong at Cragside, ROTHBURY, courtesy of the National Trust, which together with the several works now in public collections, show Emmerson to have been one of Northumbria's outstanding artists of the nineteenth century. This fact was widely recognised in his lifetime, resulting in his election as first President of the Bewick Club, and his service in this capacity until his death. Represented: Laing A.G., Newcastle; Shipley A.G., Gateshead; Sunderland A.G.

EMMERSON, Percy (fl. late 19th, early 20th cent.)

Portrait and landscape painter in oil. He was one of the two artist sons of Henry Hetherington Emmerson (q.v.), and received his early tuition in art from his father, in the company of his brother Henry Bewick Emmerson (q.v.). He was an exhibitor along with his father and brother at the 1884 exhibition of the Bewick Club, NEWCASTLE, sending a bird study and a flower study from the family home at CULLERCOATS. He

Henry Hetherington Emmerson: Evangeline, 1857. Oil 40×60. *Tyne & Wear County Council Museums, Laing Art Gallery.*

John Wilson Ewbank: Tantallon Castle. Oil 11×16. *Tyne & Wear County Council Museums, Shipley Art Gallery.*

remained a regular exhibitor at the Bewick Club until the outbreak of the Boer War, when he enlisted in the Army and went to South Africa. It is believed that he remained in South Africa following the end of the war, and became a member of the military police, painting portraits in his spare time. One of the best works which he produced before leaving for South Africa was the portrait of his father shown at the Grainger Street Gallery of Mawson, Swan & Morgan on the occasion of their showing of his father's *God's Nursery*, in the 1890's. "It is an exceedingly interesting work of art", commented the local press at the time "and is evidence of Mr. Percy Emmerson's ability in portraiture . . .". Among his portrait subjects while painting in South Africa was Cecil Rhodes.

ENGELBACH, Mrs. Florence A. (née Neumegen), R.O.I., N.S. (1872-1951)

Portrait, figure and flower painter in oil. She was born at Jerez de la Frontera, Spain, of English parents, and studied at Westminster School of Art, the Slade, and in Paris, before becoming a professional artist. Following her marriage in 1902 she settled at NEWCASTLE, remaining in the city for many years, and establishing a considerable reputation as an artist. She first began exhibiting her work publicly in 1892, showing at the Royal Academy, the Royal Scottish Academy, The Royal Institute of Oil Painters, the Royal Society of British Artists and various leading London galleries. She also exhibited her work at several provincial galleries, including the Laing Art Gallery, NEWCASTLE, at which she showed a large number of portrait and figure studies both before and after her stay in the city. Some time after the First World War she moved to London, where she died in 1951. She was a member of the Royal Institute of Oil Painters, and the National Society of

Painters, Sculptors and Gravers. The Laing Art Gallery has her *Old Woman Knitting*, exhibited at the Paris Salon in 1910, and for which she was awarded the bronze medal at the Women's International Exhibition in London.

ERRINGTON, Isabella (1806-1890)

Portrait and genre painter in oil and watercolour. She was born at TYNEMOUTH, but practised as a professional artist at NORTH SHIELDS, from her early twenties until her death. She first began exhibiting her work at NEWCASTLE, where, in 1835, she showed her *St. Cecilia at the organ*, at the First Exhibition of the Newcastle Society of Artists. She continued to exhibit exclusively at NEWCASTLE until 1846, when she sent work to both the Suffolk Street Gallery, and to Carlisle Athenaeum, at the former showing: *A Boy carrying Bait – from life*, and *A Cullercoats Girl with Fish*, and at the latter: *A Sea Swallow fallen after a shot*; *A Travelling Besom Seller*, and *The New Ribbon for a Sunday Bonnet*. Following this she exhibited outside Northumbria on only one further occasion, this being when she again sent work to Carlisle Athenaeum. She exhibited at NEWCASTLE until late in her life, and evidently became quite well known for her portrait work in the area around NORTH SHIELDS. She died a spinster in the town, at the age of eighty-four. Some exhibition records show her as "J. Errington"; her full name was Isabella Cecilia Errington. Some of her work is reproduced in Hodgson's *History of Northumberland*.

*EWBANK, John Wilson, R.S.A. (1799-1847)

Landscape, coastal and marine painter in oil; architectural and topographical draughtsman. Ewbank was born at DARLINGTON, the son of an inn-keeper who later moved to GATESHEAD. Before his parents moved to

64

Tyneside, in 1804, Ewbank was adopted by a wealthy uncle at WYCLIFFE, near BARNARD CASTLE, and later sent by his guardian to Ushaw College, near DURHAM, to train for the Roman Catholic priesthood. He absconded from the College after only a short period of study, however, and rejoining his parents, had himself bound as an apprentice to house painter Thomas Coulson (q.v.), at NEWCASTLE, in 1813. In the following year Coulson left Newcastle to set up business in Edinburgh, and took his apprentice with him. Here Ewbank began to display such a talent for painting that his master allowed him time to study under Alexander Nasmyth, one of the leading Scottish landscapists of the day. He first exhibited his work publicly at Edinburgh in 1821, while still working for Coulson, showing: *Newcastle upon Tyne from the Byker Hill*, and two black lead drawings, at the city's Institution for the Encouragement of the Fine Arts in Scotland. In the following year, and now in his own studio, he again exhibited at the Institution, and sent five works to the First Exhibition of the Northumberland Institution for the Promotion of the Fine Arts, NEWCASTLE. He continued to exhibit at Edinburgh, and NEWCASTLE, for the next eleven years, also in this period sending his first work to the Royal Academy: *Alexander's triumphal entry into Babylon*, (1826), and showing some twenty-seven works at the Carlisle Academy. These years saw his reputation as an artist in Edinburgh reach dizzy heights, then plunge into the mediocre.

In 1823, a series of views of the city by Ewbank were engraved by Lizars; in 1826 he became a founder member of the Scottish Academy, and following his showing at the Academy's first exhibition in 1827, of his *View of Edinburgh from Inchkeith*, and *The Entry of George IV into Edinburgh*, he became the city's wealthiest teacher of painting, earning £2,500 in one year alone. Towards the end of his Edinburgh period he began to paint larger and more ambitious works, then suddenly overwhelmed by his success, he took to drinking, and careless behaviour, and his work deteriorated rapidly. In 1834 he left the Scottish capital in disgrace, and returning to NEWCASTLE, took a "squalid lodging in Denton Chare" and "worked mostly at lead pencil drawings . . . executed from recollections of the fine works of his best days". He exhibited at NEWCASTLE in the year of his return, and continued to exhibit in the town until the early 1840's, but his work attracted little attention. Much of his later work was executed on pieces of tin, his daughters assisting him in their painting, and afterwards hawking the pictures around the town, and sometimes as far afield as NORTH SHIELDS and SOUTH SHIELDS. He also did many lead pencil drawings on scraps of cardboard, which were disposed of in a similar manner, or by Ewbank himself, when on visits to nearby villages with his friend of later years, William Weddell (q.v.). In 1838 he was obliged to forfeit his status as a Royal Scottish Academician. Some time after 1841 he moved to SUNDERLAND, where he died in extreme poverty in Bishopwearmouth Infirmary. Represented: British Museum; National Gallery of Scotland; Dundee A.G.; Laing A.G., Newcastle; North Tyneside Public Libraries; Shipley A.G., Gateshead; Sunderland A.G.

*FAIRLESS, Thomas Kerr (1825-1853)

Landscape, coastal and genre painter in oil and water-colour; drawing master. He was born at HEXHAM, the son of Joseph Fairless, "perpetual churchwarden" to the town's Abbey Church, and well known local anti-quary. He was interested in drawing from his boyhood, and keenly studied the work in engraving of Thomas Bewick (q.v.), later becoming a pupil of one of Bewick's apprentices, Isaac Nicholson (q.v.), at NEWCASTLE. He soon became dissatisfied with wood engraving, however, and went to London to develop his skill as a painter. Here his progress was rapid. By 1848 he had commenced exhibiting at the Royal Academy, showing a coastal view: *Vessel Ashore*, and in the following year he began exhibiting at the British Institution, and the Suffolk Street Gallery, at the former showing a landscape: *Gordale*, and at the latter a coastal view: *Sunset at Sea – Tynemouth Castle*. He exhibited at all three establishments until 1851, and sent three works to Carlisle Athenaeum, in 1850, his exhibits being well enough received to enable him to establish a considerable practice as a teacher of drawing and painting in London. It was his ambition eventually to practise in Scotland, and on the continent, but ill-health forced him to return to HEXHAM in August, 1851, and here he died two years later, at the age of twenty-eight. In the year of his death his father published *A Guide to the Abbey Church at Hexham*, containing illustrations which may have been his work.

Thomas Kerr Fairless: Pedlars resting in the square of St. Andrews, Fife, Scotland. Oil 15½×17½. Mr. & Mrs. Denis Hindmarsh.

FALLAW, Thomas Penman (1875-1922)
Landscape and seascape painter in oil and watercolour. Born at GATESHEAD, Fallaw practised in the town as an estate agent until 1918, painting in his spare time. He was largely a self-taught artist, although he did receive some assistance in improving his work from his friend for many years, John Falconar Slater (q.v.). He occasionally exhibited at the Artists of the Northern Counties exhibitions at the Laing Art Gallery, NEWCASTLE, until his retirement due to ill-health, at the end of the First World War, when he moved to Torquay. He painted a number of coastal scenes in watercolour while living at the resort, dying there in 1922.

FARRER, Nicholas (1750-1805)
Portrait painter in oil. Farrer was born at SUNDERLAND, and studied art under Robert Edge Pine, the historical and portrait painter, and in the schools of the Society of Artists, London. He was befriended by Reynolds and Northcote, and painted portraits much in the style of the former. His main patron was the Duke of Richmond, for whom he painted a number of family portraits.

FENWICK, Thomas (d. 1850)
James L. Caw, in his *Scottish Painting, 1620-1908*, published 1908, describes Fenwick as a friend, and fellow apprentice of John Wilson Ewbank (q.v.), under Thomas Coulson (q.v.), at Edinburgh. He also states that Fenwick shared "North of England birth" with Ewbank.

*FLINTOFF, Thomas (1809-1891)
Portrait and landscape painter in oil, watercolour and crayon; photographer. Flintoff was born at NEWCASTLE, and practised in the town as a professional artist until the middle of the century, when he emigrated first to Texas, U.S.A., later to Ballarat, near Melbourne, Australia. Prior to leaving Britain, Flintoff established a moderate demand for his work at NEWCASTLE, and also gave lessons in dancing. He occasionally exhibited his work in the town from his early thirties, among these works being the *Fruit Piece* which he showed at the North of England Society for the Promotion of the Fine Arts, in 1839, and the *Portrait of a Lady*, at the "Exhibition of Arts, Manufactures & Practical Science", in 1848. About 1850 he left Britain for the U.S.A., and by 1851 was painting in Texas, where one of his portrait subjects was Senator Sam Houston; he also painted portraits of other members of the State Legislature, and leading dealers in cattle and slaves. After leaving Texas he painted his way through Mexico, possibly California, and the Society Islands. In Australia by 1856, he set up practice at Ballarat, where he undertook to make portraits in oil, crayon and watercolour. After leaving Ballarat he established himself in Melbourne in 1872, and for the next nineteen years

Thomas Flintoff: Portrait of Mrs. Edward White, *c*.1873. 32×28. *La Trobe Collection, State Library of Victoria, Australia.*

took commissions for portraits of mayors, members of Parliament, farmers and their prize bulls, and worthy matrons. At the age of eighty-two he died during the 1891 influenza epidemic at Melbourne, by swallowing a glass of ammonia in mistake for a tonic. Flintoff was evidently highly successful as a portrait painter in Australia, judging by his impressive list of sitters. Several examples of his work in this field are in the La Trobe Collection in the State Library of Victoria, Melbourne, Australia. Information on his career in the U.S.A., is contained in *Painting in Texas*, by Pauline Pinckney, University of Texas, 1967, while his career in Australia, omitting, however, the above detail of his work at NEWCASTLE, appeared in the *Age*, 28th July, 1979.

*FOSTER, Myles Birket, R.W.S. (1825-1899)
Landscape and figure painter in oil and watercolour; illustrator; wood engraver; etcher. One of the most popular British artists of the 19th century, Foster was born at NORTH SHIELDS, the son of a Quaker. When he was five his family moved to London, and here he received his first formal tuition in drawing while attending an academy at Tottenham. Later he attended school at Hitchin, Hertfordshire, where he received instruction in painting, as well as drawing, from Charles Parry. He left this school at fifteen, and joining the beer bottling company which his father had established in the capital,

spent some ten months there before deciding that he would prefer a career in art. Foster's father persuaded an engraver named Stone to accept his son as an apprentice, but Stone committed suicide before the indentures were completed, and the boy was apprenticed instead to Ebenezer Landells (q.v.). Landells introduced him to the technique of wood engraving, but quickly recognising that his talents lay in the direction of drawing on wood for reproduction, increasingly employed him in this field. By the close of his apprenticeship in 1846, his work as an illustrator was beginning to attract attention, and when he left Landells he obtained an appointment in this capacity under Henry Vizetelly. His first success in illustrating came with his work for Longfellow's *Evangeline*, 1850, and in this year also, he married his cousin Ann Spence – a member of the well known Spence family of NORTH SHIELDS, several members of which later became artists (see entries). Over the next nine years his work for *Evangeline* led to his receiving many other illustrative commissions, notably for the classics, and books of modern poetry. Some of this work came from George Dalziel (q.v.), and Edward Dalziel (q.v.) – "The Brothers Dalziel", who employed him from 1851.

Although moderately prosperous as an illustrator by the late 1850's, Foster became increasingly ambitious to succeed as a landscape painter in watercolour. He had painted in the medium as a relaxation for many years, and much like Thomas Bewick (q.v.), frequently composed his illustrations in watercolour before interpreting them in line on the wood. In 1859 he commenced exhibiting his work, showing examples at the Royal Academy, and the Old Water Colour Society (later the Royal Society of Painters in Watercolours). In the following year he was elected an associate of the latter body, and with his election as a full member of the Society in 1862, he committed himself fully to his new career. His wife had meanwhile died, and when, in

1863, he came into a handsome fortune by the death of his uncle, he built a house at Witley, near Godalming, Surrey, for which the interior was designed with the help of William Morris, and Dante Gabriel Rossetti, and decorations provided by Edward Burne-Jones. In 1864 he remarried, choosing as his second wife Fanny Watson, sister of painter and illustrator John Dawson Watson, and over the next thirty years at Witley produced literally thousands of watercolours, and occasional oils, depicting scenery in Britain and on the continent. His work became so popular that he could scarcely meet the demand, and publishers clamoured to reproduce his work by chromolithography. Meanwhile, he continued to exhibit at the Royal Academy, and the Old Water Colour Society, and contributed examples of his work to many leading London and provincial exhibitions. He also exhibited at NEWCASTLE, notably at the Arts Association in 1878, the Bewick Club in 1884, and the Royal Jubilee Exhibition in 1887.

Most of Foster's work was executed in watercolour, working with as fine and dry a brush as possible, and in a minutely stippled style which was in marked contrast to that of most earlier British watercolourists. He could, however, paint in a much looser and spontaneous style, as in the *Windmill Hills, Gateshead*, reproduced. He mainly worked on the small scale to which he had become accustomed in book illustration, but sometimes produced quite large works in watercolour, such as his *Ben Nevis*, in the collection of the Laing Art Gallery, NEWCASTLE, which measures $31'' \times 46\frac{1}{2}''$. He also worked in oil, and was a skilful etcher on steel and copper. The high prices paid for his watercolours in his lifetime inevitably led to widespread forgery of his work, this once prompting him to write to his brother-in-law Robert Spence, at NORTH SHIELDS (31st January, 1880):‡ ". . . I am constantly having pictures brought to me for recognition – all forgeries. One man the other day gave 150 gns. for a little oil picture sold to him as

Myles Birket Foster:
Newcastle upon Tyne from
Windmill Hills,
Gateshead. Watercolour
$5\frac{3}{4} \times 9$. *Tyne & Wear
County Council Museums,
Laing Art Gallery.*

mine. It was a copy of a small drawing which had been forged several times." Forgers were, of course, considerably helped by the fact that his work could easily be studied in colour reproduction. Indeed, Foster's work was among the first by any artist to be reproduced in colour, and its reproduction continues unabated to the present time. He painted vigorously until just short of seventy, when ill-health drove him to retire to Weybridge, Surrey, where he spent the final years of his life. He died at Weybridge and was buried at Witley. An excellent account of his life and work, together with many colour plates of his watercolours, is contained in *Birket Foster R.W.S.*, by H. M. Cundall, 1906. A special loan exhibition of his work was held at the Laing Art Gallery in 1925, at which many of his Northumbrian, South of England, and continental watercolours were shown. His son, WILLIAM FOSTER (1853-1924), was also a talented painter and illustrator. Represented: British Museum; Victoria and Albert Museum; Laing A.G., Newcastle; Middlesbrough A.G.; North Tyneside Public Libraries; Shipley A.G., Gateshead, and various provincial and overseas art galleries.

‡ *Newcastle Central Library collection of letters from Foster to the Spence family, covering most of his career as an artist.*

FOTHERGILL, George Algernon (1868-1945)
Sporting, landscape and architectural painter in oil and watercolour; draughtsman; illustrator. He was born at Leamington, Warwickshire, and received his education at Uppingham School, Rutland, where he received first prize for his drawings from the antique and life three years in succession. He later studied medicine at Edinburgh University, qualifying as Bachelor of Medicine and Master of Surgery in 1895. About three years after receiving these qualifications he commenced practice as a doctor at DARLINGTON, and within a short time began to take a keen interest in the sporting and artistic life of the surrounding area, contributing many articles on these topics to the national and regional press of the day, including *Bailey's Magazine of Sports and Pastimes*, and the *County Monthly*. He also wrote and illustrated several books while in practice at DARLINGTON, notable among which are his *Notes from the Diary of a Doctor, Sketch Artist and Sportsman*, 1901; *North Country Album . . .*, 1901; *Darlington in Silhouette*, 1902; *Fothergill's Sketch Books*, 1901-3, and *A Pictorial Survey of S. Cuthbert's Darlington*, 1905.

By 1904 more than 1000 of his drawings and sketches had been published, and such was his reputation as an artist that his collection of "engraver's proofs, together with original drawings and the books and magazines themselves" was purchased for £200 by seventy leading Darlingtonians, and presented to the town. He had also widely exhibited his work, showing examples at the Dudley Gallery, London, and the Walker Art Gallery, Liverpool. Just before the First World War, and having by then moved to Cramond Bridge, near Edinburgh, and commenced exhibiting at the Royal Scottish Academy, he decided to give up medicine to become a full-time professional artist. It was not, however, until after the War, and service as Medical Officer in charge of the 1st Cavalry Brigade, that he fully achieved this ambi-

tion, and returning to Cramond Bridge, practised as an artist until his death. While at Cramond he continued to exhibit at the Royal Scottish Academy, and in 1938 enjoyed a major exhibition of his work at Walker's Gallery, London. He also continued to write and illustrate sporting and other works, one of the last of these being *Hunting, Racing, Coaching and Boxing Ballads*, published in 1926. In addition to being a superb if little known sporting illustrator, Fothergill was keenly interested in experimenting with various methods of reproducing his work, these including auto-lithography, collotype and tri-colour process printing. He also dabbled in wood engraving, and painted pottery. Darlington Art Gallery has a large collection of his work.

GAHAN, George Wilkie (1871-1956)
Landscape painter in oil and watercolour; etcher. He was born at NEWCASTLE, and studied at Dundee School of Art before practising as a professional artist in Scotland. He exhibited his work at the Royal Scottish Academy, and at several provincial exhibitions. His home was for many years at Broughty Ferry, Angus. Dundee Art Gallery has two examples of his work in oil: *Landscape with Sheep*, and *The Old Vault, Dundee, Saturday Afternoon*.

GARBUT, J. "Putty" (c.1820- c.1885)
Amateur coastal, seascape and landscape painter in oil and watercolour. Garbut was born at SOUTH SHIELDS, where by 1850 he was working as a painter and glazier in the town's Thrift Street. Most of his paintings appear to have been produced in his later years, perhaps after the admission of his son to the business, and include a *Self Portrait*, 1870; *Sea Scene with Castle in Background*, 1872; *Going to the Wreck*, 1875, and *The County Hotel, Westoe*, 1884, all of which are in the collection of South Shields Museum & Art Gallery. Some of his work reflects considerable ability as an artist. Although he is described in local directories as "James Garbutt", there are other references to him as "Joseph Garbut". The name "Putty" obviously derived from his trade as glazier.

*GARVIE, Thomas Bowman (1859-1944)
Portrait, genre and landscape painter in oil and watercolour. Garvie was born at MORPETH, and studied art at the evening classes of the local Mechanics' Institute before attending Calderon's School in London. While at Calderon's he won a scholarship to the Royal Academy Schools, where he won a First Silver Medal for his painting of a head, and an extension of his scholarship by three years. On leaving the Schools he studied at the Academie Julian, Paris, under Fleury and Bouguereau, then returning to Britain he practised briefly in London before settling at MORPETH. He first began exhibiting his work publicly in 1884, sending a

portrait of the Rev. F. R. Grey, Rector of MORPETH, to the inaugural exhibition of the Bewick Club, NEW-CASTLE. In 1886 he exhibited the same work at the Royal Academy, and for the next twenty years remained a regular exhibitor at both the Academy, and the Bewick Club, also sending two works to the Royal Society of British Artists' exhibitions. During the first ten of these years he practised at MORPETH, later moving to ROTHBURY, where he remained until c. 1920, although spending several long periods in Italy in the early years of the century.

While practising at ROTHBURY, Garvie was considerably patronised by Lord Armstrong, for whose home at nearby Cragside he painted several family portraits, and a number of landscape and other works, several of which can still be seen there today, courtesy of the National Trust. He also exhibited widely throughout Britain, showing work at the Royal Academy, the Royal Scottish Academy, the Glasgow Institute of Fine Arts, the Walker Art Gallery, Liverpool, and various other provincial art galleries, including the Laing Art Gallery, NEWCASTLE, whose Artists of the Northern Counties exhibitions he contributed to from their inception in 1905. He last exhibited outside Northumbria in 1914, from that date onwards exhibiting almost exclusively at the Artists of the Northern Counties exhibitions, and the Pen & Palette Club, NEWCASTLE, of which latter he was a member 1914-44, and for some time Master of Paintings. On leaving ROTHBURY, Garvie practised briefly at CULLERCOATS, then moving to FOREST HALL, near NEWCASTLE, he remained there until his death in 1944. Garvie was one of Northumbria's most successful portrait painters this century, and included some of the best known local men of his day among his sitters. He also painted many genre subjects, and was particularly fond of interiors with figures.# Many of the works which he exhibited both locally and in London from 1900 reflected his keen interest in Italy, in which he is said to have painted some of his finest works. In 1934 he shared a loan exhibition of his work at the Laing Art Gallery with Francis Thomas Carter (q.v.), George Edward Horton (q.v.), and John Falconar Slater (q.v.). Represented: Laing A.G., Newcastle; Sunderland A.G.

GAULD, John Richardson, A.R.C.A. (c.1886-1962)
Landscape and portrait painter in oil and watercolour; muralist; illustrator. Born at GATESHEAD, Gauld studied art at evening classes in the town, and later at Armstrong College (later King's College; now Newcastle University). Between 1910 and 1914 he studied at the Royal College of Art, after which he attended the London County Council School of Lithography. He first began exhibiting his work publicly in 1905, showing *The Cottage on the Cliff*, at the first exhibition of the Artists of the Northern Counties at the Laing Art Gallery, NEWCASTLE. He continued to exhibit at NEWCASTLE, and in 1911 sent his first work to the Royal Academy: *Newcastle upon Tyne*. Following his training as an artist he was appointed Chief Assistant at the Huddersfield School of Art. He remained based in the Midlands for the rest of his life, and in addition to establishing a high reputation as an art teacher, was widely recognised for his abilities as an artist, serving as President of the

Thomas Bowman Garvie: Quiet Consolation, 1889. Oil 36×20. *Private collection.*

Manchester Academy of Fine Arts, and from 1930-51, the Bolton Art Circle. Besides exhibiting at the Royal Academy, Gauld also showed work at the Goupil Gallery, London, and in the provinces, and enjoyed one-man shows at NEWCASTLE, Huddersfield, Halifax and Bolton. Examples of his work were included in the "Contemporary Artists of Durham County" exhibition staged at the Shipley Art Gallery, GATESHEAD, in 1951, in connection with the Festival of Britain. His work was also reproduced, examples appearing in *Colour Magazine*, *The Yorkshire Evening Post*, the *Leeds Mercury*, and the *Newcastle Chronicle*. He was an associate of the Royal College of Art. A relative, ALEXANDER GAULD, was a talented amateur artist and was a regular exhibitor at NEWCASTLE early in this century. Represented: British Museum; Victoria and Albert Museum; Bolton A.G.; Darlington A.G.; Laing A.G., Newcastle; Rochdale A.G.; Salford A.G.

GEORGE, Charles (1872-1937)
Landscape and marine painter in oil and watercolour; art teacher; decorator. He was born at TYNEMOUTH, the son of John Reed George (q.v.), a well known local decorator and spare-time artist. He showed a talent for art from his teens and became a protégé of a Tyneside shipping chief, who sent him to Brussels to study art for a time. On his return to TYNEMOUTH he set up a studio, but on the death of his father in 1890 he was obliged to give up art as a full-time occupation and devote himself to the family decorating business, painting in his spare time, and teaching art at local evening classes. George

painted prolifically throughout his life, forming many friendships with local artists such as John Falconar Slater (q.v.), George Edward Horton (q.v.), and John Davison Liddell (q.v.), and developing considerable skill as a painter, particularly in watercolour. He is not known to have exhibited his work outside Northumbria, but was a regular exhibitor at the Bewick Club, NEW-CASTLE, mainly showing examples of his marine work. The Laing Art Gallery, NEWCASTLE, has his oil: *Seascape with Storm*, and the Library at NORTH SHIELDS has his oils: *Seaton Sluice*, and *The Royal Yacht off Spithead, bringing Queen Victoria's body from the Isle of Wight*. He died at TYNEMOUTH.

GEORGE, John Reed (1832-1890)

Amateur coastal and landscape painter in watercolour; decorator. George was born at TYNEMOUTH, a member of a well known local family. He worked all his life in the family painting and decorating company in the town, painting in his spare time. He mainly painted local coastal views, in many of which he displayed considerable ability as an artist. He died at TYNEMOUTH. He was the father of Charles George (q.v.).

GIBB, Henry William Phelan (1870-1948)

Architectural, figure and landscape painter in oil and watercolour; potter. He was born at ALNWICK, the son of Thomas Henry Gibb (q.v.), and brother of Sadie Gibb (q.v.). He received his early artistic training under his father, and later at NEWCASTLE, and Edinburgh. While living at ALNWICK he exhibited his work at the Royal Scottish Academy in 1894, Carlisle Art Gallery in 1896, and the Bewick Club, NEWCASTLE, between 1893 and 1896. Until 1895 he exhibited his work as "H. W. Gibb", but in that year he began to use his grandmother's maiden name of "Phelan", after the initals "H. W."; later describing himself as "Harry Phelan Gibb", or simply "Phelan Gibb". Most of the works which he exhibited until leaving ALNWICK, to study in Paris, were similar in subject matter to those painted by his father, and sister, including a work entitled: *Far o'er those distant hills my longing fancy flies*, which he showed at the Artists of the Northern Counties exhibition, at the Laing Art Gallery, NEW-CASTLE, in 1905.

Following a visit to the Cezanne exhibition at the Salon d'Automne, in Paris in 1906, Gibb became much influenced by the work of the great French artist, and began to paint in a much more modern and spontaneous style. After studying in Antwerp and Munich he settled in Paris for twenty-five years, becoming a close friend of Gertrude Stein, and taking an active part in the artistic life of the city. He continued to exhibit in the British Isles throughout, and following his stay in Paris, showing his work at the Royal Hibernian Academy, the Alpine Club, and several other London galleries, including the Baillie Gallery, at which his first one-man show was held in 1911. In Paris he exhibited at the Salon d'Automne (Sociétaire 1909), and had a further one-man show at Bernheim Jeune, in 1913. He died at Great Hampden, Buckinghamshire. The Tate Gallery has his monochrome wash on paper: *Belgrave Square and Wilton Crescent*, dated 1928.

GIBB, Sadie (1869- after 1916)

Landscape painter in oil. The daughter of Thomas Henry Gibb (q.v.), and sister of Henry William Phelan Gibb (q.v.), she was born at ALNWICK, and received her early artistic training under her father. She first began to exhibit her work publicly when she sent a work: *In the gloaming*, to the Bewick Club, NEWCASTLE, in 1893. She continued to exhibit her work at the Bewick Club for some years, but later moved to Glasgow, from which she began to exhibit at the Walker Art Gallery, Liverpool, sending nineteen works between 1913 and 1916.

*GIBB, Thomas Henry (1833- after 1893)

Landscape and animal painter in oil; modeller. He was born at ALNWICK, the son of Henry Gibb, County Court Official, house agent, and one-time proprietor of the celebrated *Northern Liberator*. Nothing is known of his early artistic training, but by 1864 he had already achieved something of a reputation by exhibiting at NEWCASTLE a full-size model: *The Fox caught in a trap*, and in 1866 this reputation as a modeller was further enhanced by two works which he sent to an exhibition at the Agricultural Hall, Islington, London. These two works were entitled: *Otter and Salmon*, and *The Biter Bitten*. The former model was considered so attractive that the *Illustrated Exhibitor*, a publication devoted to the exhibition, honoured him by illustrating it by means of a specially commissioned wood engraving. In 1870 he sent examples of his work in both modelling and painting to the "Central Exchange News Room, Art Gallery, and Polytechnic Exhibition", NEWCASTLE. These included a *Dutch Scene*, and two coastal scenes. He sent four landscapes to the exhibition of works by local painters, at the Central Exchange Art Gallery, NEWCASTLE, in 1878, and also showed work at the Arts Association exhibition, NEWCASTLE, in 1881, and the Alnwick Mechanics' Institute "Exhibition of Art & Science", 1882. From the latter date until 1885, however, he appears to have exhibited mainly outside Northumbria, showing two works at the Royal Scottish Academy, one work at the Royal Hibernian Academy, and one work at Tooth & Sons Gallery, London. He subsequently resumed exhibiting at NEWCASTLE, on one occasion showing work alongside that of his daughter Sadie Gibb (q.v.), and son Henry William Phelan Gibb (q.v.), at the Bewick Club exhibition of 1893. His works were entitled: *In Alnwick Park*; *Evening*, and *The Peace of an Autumn Evening*. In addition to painting and modelling, Gibb carried on his father's business as house agent, and was also a taxidermist of note. He died at ALNWICK. Represented: Darlington A.G.; Shipley A.G., Gateshead.

GIBBS, John Binney (1859-1935)

Portrait and landscape painter in oil and watercolour; art teacher. He was born at DARLINGTON, and later studied at the town's School of Art. On leaving DAR-LINGTON he studied at South Kensington School of Art, and the Academie Julian, Paris. Returning to Britain in his twenties, he accepted a teaching appointment at

Thomas Henry Gibb:
Otter Hunt on the Tweed.
Oil 24×36. *Darlington Art
Gallery.*

Liverpool College. While teaching at the College he established a studio in the city and became a regular exhibitor at its Walker Art Gallery. Some time in the late 1890's he returned to DARLINGTON, but left after a short while to become art master and director of technical studies at an establishment at Congleton, Cheshire, remaining there for almost thirty years. Following his retirement in 1928 he returned to DAR-LINGTON, where he mainly exhibited at the Darlington Society of Arts, also serving as secretary for some years. He was the elder brother of Thomas Binney Gibbs (q.v.). Darlington Art Gallery has his oil: *High Row, Darlington*, dated 1896. Represented: Imperial War Museum; Darlington A.G.

GIBBS, Thomas Binney (1870- after 1938)
Portrait and landscape painter in oil; art teacher. He was born at DARLINGTON, the younger brother of John Binney Gibbs (q.v.), and received his artistic education at Liverpool School of Art. On completing his education at Liverpool, he moved first to Manchester, remaining there several years, then to London, where he appears to have spent the remainder of his life. He first began to show his work publicly in 1901, from that date regularly exhibiting at the Royal Academy, the Royal Institute of Oil Painters, the International Society of Sculptors, Painters and Gravers, and at various London and provincial galleries. His Royal Academy contributions totalled seventeen, and consisted of portraits and landscapes. He sent his last work to the Academy while living in London in 1938.

GIBSON, Ethel Kate – see MANVILLE, Mrs. Ethel Kate.

GIBSON, John (1794-1854)
Landscape, portrait and genre painter in oil; stained glass designer; ornamental and house painter. Gibson was born at NEWCASTLE, and practised as an "ornamental and house painter" for many years before devoting himself to stained glass designing. During his early years he frequently painted landscape and other works in his spare time, showing the first of these: *View of the Shot Tower from Thornton Street*, at the 1823 exhibition of the Northumberland Institution for the Promotion of the Fine Arts, NEWCASTLE, at the age of twenty-nine. He next exhibited at NEWCASTLE in the early 1830's by sending three works to the 1833 exhibition of the Newcastle upon Tyne Institution for the General Promotion of the Fine Arts, and exhibited at the Institution in 1834, and at the Newcastle Society of Artists in 1835 and 1836, showing such works as: *Gipsies* (1834); *Evening* (1835), and *Bywell Ferry* (1836). Also in this period he acquired a considerable reputation for his taste in art, and is said to have played an important part in its promotion in NEWCASTLE. He later spent much time on his stained glass work, many churches in NEWCASTLE still displaying examples of his skill. Gibson was elected a Town Councillor for North St. Andrew's Ward, and in 1854 served the office of Sheriff of NEWCASTLE. He died shortly after vacating his office.

GIBSON, Thomas (1810-1843)
Portrait and landscape painter in oil and watercolour. Gibson was born at NORTH SHIELDS, the third son of James Gibson, and appears to have become a largely self-taught artist before practising in his native town by the age of twenty. He first exhibited his work at NEWCASTLE, showing examples at the Newcastle upon Tyne Institution for the General Promotion of the Fine Arts in 1833. He again exhibited at this Institution in the following year, and after moving to NEWCASTLE early in 1836, was a regular exhibitor in the town for the next four years, showing examples of his work at the exhibitions of the Newcastle Society of Artists, and the North of England Society for the Promotion of the Fine

71

Arts. He last exhibited at NEWCASTLE in 1840, when he contributed two local landscapes and a *Lake Scene, near Penrith*, to the "Exhibition of Arts, Manufactures & Practical Science" in the town. In 1841 he went to London, where he exhibited at the Suffolk Street Gallery exhibition of that year showing four Westmorland landscapes. Much of his two remaining years of life was spent at Carlisle, Cumberland, where he established a considerable reputation as a portrait painter. He last exhibited in the year of his death, showing examples of his work at Carlisle Athenaeum. He died in London, where according to Carlisle newspaper reports of his death he was "pursuing his professional studies". Seventy of his paintings were sold at Carlisle in the year following his death.

GIBSON, William Sidney, M.A. (1814-1871)

Amateur landscape and coastal painter in watercolour; architectural and antiquarian draughtsman. He was born at Fulham, the son of a merchant, and after studying for the Bar for some time was admitted to Lincoln's Inn in 1839. Four years later he moved to NEWCASTLE to take up the appointment of registrar of the Newcastle upon Tyne District Court of Bankruptcy, retaining this title until the Bankruptcy Act of 1869 abolished the Court. Throughout his period in Northumbria, Gibson took a keen interest in antiquarian matters, and in addition to writing dozens of articles for magazines and newspapers on these and other topics, published many books, several of which were associated with TYNEMOUTH, where he lived after moving from NEWCASTLE c. 1856, until just short of his death. Notable among these books were his *The History of the Monastery founded at Tynemouth*, Two Volumes, 1846 and 1847, and *A Descriptive & Historical Guide to Tynemouth*, 1849. He was, however, the author of many other books on the archaeology of the North, and in recognition of his contributions to the literature of this subject received an honorary Master of Arts Degree from Durham University in 1857. Gibson led a reclusive existence while living at NEWCASTLE, and later TYNEMOUTH, and the fact that he was in addition to being a scholarly writer on a miscellany of subjects, an accomplished spare-time painter in watercolour appears to have gone entirely unnoticed. He died at London, and in accordance with a wish long and frequently expressed during his lifetime, was buried in the disused grounds of the old Priory at TYNEMOUTH. He is interred in a vault close to the Lady Chapel. The Laing Art Gallery, NEWCASTLE, has a rare example of Gibson's watercolour work: *At Newhaven*.

GIBSONE, (GIBSON), George (1762-1846)

Sea shell, plant and mineral specimen painter in watercolour; draughtsman; drawing master. Gibsone was born at Deptford, Kent, the son of an architect, and joined his father's practice on leaving school. Like his father, he travelled Italy before commencing practice, later designing several London residences and country mansions. In 1796 he married, and shortly afterwards moved with his wife and the rest of his family to NEWCASTLE, where local lead works owner Richard Fishwick wished father and son to help design and erect an iron works at nearby LEMINGTON. A company was formed in 1800 in which Fishwick and the two Gibsones were partners, but in June, 1803, the enterprise collapsed, ruining all three. Gibsone then became manager of his brother John's colour works at BILL QUAY, near GATESHEAD. However, his wife later opened an "upper class girls' school" at NEWCASTLE, and with Gibsone's help as drawing master this enterprise proved so successful, that the couple were able to retire in 1831 to a house which they had erected at LOW FELL, near GATESHEAD.

For many years after first moving to NEWCASTLE, Gibsone had taken a keen interest in the natural sciences, and was a member of what is today the Natural History Society of Northumbria. He was also a keen spare-time painter in watercolour, painting "coins, plants, minerals, shells, etc., etc.,", and acquiring "great dexterity in illustrating conchology". Before his retirement from the school he had begun to concentrate on the last named activity, and to obtain specimens for illustration travelled the coasts of England, Scotland and France, also obtaining specimens from other collectors. When he died at LOW FELL in 1846 he left behind him a vast number of watercolours depicting his collection. These watercolours, numbering some 7,260, in sixteen portfolios, were purchased by public subscription in 1890, and presented to Newcastle Public Library. Altogether, they represent a monumental work, and one of the most unusual preoccupations of any Northumbrian artist. Gibsone was also a keen gardener, and at the Northumberland Institution for the Promotion of the Fine Arts, NEWCASTLE, 1827, exhibited a watercolour portraying *Wilmot's superb strawberry, forced at Fenham 10.5.27*. Represented: Newcastle Central Library.

*GILROY, John Thomas Young, A.R.C.A., F.R.S.A. (b.1898)

Portrait and landscape painter in oil; cartoonist; illustrator; art teacher. He was born at NEWCASTLE, the son of John William Gilroy (q.v.), and received some tuition in art from his father before attending Armstrong College (later King's College; now Newcastle University). After serving in the First World War he won a scholarship to the Royal College of Art, winning his Diploma in 1920, and the Travelling Scholarship in Mural Painting, in 1921. He later settled in London, where he has since practised mainly as a portrait painter, also producing commercial design work, and for some years serving on the staff of Camberwell School of Art. He has exhibited his work widely in Britain, showing some twenty-three works at the Royal Academy since 1930, more than 100 works at the Fine Art Society, London, and a number of works at the Royal Society of Portrait Painters, The Royal Institute of Oil Painters, the New English Art Club, and at several provincial exhibitions, including those of the Artists of the Northern Counties at the Laing Art Gallery, NEWCASTLE. He has painted many famous portraits throughout the world, including several members of the Royal Family. He was the creator of the famous series of Guinness posters which appeared 1925-60, and has also produced illustrations for a number of publications, among these *McGill, The Story of a University*, 1960. He is an associate of the Royal College of Art, and a Fellow of the Royal Society of Arts. His portrait commissions since 1977 have included Her Majesty the Queen, Prince Philip, Prince Charles, and three portraits of the late Earl Mountbatten of Burma, all taken at Buckingham Palace. Represented: National Portrait Gallery; Belfast A.G.; Laing A.G., Newcastle; Leeds A.G.; Walker A.G., Liverpool, and various British and overseas art galleries.

GILROY, John William (1868-1944)

Landscape, marine, portrait and genre painter in oil and watercolour. He was born at NEWCASTLE, and became a largely self-taught artist before setting up practice in the city. He first began exhibiting his work publicly at the Bewick Club, NEWCASTLE, in his early twenties. He exhibited one work at the Royal Academy in 1898: *Trawlers Resting*, but thereafter exhibited almost exclusively in the provinces, and mainly at the Artists of the Northern Counties exhibitions at the Laing Art Gallery, NEWCASTLE, from their inception in 1905, until only a few years short of his death. Typical exhibits at the Laing Art Gallery during this period were his *Pittenweem Harbour, Fifeshire* (1910); *Aquatania in the Tyne* (1920); *Passing Ships*, and *Corner of the Stackyard* (1940). He also painted and exhibited a substantial number of portraits. Gilroy practised at NEWCASTLE until the early 1920's, when he moved to WHITLEY BAY. He was still living at WHITLEY BAY when he last exhibited at the Artists of the Northern Counties exhibition of 1940. He was the father of the distinguished portrait painter John Thomas Young Gilroy (q.v.). Represented: Laing A.G., Newcastle; Shipley A.G., Gateshead.

GLASGOW, Edwin (1874-1955)

Amateur landscape painter in oil and watercolour; draughtsman; illustrator. Born at Liverpool, Glasgow was educated at University College, Liverpool, and Wadham College, Oxford. On leaving College he took a post as Sixth Form Master, Forest School, and became a keen spare-time painter in watercolour and pen and ink artist, exhibiting examples of his watercolours at the Walker Art Gallery, Liverpool, from 1896, and publishing books of his drawings in 1900 and 1901. By the early years of the present century he had exhibited his work widely throughout the provinces and handled several illustrative commissions, this activity, allied to his experience as a teacher, securing for him an appointment as Inspector under the Board of Education. He first worked in this capacity at NEWCASTLE, in 1909, later acting as H.M.I. for the City, Northumberland County and Boroughs 1912-26. During his period in Northumbria he continued to take an active interest in painting and drawing, becoming a member of the Pen & Palette Club, NEWCASTLE, and exhibiting his work at the Royal Academy, the Royal Institute of Painters in Water Colours, the Paris Salon, and widely in the provinces, including the Artists of the Northern Coun-

John Thomas Young Gilroy: Dr. Crofton, 1951. Oil 60×50. *Private collection.*

ties exhibitions at the Laing Art Gallery, NEWCASTLE, and enjoying several one-man exhibitions of his work at various London and other galleries. On leaving NEWCASTLE he worked in Warwickshire and at Gibralter for some years, then took the post of Secretary and Keeper of the National Gallery, London, 1933-35. He retired on reaching Civil Service pensionable age, and devoted himself in the immediately following months to the completion of his book *The Painter's Eye*, published in 1936. He remained a keen painter and draughtsman until his death at Charlbury, Oxford, in 1955. Represented: Cheltenham A.G.; Laing A.G., Newcastle; Shipley A.G., Gateshead.

*GOOD, Thomas Sword, H.R.S.A. (1789-1872)

Portrait, genre and landscape painter in oil and watercolour; draughtsman; cartographer. Good was born at BERWICK-UPON-TWEED, and first found employment for his artistic talents as a house painter. He later began to paint coastal and landscape works in his spare time, exhibiting the first of these at the Edinburgh Exhibition Society in 1815, comprising: *Fishermen going out: Morning*; *Landscape*, and *Sea-Beach: Fresh Breeze*. Two years later he was engaged to draw and illustrate a map for Johnsone's history of BERWICK-UPON-TWEED, and in 1820 he showed his first work at the Royal Academy: *A Scotch Shepherd*. In the following year he again exhibited at the Academy, and sent two portraits and one genre work to the Institution for the Encouragement of the Fine Arts in Scotland, Edinburgh, and heartened by his success to date decided to become a

Thomas Sword Good: The expected Penny. Oil 14½×17½. *Tyne & Wear County Council Museums, Laing Art Gallery.*

professional artist in London. Working in the capital from 1822 until 1824, he exhibited at the Royal Academy, the British Institution and the Suffolk Street Gallery, but finding that he was not making the progress he desired, he returned to BERWICK-UPON-TWEED. He remained a regular exhibitor at the Royal Academy and the British Institution over the following nine years, also in this period exhibiting at the Scottish Academy, the Suffolk Street Gallery, the Carlisle Academy, and the Northumberland Institution for the Promotion of the Fine Arts, NEWCASTLE, and later the town's Northern Academy. In 1828 he was made an honorary member of the Scottish Academy. He exhibited little after 1834, though what little work he did exhibit contradicts the popular belief that he gave up painting entirely about that year. In 1838 he showed at the First Exhibition of the North of England Society for the Promotion of the Fine Arts, NEWCASTLE: *The Industrious Mother*; at Carlisle Athenaeum, in 1846, a genre work; at the Royal Scottish Academy in 1850: *Boy Fiddling*, and *The Sleeping Fisherman*, and at "The Exhibition of Paintings and other Works of Art", at the Town Hall, NEWCASTLE, in 1866: *The Sailor Boy*.

Good was a contemporary and imitator of Sir David Wilkie (1785-1841), the Royal Academician, and chose to paint many of Wilkie's favourite subjects – fishermen, rustics in the field, and ordinary people about their everyday lives. Like Wilkie he also painted many portraits, among these at least two of Thomas Bewick (q.v.), with whom he was evidently on terms of some familiarity. Bewick's daughter, Jane Bewick (q.v.), writing of one of these portraits in not very flattering terms, remarked of Good: ". . . a painter of some eminence he got out of his depths by painting in Wilkie's

style; as soon as these would not sell he threw by the brush & married a Woman with money – & now enjoys the fruit of his industry . . .". Good married in 1839, and his output of work certainly dropped considerably after this event, but as evidenced by the exhibiting activity detailed above, he did not give up painting entirely. He died at his home on the Quay Walls, BERWICK-UPON-TWEED, at the age of eighty-two. On her death two years later, his widow Mary Evans Good, bequeathed four examples of his work to the National Gallery, London. Represented: National Gallery, London; National Portrait Gallery; Scottish National Portrait Gallery; Victoria and Albert Museum; Tate Gallery; Gray A.G. & Museum, Hartlepool; Laing A.G., Newcastle; Natural History Society of Northumbria, Newcastle; Newcastle Central Library; North Tyneside Public Libraries.

GORDON, Thomas Watson (c.1863- after 1893)
Landscape painter in watercolour. This artist practised at NEWCASTLE in the late 19th century. He first exhibited his work publicly at the "Gateshead Fine Art & Industrial Exhibition", in 1883, showing a watercolour: *Misty Morning*, and a charcoal study: *Bill Sykes*. He later became a regular exhibitor at the Bewick Club, NEWCASTLE, and in 1892 was one of the signatories to the incorporation of the Club as the Northumbrian Art Institute, describing himself as a lithographic artist. He painted and exhibited a number of watercolour studies of scenery along the River Derwent.

GOWDY, William (1827-1877)
Portrait painter. Two examples of this artist's work were included in the exhibition of works by local

74

painters, at the Central Exchange Art Gallery, NEW-CASTLE, in 1878. These works were both head studies.

GRAHAM, Anthony (1828-1908)

Landscape painter in oil. He was the son of William Graham of ALNWICK, a carrier between the town and NEWCASTLE in the days before the railways. Little is known of Graham's artistic career except that he was for some years drawing master at the Rev. Canon Moore's School, ALNMOUTH, and that he was well known for his landscape and coastal works in his day. Several views of Bamburgh Castle are known.

GRAHAM-THOMPSON, Eva (c.1898- after 1955)

Amateur landscape painter in watercolour. This artist painted on Tyneside from the early years of this century, until the late 1950's and exhibited her work at the Artists of the Northern Counties exhibitions at the Laing Art Gallery, NEWCASTLE, and later the Federation of Northern Art Societies exhibitions at this gallery. She married in the early 1950's, and thereafter exhibited her work as Mrs. Eva Graham-Wood. Her work included many Tyne Valley views painted near her home at STOCKSFIELD in the early years of the century, and Lake District views painted after she had moved to NEWCASTLE c.1922. She appears to have spent most of her later life at NEWCASTLE.

GRAY, Ethel (1879-1957)

Landscape painter in oil and watercolour; etcher; wood-cut artist; art teacher. She was born at NEW-CASTLE, and studied at York, Leeds, the Royal College of Art, and under Leonardo Garrido, and Stanhope Forbes, before practising as a professional artist. She later served as art mistress at York and Leeds Schools of Art, and Leeds Training College. She exhibited her work at the Royal Academy 1935-50, showing such titles as: *The Old Bridge, Richmond*, and *A Coniston Waterfall*, and also sent work for exhibition in Yorkshire and Cornwall. Most of her later life was spent at Leeds.

*GRAY, George (1758-1819)

Fruit, still-life and portrait painter in oil and crayon; drawing master. Gray was born at NEWCASTLE, the son of a bookbinder, and received his education at the town's Grammar School. He showed an interest in drawing from an early age, and on completing his education was placed as an apprentice to an "eminent fruit painter" named Jones, who had temporarily settled at NEWCASTLE. Before completing his apprenticeship, however, Gray's master decided to move to York, taking his apprentice with him, and when Jones decided to move on again, Gray returned to NEWCASTLE. On returning to his native town he began to take a keen interest in botany, mineralogy and chemistry, and having acquired a considerable knowledge of the first named subject, resolved to go to North America on a "botanizing expedition". He sailed from Whitehaven, Cumberland, in 1787, and after "traversing the northern wilds of the New Continent, and observing the modes of savage life", returned to NEWCASTLE. In 1791, he was

engaged with a Mr. McNab, by Prince Pontiatowsky, to examine and report upon the geology of Poland, but his companion's extravagances of behaviour so offended Gray that he decided to abandon his commission at Cracow. A Major Anderson later asked him to accompany an expedition through Iceland as botanist, geologist and draughtsman, but he eventually declined this offer because of the subordinate position he would have had to accept, and in 1794 opened a shop in Dean Street, NEWCASTLE, as "portrait, fruit, house, and sign painter". His lack of capital, and inability to organize his business activities, soon caused him to abandon his shop, and he thereafter occupied himself with his chemical and other researches, only following his profession of painter and drawing master as much as needed to pay for the necessities of life.

Gray's talents as a fruit painter were highly regarded in his day, and his portraits show him to have been as capable in this type of work. Two of his sitters, of whom portraits still exist, were Thomas Bewick (q.v.), of whom he painted the earliest known portrait, and Bewick's brother John Bewick, The First (q.v.), whose portrait in crayon by Gray is one of the very few known to have been executed. Gray's eccentricities of behaviour and general popularity made him a popular subject of portraits himself, both Henry Perlee Parker (q.v.), and William Nicholson (q.v.), taking his likeness. Gray lived briefly at SUNDERLAND, and in London, in the early nineteenth century, and was working in the latter when he sent a fruit painting to the Royal Academy in 1811. He spent his final years in NEWCASTLE, however, dying at his home in Pudding Chare in 1819. Gray was a close friend of Thomas Bewick and is referred to in the latter's autobiographical *Memoir*, published posthumously in 1862. Represented: Laing A.G., Newcastle; Natural History Society of Northumbria, Newcastle; Shipley A.G., Gateshead.

George Gray: Fruit study. Oil 16×19. *Dean Gallery.*

GRAY, Joseph (1890-1963)

Portrait and landscape painter in oil; draughtsman; illustrator; etcher. Gray was born at SOUTH SHIELDS,

the son of a sea captain, and trained as a sea going
engineer before enrolling as a student at South Shields
Art School under John Heys (q.v.). At the conclusion
of his studies he received an appointment as an illustrator with the *Dundee Courier*, remaining with the paper
until the outbreak of the First World War, when he
enlisted in the Black Watch Regiment. He was invalided
out of the Regiment before the end of the war, and
obtained an appointment as a war illustrator with *The
Graphic*. At the end of the war he turned to etching
French, Dutch and Belgian subjects, many of which he
had sketched on holidays before the outbreak of hostil-
ities. He also began portrait painting, taking over the
old studio of John Singer Sargent in Chelsea, London,
and quickly establishing a demand for this type of work,
and for his war memorial paintings. During the Second
World War he once more enlisted in the Army, first as
an artist attached to the Camouflage Department of the
War Office and Ministry of Supply; later as an officer in
the Royal Engineers. Following the war he practised at
Marlow, Norfolk, Bath, Deal, Suffolk, Dorset, and for
some years at Broughty Ferry, Angus, producing
paintings, drawings and etchings, and exhibiting his
work at the Royal Scottish Academy, and at various
London and provincial art galleries. He also exhibited
in Europe and America. Represented: British Museum;
Victoria and Albert Museum; Imperial War Museum;
Dundee A.G.; South Shields Museum & A.G.

*GREEN, Arthur (b.1894)

Amateur landscape, portrait, cattle, still-life and flower
painter in oil and watercolour. Green was born at
Nottingham, the son of an officer in the 33rd Sussex
Regiment, but moved in his infancy to GATESHEAD,
with his family. While receiving his general education
at Gateshead Secondary School he won a scholarship to
the town's School of Art, where he studied for several
years under William Fitzjames White (q.v.). On leaving
the School he began to dabble on his own account in
building motor cycles, attending classes at King's College (now Newcastle University) under Ralph Bullock
(q.v.), in his spare time. Following service in the First
World War as a Technical Sergeant Major in the Royal
Flying Corps, however, he decided on a full-time career
in the aircraft industry, remaining in this field until his
retirement as works manager for De Havilland, at the
age of seventy-one. Green has remained interested in
painting throughout his life, and although frequently
called by his employment to spend long periods outside
Northumbria, has always made his home here, and
taken a keen interest in local artistic activities. He has
exhibited his work at the Royal Academy, he was an
exhibitor for several years at the Artists of the Northern
Counties exhibitions at the Laing Art Gallery, NEW-
CASTLE, and enjoyed several exhibitions at the city's
Mawson, Swan & Morgan gallery, in association with
leading local professional artists, such as Thomas William Pattinson (q.v.), and Robert Leslie Howey (q.v.).
At eighty-eight he still paints every day, producing work
of high professional competence.

GREEN, Benjamin (c.1812-1858)

Architectural draughtsman. He was the son of John
Green (q.v.), and trained under the Elder Pugin in
London before joining his father's practice as architect
and civil engineer at NEWCASTLE. While still in London
he exhibited at the Northern Academy, NEWCASTLE, in
1829, showing one of his designs. By 1833, and exhibiting his: *Interior of the Literary and Philosophical
Society*, at the Newcastle upon Tyne Institution for the
General Promotion of the Fine Arts, NEWCASTLE, he
had joined his father's practice in the town. He later
exhibited at NEWCASTLE on several occasions, showing

76

his designs for buildings, one of these works being the *Suggested Appearance of Grey Street*, with colour and figures added by Thomas Miles Richardson, Senior (q.v.), shown in 1838. He collaborated much with his father in designing local buildings, amongst these joint works the street front of the Theatre Royal, NEWCASTLE, and part of the south side of neighbouring Market Street. A later joint work was their Penshaw Monument, which stands on a small hill overlooking PENSHAW, near CHESTER-LE-STREET. He died in a mental home at Dinsdale Park, near DARLINGTON. The Metropolitan Museum of Art, New York, has the designs produced by John Green, Senior, and Benjamin Green, for the Theatre Royal. The Laing Art Gallery, NEWCASTLE has Green's *Suggested Appearance of Grey Street*.

GREEN, John (1787-1852)

Architectural draughtsman. Green was born at NAFFERTON, near OVINGHAM, the son of a carpenter and agricultural implement maker. Shortly after his coming of age he joined his father's business, helping to make it so successful that it was soon found necessary to establish larger premises at nearby CORBRIDGE. Here they extended the business to include general building, and after taking responsibility for this department for some time, Green moved to NEWCASTLE to practise as an architect and civil engineer. By 1822 he had established himself well enough in the town to receive the prestigious commission of designing new headquarters for its Literary and Philosophical Society. He later designed many other important structures in Northumbria, amongst these the Scotswood Suspension Bridge, opened just west of the town in 1831, and a miscellany of public and private buildings, bridges etc.

Like many architects, Green exhibited his designs, showing his first such work at the Northern Academy, NEWCASTLE, in 1828. In the following year, and with scenery painted by Thomas Miles Richardson, Senior (q.v.), he exhibited his Scotswood Bridge design. He exhibited at NEWCASTLE on several occasions subsequently, and in 1837 sent his first exhibits to the Royal Academy; his Scotswood Bridge design, and his design for Grey's Monument, NEWCASTLE. Green increasingly collaborated with his son Benjamin Green (q.v.), in his later architectural and civil engineering projects, having taken his son into the practice about 1833. He exhibited little work produced by the practice under his own name after 1837, preferring to exhibit it jointly with his son, or under the latter's name alone. Among the works for which they jointly produced designs were the street front of the Theatre Royal, NEWCASTLE, and part of the south side of neighbouring Market Street. A later joint work was the Penshaw Monument, which stands on a small hill overlooking PENSHAW, near CHESTER-LE-STREET. He died at NEWCASTLE. His son, JOHN GREEN, JUNIOR (c.1807-1868), also practised as an architect at NEWCASTLE, and exhibited his designs, but does not appear to have become as involved in his father's practice as his brother Benjamin. The Metropolitian Museum of Art, New York, has the designs prepared by John Green, Senior, and his son Benjamin, for the Theatre Royal.

GREY, Edith F. (*c.*1865- *c.*1914)

Landscape, portrait and flower painter in oil and watercolour. She was born on Tyneside, and studied at the School of Art, NEWCASTLE, and privately in London, before practising as a professional artist in Northumbria. She first began exhibiting her work publicly when she sent four works to the Royal Jubilee Exhibition, NEWCASTLE, in 1887, while living at MONKSEATON. Encouraged by the sale of three of these works she moved her studio to NEWCASTLE, remaining in the city throughout her career, and establishing a considerable reputation as a painter of a wide variety of subjects. She was very successful in selling her work from exhibitions, her first contribution to the Royal Institute of Painters in Water Colours being bought by a South Country patron at the private view, and all but one of her sixteen contributions to the Royal Academy between 1891 and 1911 enjoying a similar fate. She also exhibited her work at the Suffolk Street Gallery, the Royal Miniature Society, and widely in the provinces, including the Bewick Club, NEWCASTLE, and the Artists of the Northern Counties exhibitions at the city's Laing Art Gallery. She died at NEWCASTLE.

*HAIR, Thomas Henry (1810-1882)

Landscape, industrial and marine painter in oil and watercolour; engraver; etcher. He was born at what was then the village of SCOTSWOOD, near NEWCASTLE, the son of John Hair, a lampblack manufacturer. Details of his early artistic training are not known, but it is possible in view of his early accomplishment in engraving and etching that he received training in these activities soon after receiving his general education, and possibly at NEWCASTLE, in the workshop of Mark Lambert (q.v.). His earliest known work is a watercolour of *Hebburn Colliery*, dated 1828, in the collection of Newcastle University, and is interesting because it demonstrates how early he became interested in the Northumbrian industrial scene which he was later to depict so superbly in his *Sketches of the Coal Mines of Northumberland & Durham, in 1839*. While working on the watercolours upon which the etchings for the latter were based, however, he frequently painted more conventional works, among these his *Prudhoe Castle*, and *Cottage at Paradise*, exhibited at the Newcastle upon Tyne Institution for the General Promotion of the Fine Arts, in 1833, and the *Mill in Blagdon Burn*, and *River Scene*, which he showed at the Institution in the following year. Hair remained at NEWCASTLE until early in 1838, by which time he had completed most of the watercolours for his coal mines' publication, and in many cases executed the etchings; also before leaving the town he had executed two engravings of the drawings of John Wilson Carmichael (q.v.), for *Views on the Newcastle and Carlisle Railway*, commenced by this artist in 1835,

and issued as engravings between 1836-8, as each section of the line was completed. It is interesting that Hair and Carmichael were working on their respective industrial illustrative works simultaneously.

Shortly after arriving in London from NEWCASTLE, in 1838, Hair exhibited at the Suffolk Street Gallery for the first time, and sent work to the First Exhibition of the North of England Society for the Promotion of the Fine Arts, NEWCASTLE. It appears that he spent most of the succeeding twelve years in the capital, during which time he continued to exhibit at the Suffolk Street Gallery, and also showed work at the Royal Academy, the British Institution, and back briefly at NEWCASTLE in 1842, the North of England Society for the Promotion of the Fine Arts. Most of the works he showed in London consisted of Northumbrian and Lake District views. His movements after 1849, when he last exhibited in London, are uncertain, but it is evident from the substantial number of Northumbrian subjects which he painted between 1850 and 1875, that he was a frequent visitor to the area. These works include his view of NEWCASTLE, after the construction of the High Level Bridge, in 1851 (later engraved for use in Fordyce's *History of Coal, etc., in the North of England*, along with many etchings pirated from Hair's earlier work on the mines); *The Barque 'Bomarsund', off Tynemouth*, 1857; *Hartley Colliery after the Disaster*, 1869,# and *The Bigg Market, Newcastle*, 1875. His work was occasionally exhibited at NEWCASTLE in his later years, his final exhibit in the town being his *Lancaster Bridge*, shown at the Arts Association exhibition of 1881. Represented: British Museum; Laing A.G., Newcastle; Shipley A.G., Gateshead.

HALFNIGHT, Richard William (1855-1925)
Landscape painter in oil and watercolour. He was born at SUNDERLAND, and following his general education went to work for the architects Jos. Potts & Son, where he soon gained a reputation for his colouring of plans, etc. He quickly tired of this occupation, however, and decided to join his father's painting and decorating business. During the evenings he attended classes at the School of Art, NEWCASTLE, under William Cosens Way (q.v.), and in spare moments copied works from his father's extensive collection of paintings. Later, an artist visiting SUNDERLAND saw his work and recommended him to adopt painting as a profession. A legacy from a relative happily made this possible, and at the age of twenty-five he went to London. His progress here was not immediately satisfactory, but following the acceptance of his first work by the Royal Academy in 1884 – a colossal watercolour entitled *Dredging* – he began to achieve success. Later in the same year he joined Yeend King in a studio at St. John's Wood, benefiting considerably from this artist's three years' sojourn in Paris, and in the following year he had two works accepted by the Academy. One of these exhibits, an oil entitled: *Streatley – Late Afternoon*, was purchased by the Art Union of London. In 1886 he made his first attempt to have his work published, choosing one of his best pictures: *Still Waters*. Within a month of its issue 300 copies were sold, and in the next few years he achieved many other notable successes in having his work published.

Halfnight exhibited widely throughout his career. Prior to his move to London about 1880, he began exhibiting at the Suffolk Street Gallery, eventually showing more than forty works; he exhibited at the Royal Academy on eight occasions, and was a frequent exhibitor at the Royal Institute of Oil Painters, the Royal Institute of Painters in Water Colours, and at various London and provincial art galleries, including the Laing Art Gallery, NEWCASTLE, whose Artists of the Northern Counties exhibitions he contributed to from their inception in 1905, until 1923. He was also a regular exhibitor at NEWCASTLE throughout the late

19th century, sending works to the various exhibitions of the Arts Association, and later the Bewick Club, while working at SUNDERLAND. Halfnight returned to SUNDERLAND in the mid 1890's, later moving to NEWCASTLE, where he maintained studios until the outbreak of the First World War. During the remainder of his life he worked at both NEWCASTLE, and London, dying at the latter in 1925. Represented: Laing A.G., Newcastle; Sunderland A.G.

HALL, George (1852- after 1918)
Amateur illustrator in pen and ink. He was born at GATESHEAD, the son of a pawnbroker, and trained as an accountant before joining his father's business in the town. Later he became a regular contributor of illustrations in pen and ink to the *Newcastle Weekly Chronicle*, mainly specialising in countryside and architectural views. Many examples of his work were later reproduced in the *Monthly Chronicle of North Country Lore & Legend*, 1887-1891. He died at GATESHEAD.

HANCOCK, Albany (1806-1873)
Amateur sea shell illustrator; flower, fruit and fish painter in watercolour; modeller. He was born at NEWCASTLE, one of the three sons of John Hancock, saddler and ironmonger, and practised as an attorney in the town before devoting his life to the study of natural history, like his brother John Hancock (q.v.). During the period immediately following the end of his legal career in 1832, he became interested in modelling in clay and plaster, and drew and painted flowers, fruit and fish with some success, these skills in art later proving of much value to him in his natural history researches. He subsequently became interested in the study of sea shells, and during the period 1845-1855 was co-author with Joshua Alder, of *Monographs of the British Nudibranchiate Mollusca*. This work was described as having "Figures of the Species by Joshua Alder and Albany Hancock", but most of the drawings and the whole of the anatomy were by Albany alone. This work brought the two men a world-wide reputation, and soon after its completion Albany commenced work alone on *The Organisation of the Brachiopoda*, which appeared in the Philosophical Transactions of the Royal Society for 1858, and further enhanced his reputation as an authority on his subject as well as an "accomplished artist". Altogether, either alone or in collaboration with friends, he published some seventy-four scientific works, and had many honours conferred upon him by learned societies, not only for his knowledge of the mollusca and brachiopoda, but of several other groups of invertebrates. He died at NEWCASTLE. He was the uncle of Thomas Archibald Hancock (q.v.). Represented: Natural History Society of Northumbria, Newcastle.

HANCOCK, John (1808-1890)
Bird illustrator in line; sculptor; wood engraver. He was born at NEWCASTLE, one of the three sons of John Hancock, saddler and ironmonger, and later joined the family business with his brother Thomas. He soon found business irksome, however, and came to an arrangement with Thomas whereby he would be free to devote his life to the study of natural history, like their brother Albany Hancock (q.v.). John had been an acquaintance in his youth of Thomas Bewick (q.v.), and from his earliest years had collected specimens of birds, insects, shells and plants. He had also formed a friendship with taxidermist at NEWCASTLE, Richard Wingate, this leading to a lifelong interest in this art himself, and eventually the reputation of Britain's finest practitioner. In 1851 he contributed a series of mounted birds to the Great Exhibition, London, two years later publishing a series of lithographic plates of these groups, drawn on the stone himself. This work was followed in 1875 by the publication of his *Catalogue of Birds of Northumberland and Durham*, with fourteen photographic copper plates from drawings by the author, and published as Volume VI. of *The Natural History Transactions of Northumberland and Durham*. He also wrote and published many other works on birds, taking a special interest in birds of prey. Some of his finest work in taxidermy was devoted to mounting specimens of these birds, modelling them in clay, and illustrating them by means of wood engravings. He was a member of many Northumbrian bodies associated with natural history study, and served as Vice-President of what is today the Natural History Society of Northumbria, NEWCASTLE. It was largely through his influence that the natural history museum at NEWCASTLE which bears his name, was opened in 1884. He died at NEWCASTLE. He was the uncle of Thomas Archibald Hancock (q.v.). Represented: Hancock Museum, Newcastle; Natural History Society of Northumbria, Newcastle.

HANCOCK, Thomas Archibald (1858-1916)
Landscape and coastal painter in watercolour. He was born at NEWCASTLE, the son of ironmonger Thomas Hancock, and nephew of Albany Hancock (q.v.), and John Hancock (q.v.). He practised as a professional artist at NEWCASTLE until 1900, when he moved to TYNEMOUTH. He was a member of the Bewick Club, NEWCASTLE, occasionally exhibiting his work with the Club from 1890, on which occasion he showed: *Cornfield near Kenton*. He was also an exhibitor at the Artists of the Northern Counties exhibitions of the Laing Art Gallery, NEWCASTLE, showing *Promontory Point, Cullercoats*, in 1906. He died at TYNEMOUTH.

*HARPER, Thomas (1820- c.1889)
Landscape painter in watercolour; drawing master. Harper was born at EIGHTON BANKS, near GATESHEAD, but at an early age moved to NEWCASTLE, where he became a pupil of Thomas Miles Richardson, Senior, (q.v.). At the age of sixteen he exhibited two landscapes at the Newcastle Society of Artists. He again exhibited at NEWCASTLE in 1838 and 1839, showing work at the North of England Society for the Promotion of the Fine Arts, but from the latter date until 1841 he is believed to have worked in London, where in 1840 he showed his only works at the Royal Academy: *Distant View of the Cheviot, Northumberland*, and *Ruins of Dunstanborough Castle, Coast of Northumberland, by Moonlight*. On returning to NEWCASTLE he resumed exhibiting in the town, mainly showing Lake District views. He

Thomas Harper: Figures on a Northumberland Beach, Sundown. Watercolour 7¾×11¼. *Abbey Antiques and Arts.*

did not exhibit again in London until 1856, when he sent three Northumbrian coastal views to the Suffolk Street Gallery. By the time that he next exhibited at the Suffolk Street Gallery, in 1875, he had moved to SOUTH SHIELDS, following a brief spell at NORTH SHIELDS, and it appears that he spent the rest of his life at the former town, dying there some time after 1888. Harper exhibited little in his later life, among his few known exhibits being the two coastal views which he sent to the exhibition of works by local painters, at the Central Exchange Art Gallery, NEWCASTLE, in 1878. Represented: Laing A.G., Newcastle; North Tyneside Public Libraries; Shipley A.G., Gateshead.

HARRISON, Amy (d.1954)

Landscape painter in watercolour. She was the daughter of Ewbank Harrison, goldsmith at DARLINGTON, and great, great granddaughter of John (Longitude) Harrison, inventor of the chronometer. In her late teens, or early twenties, she left DARLINGTON to study under the Cornish Group of Painters, and further developed her art under Sir Frank Brangwyn. She later settled permanently at DARLINGTON, where she became well known for her studies of local churches, and Northumbrian views. She exhibited her work at the Royal Institute of Painters in Water Colours, and the Society of Women Artists from 1920, and was a frequent exhibitor at the Artists of the Northern Counties exhibitions at the Laing Art Gallery, NEWCASTLE, from 1911, her first exhibits being entitled: *Old Pilchard Curing House, Newlyn*, and *Croft Church, with Hunlaby Pew*. Three examples of her work were shown at the North East Coast Exhibition, Palace of Arts, in 1929, and she was a regular exhibitor at the Darlington Society of Arts throughout her life. Darlington Art Gallery has several of her large watercolour studies of local churches. She was the sister of John Brown Harrison (q.v.).

HARRISON, James (b.1873)

Marine draughtsman. Harrison was born at HARTLEPOOL, the son of a master mariner. His first attempts at drawing sailing ships were made in his very early years, encouraged by his father, who assisted him with the technical details of the masting, sparring and rigging. In later years his own experience at sea intensified his desire to draw ships under varying conditions of wind and weather, and to help develop his capabilities in this direction he studied under Richard George Hatton (q.v.) at Armstrong College (later King's College, now Newcastle University). A major exhibition of his work, comprising more than sixty ink and pencil drawings of sailing ships, was staged at Sunderland Art Gallery in 1950.

*HARRISON, John Brown (1876-1958)

Landscape painter in oil, watercolour and pastel. He was the son of Ewbank Harrison, goldsmith at DARLINGTON, and great, great grandson of John (Longitude) Harrison, inventor of the chronometer. On concluding his general education he was allowed to enrol as a pupil at the School of Art, DARLINGTON, under Edgar Averill Elton (q.v.), where he soon distinguished himself as a talented painter in watercolour and pastel. After leaving the School, however, Harrison was introduced into the family business, remaining a spare-time painter until his retirement about 1931. He exhibited his work widely, showing examples at the Royal Academy, the Paris Salon, the Royal Cambrian Academy, the Royal Institute of Painters in Water Colours, the Pastel Society, and at various London and provincial galleries. He also took an active interest in local artistic matters, in 1922 helping to found the Darlington Society of Arts, and serving as secretary for almost thirty years. Under the nom-de-plume "Xamon", he also wrote art criticisms for the *Darlington & Stockton Times*. One of his Royal Academy exhibits: *The morning after* – a study of a bombed area of the North East Coast – was a chief exhibit at Burlington House in 1941, and much of his other work received special attention for its accomplishment. He died at DARLINGTON. He was the brother of Amy Harrison (q.v.). Darlington Art Gallery has a substantial collection of his watercolours, including: *Pool on the Swale*, 1926,# and *The Meadows, High Coniscliffe*, 1936. Represented: Darlington A.G.; Middlesbrough A.G.

HARRISON, Thomas (d. 1945)

Landscape, architectural and coastal painter in watercolour; architectural draughtsman. Harrison was born at NEWCASTLE, and practised as an architect in the city in partnership with Sidney Ash (q.v.), following an apprenticeship in London, and some time as assistant of J. H. Morton of SOUTH SHIELDS. He went to France with the Artists' Rifles in the First World War, and on his return rejoined the partnership, retiring in 1936 to take a post as Borough Architect at WALLSEND, near NEWCASTLE. From his early days he had been a keen student of architecture and spent most of his spare time sketching and making drawings of historical and interesting buildings. In this way, it has been said, he acquired a vast knowledge of architectural details which was of great value to him in his career as an architect. Later he became an enthusiastic painter in watercolour, and frequent exhibitor of his work at the Artists of the Northern Counties exhibitions at the Laing Art Gallery, NEWCASTLE, and the city's Pen & Palette Club. He was also an exhibitor at the North East Coast Exhibition, Palace of Arts, in 1929. Harrison was a member of the Newcastle Society of Artists, and as a member of the Pen & Palette Club served as Honorary Secretary from 1919 until 1931. He was the son-in-law of John Atkinson (q.v.), having married Atkinson's daughter Mabel, in 1923.

HARVEY, William (1796-1866)

Wood engraver; draughtsman. Born at NEWCASTLE, the son of the keeper of the town's public baths, Harvey showed a remarkable talent for drawing from an early age, and was apprenticed to Thomas Bewick (q.v.), at the age of fourteen. He made remarkable progress under Bewick, and was soon allowed to give up the drudgery of engraving bar bills, invoice headings, etc., for the more demanding work of engraving with fellow apprentice William Temple (q.v.), cuts for Bewick's *Fables of Aesop*, published in 1818. On completing his apprenticeship in 1817, Harvey decided to develop his skills as an artist yet further, and moving to London placed himself as a pupil of the rapidly rising historical and genre painter Haydon. Like Haydon's other Northumbrian pupil, William Bewick (q.v.), he also attended the dissecting rooms of Sir Charles Bell. At Haydon's studio he worked with the Landseers and others, maintaining himself meanwhile by "furnishing designs for the engravers, and labouring with the burin on his own account". One of his most outstanding works in wood engraving while with Haydon, was his interpretation of his master's *Death of Denatus*, later described by Chatto in his *The History of Wood Engraving*, 1848,

John Brown Harrison: Pool on the Swale, 1926. Watercolour 18¾×23. *Darlington Art Gallery.*

as one of the most elaborately engraved wood cuts, for a large subject, that had ever appeared. Harvey went on to become the successor of John Thurston as the principal designer for the wood engraving trade in London. His work appeared in innumerable books, but is seen to its best advantage in only a few of these, notably: *Northcote's Fables*, 1828 and 1833; Lane's *Arabian Nights*, 1838-40, and *The Gardens and Menagerie of the Zoological Society*, 1829. In addition to designing and engraving for a wide range of books, Harvey also contributed to a number of popular periodicals of his day, including *The Observer*, 1828; *Punch*, 1841-2; the *Illustrated London News*, 1843-59, and *The Illustrated London Magazine*, 1854. Like several of Bewick's pupils, Harvey prepared water colour designs for several of his book illustrations. Some of this work survives in public collections. He exhibited on only one occasion, this being when he showed his "Impressions from Wood Cuts, chiefly illustrative of the History of Bacchus. Designed and engraved for Dr. Henderson's 'History of Wines'", at the Northumberland Institution for the Promotion of the Fine Arts, NEWCASTLE, 1824. He died at Richmond, Surrey. He was the last of Bewick's major pupils to die, his passing later being commemorated just inside the north porch of St. Nicholas' Cathedral with a stone carved with the design of a palette, and a set of engraver's tools. Represented: British Museum; Victoria and Albert Museum; Fitzwilliam Museum, Cambridge; Natural History Society of Northumbria, Newcastle; Newcastle Central Library.

*HASTINGS, Edward (Edmund) (1781-1861)

Portrait, genre and landscape painter in oil and watercolour. He was born at ALNWICK, but received his education at BAMBURGH. He was later taught painting under the patronage of Archdeacon of Northumberland, Reynold Gideon Bouyer, probably before Bouyer's attainment to this position in 1812, as Hastings was then working as a professional artist in London. By 1804 he had commenced exhibiting at the Royal Academy, showing his *Portrait of a Lady*, and in 1807 he

Edward Hastings: Prideaux John Selby. Oil 30×22. *Private collection.*

exhibited his first work at the British Institution: *South West View of Durham Cathedral*. In the next twenty-three years he continued to exhibit at the Academy and the Institution, also sending work to the Suffolk Street Gallery, and the Old Water Colour Society. His exhibits at the first two of these establishments were contributed as "Edward Hastings", while those to the second two were contributed as "Edmund Hastings". Some confusion has arisen as a consequence of this practice, but all available evidence supports the conclusion that Edward and Edmund Hastings were one and the same artist. Hastings' exhibits at the Royal Academy were all portraits, entered as the work of "Edward Hastings", and it is significant that the obituary of "Edmund Hastings", when he died at DURHAM in 1861, described him as a portrait painter; also, most of the Suffolk Street exhibits entered as by "Edmund Hastings", were portraits.

Hastings' early association with DURHAM, (as evidenced by his British Institution exhibit of 1807) was developed following his marriage to a local girl about 1805, and by 1829 he was describing his address as "London and Durham". By that date he had become a regular exhibitor at NEWCASTLE, where he had shown portraits, animal, coastal and landscape paintings at the Northumberland Institution for the Promotion of the Fine Arts, from 1823. In 1829 he commenced exhibiting at the town's Northern Academy, and from that date until the early 1840's he remained a regular exhibitor at NEWCASTLE, from 1834 showing his address as DURHAM.

His work attracted considerable interest among fellow artists in Northumbria, and he painted several portraits of these men, including Thomas Miles Richardson, Senior (q.v.), John Prideaux Selby (q.v.),# and Henry Perlee Parker (q.v.). He also took a prominent part in various of the art promoting ventures of the period, and chaired the first meeting of The Northern Society of Painters in Water Colours, held at NEWCASTLE, 24th November, 1830. In the last twenty-five years of his life Hastings appears to have concentrated mainly on painting portraits of well known people at DURHAM, among these the famed Count Boruwalski, the three-feet-high son of a Polish nobleman, who spent the last seventeen years of his life in the city. But he also produced occasional informal portraits, such as his *Houghall Milk Boy*, painted on wood in 1855. He died at DURHAM. His elder brother CAPTAIN THOMAS HASTINGS, and son W. A. HASTINGS, were both talented artists, and exhibited their work. Represented: Old Town Hall, Durham.

HASWELL, John (1855-1925)
Amateur landscape painter in oil. Haswell was born at SUNDERLAND, the eldest son of a clergyman, and later practised as a solicitor in the town, taking a keen spare-time interest in painting and writing. He did not begin to exhibit his work widely until quite late in life, sending two works to the Royal Academy, one work to the Royal Scottish Academy, and various works to London and provincial exhibitions, between 1908 and 1914. His two Royal Academy contributions were entitled: *Mountain Torrent: melting snow* (1908), and *After the Storm* (1909). His exhibits at the Artists of the Northern Counties exhibitions at the Laing Art Gallery, NEWCASTLE, 1909-14, included his two Royal Academy exhibits, and a wide range of Lake District views. Haswell was President of the Stanfield Art Society in 1908, and wrote a book: *Pages from my past*. He was also a poet, musician, astronomer, and photographer of some ability. He died at Leamington Spa. Sunderland Art Gallery has his two Royal Academy exhibits in its collection. His daughter, VIOLET M. HASWELL, was also a talented amateur artist, and showed one work at the Royal Academy in 1911, and several works at the Artists of the Northern Counties exhibition in 1912; her work was in portraiture.

HATTON, Richard George, A.R.C.A. (1865-1926)
Landscape, genre and portrait painter in oil and watercolour; art teacher. Hatton was born at Birmingham and received his early training in art at Birmingham School of Art. In 1890 he was appointed to the position of second art master at the College of Physical Science, NEWCASTLE, becoming headmaster five years later, on the retirement of William Cosens Way (q.v.). He remained with the College until its absorption into Armstrong College (later King's College; now Newcastle University), and in 1912 received the appointment of Director of the School of Art at King's College, becoming Professor of Fine Art five years later. He was responsible for encouraging and instructing many Northumbrian artists during his long period of association with the city's Schools of Art, and was himself an

accomplished artist, though he did not frequently exhibit his work. He exhibited at the Royal Society of Artists, Birmingham, between 1887 and 1895, the Bewick Club, NEWCASTLE, for a few years after his move to Northumbria, and he was an occasional exhibitor at the Artists of the Northern Counties exhibitions at the city's Laing Art Gallery, from 1906. In addition to teaching art, Hatton published several books of use to the art student, these including: *Perspective for Art Students*, 1902; *Figure Drawing* 1905, and *Principles of Decoration*, 1925. He was an associate of the Royal College of Art, and was President of the National Society of Art Masters in 1911. He died at NEWCASTLE. The Hatton Gallery at Newcastle University was named in memory of his great contribution to the teaching of art on Tyneside. Represented: Laing A.G., Newcastle.

HAVELOCK-ALLAN, Sir Henry Spencer Moreton, Bart. (1873-1953)
Amateur landscape painter in oil and watercolour. He was born at Dublin, the son of General Sir H. M. Havelock-Allan, Baronet, V.C., and grandson of General Havelock of Indian Mutiny fame. He succeeded to the Baronetcy in 1897, and after taking up residence at Blackwell Grange, DARLINGTON, became intimately involved in the civic and cultural life of the town, also painting in his spare time. He held several offices connected with the judiciary at DARLINGTON during his many years at Blackwell Grange, and also served as M.P. for BISHOP AUCKLAND 1910-18. He was a leading member of Darlington Society of Arts for many years, and was an enthusiastic patron of the music, literature and painting.

HAWARD, Arthur (1857-1937)
Landscape painter in watercolour. Born and educated in London, Haward moved to DARLINGTON in 1874 to assist in his father's cabinet making and upholstery business, eventually becoming senior partner. He was a keen spare-time painter, and frequently contributed work to the exhibitions of the Darlington Society of Arts from its foundation in 1922, until his death fifteen years later. He was also an occasional exhibitor at the Artists of the Northern Counties exhibitions at the Laing Art Gallery, NEWCASTLE, and had two examples of his work accepted for showing at the North East Coast Exhibition, Palace of Arts, in 1929. He died at his home for many years at EGGLESTON, near MIDDLETON-IN-TEESDALE. Represented: Darlington A.G.

HAY, Charles William (fl. 19th cent.)
Landscape and portrait painter in watercolour. He was born at NEWCASTLE, the son of a schoolmaster. He was an acquaintance from his youth of Thomas Miles Richardson, Senior (q.v.), and may have had some tuition from this artist before taking up the profession of watercolour painter at NEWCASTLE. He occasionally exhibited his work here in the 1840's, examples being the *Portrait*, and *Cottages near Gosforth*, which he showed at the North of England Society for the Promotion of the Fine Arts, in 1843. The Laing Art Gallery, NEWCASTLE, has his *Landscape with river and bridge*.

HEATH, William "Paul Pry" (1795-1840)
Genre, landscape and subject painter in watercolour; caricaturist; engraver. This artist was born in Northumbria, and started his professional career as an artist working as a draughtsman, later claiming to be "Portrait and Military Painter". His main claim to fame rests on his having produced the first caricature magazine in Europe, *The Glasgow*, later *Northern Looking Glass*, 1825-6, but he enjoyed considerable popularity as a caricaturist throughout the years 1809-34, under the pseudonym of "Paul Pry". Heath was reputed to have spent his early years as a Captain of the Dragoons, but is not recorded in the Army List. His movements after his early years in Northumbria are uncertain, but he was working at NEWCASTLE, in 1827, when he contributed six genre, landscape and other works to the Northumberland Institution for the Promotion of the Fine Arts, in the town. Following his fall from popularity as a caricaturist about 1834, Heath concentrated on topographical work, and straight illustration. His works in illustration include: *The Looking Glass*, 1830; *The Life of a Soldier*, 1823; *Minor Morals*, 1834, and *The Martial Achievements of Great Britain and Her Allies and Historical Military and Naval Anecdotes*. He died in London. His watercolour: *Merry Wives of Windsor*, was included in the exhibition of works of local painters, at the Central Exchange Art Gallery, NEWCASTLE, in 1878. Represented: British Museum; Victoria and Albert Museum; National Gallery of Scotland.

HEAVISIDE, John Smith (1812-1864)
Wood engraver. He was born at STOCKTON ON TEES, the son of a builder, and did not become an artist until the age of twenty-six. Following this he spent a short time in London, then settled at Oxford, where he mainly worked on cutting illustrations for archaeological works, many of them by John Henry Parker. He died at Kentish Town. Two of his brothers also practised as engravers; one of these was Thomas Heaviside (q.v.).

HEAVISIDE, Thomas (fl. early 19th cent.)
Wood engraver. He was the brother of John Smith Heaviside (q.v.), and also practised as a wood engraver. Among his best known work in this field was his portrait of Thomas Bewick (q.v.), after William Nicholson (q.v.); this portrait, with a short memoir by William Howitt, appeared in *Howitt's Journal*, No. 38, Vol. II, September, 1846. He also engraved other portraits, and contributed work to the *Illustrated London News*, 1849-51. Another brother was also a wood engraver.

HEDLEY, Johnson (d. 1914)
Amateur landscape and genre painter in oil and watercolour. The brother of Ralph Hedley (q.v.), he was born at Gilling, near Richmond, North Yorkshire, and joined his brother on Tyneside by 1880. He settled first at GATESHEAD, where he started a confectionery business, and began exhibiting his work by sending two genre paintings to the Arts Association, NEWCASTLE, in 1880: *The Rosary*, and *Past Redemption*. He exhibited at the Arts Association in 1881, and 1882, and contributed a view of the River Tyne at Dunston to the

"Gateshead Fine Art & Industrial Exhibition", in 1883, and several landscape and genre works to the Bewick Club, in 1885 and 1886. Following the latter date he removed to SUNDERLAND, where his family continued his confectionery business and he took an increasing interest in painting. He was Vice-President of the Stanfield Art Society at SUNDERLAND, and regularly showed work at its exhibitions until his death in the town in 1914. Sunderland Art Gallery has his watercolours: *Girdle Cake Cottage, Biddick* (1912-14), and *Field Path to Whitburn*, 1914.

*HEDLEY, Ralph, R.B.A. (1848-1913)

Genre, portrait and landscape painter in oil and watercolour; illustrator; sculptor; wood carver. Born at Gilling, near Richmond, North Yorkshire, Hedley began his career in art as an apprentice to Thomas Hall Tweedy (q.v.), wood carver at NEWCASTLE. While working as an apprentice, however, he attended the Government School of Design in the town, and the evening classes of the Life School, where he received tuition in drawing and painting under William Bell Scott (q.v.), and William Cosens Way (q.v.). At the end of his apprenticeship and art studies he decided to become a professional painter, and leaving Tweedy he set up a studio in the town and began to paint genre, portrait and landscape subjects. He quickly established a demand for his work, and in 1878 sent eight works to the exhibition of works by local painters, at the Central Exchange Art Gallery, NEWCASTLE, and three works to

Ralph Hedley: The Sleeping Model, 1888. Watercolour 23×18. *Christopher Wood Ltd.*

84

the first exhibition of the town's Arts Association. In the following year he commenced exhibiting at the Royal Academy, showing his *News Boy*, between that date and his death in 1913, contributing some fifty-two works, and also exhibiting at the Royal Scottish Academy, the Royal Institute of Painters in Water Colours, the Royal Society of British Artists, and widely in the provinces, where he was a regular exhibitor at the Bewick Club, NEWCASTLE, and later the Artists of the Northern Counties exhibitions at the city's Laing Art Gallery.

Early in his career as a painter, Hedley founded a wood and stone carving firm at NEWCASTLE, which became one of the best known in the area, though he only occasionally handled its commissions himself. A notable example of his work for the firm is the wood carving of the pulpit, rood screen, choir stalls, the panelling in the sanctuary and the Bishop's Chair, in St. Andrew's, NEWCASTLE. This firm employed William Robinson (q.v.), for some thirty years, and Hedley's sons, FREDERICK HEDLEY, and ROGER HEDLEY, who were also talented wood carvers, carried on the family business until well into the present century. Hedley was one of the most popular and well respected local artists of his day, and in addition to enjoying membership of the Royal Society of British Artists from 1899, served as President of the Bewick Club from 1895, in succession to Henry Hetherington Emmerson (q.v.), and was either President or Vice-President of several other Northumbrian art clubs. His work is today particularly valued for the record it provides of everyday life on Tyneside in the late 19th and early 20th centuries, as well as for its excellence of execution. He died at NEWCASTLE. He was the elder brother of Johnson Hedley (q.v.). A major loan exhibition of Hedley's work was staged at the Laing Art Gallery in 1938, including examples of his work in oil, watercolour, and wood carving. On this occasion more then twenty of his surviving models took tea at the Gallery with the establishment's chairman, and the artist's sons. The Laing Art Gallery has a large collection of his work. Represented: Gray A.G. & Museum, Hartlepool; John George Joicey Museum, Newcastle; Laing A.G., Newcastle; Shipley A.G., Gateshead; South Shields Museum & A.G.; Sunderland A.G.

*HEMY, Bernard Benedict (1845-1913)

Marine and coastal painter in oil and watercolour. He was born at NEWCASTLE, the second son of Henri F. Hemy, music teacher and composer. At the age of seven he travelled with his family to Australia, where they remained some two and a half years, and his father worked on the goldfields at Ballarat, near Melbourne. When the family returned to NEWCASTLE he studied for some time at the School of Art in the town under William Cosens Way (q.v.), then decided to lead a seafaring life while preparing for the priesthood. Neither seafaring, nor the priesthood, retained his interest, however, and he returned to his first love of painting. He first practised as a professional artist at NORTH SHIELDS, from which in the period 1875-7 he sent

Bernard Benedict Hemy:
Mending the boat.
Watercolour 20×30. *G. R.
McArdle.*

his first work for exhibition, showing *A boat builder's shop on the Tyne*, and *On the Tyne, South Shields*, at the Suffolk Street Gallery, and two works at the Dudley Gallery, London. He next showed his work at the exhibition of works by local painters, at the Central Exchange Art Gallery, NEWCASTLE, in 1878, and on finding his six marine and coastal views so well received there, decided to return to his native town. He remained at NEWCASTLE until the late 1880's, when he again settled at NORTH SHIELDS, meanwhile exhibiting at the "Gateshead Fine Art & Industrial Exhibition", in 1883, and showing his first work at the Bewick Club, NEW-CASTLE: *Shipping on the Tyne*. He remained a regular exhibitor at the Bewick Club throughout his stay at NORTH SHIELDS, and later SOUTH SHIELDS, also sending work to the art club at the latter, and for some years the Walker Art Gallery, Liverpool. He spent his final years at SOUTH SHIELDS, dying there in 1913. He was the younger brother of Charles Napier Hemy (q.v.), and the elder brother of Thomas Marie Madawaska Hemy (q.v.). Represented: Bootle A.G.; Laing A.G., Newcastle; North Tyneside Public Libraries; South Shields Museum & A.G.; Sunderland A.G.

*HEMY, Charles Napier, R.A., R.W.S. (1841-1917)
Marine, coastal and landscape painter in oil and water-colour; illustrator. He was born at NEWCASTLE, the eldest son of Henri F. Hemy, music teacher and composer. Here he attended the Grammar School, and took lessons in art at the town's School of Art, under William Cosens Way (q.v.), before leaving with his family for Australia, where they spent some two and a half years. In this period Hemy's father worked in the goldfields at Ballarat, near Melbourne, Charles Napier

helping him as a rough digger in this work. On the return trip to England he helped man the ship on which the family travelled, this activity infecting him with a lifelong love of the sea, and a desire later to paint it in all its moods. On arriving back at NEWCASTLE, however, he decided to enter the priesthood, and was sent to Ushaw College, near DURHAM, but his love of the sea was too strong, and he left the college to work until the age of nineteen on a collier brig. At the end of this period he again felt a strong urge to become a priest and spent the next two years in a Dominican House at NEWCASTLE, and in a monastery of the same Order, at Lyons, France. His health proved too precarious for his calling, and he abandoned it to become a full-time professional artist.

Hemy first practised at GATESHEAD, from which in 1863 he sent four marine and coastal views, and a view of Jesmond Dene, NEWCASTLE, to the Suffolk Street Gallery. He next practised at NORTH SHIELDS, sending his first work to the Royal Academy from this town in 1865: *The lone sea shore . . .*, and *Among the Shingles at Clovelly*, this latter work, painted in 1864, indicating a period in North Devon, and stylistically, the influence of the Pre-Raphaelite movement in its attention to detail, and general handling. In 1865 Hemy married a woman of independent means, and in the next five years spent much time studying at the Antwerp Academy of Arts, under Baron Leys, meanwhile continuing to exhibit in London, and showing work at the "Exhibition of Paintings and other works of Art", at the Town Hall, NEWCASTLE, in 1866. In 1867 he sent his only contribu-tion to the British Institution: *Tynemouth, Low Water*. After settling in London in 1871, he continued to exhibit at the Royal Academy and the Suffolk Street Gallery,

Charles Napier Hemy: Uninvited Guests, 1916. Oil 54×32. *Sotheby, King & Chasemore.*

and began to show his work widely in London and the provinces, mainly showing river and coastal scenes. By the beginning of the 1880's, however, he was starting to feel the need of different inspiration for his work, and after visiting Venice, and touring the coastal resorts of the South Coast of England, settled at Falmouth, where he converted a forty-foot, broad beamed fishing boat into a floating studio, christening it the "Van de Velde". From this vessel and its successor, the "Van der Meer", he painted the sea and sailing studies for which he is now most famous. The vivid realism of these paintings attracted considerable attention, and in 1897 his *Pilchards* was purchased by the Chantrey Bequest for the Tate Gallery, and in the following year he was elected an associate of the Royal Academy, and a member of the Royal Society of Painters in Water Colours. In 1904 his *London River* was the subject of a second Chantrey purchase for the Tate, and in 1910 he was elected a full member of the Royal Academy.

Although Hemy showed his work at all the leading exhibiting establishments in Britain from early in his career, he never forgot his native Tyneside, and was an exhibitor at NEWCASTLE until close to his death, showing many works at the Artists of the Northern Counties

exhibitions at the city's Laing Art Gallery. Indeed, the last work which he exhibited was shown at NEWCASTLE: *The Black Flag*, in 1916. He died at Falmouth. A memorial exhibition of his work entitled: *Life on the Sea*, was held at the Fine Art Society, London, in the year following his death, and examples of his work have been included in several other marine exhibitions since that date, most recently: *The Restless Wave*, mounted by Tyne & Wear Museums Service, 1978. He was the elder brother of Bernard Benedict Hemy (q.v.), and Thomas Marie Madawaska Hemy (q.v.). Represented: British Museum; Tate Gallery; National Maritime Museum; Gray A.G. & Museum, Hartlepool; Laing A.G., Newcastle; South Shields Museum & A.G.; Sunderland A.G.; Walker A.G., Liverpool.

HEMY, Thomas Marie Madawaska (1852-1937)

Marine and coastal painter in oil and watercolour. He was born on the passenger ship "Madawaska", the sixth son of Henri F. Hemy, music teacher and composer, while his family were en route from NEWCASTLE to Australia. His family remained in Australia for some two and a half years, his father working for part of this time in the goldfields at Ballarat, near Melbourne. On his family's return to NEWCASTLE he was sent to school in town, and when he later moved to NORTH SHIELDS, he received some tuition in art from his uncle, Isaac Henzell (q.v.). About the age of fourteen, however, he became "fed up" with life ashore, and spent the next seven years at sea, travelling widely throughout the world. At the end of this period, and having suffered a shipwreck on his way back to England from San Francisco, he decided to return to NEWCASTLE, where he enrolled as a pupil at the town's School of Art, under William Cosens Way (q.v.). While still at the School he exhibited for the first time, showing his *Old Houses on the Tyne*, at the Suffolk Street Gallery, in 1873. In the following year his works were hung on the line at the Dudley Gallery, London, and in 1874 he showed his first work at the Royal Academy: *The herring fishery at North Shields*. At this point in his career he came to the attention of John George Sowerby (q.v.), who sent him to Antwerp for two years to study drawing under Verlat.

On returning to Tyneside he found some difficulty in living from his art, but shortly after showing an Irish coastal view at the exhibition of works by local painters, at the Central Exchange Art Gallery, NEWCASTLE, in 1878, he moved to SUNDERLAND, and from then on his fortunes steadily improved. While on a visit to London from SUNDERLAND, he received his first major commission – a picture in commemoration of "Lord Charles Beresford and Engineer Benbow's gallantry up the Nile". His work was titled: *Running the Gauntlet*, and after its purchase by Lord Beresford, was despatched on a tour of the provinces, and widely reproduced as an engraving. His career from this point forward suffered few reverses. Many other commissions followed his move to London, about 1883, several of which were also reproduced as engravings. He continued to exhibit at the Royal Academy until 1915, when one of his final exhibits was *The Ard Lects o' Shields*, and also showed work at the Royal Institute of Painters in Water Colours, and widely in the provinces, including the exhibitions of the Bewick Club, NEWCASTLE, and later the Artists of the Northern Counties exhibitions at the city's Laing Art Gallery. Although most of his later life was spent in London he frequently spent time working away from the capital on commissions, and pursuing his personal interests in painting. Towards the end of his life he settled at St. Helen's, Isle of Wight, where he died in 1937.

Much interesting information about Hemy's early life at sea, his later periods at sea on painting expeditions, and several of his more important works, are contained in his *Deep Sea Days – The Chronicles of a Sailor and Sea Painter*, 1926. This book also contains twelve monochrome illustrations by him. He was the younger brother of Charles Napier Hemy (q.v.), and Bernard Benedict Hemy (q.v.). His daughter, GWENYTTH HEMY (Mrs. Harold de Brath), was also a talented artist, and exhibited her work at the Royal Academy, and the Artists of the Northern Counties exhibitions. Represented: Laing A.G., Newcastle; Shipley A.G., Gateshead; Sunderland A.G.

*HENZELL, Isaac (1815- after 1875)

Genre, landscape and portrait painter in oil. Although Henzell was born at Sheffield, Yorkshire, there is little doubt that he was descended from the De Henzell, or Hensey, Huguenot family brought to Tyneside in 1619 from Lorraine, Germany, to help found a local glass industry. He is first recorded as an artist at NEWCASTLE in 1841, where he practised as a portrait painter in the town's Grainger Street. He appears to have spent the next thirteen years on Tyneside, later moving to Lon-

Isaac Henzell: By the Cottage Door. Oil 17¼×13¼. *Private collection.*

don, where he practised until 1865. He next practised at NEWCASTLE for six years, then returned to London, after which no records of him are traceable beyond 1875. He first began exhibiting his work publicly in 1841, when he sent three portraits to the North of England Society for the Promotion of the Fine Arts, NEWCASTLE. These were among his few known portrait works, however, as the work which he subsequently showed at the Royal Academy, the British Institution, the Suffolk Street Gallery, and at NEWCASTLE, were almost all genre and other works, with such titles as: *The Seaside Rustics* (Royal Academy, 1854); *The Prawn Fishers* (British Institution, 1862), and *R. Lambton and his Hounds* ("Central Exchange News Room, Art Gallery, and Polytechnic Exhibition", NEWCASTLE, 1870). Indeed, all but six of the some sixty-one works which he showed at the Suffolk Street Gallery from the year before his election as member of the Society of British Artists in 1855, could be firmly classed as genre paintings. His place of death is not known, but he was certainly dead by 1878, as he was referred to as such when his work: *The Fisher Girl*, was included in the exhibition of works by local painters, at the Central Exchange Art Gallery, NEWCASTLE, in 1878. Henzell was the uncle of Charles Napier Hemy (q.v.), Bernard Benedict Hemy (q.v.), and Thomas Marie Madawaska Hemy (q.v.). Represented: Laing A.G., Newcastle; Shipley A.G., Gateshead; York A.G., and various provincial art galleries.

HEPPER, George (1839-1868)

Portrait, genre, landscape and animal painter in oil. He was born at NEWCASTLE, and after practising as an animal painter in the town for some years, went to London, where he quickly established himself as a professional artist. In 1866 he began to exhibit his work at the British Institution, and the Suffolk Street Gallery, at the former showing: *Uncle Charlie's Favourites*, and *Auntie Peggie's Pets*, and at the latter: *The Young Anglers*. He again exhibited at the British Institution in 1867, and at the Suffolk Street Gallery in 1868. He died in London. Three of his works were included in the exhibition of works by local painters, at the Central Exchange Art Gallery, NEWCASTLE, in 1878; these comprised: *Showing the way*; *Sheep*; and *View of the Thames*. He was the elder brother of William James Hepper (q.v.).

HEPPER, William James (d. 1882)

Portrait and animal painter in oil. He was born at NEWCASTLE, the younger brother of George Hepper (q.v.), and practised as an artist in the town from his early twenties. He exhibited two works at the exhibition of works by local painters, at the Central Exchange Art Gallery, NEWCASTLE, in 1878: *Moonlight after the storm*, and *Humble Life*. He appears to have exhibited in the town on only one further occasion before his death, at the Arts Association exhibition, NEWCASTLE, in 1881, showing his *Ten Miles from Home*. He died at NEWCASTLE. Two examples of his work were included posthumously in the inaugural exhibition of the Bewick Club, NEWCASTLE, in 1884: *Dog's Head*, and *Frenchman's Bay*.

HEPPLE, John Wilson (1886-1939)

Amateur landscape painter in oil and watercolour. The
son of Wilson Hepple (q.v.), he was born at WHICKHAM
near GATESHEAD, and although a talented artist from an
early age, chose to enter the teaching profession. He
became an English master at Atkinson Road Technical
School, NEWCASTLE, and remained in the teaching
profession until his death. Throughout his teaching
career Hepple was a keen amateur painter in watercolour, exhibiting his work almost exclusively on Tyneside,
and mainly at the Artists of the Northern Counties
exhibitions at the Laing Art Gallery, NEWCASTLE. He
spent much of his life at GATESHEAD, but about 1928
moved to CULLERCOATS, where he lived with his family
until his death while on holiday at this father's former
home at ACKLINGTON, in 1939. He was buried in the
village churchyard at ACKLINGTON. His son, Reginald
Watson Hepple, is an art teacher, and a talented painter
of landscapes and hunting scenes.

*HEPPLE, Wilson (1853-1937)

Landscape, animal, sporting and historical subject
painter in oil and watercolour; illustrator. He was born
at NEWCASTLE, and is said to have received his early
tuition in art from William Cosens Way (q.v.), who was
visiting art master at Hepple's school, and later taught
him at evening classes. At thirteen he was apprenticed
to a grocer, but his artistic inclinations were such that
he quickly left the grocery trade and entered the service
of Gerrard Robinson (q.v.), to learn wood carving.
After less than a year, however, he tired of wood
carving and decided to become a full-time professional
painter. Helped in his early efforts in this direction by
John Blower, of Gallowgate, NEWCASTLE, he quickly
established himself in his profession, and by the age of

twenty-two had produced his first major work: *Gallowgate Hoppings*. This work is said to have "astounded
the art world of Newcastle", and led Hepple to devote
himself to genre painting for some time, only later
specialising in the type of animal painting for which he
is now best known. In 1878 he contributed work to two
major exhibitions at NEWCASTLE; the first exhibition of
the Arts Association, and the exhibition of works by
local painters, at the Central Exchange Art Gallery.
From this point forward he remained a regular exhibitor
in the city, showing many examples of his work at the
Bewick Club, and later the Artists of the Northern
Counties exhibitions at the Laing Art Gallery.

Until 1895 Hepple lived and worked on Tyneside,
living for some years at WHICKHAM, near GATESHEAD.
His increasing preoccupation with animal painting,
however, made him wish to work in the country, and
while he maintained a studio in the city for some years
after this date, his home for the rest of his life was a
small cottage on the banks of the River Coquet, near
ACKLINGTON. Hepple's work varied widely throughout
his career, and although he never exhibited outside
Northumbria he was able to establish a considerable
reputation as an artist in the area of his birth. He made
drawings for Dr. Bruce's work on the Roman Wall;
executed many paintings for local hunts; painted several
major works portraying incidents in the history of
Tyneside (some of which were reproduced by lithography), and produced hundreds of horse, dog and kitten
paintings.# One of his most unusual works was the
highland cattle scene which he painted jointly with
George Blackie Sticks (q.v.), for the Royal Jubilee
Exhibition at NEWCASTLE in 1887; Hepple painted the
cattle; Sticks the landscape. He personally considered
that his best work was his painting of the visit of King

Edward VII to NEWCASTLE to open the new infirmary, and Armstrong College (later King's College; now Newcastle University). He died at his cottage near ACKLINGTON, at the age of eighty-four, and is buried in the village churchyard. Represented: Laing A.G., Newcastle; Shipley A.G., Gateshead.

HESKETH, Richard (1867-1919)
Landscape painter in oil. This artist practised on Tyneside in the late 19th and early 20th centuries, where he became an acquaintance of several leading local artists, including Ralph Bullock (q.v.), David T. Robertson (q.v.), Francis Thomas Carter (q.v.), and J. Edgar Mitchell (q.v.). He exhibited his work at the Bewick Club, NEWCASTLE, and later at the Artists of the Northern Counties exhibitions at the city's Laing Art Gallery, from their inception in 1905, until a year before his death. Hesketh lived for many years at RIDING MILL, but spent his final years in NEWCASTLE. The Shipley Art Gallery, GATESHEAD, has his *Harter Fell, Eskdale*. He died at NEWCASTLE.

HESLOP, Arthur (1881-1955)
Landscape and marine painter in oil and watercolour; etcher; art teacher. Heslop was born at NEWCASTLE, but spent his early years living in Egypt with his parents and sisters. At the age of ten he was sent to a private school in Jersey, remaining there until he was seventeen, when he became an art student at Armstrong College (later King's College; now Newcastle University), under Richard George Hatton (q.v.). At the end of his studies he remained as a member of staff, subsequently becoming Master of Engraving and Design at the School of Art at King's College. Heslop was one of the finest etchers produced by Northumbria, and in addition to teaching many young local artists his skills, exhibited his work at the Royal Scottish Academy, the Walker Art Gallery, Liverpool, and the Laing Art Gallery, NEWCASTLE, whose Artists of the Northern Counties exhibitions he contributed to for many years. Many of his etchings and paintings were based on continental subjects, several of his annual holidays being spent abroad. He was also extremely fond of marine subjects, and was an active member of the Society for Nautical Research, Greenwich, London, which showed a warm appreciation of his accurate drawings of boats and ships. One of his sketch books of cobles, each sketch of which was carefully annotated by Heslop, is in the collection of this Society, and has been used as a source of valuable information on the history and development of this type of craft. Heslop continued to etch, sketch and paint following his retirement from the College. In 1953, two years before his death at NEWCASTLE, he shared an exhibition of his work with Sophia Mildred Atkinson (q.v.) – one-time fellow pupil at Armstrong College – at the city's Hatton Gallery. Represented: Laing A.G., Newcastle.

HESLOP, B. H. (fl. late 19th, early 20th cent.)
Landscape and genre painter in watercolour. This artist practised at STOCKTON ON TEES in the late 19th and early 20th centuries, and exhibited his work at the Bewick Club, NEWCASTLE, and later the Artists of the Northern Counties exhibitions at the city's Laing Art Gallery.

HESLOP, T. R. (fl. early 19th cent.)
Landscape, architectural, coastal and figure painter in oil and watercolour; illustrator; etcher. This artist practised at TYNEMOUTH in the early 20th century, and was a regular exhibitor at the Artists of the Northern Counties exhibitions at the Laing Art Gallery, NEWCASTLE, from 1914. He mainly exhibited Northumbrian views in watercolour, but also showed designs for book illustrations, etchings, and examples of needlework and embroidery. Among his last exhibits at the Artists of the Northern Counties exhibitions were the oil painting: *Punch and Judy* and the embroidery work: *At the Zoo*, which he showed in 1935, while still living at TYNEMOUTH.

HEYS, John (1864-1952)
Landscape painter in oil and watercolour; art teacher. Heys' place of birth is not known, but by 1880 he was a pupil teacher at the Old Friends School, SOUTH SHIELDS. He was appointed art teacher at South Shields High School in 1889, and later became first Principal of South Shields Art School, retiring in 1929. Throughout his career as a teacher Heys was an enthusiastic painter, and regularly exhibited his work at the Bewick Club, NEWCASTLE, and later at the Artists of the Northern Counties exhibitions at the city's Laing Art Gallery. He married three times, his first wife, ANNIE E. HEYS, also being a gifted landscape painter, and exhibitor alongside her husband at the Laing Art Gallery. Heys continued to live at SOUTH SHIELDS for some eleven years following his retirement, then moved to Sussex, where he became a member of the Association of Sussex Artists.

HIGGINBOTTOM, William Hugh (1881- after 1936)
Landscape portrait and figure painter in oil and watercolour. He was born at NEWCASTLE, the son of wine and spirit merchant Albert H. Higginbottom, and received his training in art at the Royal Academy Schools, and at the Academie Julian, Paris. He first began to exhibit his work publicly in 1908, when he showed a portrait work in oil: *Elsie*, at the Royal Academy, and subsequently at the Artists of the Northern Counties exhibition at the Laing Art Gallery, NEWCASTLE, of that year. He did not exhibit at the Royal Academy again until 1926, meanwhile continuing to exhibit at the Artists of the Northern Counties exhibitions, and on one occasion at the Royal Institute of Oil Painters. He last exhibited at the former venue in 1936, when he showed two oils: *Jevington*, and *Sussex Downs*. Higginbottom lived at Chiswick, London, for much of his later life. His father was a keen collector of Japanese objects and prints, and bequeathed his collection to the Laing Art Gallery, NEWCASTLE.

HINGLEY, Oswin F. (b. 1884)
Landscape and coastal painter in oil. Hingley lived at CULLERCOATS, from which in 1906 he began exhibiting his work at the Artists of the Northern Counties exhibitions at the Laing Art Gallery, NEWCASTLE, showing: *A Study of the Sea*. He remained an exhibitor at NEWCASTLE for several years, showing a wide variety of seascapes and coastal views.

*HOBSON, Victor William (1865-1889)
Portrait and landscape painter in oil. Hobson was born at DARLINGTON, and studied art at the town's Mechanics' Institute under Samuel Averill Elton (q.v.), following his general education. A Queen's Prizeman in examinations for the South Kensington School of Art, he won the bronze medal in 1883, and in the same year gained a place at the Royal Academy Schools, winning a silver medal for drawing in 1884. He exhibited one work in Manchester in 1888, while living at DARLINGTON. He died at Lugana, Tenerife. Represented: Bowes Museum, Barnard Castle; Darlington A.G.

HODGE, Robert (c. 1875- after 1926)
Marine, landscape and coastal painter in oil. This artist practised at SOUTH SHIELDS from 1895 until c. 1926, in the town's Fowler Street. South Shields Museum & Art Gallery has several examples of his work. His marine work is particularly accomplished.

HODGES, Florence Mary (fl. late 19th, early 20th cent.)
Landscape and animal painter in oil. She was born at DURHAM, and later studied at the Royal Female School of Art, Calderon's School of Animal Painting, and under Frank Short. She exhibited one work at the Royal Academy in 1890, while living in London: *Door in Henry VII's Chapel, Westminster*, and in the following three years also sent work to the Society of Women Artists, and the Walker Art Gallery, Liverpool. She lived for some years in the 1920's at Petersfield in Hampshire.

HODGKIN, Jonathan Edward, R.B.A. (1875-1953)
Amateur landscape painter in watercolour. He was born at DARLINGTON, the son of Jonathan Backhouse Hodgkin, and received his education at Bootham School, York, and Leighton Park School, Reading. He later trained as an engineer, and on returning to DARLINGTON to take up business, became a keen spare-time painter, proving so successful that his work was widely accepted for exhibition. He exhibited at the Royal Institute of Painters in Water Colours, the Royal Society of British Artists, the Paris Salon, and at various London and provincial galleries, including the Laing Art Gallery, NEWCASTLE, whose Artists of the Northern Counties exhibitions he contributed to for many years. Hodgkin was elected an associate of the Royal Society of British Artists in 1926, and became a full member two years later. He took an active interest in local artistic matters, in 1922 helping to found the Darlington Society of Arts, and serving as its chairman for thirty years. He was also a Trustee of the Bowes Museum, BARNARD CASTLE, and was at one time a Councillor at DARLINGTON, and President of the town's Rotary Club. In addition to his artistic, business and town council activities, Hodgkin was also deeply interested in local history and archaeology, and was author of *A little guide to the County of Durham*. Represented: Bowes Museum, Barnard Castle; Darlington A.G.

HODGSON, Edward (fl. late 19th, early 20th cent.)
Landscape and coastal painter in watercolour. This artist practised at NEWCASTLE, GATESHEAD and TYNEMOUTH. He appears to have exhibited his work exclusively in Northumbria, and principally at the Bewick Club, NEWCASTLE, at whose inaugural exhibition in 1884, for instance, he showed two works: *Stella Coal Staithes*, and *Scotswood Suspension Bridge*. Many of his later works were painted along the coast near his home at TYNEMOUTH, and exhibited at the early Artists of the Northern Counties exhibitions at the Laing Art Gallery, NEWCASTLE.

HODGSON, William (fl. late 18th cent.)
Portrait and landscape painter in watercolour; copyist. Hodgson's parents lived at GATESHEAD, and he was sent as a boy to study drawing under Boniface Muss (q.v.), at NEWCASTLE, where he is said to have become an "exquisite painter in water colours". On later moving to London he was patronised by Lewis Schiavonetti, the engraver, who gave him lessons both in drawing and Italian. He quickly established a reputation for accurate copying, and was commissioned to visit Castle Howard, in Yorkshire, to copy the *Three Mary's*. He died there before completing his commission.

Victor William Hobson: Portrait of an old man, 1887. Oil 20×15½. *Darlington Art Gallery.*

HOLE, Henry Fulke Plantagenet Woolcomb (c.1781-c.1830)

Wood engraver. He was the son of a Captain in the Lancashire Militia, and served an apprenticeship with Thomas Bewick (q.v.), from 1795 until 1801. On completing his apprenticeship he left for Liverpool, taking with him a letter of introduction from Bewick to a picture merchant in the town, remarking: "The bearer of this my late pupil – Mr. Henry Hole – intends to begin business in Liverpool. I hope, from his sobriety and attention, that he will, when more settled, make a Figure in the line of his profession". Hole, who had cut a few engravings for Bewick's "Birds", before his departure from NEWCASTLE, was moderately successful at Liverpool, where he was patronised by several leading local men, and even called on Bewick to help him complete one particularly large commission. He also became a member of the Liverpool Academy, and at its exhibition in 1814, contributed: *An Attempt to restore the Old Method of Cross-lining on Wood*. He later inherited a large estate in Devon, his sudden good fortune leading him to give up wood engraving, and take to a life of drinking and self indulgence. He cut illustrations for several works in his brief career as a professional wood engraver, among these Ackerman's *Religious Emblems*, 1809.

HOLMES, Charles Clement (1852-1932)

Amateur architectural and antiquarian draughtsman. Holmes was born at Wentworth, Yorkshire, the son of a curate and received his education at Oxford, and later Manchester. At the age of seventeen he joined the drawing office staff of the iron works at CONSETT, remaining there for seven years before moving to HEXHAM, where he set up practice as an architect. He had been interested in architecture and archaeology from an early age, and had become particularly fond of HEXHAM on visits to the town from CONSETT. HEXHAM remained his home and business base for most of his life, and here he took a special interest in the Abbey, serving for many years as architect to the building, and writing and illustrating several works on its history, notable among which was his *The Abbey of St. Andrew, Hexham*, 1888, described by William Greenwell as "the grandest and most exhaustive illustration of an ecclesiastical establishment which has been published in England". The restoration of the Abbey is generally regarded as his most important work as an architect. In his later years he was associated with William Henry Knowles (q.v.), in his architectural and antiquarian work. He died at GATESHEAD.

HOLMES, Sheriton (1829-1900)

Amateur landscape painter in watercolour; antiquarian draughtsman. Holmes was born at SOUTH SHIELDS, and following his education at Wharfedale in Yorkshire, was articled to John Bourne, civil engineer and land agent of NEWCASTLE. While working with Bourne he surveyed several important sections of railway line in the North East of England. After serving his time he became connected with a number of other railway enterprises throughout the North of England, then went

to work in London, where he continued his railway work. On his return to the North East he became responsible for several major projects, mainly associated with the construction of shipbuilding and repair facilities on Tyneside, and served as resident engineer to the Border Counties Railway Line. Throughout his professional career as a civil engineer Holmes maintained a strong interest in antiquarian matters, and contributed many articles and sketches to the publications of the Society of Antiquaries, NEWCASTLE, also serving as treasurer for some years. He also took an interest in artistic activities in the city, and was a founder member of the Arts Association, NEWCASTLE, as well as an exhibitor in 1881 and 1882. He was responsible for writing and illustrating several publications associated with old buildings on Tyneside, amongst these *The Walls of Newcastle*, 1895, and with Heslop, *A Short Guide to the Castle and Black Gate*, 1899. Some of his drawings were issued as lithographs by Akerman of London. Newcastle University Library has a copy of Mackenzie's *History of Newcastle*, containing six watercolour, twenty sepia, and three black and white drawings, of NEWCASTLE, executed in the last twenty years of his life. Represented: Laing A.G., Newcastle.

HORSLEY, Thomas John (1795-1844)

Miniature painter. Born at SUNDERLAND, Horsley practised as a painter of portrait miniatures in London from his early twenties. He exhibited five works at the Royal Academy between 1820 and 1833, the first of which was a self portrait; the last: *Portrait of a gentleman*. He also in this period exhibited one work at the New Water Colour Society (later the Royal Institute of Painters in Water Colours). It is believed that he died in London.

*HORTON, George Edward (1859-1950)

Marine, coastal and landscape painter in oil and watercolour; illustrator; etcher. Horton was born at NORTH SHIELDS, the son of a butcher. When he left school he became a delivery boy for his father, but spent every spare moment drawing. One day his mother found him drawing an animal skull which he had borrowed, and disgustedly asked him to leave the family home. Then aged about seventeen, he moved in with a relative, and deciding to become a full-time professional artist, produced his first significant work in watercolour and pencil. He first exhibited his work in 1881, showing his watercolour: *Harrowed Fields*, at the Arts Association, NEWCASTLE. He again exhibited at the Association in the following year, then in 1884 exhibited his first work at the Bewick Club, NEWCASTLE; an oil entitled: *Morning Light*. He continued to exhibit at the Bewick Club over the next eight years, and encouraged by older artists such as Robert F. Watson (q.v.), and Henry Hetherington Emmerson (q.v.), made rapid progress as a painter. Towards the end of this period, however, he became increasingly interested in producing drawings for illustration, achieving his first success in this field with the publication in 1892, of *South Shields: A Gossiping Guide*, written by his friend, art writer Aaron Watson. In that year also he was commissioned to supply his first illustrations for *The Banks O' Tyne: A*

George Edward Horton: On the beach at Scheveningen.
Watercolour 20×14. *Dean Gallery.*

Christmas Annual, published by the *South Shields Daily Gazette*, subsequently illustrating its 1893 and 1894 numbers entirely himself. About 1895 he decided to move to SOUTH SHIELDS, and from there in 1896 sent his first work for exhibition at the Royal Academy: *The Fish Quay, North Shields*. It would appear that he made his first sketching trip to Holland in the following year, later preparing an illustrated article on his experiences, which was published in ''The Studio'', Volume II, 1897. In 1902, and having by then exhibited his work widely in England, Horton sent his first work to the Royal Scottish Academy. Three years later, and still living at SOUTH SHIELDS, he sent his first work to the Artists of the Northern Counties exhibitions at the Laing Art Gallery, NEWCASTLE, showing his *On the beach at Scheveningen,#* and *Autumn*. In 1918, and with the encouragement of the Laing Art Gallery's Curator, C. Bernard Stevenson, Horton left SOUTH SHIELDS, and settled in London. Here he quickly established a demand for his work, helped by one-man exhibitions at the Greatorex Gallery in 1922, and the Fine Arts Society in 1927. Throughout his early years in London he continued to make regular trips to Holland, and in 1921 made his only trip to Venice, where he made a large number of pencil sketches, and a few watercolours.

Horton exhibited his work until late in his life, showing examples at the Royal Academy, the Royal Scottish Academy, the Royal Institute of Painters in Water Colours, the Paris Salon, the International

Society of Aquarellists, and at many leading London and provincial galleries. He enjoyed several exhibitions of his work in Holland, and in 1934 shared a loan exhibition at the Laing Art Gallery, NEWCASTLE, with Francis Thomas Carter (q.v.), Thomas Bowman Garvie (q.v.), and John Falconar Slater (q.v.). While obviously infatuated with the scenery around Rotterdam and Dordrecht for much of his life, Horton never forgot his native Northumbria, and, indeed, every one of his Royal Academy exhibits 1930-38, portrayed subjects from the area. His Academy exhibit of 1930 was entitled: *Winter in Newcastle upon Tyne;* that of 1938: *The Fish Quay, North Shields*. He also retained many contacts among artist friends, particularly Joseph Henry Kirsop (q.v.), with whom he shared a deep interest in the art of etching, and with whom he corresponded for many years on this subject. Following his last showing of work at the Royal Academy in 1938, he exhibited almost exclusively at the Artists of the Northern Counties exhibitions, showing his last works in the year before his death. Following the bombing of his London studio in 1940, he spent five years at NEWCASTLE. At the end of the Second World War, however, he returned to the capital, dying there in 1950, at the age of ninety. Horton was one of the most individual Northumbrian watercolourists working in the 20th century, and exhibited his work for a longer period than any other artist from the area; a total of sixty-eight years. South Shields Public Libraries held major exhibitions of his work in the year following his death, and in the centenary year of his birth. Important exhibitions of his work were held at the Moss Galleries, HEXHAM, and the Laing Art Gallery, NEWCASTLE, in 1982. Represented: British Museum; Laing A.G., Newcastle; North Tyneside Public Libraries; Shipley A.G., Gateshead; South Shields Museum & A.G.

HOWEY, John William (1873-1938)

Amateur landscape, coastal and genre painter in oil, watercolour and pastel. Howey was born at WEST HARTLEPOOL (now HARTLEPOOL), and trained for some time at the local School of Art. Lacking confidence in his ability to succeed as a professional artist, however, he joined the West Hartlepool Gas & Water Company, eventually rising to the position of Head Collector. He maintained a lifelong interest in painting, and was accepted as the equal of many professional artists. He built a studio at the top of his house, at which he painted alongside many now well known artists, including Rowland Hill, and was particularly fond of painting along the Yorkshire coast in the company of Hill, Mark Senior and Florence Hess. Runswick Bay and Staithes were among his favourite subjects, but he also painted along the Scottish coast, and produced a large number of Northumbrian landscapes, genre works, and portraits. He is known to have exhibited his work outside Northumbria on only one occasion, this being at the Royal Institute of Oil Painters in 1923, but he was a regular exhibitor at the Artists of the Northern Counties exhibitions at the Laing Art Gallery, NEWCASTLE, from 1909 until his death, and also showed work at the Gray Art Gallery, WEST HARTLEPOOL, enjoying a special one-man show there in 1925. This exhibition contained some thirty works in oil, including his Royal Institute of Oil Painters' exhibit of 1923, and two works said to have been exhibited at the Royal Academy in 1924 and 1925, but of which no records exist. He died at HARTLEPOOL. His son, Robert Leslie Howey (q.v.) was a talented professional artist. Represented: Gray A.G. & Museum, Hartlepool; Pannett A.G., Whitby.

HOWEY, Robert Leslie (1900-1981)
Landscape, coastal and portrait painter in oil, watercolour and pastel; linocut artist. The son of John William Howey (q.v.), he was born at WEST HARTLEPOOL (now HARTLEPOOL), and studied at the local School of Art before practising as a professional artist in the town. In his youth he frequently accompanied his father on family holidays to Runswick Bay and Whitby, on the Yorkshire coast, and in this way became acquainted with several of the well known artists then working in these areas. He exhibited his work at the Royal Scottish Academy, the Redfern Gallery, London, and at various provincial public and private galleries, including among the former, the Laing Art Gallery, NEWCASTLE, whose Artists of the Northern Counties exhibitions he contributed to for many years. A one-man exhibition of his work was staged at the Gray Art Gallery, WEST HARTLEPOOL, in 1949, at which a large number of his watercolours, pastels, and lino-cuts were shown. Howey was one of the first British artists to produce significant work in the last named medium. He died at SEATON CAREW. Represented: Gray A.G. & Museum, Hartlepool.

*HUDSON, John (1829-c.1896)
Marine painter in oil and watercolour. Hudson was born at SUNDERLAND, the son of mariner James Hudson. At the age of fourteen he was apprenticed as a shipwright, but by the time he was sixteen he was already producing marine studies such as his *Launch of the*
'*Polka*', *1841* (painted from memory), in the National Maritime Museum, albeit with little accomplishment. He remained a shipwright until after his marriage in 1851, painting ship portraits in his spare time, but in 1880, and now having moved from the Monkwearmouth to the Bishopwearmouth district of the town, he was describing himself as a marine artist. Hudson painted ship portraits well into the 1890's, one of his latest dated works being his oil: *2nd Royal Yacht, Victoria & Albert, Spithead*, 1895.‡ He died at SUNDERLAND. Represented: National Maritime Museum; Sunderland A.G.

HUDSON, R. M. (1899- after 1956)
Amateur landscape and coastal painter in oil. Hudson was a builder at SUNDERLAND who painted in his spare time, and exhibited his work with the art club in the town. His *North Dock, Sunderland*, 1955, is in the collection of Sunderland Art Gallery.

HUMBLE, Stephen (1793-1853)
Landscape, figure, portrait and flower painter in oil and watercolour; miniature painter; draughtsman; drawing master. He was born at NEWCASTLE, the son of Edward Humble, bookseller, stationer and circulating library owner, and the grandson of engraver Joseph Barber, Senior (q.v.). He began his career in art as an engraver in London, but by 1819 had returned to NEWCASTLE where he established a picture gallery, and began describing himself as "miniature painter and engraver." His father died in 1820, and when the business was later sold off, he led a precarious existence, advertising himself variously as bookseller, hatter and picture dealer, and evidently painting theatrical portraits, for he showed four such works at the First Exhibition of the Northumberland Institution for the Promotion of the Fine Arts, NEWCASTLE, in 1822. He was still at NEWCASTLE when he showed his copy of *The Death of Wolfe*, at the Institution in 1823, but when he next

John Hudson: 2nd Yacht, "Victoria & Albert", Spithead, 1895. Oil 24×36. *Simon Carter Gallery.*

93

exhibited at the Institution in 1826 he was practising at ALNWICK as a drawing master, having left NEWCASTLE two years previously as a bankrupt. He exhibited at the Institution in 1827, while still showing his address as ALNWICK, but when he next exhibited at NEWCASTLE in 1831, showing his *Head of Walter Scott*; *Varieties of Dahlia*; *Varieties of Camellia Japonica*; *Group of Shells*, and *View of Alnwick Castle*, at the Northern Academy, he was practising at Edinburgh. His movements over the next sixteen years are uncertain. By 1848, however, he was practising at DARLINGTON, evidently spending several years in the town, for close to his death he produced what is today his best known work: *St. Cuthbert's Church, Darlington*. This work was drawn on the stone by Thomas Picken, and published as a large lithograph in the year following Humble's death at Scarborough, North Yorkshire.

HUMBLE, Stephen (1812-1858)
Portrait painter in oil. He was born at NEWCASTLE, and did not become a professional artist until he had spent some years working as a bricklayer, like his father. Legend has it that while he was working on structural alterations to the property of John Balmbra, the town's music hall proprietor, Balmbra saw some of Humble's sketches and was so impressed that a commission to paint Balmbra's portrait resulted. Following this evidently successful venture, Humble received many other portrait commissions in the town, eventually including amongst his sitters some of its leading citizens. He exhibited his work sparingly, showing a *Portrait of a Gentleman* at the 1843 exhibition in NEWCASTLE of the North of England Society for the Promotion of the Fine Arts, and two further portraits at its 1850 exhibition. He lived and worked in the town's Brunswick Place for most of his professional life, and died there at the age of forty-six, when by all accounts he was at the height of his powers as a portrait painter. The Literary and Philosophical Society, NEWCASTLE, has his portrait of the Rev. William Turner.

HUNTER, Abraham (d. 1799)
Engraver. This engraver practised at NEWCASTLE in the late 18th century, following an apprenticeship with Ralph Beilby (q.v.), and Thomas Bewick (q.v.), c. 1778-84. The brother of William Nicholson (q.v.), was taught engraving by Hunter, and while Robert Johnson (q.v.), was working at NEWCASTLE, after his apprenticeship to Bewick, he made a drawing of the bridge at SUNDERLAND, which he engraved with Hunter.

*HUTTON, Thomas Swift (fl. 1865-1935)
Landscape and coastal painter in watercolour. Hutton's place of birth is not known, but is believed to have been Glasgow, as it was from this city that he sent his first work for public exhibition in 1887. His work is well known in Northumbria for its portrayal of a wide variety of local beauty spots, predominantly along the coastline, and up various river valleys. He also exhibited his work in Northumbria, in addition to sending work to the Royal Academy in 1895, 1898 and 1899, and the Royal Scottish Academy, and various London and provincial galleries between 1887 and 1906. His Royal Academy exhibits comprised: *A peep on the River Derwent*, sent from NEWCASTLE in 1895, and *St. Abb's Head, North East Coast* (1898), and *The Glories of departing day – Needles Eye* (1899), sent from his home for a number of years at the turn of the century, Hoylake in Cheshire. He exhibited his work regularly at the Bewick Club, NEWCASTLE, in the 1890's, and is believed to have returned to the city following his sojourn at Hoylake, to continue practising in the area until about 1935. Many of his works were painted on small boards which are said to have come from shirt boxes. Represented: Shipley A.G., Gateshead; South Shields Museum & A.G.

Thomas Swift Hutton: Durham. Watercolour 15×20. *Dean Gallery.*

94

IONS (I'ONS), Algernon (c.1860- after 1910)

Landscape painter in oil and watercolour. He was born at NEWCASTLE, the son of Walter J. Ions, organist at St. Nicholas' Church, in the town. He first began exhibiting his work at the Bewick Club, NEWCASTLE, showing a number of Northumbrian and Irish landscapes between 1890 and 1900. He later moved to London, where he exhibited one work at the Royal Academy in 1910: *A fishing haven in Cornwall*.

IRELAND, Mrs. Jennie Moulding (d.1945)

Amateur landscape and portrait painter in oil and watercolour. This artist painted at NORTH SHIELDS in the early years of this century, contributing one work to the Artists of the Northern Counties exhibition at the Laing Art Gallery, NEWCASTLE, in 1913. She later moved to SOUTH SHIELDS, from which in 1942, 1944 and 1945, she again sent work to the Artists of the Northern Counties exhibitions. These works included: *Self Portrait* (1942); *Lillian* (1944), and *Seascape* (1945). Her works: *The Island, Marsden*, and *Thrift on the Cliffs –*

Frenchman's Bay, were bequeathed to South Shields Public Library & Museum in 1952, by her husband David Ireland.

*IRVING, William (1866-1943)

Portrait, landscape and genre painter in oil and watercolour; illustrator. Born at Ainstable, Cumberland, the son of a farmer, Irving moved with his parents to Tyneside in his infancy, and later attended the School of Art, at NEWCASTLE, under William Cosens Way (q.v.). At the end of his tuition he was recommended by Cosens Way for a position with the *Newcastle Weekly Chronicle* as an illustrator, and he remained in this occupation for many years while building up a reputation as a portrait painter. He also in this period became a member of the Bewick Club, NEWCASTLE, showing at its exhibition in 1891 his first important landscape with figures: *The End of the Season*. Later he began exhibiting his work at the Royal Academy, showing his *Ducks and Darlings*, in 1898, and his *Happy Days*, in 1901. In 1903 he painted what is today regarded as one of the North East of England's most popular and famous paintings: *Blaydon Races – a study from life*.# It is said of this painting (which now hangs in the County Hotel, NEWCASTLE) that when it was exhibited in the window of an art dealer's shop at NEWCASTLE it attracted the attention of such a large crowd that the manager was

William Irving: Blaydon Races – a study from life. Oil 38×56. *Scottish & Newcastle Breweries.*

95

asked by the police to draw the blinds.

While employed by the *Chronicle*, and its separate publication: *Monthly Chronicle of North Country Lore and Legend* (later reprinted in five volumes covering its life from 1887-1891), Irving was frequently called upon to prepare portraits of local celebrities as pen and ink drawings, for line reproduction. Many of these assignments subsequently led to portrait commissions in oil, from either the sitters, or other interested parties. Shortly after painting his *Blaydon Races* he was commissioned to paint two portraits of Newcastle M.P. and newspaper proprietor Joseph Cowen (one for the *Chronicle*, and one for Cowen's family). On receiving payment for this commission he decided that he would increasingly look to portraiture for his living, and further to enhance his reputation in this field he would study in Paris. About 1905 he left NEWCASTLE and enrolled as a pupil in the Academie Julian, where he had amongst his tutors some of the leading French painters of the day. Returning to Tyneside about 1908, he resumed his profession with renewed vigour and, according to contemporary accounts, with a marked improvement in his skill. Irving painted portraits until close to his death, but with the growing competition of photography found it increasingly difficult to find sitters. In his final years he frequently turned to picture restoration as a source of income, and was responsible for extensive work on the painting by Luca Giordano in St. Andrew's Church, NEWCASTLE. After last exhibiting at the Royal Academy in 1908, Irving mainly exhibited

at the Artists of the Northern Counties exhibitions at the Laing Art Gallery, NEWCASTLE. He died at NEWCASTLE. His son, STANLEY ROLLINGS IRVING, was a keen amateur painter in oil and watercolour. Represented: Carlisle A.G.; Laing A.G., Newcastle.

IRWIN, Annie L. (d.1894)
Flower, landscape and figure painter in oil and watercolour. This artist practised at SUNDERLAND in the late 19th century, and first began exhibiting publicly when she sent two works to the Arts Association exhibition, NEWCASTLE, in 1882, entitled *Rose of Sharon*, and *Autumn Leaves*. She was a regular exhibitor at the Bewick Club, NEWCASTLE from 1884 until her death, also sending one work to the Royal Academy in 1890: *Chrysanthemums*, and showing her work on several occasions at the Royal Institute of Oil Painters, the Society of Women Artists, and various provincial exhibitions. Her Bewick Club exhibits included flower studies, British and continental landscapes, and occasional genre works. She last exhibited with the Club in the year of her death at SUNDERLAND, when her contributions were entitled: *A Normandy Peasant*, and *Pink Peonie Rose*.

*JACK, Richard, R.A., R.I., R.M.S., R.P. (1866-1952)
Portrait, figure and landscape painter in oil and watercolour. Born at SUNDERLAND, Jack was educated at York, and later studied at the city's School of Art, where he won a national scholarship to South Kensington. While at South Kensington he gained the gold medal travelling scholarship, afterwards studying at the Academie Julian, and at Calarossi's, Paris. He first began exhibiting his work publicly while still studying in Paris, showing his *Portrait of a Lady*, at the Royal Academy, in 1893. Two years later he settled in London, and resumed exhibiting at the Academy, showing more than 160 works there between 1895 and 1951. During this period he also exhibited at the Royal Scottish Academy, the Royal Institute of Painters in Water Colours, the Glasgow Institute of Fine Arts, and at many leading London and provincial galleries.

While practising in London as a portrait painter, Jack handled a number of commissions in his native Northumbria, and was an occasional exhibitor in the area, showing examples of his work at the Artists of the Northern Counties exhibitions at the Laing Art Gallery, NEWCASTLE, and the North East Coast Exhibition, Palace of Arts, 1929. He also achieved considerable distinction in his profession, becoming a member of the Royal Miniature Society in 1896, a member of the Royal Society of Portrait Painters in 1900, an associate of the Royal Academy in 1914, a member of the Royal Institute of Painters in Water Colours in 1917, and a full Royal Academician in 1920. Several of his works were purchased for public collections, notably his *Re-*

Richard Jack: Loup Scar, Wharfedale. Oil 49½×39½. *Gray Art Gallery & Museum.*

hearsal with Nikisch, for the Tate Gallery, through the Chantrey Bequest, in 1912. In 1930 he visited Canada, where he painted several landscapes, among other subjects, and in 1932 he decided to move permanently to that country, remaining based at Montreal until his death in 1952. Among his last exhibits were two portraits shown at the Royal Academy in 1951, and his landscape in oil: *Anglesey*, which was included in the "Contemporary Artists of Durham County" exhibition, staged at the Shipley Art Gallery, GATESHEAD, in that year, in connection with the Festival of Britain.

Jack was Northumbria's most successful portrait painter of this century, and included some of the most famous men of his day among his sitters. He received many medals for his work in portraiture, including several in his student days in Paris; the silver medal for portraiture at the Paris International Exhibition in 1900, and the silver medal at Pittsburgh, U.S.A., in 1914, for his *String Quartette*. Like many well known portrait painters, however, Jack was also an able painter of other subjects, his landscape work, for instance, bearing favourable comparison with that of many professionals in this field.# Represented: Tate Gallery; Gray A.G. & Museum, Hartlepool; Laing A.G., Newcastle; Sunderland A.G.

JACKSON, John (1801-1848)
Wood engraver; draughtsman. He was born at OVINGHAM, and is said to have worked for George Armstrong (q.v.), and James Walker (q.v.), at NEWCASTLE, before joining Thomas Bewick (q.v.), as an apprentice at the age of twenty-three. He remained with Bewick only a year, however, leaving NEWCASTLE following a dispute with his master to work in London under former Bewick apprentice William Harvey (q.v.). Here he worked principally as a wood engraver, reproducing the work of others. His first work of note in this field was for *Northcote's Fables*, 1828, while from 1832 he worked for Charles Knight on the *Penny Magazine*. He later prepared wood engravings for Lane's *Arabian Night's*, 1849-51, but is now best remembered for *A Treatise on Wood Engraving*, 1839, which he prepared with W. A. Chatto. Some excellent examples of his work may be seen in this book, including a portrait of Bewick from memory. According to Robert Robinson in his *Thomas Bewick – his life and times*, 1887, Jackson "drew and painted domestic subjects with much originality of feeling, and he always had a strong desire to be a painter". He died in London. His younger brother, Mason Jackson (q.v.), was also a wood engraver, in addition to painting landscapes, and working as an illustrator.

JACKSON, Mason (1819-1903)
Landscape painter in oil and watercolour; wood engraver; illustrator. He was born at OVINGHAM, and studied wood engraving under his brother, John Jackson (q.v.), in London, before taking up the profession in the capital. A man of miscellaneous talents, he also executed illustrations for books and periodicals, and between 1856 and 1879 exhibited two works at the Royal Academy, and some fourteen works at various London exhibitions. In 1860 he became Art Editor of

the *Illustrated London News*, succeeding to the editorship of the paper in 1875. He is credited with being the first historian of illustrated journalism. Jackson's two Royal Academy exhibits were entitled: *Black Gang, Isle of Wight*, (1858), and *Warkworth Castle, Northumberland*, (1859). He illustrated *Walton's Compleat Angler*, and *Ministering Children*, and contributed illustrations to *Cassell's Illustrated Family Paper*, 1857, and the *Illustrated London News*, 1876-78. He died in London.

JACKSON, Robert Story (c.1880-c.1945)
Amateur landscape and coastal painter in watercolour. Jackson was born on Tyneside and took up a career in commerce at NEWCASTLE on leaving school. He was a keen painter in watercolour from his youth, and is believed to have received some tuition in the use of this medium from Thomas Swift Hutton (q.v.), before becoming a regular exhibitor of his work at the Bewick Club, NEWCASTLE, and later the Artists of the Northern Counties exhibitions at the city's Laing Art Gallery. Jackson rose to the position of manager in the company at NEWCASTLE in which he was employed, then moving to WHITLEY BAY after the First World War, he became a timber merchant. It is believed that he died at WHITLEY BAY during the Second World War.

JAMESON, Thomas (fl.18th century)
Engraver. Jameson practised as an engraver at NEWCASTLE in the late 18th century, and was said by Thomas Bewick (q.v.), in his autobiographical *Memoir*, to have "had the whole stroke of business in Newcastle", when, "having been detected in committing a Forgery upon the old Bank . . . left the town". Jameson's misfortune made way for Bewick's master, Ralph Beilby (q.v.), enabling him to "get forward in his business unopposed by anyone in Newcastle". Jameson's work included the engraving of several landscape and architectural views such as his *Tanfield Arch*, and a portrait of Dr. Isaac Watts, which was prefixed to an edition of the *Psalms of David*, published by William Charnley of NEWCASTLE. In collaboration with Whitehead, of NEWCASTLE, he published in 1776 an "Explanation of the Arms of the Incorporated Companies of Newcastle".

JARVIS, John Wesley (1780-1840)
Portrait painter in oil; miniaturist; engraver. He was born at SOUTH SHIELDS, a nephew of John Wesley, the famous evangelist. At the age of five he emigrated to Philadelphia, U.S.A., joining there his father, who had left SOUTH SHIELDS some years earlier. He was apprenticed as a youth to an engraver, and moved with his master to New York in 1802 before setting up his own engraving establishment. While working in New York he learned of the success in the field of portraiture of another immigrant artist called Martin, and decided himself to become a professional portrait painter. He met with immediate success in his new profession, but contemporaries recorded him as "extravagant, irascible, and unpredictable". He made several trips to the south of the U.S.A., with his pupil, Henry Inman, and is said

on one occasion to have finished six portraits in a week. Following his final visit south he received a commission which made him famous as a painter on the western seaboard of the continent. He was asked by the City of New York authorities to paint a series of full-length portraits of American military and naval heroes. Meanwhile, he continued to live in New York, and to pursue his interests in engraving. His success in portrait painting and engraving was short lived, however, and he died in extreme poverty. Dunlap, in his *A History of the Rise and Progress of the Arts of Design in the United States*, 1834, described Jarvis as an artist of "astonishing powers, but unfortunately of the most depraved habits". He was also described as one of the best portrait painters of his day, and eccentric, witty and convivial. His work is well represented in galleries and museums in the U.S.A.

JEFFERSON, Charles George (1831-1902)

Landscape and coastal painter in oil and watercolour. Jefferson was born at SOUTH SHIELDS, the son of an old and respected local family. A man of independent means, he was able to devote himself to drawing and painting from his youth without any of the difficulties normally attendant on a career in art, and quickly developed into an accomplished artist. It appears that he first exhibited his work while living at Glasgow in 1880, sending examples to the Glasgow Institute of Fine Arts, and the Royal Scottish Academy. He continued to exhibit in Scotland following his return to SOUTH

Isa Jobling: A Cottage Garden. Oil 11×7. *Dean Gallery.*

SHIELDS, also sending work to the town's Art Club exhibitions of 1892, 1893 and 1894, and to the Bewick Club, NEWCASTLE. He last exhibited in the year of his death. He died at SOUTH SHIELDS. Represented: South Shields Museum & A.G.

JEFFERSON, John (fl. late 18th, early 19th cent.)

Portrait and landscape painter in oil. This artist practised in Northumbria in the early 19th century, and is first recorded practising at St. Nicholas' Churchyard, NEWCASTLE, in 1811. He was practising at NORTH SHIELDS in 1818, when the *Northumberland & Newcastle Monthly Magazine* recorded the birth of his son on January 17th of that year, but by 1822, and exhibiting at the Northumberland Institution for the Promotion of the Fine Arts, NEWCASTLE, he had moved to SUNDERLAND. He exhibited at the Institution throughout its early life, showing a number of portraits of sitters from SUNDERLAND, and in 1824, a *Landscape Study*, but does not appear to have exhibited subsequently. Sunderland Art Gallery has his portrait of Robert Thompson, dated 1825.

JENNINGS, Charles Henry (c.1875-c.1940)

Landscape, genre and portrait painter in oil and watercolour; lithographer. Jennings was born at NEWCASTLE, the son of a builder from Gloucester, and received his education at the city's Rutherford College. He appears to have become a largely self-taught artist before becoming a lithographer, painter, and producer of illuminated addresses at NEWCASTLE, and exhibiting his work at Rutherford College Art Club, and later the city's Laing Art Gallery, to whose Artists of the Northern Counties exhibitions he was a regular contributor, 1909-1936. He died at NEWCASTLE.

JEVONS, Mrs. Louisa E. (fl. late 19th, early 20th cent.)

Miniature painter. She contributed two works to the Royal Academy, and one work to the Royal Miniature Society, in the period 1893-1901, while living at DURHAM. Her two Royal Academy exhibits were entitled: *Mrs. Fitzhugh Whitehouse*, and *Principal Jevons, M.A.* It is believed that she was the wife of the latter, who was head of a college at DURHAM.

*JOBLING, Mrs. Isa (née Thompson) (1850-1926)

Landscape and genre painter in oil and watercolour. She was born at SUNDERLAND, and appears to have become a largely self-taught artist before practising in the town. She first began to exhibit her work publicly when she sent her *Study of a Head* to the "Gateshead Fine Art & Industrial Exhibition", in 1883. In 1884, and now having moved to CULLERCOATS, she sent four works to the first exhibition of the Bewick Club, NEWCASTLE, these consisting of two oils and two watercolours. In 1885/6 she began exhibiting at the Suffolk Street Gallery, showing a watercolour: *Jack and His Mates*, and in 1892 she sent to the Royal Academy from her studio at NEWCASTLE, a work entitled: *Blossom*. She continued to exhibit at the Academy until 1912, also showing work at the Royal Scottish Academy, and at

Robert Jobling: Daddy's
Boat. Oil 12×18. *Dean
Gallery.*

various London and provincial exhibitions, including
the Artists of the Northern Counties exhibitions at the
Laing Art Gallery, NEWCASTLE, to which she contributed from their inception in 1905, until her death. In
the middle 1890's she became the second wife of Robert
Jobling (q.v.), and thereafter signed her work using her
married name. Husband and wife frequently accompanied each other on painting expeditions, one of their
favourite haunts being the North Yorkshire fishing
village of Staithes. Here they painted many pictures
similar in subject matter to those which they both
produced at CULLERCOATS throughout their respective
careers. She died at WHITLEY BAY. Represented: Shipley
A.G., Gateshead.

JOBLING, Joseph (1870-1930)

Coastal, landscape and bird painter in oil and watercolour; draughtsman. One of the three sons of Robert
Jobling (q.v.), by his first wife, Jobling was born at
NEWCASTLE, and received some tuition from his father
before becoming a professional artist. He first began
exhibiting his work publicly at the Bewick Club, NEW-
CASTLE, following his family's move to WHITLEY BAY;
here he exhibited on several occasions alongside his
father choosing much the same subjects as Jobling,
Senior, and often displaying equal competence as an
artist. Later, however, he turned to photography as a
career, and after taking a studio at NEWCASTLE in the
early years of the century, he only painted in his spare
time. He was an occasional exhibitor at the Artists of
the Northern Counties exhibitions at the Laing Art
Gallery, NEWCASTLE, from 1908 until the death of his
father, but thereafter exhibited little. In his later life he
worked mainly in the area around his home at WHITLEY
BAY, handling technical photography, and producing a
large number of drawings and paintings of bird life. He

also painted several studies of the fish quay at NORTH
SHIELDS for illustrative purposes. He died at WHITLEY
BAY. His wife ELIZABETH JOBLING (née Ewen),
was also talented artistically, and was an accomplished
picture restorer. His stepmother was Isa Jobling (née
Thompson) (q.v.).

JOBLING, Robert (1841-1923)

Marine, landscape and figure painter in oil and watercolour; illustrator; art teacher. Jobling was born at
NEWCASTLE, the son of a glassmaker employed in the
glassworks of Sir Matthew White Ridley & Co., on the
banks of the Tyne. His first employment was alongside
his father, where he remained until the age of sixteen.
He next became a ship painter in the Tyne General
Ferry Company's yard on the Tyne, attending the art
classes of the Government School of Design in his spare
time. He rose to become foreman in the shipyard, but
became increasingly disillusioned with his occupation,
and decided to become a full-time professional artist.
The date at which he made this decision is unknown,
but by 1866 he was exhibiting a work entitled: *Sea
Piece*, at the "Exhibition of Paintings and other Works
of Art", at NEWCASTLE, following this with his *Shields
by Moonlight*, at the "Central Exchange News Room,
Art Gallery, and Polytechnic Exhibition", in the town,
in 1870. His work was included in several important
local exhibitions over the next few years, including the
exhibition of works by local painters, at the Central
Exchange Art Gallery, and the first exhibition of the
Arts Association, in 1878. By 1883 he had a studio in
Shakespeare Street, NEWCASTLE, and in this year sent
his first works to the Royal Academy, and the Suffolk
Street Gallery; an oil entitled: *Moonlight*, and a water-
colour: *North Sea Fishers*. He remained at Shakespeare
Street for more than eleven years, later moving to the

old Academy of Arts' building at Blackett Street, where he stayed until about three years before his death. He then began to paint at his home for many years, at WHITLEY BAY.

Jobling remained an exhibitor at the Royal Academy until 1911, also exhibiting his work at various London and provincial galleries, and for many years at the Bewick Club, NEWCASTLE, of which he was one of the founders, and later President. For the last eighteen years of his life he exhibited mainly at the Artists of the Northern Counties exhibitions at the Laing Art Gallery, NEWCASTLE, and as one of the founders and lifelong members of the city's Pen & Palette Club, his work inevitably appeared at various of its exhibitions. Two major exhibitions of his work were held in NEWCASTLE during his lifetime; one in 1899; the other just a few months before his death, at Armstrong College (later King's College; now Newcastle University), in honour of his great assistance in conducting its art classes. Jobling married twice, his second wife being the artist Isa Thompson (q.v.). Joseph Jobling (q.v.), a son by his first wife, was also artistically gifted. Most of Jobling's work was associated with the sea, and featured fishing boats, # fishermen and their activities, and figure studies, many of these works painted at CULLERCOATS, or at the North Yorkshire fishing village of Staithes. In addition to painting pictures of these subjects, however, he was also much interested in illustration, several of his drawings of the Tyne, and its shipping, appearing in books and periodicals. Examples of his work in illustration also appeared in *Wilson's Tales of the Borders*, and editions of Burns's poems. He died at WHITLEY BAY. Represented: Carlisle A.G.; Laing A.G., Newcastle; Shipley A.G., Gateshead.

JOHNSON, Alfred (d.1944)

Landscape painter in watercolour. This artist practised at SOUTH SHIELDS in the first half of the present century. He exhibited his work at the Artists of the Northern Counties exhibitions at the Laing Art Gallery, NEWCASTLE, in the later years of his life. His last work, shown in 1944, was bequeathed to South Shields Museum. This work was entitled: *Durham Cathedral*. He died at his home at SOUTH SHIELDS.

JOHNSON, James (d. before 1822)

Sculptor. This artist practised at STAMFORDHAM in the late 18th century, but from 1750 was mainly engaged in cutting stone figures for the battlements of the castle at ALNWICK. These figures were all life-size, and represented men in the act of defending the building with such arms as were then in use. Johnson began his work about 1750, and took twenty years to complete it.

JOHNSON, John (c.1769-1794)

Wood engraver; draughtsman. He was born at STANHOPE, in Weardale, and was apprenticed to Ralph Beilby (q.v.), and Thomas Bewick (q.v.), in their workshop at NEWCASTLE, in 1782. Bewick later wrote of Johnson, in his autobiographical *Memoir*: "John Johnson . . . we put to do engraving on Wood, as well as other kinds of work – I think he would have shone out in the former branch – but he died of a fever, at about the Age of 22 when only beginning to give great promise of his future excellence".‡ While working for Beilby and Bewick he prepared a design for *The Hermit at his Morning Devotion*, for *Poems of Goldsmith and Parnell*. Bewick engraved this design for the publication, which appeared in the year following Johnson's death. Some of the engravings in Bewick's *Birds* have been credited to Johnson by John Jackson (q.v.), in his book with W. A. Chatto: *A Treatise on Wood Engraving*, 1839. He died at NEWCASTLE. He was the cousin of Robert Johnson (q.v.).

‡ *See p. 195, "A Memoir of Thomas Bewick Written by Himself", edited and with an introduction by Iain Bain, Oxford University Press, 1975.*

Ralph Johnson: River Allen, near Staward. Watercolour 14×20. *Hexham Antiques.*

*JOHNSON, Ralph (1896-1980)

Landscape painter in oil and watercolour. Johnson was born at ANNFIELD PLAIN, near CONSETT, and was a builder by trade, who painted in his spare time. Until 1930 he painted in both oil and watercolour, but following this date he increasingly concentrated on watercolour alone. He exhibited his work for many years at the Artists of the Northern Counties exhibitions at the Laing Art Gallery, NEWCASTLE, and regularly showed his work with the Durham & District Artists Society, of which he was for some time vice-president. He painted mainly Northumbria, Lake District and Scottish scenes, many with outstanding accomplishment. He died at ANNFIELD PLAIN.

JOHNSON, Robert (1770-1796)

Landscape painter in watercolour; draughtsman; engraver. Born at SHOTLEY, near CONSETT, the son of a joiner and cabinet maker, Johnson is said to have shown such promise as an artist as a youth that his parents moved to GATESHEAD, where they thought his abilities could receive greater encouragement than in his native village. This story, like the one told of a lady at NEWCASTLE paying for his instruction in drawing at a local academy, must be treated with some reservations, however, if we are to believe the account of his training given in the autobiographical *Memoir* of Thomas Bewick (q.v.).‡ According to this account, Johnson through his mother's friendship with the Bewick family, was led to believe from his earliest years that he would one day become Bewick's apprentice. To equip himself for this day he therefore "at every opportunity kept closely employed in drawing". At thirteen, and although still too young to become an apprentice, he was taken into Bewick's home "till the proper time arrived". Curiously, this day did not arrive until some four years later, Johnson not becoming apprenticed to Bewick, and his partner Ralph Beilby (q.v.), until 23rd August, 1787. He then served his full seven years as an apprentice, during this period receiving special treatment from his masters because of his obvious aptitudes as an artist, and delicate health. "He was mostly employed in drawing", says Bewick, "& was also at intervals practising himself in the use of the graver & in etching on copper – but being very delicate in his health, we were carefull not to confine him too closely at any thing." Bewick next gives a detailed account of his training of Johnson, from copying his own designs, to colouring them, and concludes by stating that "He soon coloured them in a style superior to my hasty productions of that kind – indeed, in this way he became super-excellent, & as I conceived he could hardly be equalled, in his water coloured drawings of views & landscapes, by any artist . . .".

While still an apprentice, Johnson accumulated a portfolio of watercolours, some of which his masters though fit to sell to the Earl of Bute, for £30. This sum the partners retained on the grounds that they were the work of an apprentice, and therefore part of the business. Johnson did not agree, however, a lawsuit ensued, and rather unjustly in the light of Bewick's help to him in developing his undoubted talents as a watercolourist, he was allowed to claim the £30, while the partners paid the costs. After leaving Beilby and Bewick, Johnson took rooms in NEWCASTLE, and followed the business of copperplate engraver, but was seemingly unsuccessful. He executed several drawings of local architectural subjects, some of which he later engraved, notable among these being his famous *A North View of St. Nicholas' Church, c.1795*, for Joseph Whitfield's *Annual Ladies' Pocket Book*. In the summer of 1796 he was recommended by Messrs Morison & Son, publishers at Perth, Scotland, to make drawings of portraits by Jamesone, the "Scottish Vandyke", at Taymouth Castle, Kenmore, the seat of Lord Breadalbane. These were intended for Pinkerton's *Scottish Portraits* of 1799. Of the some nineteen copies of portraits by Jamesone required, Johnson had completed fifteen when he was taken ill with a fever. His illness was taken to be a form of madness, and he was bound with ropes and beaten. A passing doctor fortunately recognised his symptoms and attempted to give him proper treatment, but he died shortly afterwards.

Johnson's abilities as a watercolourist were second only to those of fellow Bewick apprentice Luke Clennell (q.v.), while in regard to his draughtsmanship Bewick once remarked to John Hancock (q.v.), that he could not draw out of perspective, so true was his eye. His work as an engraver though slight, was keenly appreciative of current techniques, and, indeed, he had very clear ideas as to how his copies of Jamesone's portraits should be handled. His contributions to Bewick's *Birds* is still a matter of debate, although much has been done by Iain Bain in recent years to clarify Johnson's likely involvement, notably in *The Watercolours & Drawings of Thomas Bewick and his Workshop Apprentices*, 1981. A tablet to Johnson's memory is situated in the exterior wall of the south transept of the Parish Church at OVINGHAM, in whose churchyard he is buried. He was the cousin of John Johnson (q.v.). Represented: Scottish National Portrait Gallery; Laing A.G., Newcastle; Natural History Society of Northumbria, Newcastle; Newcastle Central Library.

‡ *See pp. 196-9, "A Memoir of Thomas Bewick, Written by Himself", edited and with an introduction by Iain Bain, Oxford University Press, 1975.*

JOHNSON, Robert James, F.S.A. (1832-1892)

Architectural draughtsman. Johnson was born near DARLINGTON, and after showing an interest in following a career as an architect, was apprenticed to John Middleton in the town. On completing his apprenticeship he moved to NEWCASTLE to complete his studies. He first followed his profession in London, but returning to Northumbria a few years later, he practised at NORTH SHIELDS, and later NEWCASTLE, remaining at the latter for many years, and taking over with Thomas Austin, the practice of John Dobson (q.v.). Most of his career as an architect was occupied in designing churches, banks and offices. He exhibited several of his designs for churches at the Royal Academy between 1862 and 1887, including among these: *St. Hilda's Church, Whitby*, and *All Saints' Church, Gosforth, Newcastle*. He also wrote on architectural matters, and in 1861 published *Specimens of French Architecture*. He was especially interested in antiquarian matters, and was a Fellow of the Society of Antiquaries, London, and a member of the Society of Antiquaries, NEWCASTLE. He died at Tunbridge Wells, Kent. Hexham Abbey Museum has examples of his pen and ink drawings of the Abbey, prepared while he was architect to the building as a member of the practice headed by Charles Clement Holmes (q.v.).

JOHNSTON, Rev. George Liddell (1817-1902)

Draughtsman. Born at SUNDERLAND, Johnston studied at University College, DURHAM, before becoming ordained as a minister in 1849. In 1850 he left DURHAM, and began his ecclesiastical career in the Exeter Diocese, remaining there until 1856, when he left Britain to take up an appointment to the British Embassy in Vienna, until 1885. In 1892 he spent a holiday at Merano in the Italian Tyrol, and there produced a sketch book of drawings upon which his reputation as an artist almost entirely rests. This sketch book was not given much attention until 1969, when it was discovered in Vienna, but subsequent study of its contents has revealed an artist of extraordinarily grotesque vision, whose drawings are far from the restrained exaltations of nature which one might have expected from a clergyman. The drawings were exhibited by the Stone Gallery, NEWCASTLE, in 1970, and superbly introduced by proprietor Ronald Marshall in his exhibition catalogue. To him more than anyone else are we indebted for a glimpse of surely some of the strangest drawings produced by a Northumbrian artist: skeletons, three-

Francis W. Doyle Jones: South Africa, 1899-1902. Bronze 19 high. *Gray Art Gallery & Museum.*

headed men, animals – legendary and otherwise – with the heads of men; kings, queens and courtiers of bizarre appearance, and a pear dressed as a ballet dancer. Johnston died in London without, it seems, leaving us any examples of his work apart from his sketchbook. Represented: Shipley A.G., Gateshead.

*JONES, Francis W. Doyle, R.B.S. (1873-1938)

Sculptor. He was born at HARTLEPOOL, the son of a monumental sculptor, and studied under his father before attending the local School of Art. He later studied at Armstrong College (later King's College; now Newcastle University), and at the Royal College of Art, under Lanteri, before becoming a professional sculptor in London by the early years of the 20th century. Jones exhibited his work regularly at the Royal Academy throughout his professional career, showing some thirty works between 1903 and 1936. He also exhibited at the Royal Hibernian Academy, and at various London and provincial galleries, including among the latter the Laing Art Gallery, NEWCASTLE, whose Artists of the Northern Counties exhibitions he contributed to from their inception in 1905. His principal works were his war and other memorials for various parts of the British Empire, amongst these his South African War Memorial for the Ward Jackson Park at HARTLEPOOL, for which the town's Gray Art Gallery, has his original bronze statuette. # This gallery also has his relief panels: *Fame & Patriotism*, exhibited at the Royal Academy in 1903. Jones spent most of his professional life in London, travelling widely to carry out commissions for his memorial and portrait work. He was a member of the Royal Society of British Sculptors. Examples of his work may be seen in parks and other public places widely throughout the North East.

JONES, John Rock, Junior (c.1836- c.1898)

Landscape painter in watercolour; art teacher. He was born in the Isle of Man, the son of JOHN ROCK JONES, SENIOR, the portrait painter. His father some time later decided to move to Tyneside, where Jones Junior, was educated privately, and evidently showed an early inclination towards art by "copying pictures by Richardson, Copley Fielding, David Cox, and others, that were lent out by Mr. Kaye, artists' colourman and stationer, Blackett Street . . .". On completing his education he became an art teacher at NEWCASTLE, remaining in this profession until his death at FOREST HALL, near NEWCASTLE, about 1898. He was one of the first members of the Newcastle Life School, which later developed into the Bewick Club, NEWCASTLE, and served on the Club's art council for many years. He first began exhibiting his work publicly in 1866, when his *On the Wansbeck* was included in the "Exhibition of Paintings and other Works of Art", at the Town Hall, NEWCASTLE. He next exhibited at the Arts Association, and at the exhibition of works by local painters, at the Central Exchange Art Gallery, NEWCASTLE, in 1878, later becoming a regular exhibitor at the city's Bewick Club. Jones was the author of: *Groups for Still-Life Drawing and Painting*, and a series of papers called *Leisure-graphs, or Recollections of an Artist's Rambles.* He also delivered several lectures on popular art sub-

John Wilson Jowsey: "R.M.S. Mauretania" leaving the Tyne, 1907. Oil 24×48. *Port of Tyne Authority.*

jects, and in 1887 was elected a member of the Society of Science, Letters, and Art, London. He is believed to have exhibited outside Northumbria on only one occasion, this being when he sent two landscapes to Carlisle Art Gallery, in 1896.

JOPLING, Isaac, Senior (1752-1827)
Sculptor; marble mason. Born on Tyneside, Jopling became a successful marble mason who occasionally turned his hand to works of sculpture. He established a marble works at GATESHEAD in 1780, one of his later trade cards describing its activities as including the execution "in the best foreign, Irish, and British Marbles, CHIMNEY PIECES, MONUMENTS, GRAVE-STONES, TOMBS, ETC.". This trade card also bore replicas of both sides of the gold medal with which he was presented by the Society of Arts in 1810, for discovering in the Highlands of Scotland a variety of fine marbles. In his later years, and following the development in skill of his son and business partner, Isaac Jopling, Junior (q.v.), he took a lesser interest in the marble works, and sold books, and ran a circulating library from this establishment. A few days after his death, however, his son disposed of this side of the business. Jopling's work embraced a large number of monuments and tablets for churches throughout Northumbria. He was for some years in partnership with his brother, John Jopling (q.v.). He died at GATESHEAD.

JOPLING, Isaac, Junior (c.1790- after 1842)
Sculptor; marble mason. He was born at GATESHEAD, the son of Isaac Jopling, Senior (q.v.), and was apprenticed to his father before becoming a partner in the family mason's works in the town. In the latter capacity he worked frequently with his father in the production of monuments and tablets for churches throughout Northumbria. There is, however, reason to suppose that he was a much more accomplished sculptor than his father, for in 1811 he was presented with the silver medal of the Society of Arts, for his plaster cast of *The Dying Gladiator*, and occasionally exhibited his work. One of his exhibits was the *Original Bust of a Child*, which he showed at the Northumberland Institution for the Promotion of the Fine Arts, NEWCASTLE, in 1823.

JOPLING, John (died c.1810)
Sculptor; marble mason; miniature painter. He was born at GATESHEAD, and was for many years partner with his brother Isaac Jopling, Senior (q.v.), in the Jopling marble works in the town. In 1806 he decided to branch out on his own, moving to NEWCASTLE, where he possibly took on Richard George Davies (q.v.) as an apprentice or helper during his few years in business there. Eneas Mackenzie in his *History of Newcastle*, Volume II, page 589, says of him: "The Late John Jopling, of Newcastle, and predecessor of Mr. Davis, marble mason, was a good sculptor, and had a fine taste for miniature painting." It is believed that he died at NEWCASTLE, his widow carrying on his business for some years following his death.

*JOWSEY, John Wilson (1884-1963)
Portrait and landscape painter in oil; muralist. He was born at ASHINGTON, the son of a shipwright and keen amateur sailor, and studied art at Edinburgh, Paris, and Newlyn, Cornwall, before practising as an artist in Northumbria, and later London. In the early part of his career he painted at ASHINGTON and NORTH SHIELDS, shortly after the First World War opening a studio at NEWCASTLE, where he painted portraits of leading Tyneside shipowners. Among these shipowners he found a patron in Lord Kirkley, chairman of the Tyne Improvement Commission, who, in addition to having his portrait painted by the artist, obtained a commission for him to paint a series of nine murals for the frieze of the Commission's headquarters at NEWCASTLE.# The murals were unveiled in November, 1927, and in the following year Jowsey moved to London, where he followed the profession of portrait painter until his death. Many notable personalities of his day were among his sitters, including Sir Winston Churchill, painted for an American patron while Churchill was serving as Prime Minister 1951-5. Jowsey first exhibited his work at the Artists of the Northern Counties exhibitions at the Laing Art Gallery, NEWCASTLE, later exhibiting at the Royal Society of British Artists, the Royal Cambrian Academy, the Royal Portrait Society and the Paris Salon. He died in London.

John Andrews Kidd: Portrait of Thomas Bewick, after Miss Kirkley. Engraving $3\frac{7}{8} \times 3$. *Private collection.*

KEEDY, Elizabeth (c.1870- after 1908)
Landscape and coastal painter in oil and watercolour; art teacher. Born at SOUTH SHIELDS, she served for some years as a teacher at the town's School of Art, painting in her spare time. South Shields Museum & Art Gallery has her *Bent's Cottage*, 1908, and an undated view of SEATON SLUICE, near BLYTH, presented by her father.

KELL, Robert John (d.1934)
Amateur landscape painter in oil, watercolour and pastel. He was born at SOUTH SHIELDS, the son of an income tax collector for the Borough, and later became a teacher, painting in his spare time. He began teaching in 1887 at SOUTH SHIELDS, but later abandoned his profession in favour of accountancy work on income tax. He resumed teaching in 1926, but retired in 1932, due to ill-health. Kell was honorary secretary of South Shields Art Club for many years, and one of its best known members. He exhibited his work regularly with the Club, and occasionally at the Bewick Club, NEW-CASTLE, and at the Artists of the Northern Counties exhibitions at the city's Laing Art Gallery. One of his best known works was his oil: *The Bents, Ballast Hills*, painted in 1901. This work was reproduced by Hodgson in his *History of South Shields*. An exhibition entitled: "Water Colour Drawings, Sketches of Old Shields Beauty Spots, Oils and Pastels, by the late Robert John Kell of South Shields", was held in his home town in the year following his death.

*KIDD, John Andrews (d.1811)
Engraver. This engraver practised at NEWCASTLE in the late 18th, and early 19th centuries, engraving many plates for locally published prints and books. His best known work is his engraving of a portrait of Thomas Bewick (q.v.), after a Miss Kirkley, published in London and NEWCASTLE, in 1798.# This engraving, of which early impressions are extremely rare, was inserted in the *Gentleman's Magazine*, for January, 1829, following Bewick's death. Kidd died at NEWCASTLE. He was the master of Thomas Fryer Ranson (q.v.).

KIDD, William A. (fl.1834-1851)
Portrait and landscape painter in oil; lithographer. This artist practised in Northumbria during the first half of the 19th century. He is first recorded at NORTH SHIELDS in 1834, from which address he sent two landscape works to the Newcastle upon Tyne Institution for the General Promotion of the Fine Arts. Both of these works were Scottish views. Later in the same year (September) he issued an announcement to the effect that William A. Kidd "portrait and landscape painter (late of London)", would be executing "a large oil painting of the opening and shipment of coals from Stanhope & Tyne Rail-way", which painting would "afterwards be published in Lithography at a modest price". This view was taken on September 10th, 1834, and was duly "drawn on the stone" by Kidd and published by Kelly of NORTH SHIELDS. He exhibited on three further occasions at NEWCASTLE; in 1838 showing four landscapes; in 1839, two landscapes, and in 1843, two landscapes. These works comprised continental and local views, and were sent from NORTH SHIELDS, and SOUTH SHIELDS. It would appear that Kidd devoted most of his later life to running a bookselling, stationery and map-selling business at SOUTH SHIELDS, painting only in his spare time. His wife was sole proprietor of the business by 1855, suggesting that the artist was by then deceased. Represented: South Shields Library.

KILVINGTON, George (1858-1913)
Landscape painter in oil. Kilvington was born at WEST HARTLEPOOL (now HARTLEPOOL), and was employed as Clerk to the Hartlepool Guardians for many years. A keen spare-time painter, he exhibited his work at the Bewick Club, NEWCASTLE, and later at the Artists of the Northern Counties exhibitions at the city's Laing Art Gallery, showing a wide range of Northumbrian, North Yorkshire and Lake District landscapes, frequently with buildings. He died at HARTLEPOOL. The Gray Art Gallery, HARTLEPOOL, has his *Thatched Cottage, Runswick.*

KINGSLEY-WOOD, Eva (1890-1976)

Amateur landscape and flower painter in watercolour. This artist lived at SUNDERLAND for most of her life, and was believed to be the last descendant of the family of the famous Captain Cook. She was a member of Sunderland Art Club, and died in the town in 1976.

*KIRSOP, Joseph Henry (1886-1981)

Landscape and architectural painter in watercolour; draughtsman; etcher. Born at NEWCASTLE, Kirsop did not become a full-time professional artist until his retirement from the city's Tyne Improvement Commission in 1951. He had, however, maintained a lifelong interest in art, receiving his early training as an artist at evening classes at GATESHEAD, under William Fitzjames White (q.v.), and later Armstrong College (later King's College; now Newcastle University). Part of his training was in the art of etching, in which he subsequently established himself as a distinguished artist, winning a gold medal in 1933 from *The Artist* magazine for the best etching submitted for its judgement in that year, and receiving much acclaim for his Royal Academy exhibit of 1943: *Sandhill, Newcastle upon Tyne.*# He was also an outstanding painter in oil and watercolour, exhibiting his first work in the former medium at the Artists of the Northern Counties exhibition at the Laing Art Gallery in 1912: *The Bridges, Newcastle upon Tyne*, and later becoming a regular exhibitor of works in a variety of media at the Laing Art Gallery, the city's Bewick Club, and the exhibitions of the Newcastle Society of Artists. Kirsop travelled widely to draw and paint until shortly after his retirement, visiting America, France, Spain, Belgium and Norway, as well as various parts of Great Britain, and often producing etchings based on this work. His home for many years before his retirement was at GATESHEAD. In the late 1950's he moved to NEWCASTLE to live and work, occupying studios successively in the Groat Market, and at Plummer Tower. He was an exhibitor at the "Contemporary Artists of Durham County" exhibition at the Shipley Art Gallery, GATESHEAD, staged in 1951 in connection with the Festival of Britain, and thereafter exhibited his work mainly with the Federation of Northern Art Societies, at the Laing Art Gallery, and with the Gateshead Art Club, at the Shipley Art Gallery. He died at WESTERHOPE, near NEWCASTLE. Represented: Laing A.G., Newcastle; Shipley A.G., Gateshead.

KNOWLES, William Henry, F.S.A. (1857-1943)

Architectural and antiquarian draughtsman; illustrator. Knowles was born at NEWCASTLE, and practised as an architect, drawing in his spare time. He was particularly interested in the old buildings of Tyneside, and published in 1890, jointly with J. R. Boyle, F.S.A., *Vestiges of Old Newcastle and Gateshead*, for which he provided the illustrations. He also illustrated several other publications, and occasionally exhibited his work, notably at the Royal Academy, the Royal Scottish Academy, and the Artists of the Northern Counties exhibitions at the Laing Art Gallery, NEWCASTLE. He was a Fellow of the Society of Antiquaries, London, a member of the Architectural Committee of the Victoria Histories for the Counties of England, and a member of the Society of Antiquaries, NEWCASTLE, in addition to being associated with several other bodies connected with the study and preservation of old buildings. Among the many local buildings for which he was architect was the major portion of Armstrong College (later King's College; now Newcastle University), including the School of Art. He died at NEWCASTLE. Represented: Shipley A.G., Gateshead.

Joseph Henry Kirsop: Sandhill, Newcastle upon Tyne. Etching 10×16. *Dean Gallery.*

LAMBERT, Mark (1781-1855)

Engraver; lithographer; draughtsman. Lambert was born at NEWCASTLE, and began his career as an apprentice to Ralph Beilby (q.v.), and Thomas Bewick (q.v.), in their workshop in the town. In 1807 he commenced business on his own account, and soon established himself as the busiest copper-plate engraver at NEWCASTLE, taking several apprentices who were later to make considerable reputations as engravers, notably Thomas Abiel Prior, of London. By the 1820's he is said to have been employing four or five men in engraving for reproduction, and on silver, etc., in addition to handling much engraving himself, sometimes in association with William Collard (q.v.). One of his best known series of engravings was that of a number of views of the Tyne executed by John Wilson Carmichael (q.v.), who produced so many drawings for Lambert that he was frequently described as the latter's "chief draughtsman". Lambert's main accomplishment, and the one to which he principally devoted himself after his son, MARK WILLIAM LAMBERT (1812-1893), joined him in 1840, was bookplate engraving, and an interesting account of his work in this field can be found in *Lambert (Newcastle upon Tyne) as an Engraver of Bookplates*, by John Vinycomb, M.R.I.A., 1896. After his son joined the business they traded as "M. & M. W. Lambert", and with the help of their new draughtsman George Finlay Robinson (q.v.), rapidly expanded into lithography. Later, they bought out the largest letterpress printer at NEWCASTLE, the new business including the *Newcastle Chronicle*. Mark William's contribution to the success of the Lambert business lay mainly in the field of management, though it published many engravings bearing the joint initials of father and son. Lambert died at NEWCASTLE in 1855, and was buried in the old cemetery at Jesmond. His son ran the business until 1890, when it was sold to his father's one-time apprentice, Andrew Reid (q.v.). Both father and son were keen collectors of works of art; the latter's daughter, KATE LAMBERT, was a talented amateur artist who exhibited her work.

LANDELLS, Ebenezer (1808-1860)

Engraver; draughtsman; illustrator. Born at NEWCASTLE, Landells is popularly believed to have served an apprenticeship with Thomas Bewick (q.v.), before leaving for London in 1829. It is, however, more likely that he served all, or most of his apprenticeship, under former Bewick apprentice Isaac Nicholson (q.v.). Whatever his training as an engraver, Landells was evidently a largely self-taught artist, and competent enough to have his work exhibited while still an apprentice. He exhibited at the Northumberland Institution for the Promotion of the Fine Arts, NEWCASTLE, in 1826 and 1827, showing views of TYNEMOUTH, and Duns, near BERWICK-UPON-TWEED, in the first of these years, and *The Young Anglers*, and *Portrait of a Gentleman*, in the second; he also exhibited at the Northern Academy, NEWCASTLE, in 1828, showing: *Vessels stranded on the coast at Durham*. On arriving in London in 1829, he looked up fellow Northumbrian engravers John Jackson (q.v.), and William Harvey (q.v.), and through their influence got a job superintending the fine art department of Branston & Vizetelly.

Landells' work for a decade after his arrival in London lay almost exclusively in the field of wood engraving, wherein he distinguished himself principally for his work for *Northcote's Fables*, 1833. Also in this period he exhibited his engravings, showing examples at the Suffolk Street Gallery in 1833 and 1837. He later became ambitious to become a publisher, however, and in 1841 started with Douglas Jerrold, the Brothers Mayhew, Mark Lemon, and others, the magazine *Punch*. This was the beginning of a long association with the publication of magazines on Landells' part, though in 1842 he left *Punch* to handle what was to prove his most important assignment as an illustrator; the coverage for the *Illustrated London News* of Queen Victoria's first tour of Scotland. The Queen was so impressed by his productions that she later bought them for her own collection. He later handled several other commissions for the *News*, but remained fascinated by publishing, and subsequently became one of the promoters of the *Illuminated Magazine*, 1843, and one of the proprietors of the *Lady's Illustrated Newspaper*, 1847. The latter publication was later incorporated into *The Queen*. Throughout his involvement in publishing Landells remained deeply involved in wood engraving, and at one time had as a pupil in his "office", Myles Birket Foster (q.v.), among several artists who were later to make their names as wood engravers, illustrators, or artists in the round. But he was not successful in his publishing ventures, and the constant strain of having to tackle onerous wood engraving and illustrative commissions is said to have led to his death in London at the early age of fifty-one. His son ROBERT THOMAS LANDELLS (1833-1877), was a talented illustrator and War Artist.

LANGLANDS, George (fl. early 19th cent.)

Marine and coastal painter. This artist practised at GATESHEAD, and later NEWCASTLE, in the early 19th century, and first exhibited his work publicly when he sent a *View of the Tyne* to the Northern Academy, NEWCASTLE, in 1831. He remained an occasional exhibitor at NEWCASTLE for several years, mainly contributing marine views, such as the *Entrance to Shields Harbour; View of Tynemouth*, and *Dutch Fishermen*, which he showed at the "Exhibition of Arts & Manufactures & Practical Science", in 1840. He was still practising at GATESHEAD when he sent three works to the North of England Society for the Promotion of the Fine Arts, in 1841, but by 1844 had moved to NEWCASTLE, where *Williams Directory* of that date shows him living in the east end of the town. He may have been the George Langlands who traded as a tin brazier at Bottle Bank, GATESHEAD, in the first few decades of the century, as this was the address given by the artist when sending works for exhibition in this period. It is possible that he was related to the famous Langlands family of silversmiths at NEWCASTLE.

LASERKY (LASCHKE), Edwin Hugo (1861-1933)
Amateur marine painter in oil. He was born at SUNDER-LAND, the second son of a Polish Count from Warsaw, who moved to the town a short time before Laserky's birth. His father described himself as an artist on his son's birth certificate, and may have taught his son to paint while himself practising as an artist in the town. Laserky, however, did not take up art as a full-time career, but worked on the railways most of his life, painting in his spare time. He was particularly fond of painting ships, and would often sketch them from a rowing boat, or while working at the Albert Edward Docks, near his home at NORTH SHIELDS. Several examples of his work are in public and private collections on the German Coast. He died at NORTH SHIELDS.

LAVENDER, Alfred J., A.T.D. (b.1900)
Landscape painter in oil and watercolour; etcher; art teacher. He was born at GOSFORTH, near NEWCASTLE, and studied at Gateshead Secondary School, and Bede College, DURHAM, before attending Armstrong College (later King's College; now Newcastle University). In 1927 he was appointed art master at Swansea Grammar School, remaining there until his retirement in 1964. Lavender has exhibited his work at the Royal Cambrian Academy, and at various London and provincial galleries, including the Laing Art Gallery, NEWCASTLE, whose Artists of the Northern Counties exhibitions he contributed to for several years. Three of his etchings: *Durham*; *Warkworth*, and *Dunstanburgh* were included in the "Contemporary Artists of Durham County" exhibition at the Shipley Art Gallery, GATESHEAD, in 1951, in connection with the Festival of Britain. He has served as a part-time lecturer at Swansea Art School, and Secretary of Swansea Art Society and South Wales Group, and was organiser of the Festival exhibitions in Swansea in 1951. He is a holder of an Art Teacher's Diploma.

LAWS, John (d.1884)
Engraver; wood carver. He was born at Breckney Hill, near HEDDON-ON-THE-WALL, and later served an apprenticeship with Ralph Beilby (q.v.), and Thomas Bewick (q.v.), at NEWCASTLE. While with the partners he mainly concentrated on the decorative engraving of silver, establishing such a reputation for his work that when he left the workshop to set up on his own account, he was inundated with work. About the end of the 19th century he visited America to recuperate from his strenuous work in engraving, remaining there several years, and clearing land for cultivation. He later returned to Northumbria, where he carried on engraving silver, and also distinguished himself as a wood carver in oak, as well as a naturalist of some note. He engraved until close to his death at Breckney Hill in 1884, where he had farmed for many years previously. Bewick, in his autobiographical *Memoir*, wrote most flatteringly of Laws' abilities as a silver engraver.‡ The Laing Art Gallery, NEWCASTLE, has an album of impressions of his work in engraving.

‡ *See p. 195, "A Memoir of Thomas Bewick, Written by Himself", edited and with an introduction by Iain Bain, Oxford University Press, 1975.*

LAWSON, Eva – see CARTER, Mrs. Eva.

*LEAR, William Henry (1860-1932)
Amateur landscape and animal painter in watercolour. He was born at DARLINGTON, the son of an ironmonger with a long established and well known business in the town. He was educated privately at DARLINGTON, and worked for an ironmonger in London for fifteen years before joining the family business. On the death of his father in 1914 he took control of the business, running it until his death at DARLINGTON in 1932. Lear was throughout his life a keen and talented spare-time painter in watercolour, much of whose work resembles

William Henry Lear:
Carting Sand. Watercolour
17×25. *Darlington Art
Gallery.*

in style and competence that of Wilson Hepple (q.v.). He mainly showed his work at the exhibitions of the Darlington Society of Arts. Darlington Art Gallery has his *Carting Sand*.#

LEE, John (c.1869- after 1934)
Portrait, genre and landscape painter in oil and water-colour. Lee's place of birth is not known, but the fact that he studied at the School of Art, DARLINGTON, under Samuel Averill Elton (q.v.), may suggest that he was a native of Northumbria. By 1889 he was working as a professional artist in London, and exhibiting at the Royal Institute of Oil Painters, and in 1891 he sent a work to the Royal Society of British Artists: *Cynthia*. He returned north just before the turn of the century, and by 1900 had settled at MIDDLETON-IN-TEESDALE, near DARLINGTON, from which he sent his only contri-bution to the Royal Academy: *Meditations*. It is believed that he died at MIDDLETON-IN-TEESDALE. The Bowes Museum, BARNARD CASTLE, has several examples of his work, and Darlington Art Gallery has his portrait of Victor Hobson (q.v.).

LIDDELL, Captain Hedworth (b.1825)
Amateur landscape and sporting painter in oil. He was born at Ravensworth Castle, near GATESHEAD, the son of Sir Henry Thomas Liddell (q.v.), and after entering the Army, occasionally exhibited his work at NEW-CASTLE. He was still in the Army when he married at Jersey, in 1856, having by then achieved the rank of Captain. His mother, Lady Isabella-Horatia Liddell (q.v.), and uncle, Thomas Liddell (q.v.), were also talented amateur artists.

LIDDELL, Sir Henry Thomas, Third Baron, and First Earl of Ravensworth (1797-1878)
Amateur painter. He was born at Ravensworth Castle, near GATESHEAD, eldest son of the Second Lord Rav-ensworth, Sir Thomas Henry Liddell, and was educated at Eton, and St. John's, Cambridge. After travelling Europe, and visiting Paris, Rome, Berlin and Vienna, he married, and settling at Ravensworth Castle, entered politics, serving as M.P. for DURHAM, and Liverpool, before entering the House of Lords on the death of his father. A deeply cultured man, Sir Walter Scott wrote of him in 1831: "I like him and his brother Tom very much . . . Henry is an accomplished artist, and certainly has a fine taste for poetry, though he may never cultivate it . . .". Sir Henry did, indeed, cultivate his "fine taste for poetry", writing considerably in verse, and translat-ing the Odes of Horace, but nothing is known of his productions as an artist, no examples of his work appearing at the Ravensworth Castle sale of 1920.* He died at Ravensworth Castle. His wife, Lady Isabella-Horatia Liddell (q.v.), his brother, Thomas Liddell (q.v.), and son Captain Hedworth Liddell (q.v.), were all talented amateur artists.

 * *It may be noted, however, that the "Illustrated London News", showing additions to Ravensworth Castle completed in 1846, said that the principal front was designed by the "Hon. H. T. Liddell".*

LIDDELL, Lady Isabella-Horatia (1801-1856)
Amateur landscape and figure painter in oil; copyist. She was the eldest daughter of Lord George Seymour,

and in 1820 married Sir Henry Thomas Liddell (q.v.), of Ravensworth Castle, near GATESHEAD. She was a keen amateur painter from her girlhood, and following her marriage travelled extensively with her husband, visiting many famous collections of paintings in Europe, and studying the styles of the Old Masters. She was particularly influenced by the work of Poussin, and later painted many landscapes in the style of this artist. She also painted abroad, including Dutch street and canal scenes, and Italian landscapes among her work. She died in London. The Ravensworth Castle Sale in 1920 included more than thirty examples of her work, some of very large proportions. Her brother-in-law, Thomas Liddell (q.v.), and her son, Captain Hedworth Liddell (q.v.), were both talented amateur artists, as were also her granddaughters, LADY LILLIAN LIDDELL (d.1962), and LADY MARY LIDDELL (d.1958). Both of these granddaughters were tutored in art by the wife of John Surtees (q.v.).

*LIDDELL, John Davison (1859-1942)
Marine and landscape painter in oil and watercolour; illustrator; art teacher. Born at NORTH SHIELDS, Liddell first worked as a tinsmith, but gave up this occupation in his twenties to devote himself to art. In 1884 he began exhibiting at the Bewick Club, NEWCASTLE, showing an oil entitled: *Sunset on the Tyne at North Shields*, and by 1895 he was describing himself as a full-time professional artist, living at Grey Street, NORTH SHIELDS. Grey Street remained his home and work place for the remainder of his life. During this period he visited the continent on several occasions to paint, and on one occasion took an exhibition of his work to Spain on a ship captained by his brother. Most of his work consisted of studies of tugs and colliers in and around the mouth of the Tyne,# but he painted many landscapes, frequently featuring cattle. Some of his coastal views were reproduced by chromolithography. He died at NORTH SHIELDS follow-ing a period in the town's Preston Hospital, and was buried in the nearby cemetery. His cousin Ralph Walter Liddell (q.v.), was also an artist. Represented: South Shields Museum & A.G.

LIDDELL, Ralph Walter (1858-1932)
Architectural, landscape and coastal painter in oil and watercolour; art teacher. He was born at NORTH SHIELDS, and appears to have taken up art as a career after some years in another employment. He was an occasional exhibitor at the Bewick Club, NEWCASTLE, in the 1890's but otherwise appears to have confined his artistic activities to his occupation as art master of Tynemouth Secondary School, where he taught Victor Noble Rainbird (q.v.), among several well known Northumbrian artists. He died at NEWCASTLE.

LIDDELL, Thomas (1800-1856)
Amateur marine and landscape painter in oil and watercolour. He was born at Ravensworth Castle, near GATESHEAD, second son of the Second Lord Ravens-worth, Sir Thomas Henry Liddell. He was a keen amateur painter from his youth, and may have received some tuition from his elder brother, Sir Henry Thomas Liddell (q.v.), before exhibiting *A composition from the*

John Davison Liddell:
Collier outward bound,
from the mouth of the
Tyne. Oil 12×18. *Private
collection.*

collection of H. T. Liddell, at the Northumberland Institution for the Promotion of the Fine Arts, NEW-CASTLE, in 1826. Three years later, and exhibiting at the Northern Academy, NEWCASTLE, his contributions were described by W. A. Mitchell, in the *Tyne Mercury*, as "two pretty pencil drawings and a beautiful piece of watercolour drawing by the Hon. T. Liddell". He continued to exhibit at NEWCASTLE until the early 1840's, showing a large number of local marine, coastal and landscape views, occasional continental landscapes, and one North American landscape. Following his marriage in 1843, however, he appears to have given up exhibiting his work. The Ravensworth Castle Sale in 1920 included his oil: *The Painter's Paradise – Jesmond Dene.* His sister-in-law, Lady Isabella-Horatia Liddell (q.v.), and nephew, Captain Hedworth Liddell (q.v.), were also talented amateur artists.

LILEY, William, A.R.C.A. (1894-1958)

Landscape and portrait painter in oil and watercolour; art teacher. Liley was born at SUNDERLAND, and after education at the Bede Collegiate School, attended the town's School of Art. Here he was an outstanding pupil, winning the National silver and bronze medals for wood engraving in 1913-14, and the King's Prize for Design, in 1922. He later attended the Royal College of Art, and the Central School of Arts and Crafts, London, before taking up an appointment as assistant master at the School of Art, SUNDERLAND. On leaving SUNDER-LAND, he became headmaster at the Heginbottom School of Art, Ashton-under-Lyme, Lancashire, re-maining there until his retirement twenty-four years later, and also serving as a national examiner for the Board of Education. He died at Bollington, Cheshire. Liley only occasionally exhibited his work, among his few known exhibits being the landscapes and portraits which he contributed to the Artists of the Northern Counties exhibitions at the Laing Art Gallery, NEW-CASTLE, 1931-34. He was an associate of the Royal College of Art.

LONGBOTTOM, Sheldon (fl. late 19th cent.)

Landscape painter in watercolour. This artist practised at BARNARD CASTLE in the late 19th century. He was an occasional exhibitor at the Bewick Club, NEWCASTLE, in 1890 showing his *Early Morning on the Tees*, and in 1891: *A bit of Egglestone Abbey near Rokeby.* He was also an exhibitor at Carlisle Art Gallery in 1896, showing a landscape. The Bowes Museum, BARNARD CASTLE, has his *Barnard Castle Church.*

LONGDEN, Major Alfred Appleby (1876-1954)

Landscape painter in watercolour. Born at SUNDER-LAND, Longden was educated at Durham School, and studied at the School of Art in his native town, and at the Royal College of Art, before becoming a profes-sional artist, and later a gallery director and art adviser. He first began exhibiting his work in 1901, while working in London, in the next seven years showing several landscapes at the Royal Academy, the Royal Institute of Painters in Water Colours, and the New Gallery. In this period he also served as British Govern-ment Representative for Fine and Applied Art, New Zealand International Exhibition, 1906-7. He was di-rector of Aberdeen Corporation Art Gallery from 1909 until 1911, then resuming his career as a professional exhibition director and art adviser, he held a variety of posts associated with British and overseas exhibitions, until his appointment as director of the Wernher Col-lection, Luton Hoo, Bedfordshire, a few years before his death. Longden only occasionally exhibited his work after the early years of the century, notable examples being his participation in the 1948 Olympic Games, International Exhibition (which he helped organise), and the "Contemporary Artists of Durham County" exhibition, staged at the Shipley Art Gallery, GATES-HEAD, in 1951, in connection with the Festival of Britain. He was the author of *British Cartoon and Caricature,* 1944, and contributed many articles on fine and applied art to magazines and newspapers. He died at Luton Hoo. Several honours were conferred on him in recognition of his service to art, and for his bravery in the Second World War, including the Order of the British Empire, and the Distinguished Service Order. Represented: Wernher Collection, Luton Hoo.

LONGSTAFFE, William Hylton Dyer, F.S.A. (1826-1898)

Architectural and antiquarian draughtsman. He was born at Norton, in Yorkshire, the son of a surgeon. Following his education at grammar school he worked briefly at York and Thirsk as an attorney's clerk, before moving to DARLINGTON, in 1845, where he remained for five years, before becoming articled to a solicitor at GATESHEAD. In 1857 he became a partner in this practice, remaining a solicitor for the rest of his life. Longstaffe had early developed an interest in old churches, and made careful drawings and notes of interesting specimens from his boyhood. This interest led to the publication of his *Richmondshire, its Ancient Lords & Edifices*, 1852, and his better known *History and Antiquities of the Parish of Darlington*, 1854, in which latter may be found several excellent examples of his draughtsmanship. Longstaffe remained interested in architectural and antiquarian matters all his life, and was a member of several societies connected with their study, including the Society of Antiquaries, NEWCASTLE, and the Surtees Society. He was also a Fellow of the Society of Antiquaries, London. He died at GATESHEAD.

*LOUGH, John Graham (1798-1876)

Sculptor; draughtsman. Lough was born at the hamlet of GREENHEAD, near CONSETT, the son of a farmer, and after a rudimentary education, began work on his father's small farm. Here he spent spare moments drawing and modelling in clay, his works one day coming to the attention of local squire George Silvertop, who helped crystallise Lough's desire to become a sculptor by showing him examples of sculpture at his home at Minsteracres. He afterwards became an apprentice to a local stone mason and builder, but disliked the work and later went to NEWCASTLE, where he found employment carving decorations for the new Literary and Philosophical Society's building then being built in the town to the design of John Green, Senior (q.v.). About 1825, and wishing to expand his talents yet further, he persuaded a collier captain to give him a free passage to London, little realising as he left the Tyne, that one of his monuments would one day dominate its mouth. Arrived at London, he took modest lodgings in Burleigh Street, studied the Elgin Marbles, and commenced work on his first sculpture of note, his bas-relief of *The Death of Turnus*. This work was accepted for showing at the Royal Academy in 1826, and in the same year he was admitted as a student to its Schools, on the recommendation, it is said, of J. T. Smith. There is little evidence that he took advantage of the lectures at the Schools, and, indeed, occupied as he was over the next few months with his giant *Milo*, it seems unlikely that he would have found the time. Commenting on this work, Haydon, the historical and genre painter friend of Lough, said in his autobiography: 1827 – May 18th. – "From me Lord Egremont went to young Lough, the sculptor, who has just burst out, and

John Graham Lough: Lord Collingwood Monument, Tynemouth. Stone.

has produced a great effect. His *Milo* is really the most extraordinary thing, considering all the circumstances, in modern sculpture. It is another proof of the efficacy of inherent genius."

Helped by Haydon, Lough subsequently held a very successful exhibition of his work, as a result of which no less a personage than the Duke of Wellington placed commissions. By the following spring he had completed other figures and in March opened a second exhibition, featuring *Milo*, *Sampson*, *Musidora*, and *Somnus and Iris*. Society again flocked to the show, but commissions came slowly. For the next four years Lough continued his practice of exhibiting privately, with moderate success, then decided to resume exhibiting at the Royal Academy by showing his *Duncan's Horses* (inspired by "Macbeth"), also in this year marrying Mary North, the daugher of a clergyman. He commenced exhibiting at the British Institution in the following year, with his *Monk*, and *Group of Horses*, then in 1834, and taking his wife with him, he began four years studying great works of sculpture in Italy. He also in this period executed several commissions for several leading British aristocrats, including the Duke of Northumberland, and a number of wealthy commoners. Returning to England in 1838, he resumed exhibiting at the Royal Academy and the British Institution, showing among his early

110

exhibits several inspired by his Italian sojourn – *Boy giving Water to a Dolphin; A Roman Fruit Girl, A Bacchanalian Revel*, and similar groups. He remained a regular exhibitor at both establishments until 1863, showing a wide range of sculpture, including a large number of portrait statues and busts, and occasional compositions based on Shakespearian themes. Several of his exhibits aroused controversy. His model of a statue of Queen Victoria (designed as a companion to his statue of the Prince Consort, for the Royal Exchange, London), when exhibited at the Royal Academy in 1845, was described by the *Art Journal* as "an obviously coarse production in which not one feature of the Queen is recognisable". This sort of attack upon him from the press did little to damage his success, however, and, indeed, some of his most accomplished and lucrative work was executed for aristocrats such as the Duke of Sutherland, Earl Grey, and Sir Matthew White Ridley. His works for Sir Matthew's home, Blagdon Hall, near SEATON BURN, and for Carlton House, London, were perhaps more numerous than for any other of these patrons; for the former including figures, busts, groups, etc., and for the latter, a bas-relief and ten statues representative of characters from Shakespeare. The Blagdon Hall works comprise some of his finest in sculpture, the best being his *Milo*, later placed by Sir Edwin Lutyens, the distinguished architect, in the ornamental water to the west of the building, when he remodelled Blagdon's gardens. In addition to his work for private patrons, Lough received several commissions as a result of public subscription; these include some of his best known work in Northumbria: the monument to Lord Collingwood, at TYNEMOUTH, 1847,# and the Stephenson monument at NEWCASTLE, 1862. The architectural base of the former was designed by John Dobson (q.v.), the statue measuring 23' tall; the pedestal, 50'.

Lough continued to work vigorously after he last exhibited in London in 1863, his latest dated work being the bust of Dr. Campbell de Morgan, which he executed in 1875 for Middlesex Hospital. He died in London, the *Art Journal* making amends for its earlier, and sometimes virulent attacks on his work, by stating in a substantially flattering obituary: "in private life no artist has been more largely esteemed and respected. His personal friends were numerous, including many of the most famous men and women of the age of science, art and letters." Lough maintained close connections with his native Northumbria throughout his life, and, apart from executing commissions for the area, donated several examples of his work to establishments on Tyneside; in 1828 he sent a cast of his *Milo* to the Literary and Philosophical Society, NEWCASTLE, and in 1838, when exhibiting at the town's North of England Society for the Promotion of the Fine Arts, he presented two of his four exhibits to this Society. Following his death his widow gave his models, etc., to the Corporation of NEWCASTLE, and these were exhibited for many years at Elswick Hall, in the west end of the city. Lough was Northumbria's most outstanding sculptor of the nineteenth century, and a well deserved study of his life and work has now been prepared by descendants of his family, J. and E. Lough. Represented: National Portrait

Gallery; Victoria and Albert Museum; Hatton Gallery, Newcastle; Laing A.G., Newcastle; Literary and Philosophical Society, Newcastle; Walker Art Gallery, Liverpool.

LOVIBOND, Mrs. Phyllis Ellen – see BICKNELL, Phyllis Ellen.

LOWTHIN, Thomas (1825-1863)
Landscape painter. This artist's work was exhibited at the exhibition of works by local painters, at the Central Exchange Art Gallery, NEWCASTLE, in 1878. Three of his landscapes were shown, among them his *Vale of Tyne*. Nothing more is known of this artist.

LUMSDEN, John (1785-1862)
Landscape, portrait and animal painter in oil. This artist practised at NEWCASTLE in the early 19th century, variously advertising himself as animal painter (1811), and landscape painter (1822-1838). He occasionally exhibited his work in the town from 1824, in which year he showed two landscape works at the Northumberland Institution for the Promotion of the Fine Arts. He again exhibited at the Institution in 1827, and at the First Exhibition of the Northern Academy, NEWCASTLE, in the following year, showed: *View on the Tyne, Evening; View from Dunston Hill*, and *Bank of the Tyne, near Benwell*. In the Academy's next exhibition, in 1829, his *Newcastle from Byker Hill*, earned from W. A. Mitchell, in the *Tyne Mercury*, the remark: ". . . this picture shows a considerable improvement in the artist". Lumsden continued to exhibit at NEWCASTLE until 1838, also exhibiting at the Carlisle Academy, in 1828, showing his *View on the Tyne*, and *Scene on the bank of the Tyne*. His *View in Pandon Dene*, painted in 1821, was engraved by J. Knox. He died at NEWCASTLE.

*LUND, Neils Moeller, R.B.A., R.O.I., A.R.E. (1863-1916)
Landscape and portrait painter in oil and watercolour; etcher; lithographer. Lund was born at Faaborg, Denmark, but moved with his parents to NEWCASTLE at the age of four. Here he studied at the town's School of Art under William Cosens Way (q.v.), before leaving for London, where he studied first at St. John's Wood, later at the Royal Academy Schools. On leaving the Schools he enrolled as a pupil in the Academie Julian, in Paris, deciding at the end of his period there to become a professional artist in London. Much of his subsequent life was spent in the capital, though he spent long periods on Tyneside while painting local landscape and portrait commissions, and in addition to showing his work at the Royal Academy, the Royal Scottish Academy, the Royal Institute of Oil Painters, and various major London and provincial venues, from 1887, he was a regular exhibitor at NEWCASTLE. He was an exhibitor at the Bewick Club, NEWCASTLE, from his early twenties, and exhibited at the Artists of the Northern Counties exhibitions at the city's Laing Art Gallery, from 1908. Several of his Royal Academy exhibits featured Northumbrian subjects, notable amongst which was his *The City of Newcastle upon Tyne*, shown in 1898.# So popular was this work that

he painted two smaller versions, and reproduced it as a lithograph. Late in life he became interested in etching, and in 1912 joined the classes of Sir Frank Short. His work in oil, watercolour and etching was well recognised in his lifetime, leading to his election as a member of the Royal Society of British Artists in 1896; member of the Royal Institute of Oil Painters, in 1897, and associate member of the Royal Society of Painter-Etchers and Engravers, in 1915. One of his exhibits at the Paris Salon – *The Land of the Leal* – was purchased by the French Government for the Luxembourg Galleries. He died in London. A major exhibition of his work, consisting of many of his Northumbrian and Scottish landscapes, portraits, and etchings, was staged at the Laing Art Gallery in the year of his death, along with works by Joseph Crawhall, The Third (q.v.). Represented: Laing A.G., Newcastle; Literary and Philosophical Society, Newcastle; Shipley A.G., Gateshead, and various provincial and overseas galleries.

MACKAY, Thomas (1851- after 1909)

Genre painter in oil and watercolour; architectural draughtsman. Mackay was born at MORPETH, later moving to NEWCASTLE, where he practised as an architect, painting in his spare time. He first exhibited his work publicly in 1878, showing *A bottle of Tom*, at the Arts Association, NEWCASTLE. In 1880 he showed his *In Trouble; Saved*, and *Birds of Prey*, at the Association, and later became an occasional exhibitor at the Bewick Club, NEWCASTLE. He last exhibited on Tyneside in 1909, showing his *Tidings of a reverse*, at the Artists of the Northern Counties exhibition in that year, at the Laing Art Gallery, NEWCASTLE. The Shipley Art Gallery, GATESHEAD, has his oil: *Contentment*, 1880. His younger brother, WILLIAM OLIVER MACKAY (b.1853), also painted, and exhibited his work on Tyneside.

MACKLIN, John Eyre (1834-1916)

Landscape painter in oil and watercolour. He was born at NEWCASTLE, of Irish parentage, and served in the Army as a Lieutenant before becoming a toy and fancy goods dealer in the town, painting in his spare time. Following the birth of his son Thomas Eyre Macklin (q.v.), he began to take an increasing interest in painting for a living and in 1878 exhibited his *Rowlands Gill*, which was included in the exhibition of works by local painters, at the Central Exchange Art Gallery, NEWCASTLE. By 1881 he was describing himself as an artist in local trade directories, continuing this practice until the First World War years, even though he exhibited little of his work. It is believed that he died at NEWCASTLE, and that in addition to being an artist of some accomplishment, he also worked as a freelance journalist for Tyneside publications. The Laing Art Gallery, NEWCASTLE, has a portrait of him painted by his son.

*MACKLIN, Thomas Eyre, R.B.A. (1863-1943)‡

Landscape, portrait and figure painter in oil and watercolour; sculptor; illustrator. He was born at NEWCASTLE, the son of John Eyre Macklin (q.v.), and displayed such a talent for drawing as a child that he was placed as a pupil at the town's School of Art at the age of ten. Here he was an outstandingly successful pupil, on one occasion gaining the first four prizes of the year. He next spent two or three years studying the Antique at the British Museum, and at Calderon's School, London, later gaining admission to the Royal Academy Schools, and largely supporting himself by acting as special artist to the *Pall Mall Budget*, and painting in his vacations at CULLERCOATS, where he met, and was befriended by, the American artist Winslow Homer. In 1889 he sent his first work to the Royal Academy: *From the Sunny South*, shortly afterwards establishing himself as a successful portrait painter in the capital. He remained in London until the early part of 1893, when he returned to Northumbria and made sketches for two publications prepared by William Weaver Tomlinson: *Historical Notes on Cullercoats, Whitley and Monkseaton*, 1893, and *Denton Hall and its associations*, 1894, and commenced exhibiting at the Bewick Club, NEWCASTLE. In 1893-4, he also prepared illustrations for *The Works of Nathaniel Hawthorne*, 1894. He next spent a short period on the northern coast of France with his journalist and artist wife ALYS EYRE MACKLIN (née Philpott), after which he settled at NEWCASTLE.

He continued to exhibit throughout his ten-year stay in his native city, showing work at the Royal Academy, the Royal Scottish Academy, the Royal Society of British Artists, the Paris Salon, and at several provincial exhibitions, including the Bewick Club. Following his election as a member of the Royal Society of British Artists in 1902, he maintained studios at NEWCASTLE and London for some twenty years, but finally settled in the capital, where he continued his success as a portrait painter, and became a popular sculptor of war memorials, illustrator for books and periodicals, and poster designer. His work in portraiture included some of the best known men of his day; that in sculpture, the South African War Memorial, in the Haymarket, NEWCASTLE, unveiled in 1908,‡ and war memorials for Auckland, New Zealand, and Bangor, Co. Down. He exhibited little after settling in London, mainly showing his work at the Artists of the Northern Counties exhibitions at the Laing Art Gallery, NEWCASTLE. Several of his works shown at NEWCASTLE were Northumbrian landscapes, indicating that he was a frequent visitor to the area in his later life. He died in London. Represented: Laing A.G., Newcastle; Shipley A.G., Gateshead; South Shields Museum & A.G.; and various provincial and overseas art galleries.

‡ Macklin's date of birth is usually given as 1867, but the Census Return completed by his father in 1871 shows his age as eight, and at least two other sources: "Monthly Chronicle of North Country Lore and Legend", 1891, page 373, and Tomlinson, in his "Historical Notes on Cullercoats, Whitley and Monkseaton", 1893, page 111, provide information which confirms the date given above.

MACKRETH, Harriet, F.S. (1803- after 1851)
Miniature painter. She was born in London, the daughter of Robert Mackreth (q.v.). After education in the capital, and some tuition in miniature painting, she joined her family in their move to Tyneside in 1823, following her father's appointment as receiving inspector of stamps and taxes at NEWCASTLE. She first began exhibiting her work in 1828, showing portrait miniatures at the Royal Academy, and the Northern Academy, NEWCASTLE. She remained a regular exhibitor at the Royal Academy until 1842, also showing work at NEWCASTLE throughout this period, and at the Suffolk Street Gallery in 1829, and the Carlisle Academy in 1833. Most of her exhibits were portrait miniatures of well known Northumbrian personalities, including John Dobson (q.v.), the Rev. John Hodgson, and William Chapman, the civil engineer. Her portrait of Hodgson was engraved for his *History of Northumberland*. She did not marry, and was still living with her family at NEWCASTLE in 1851. One of her sisters, "Miss J. Mackreth", was also talented artistically, and exhibited her work briefly at NEWCASTLE.

MACKRETH, Robert (1766- c.1860)
Amateur landscape, coastal and genre painter in oil; lithographer. He was born at Northfleet, Kent, and after working as a government official in London, took up an appointment as receiving inspector of stamps and taxes at NEWCASTLE, in 1823. He first began exhibiting his work at NEWCASTLE, showing four North Country landscapes at the First Exhibition of the Northumberland Institution for the Promotion of the Fine Arts, in the year before his appointment. In 1823, and now settled at NEWCASTLE, he again exhibited at the Institution, and sent his first work to the Carlisle Academy. In the following year he commenced exhibiting at the British Institution, showing his *The Entrance to Shields Harbour*, and from 1824 until 1833, was a regular exhibitor at NEWCASTLE, Carlisle and London, mainly showing Northumbrian landscape works. From 1826, however, he exhibited a number of Rhine Valley subjects, and occasional genre works, such as his *Fisher Girl* (British Institution, 1829), and *A Monk at his Devotions* (Carlisle Academy, 1833). After 1833, and his retirement from his official position, he exhibited

Thomas Eyre Macklin: South African War Memorial, 1908. Haymarket, Newcastle upon Tyne. Bronze.

113

exclusively at NEWCASTLE, and appears to have become a semi-professional artist, possibly working in the same studio as his artist daughter Harriet F. S. Mackreth (q.v.), and undertaking both oil painting and lithographic commissions, amongst the latter several for the Rev. John Hodgson's *History of Northumberland*. He died at his home for many years, High Swinburne Place, NEWCASTLE.

MADDISON, John (c.1875- c.1925)

Still-life, landscape and portrait painter in oil and watercolour; art teacher. He was born at Great Ayton, North Yorkshire, and studied at South Kensington Art School, and the Royal College of Art, before practising as a professional artist and art teacher at MIDDLESBROUGH. He achieved considerable recognition for his work in painting and teaching in his day, and exhibited both in Britain and abroad. He exhibited his work at the Royal Academy 1896-1901, first showing a still-life: *Brown Jar and Onions*, and later attracting much attention with his *Batchelor's Breakfast* (1898). He exhibited widely in the provinces, showing examples of his work at Bradford, York, Leeds and Manchester, and was specially invited to exhibit at the Copenhagen International Art Exhibition, in 1891. Represented: Middlesbrough A.G.; Walker A.G., Liverpool.

*MAHER, Frederick J. (1871-1963)

Portrait and landscape painter in oil and watercolour. Maher was born at NEWCASTLE, and later became a teacher of art at the city's Rutherford Grammar School. He was a frequent exhibitor at the Bewick Club, NEWCASTLE, from his early twenties, and showed work

Frederick J. Maher. Portrait of Esme. Oil 30×20. *Private collection.*

at the Artists of the Northern Counties exhibitions at the city's Laing Art Gallery, for several years from 1910. Among his exhibits at the Bewick Club, was his *Wayside Inn, Lincolnshire* (1893), while typical of his Laing Art Gallery exhibits were his *Wicklow Hills, Showery Day*, and *On the River Teith* (1910), and *Summer Sunset, Loch Arklet* (1914). After leaving Rutherford College, Maher taught for many years at Armstrong College (later King's College; now Newcastle University). He was well known in Tyneside art circles, and was a member of several local art societies, and clubs, including the Benwell Art Club. He painted well into his late life, dying at NEWCASTLE at the age of ninety-two.

MAINDS, Allan Douglass, A.R.S.A. (1881-1945)

Portrait, landscape and figure painter in oil and watercolour; costume designer; commercial designer; art teacher. He was born at Helensburgh, Dumbartonshire, Scotland, the son of an artist. On completing his general education he studied at Glasgow School of Art, where he received the Haldane Travelling Scholarship, enabling him to study in Brussels under Jan Delville, then in Rome. He then returned to Glasgow, where, in 1909, he was appointed to the staff of the city's School of Art. In 1931 he left the School to take up an appointment as Professor of Fine Art, at King's College (later Newcastle University), remaining there until his death at Gosforth, near NEWCASTLE, in 1945. Mainds first exhibited his work publicly in the year in which he took up his teaching appointment at Glasgow, later showing work at the Royal Academy, the Royal Scottish Academy, the Glasgow Institute of Fine Arts, and the Royal Scottish Society of Painters in Water Colours. He was a member of the Glasgow Art Club for much of his teaching life in the city, and in 1929 was elected an associate of the Royal Scottish Academy. Following his move to Tyneside he exhibited almost exclusively at the Artists of the Northern Counties exhibitions at the Laing Art Gallery, NEWCASTLE, and the city's Pen & Palette Club, of which latter he was a member, and for some time Master of Pictures. He last exhibited at the Laing Art Gallery in the year of his death, showing: *Spring Morning; Peasant*, and *Chess Players*. Represented: Laing A.G., Newcastle.

MANVILLE, Mrs. Ethel Kate (née Gibson) (1880-1942)

Portrait, flower and decorative painter in oil and watercolour. She was born at NEWCASTLE, the great granddaughter of William Dalziel (q.v.), and studied art at Armstrong College (later King's College; now Newcastle University), under Richard George Hatton (q.v.). She exhibited her work at the Artists of the Northern Counties exhibitions at the Laing Art Gallery, NEWCASTLE, from 1906 until her death, mainly showing portraits. Her *Head of a Young Girl*, exhibited in 1934, was singled out for comment and illustration in *Moderne Illustrée Des Arts et de la Vie* (Paris), 28th February, 1935, a correspondent writing: "I know too little of the work of Mrs. Ethel K. Manville to pass any judgement on her. I have only the impression of good art applied with a sincere sensitivity and free from all influence."

She contributed one work to the 1929 North East Coast Exhibition, Palace of Arts. She died at NEWCASTLE, where she had spent all her life.

MARKS (MARK), George (fl. early 19th cent.)

Landscape and portrait painter in oil; engraver. Marks is best remembered as the artist at DARLINGTON, who was one of the earliest teachers of William Bewick (q.v.). In a lengthy passage in *The Life and Letters of William Bewick (Artist)*, edited by Thomas Landseer, 1871, Bewick delightfully describes his acquaintance-ship with this "bookbinder, bird-stuffer, botanist, herbalist, geologist, mineralogist, geographer, astronomer, surveyor, engraver", and states: "It was by him that I was initiated into the mysteries of 'oil'; it was by him I was told of the wonders of the palette, its mixtures and compound tints, those which were evanescent and those which stood the test of time . . .". William Hylton Dyer Longstaffe (q.v.), also makes reference to Marks in his *History and Antiquities of the Parish of Darlington*, published in 1854.

MARSH, Arthur Hardwick, A.R.W.S. (1842-1909)

Portrait, genre, landscape and coastal painter in oil and watercolour; illustrator; stained glass designer. Marsh was born at Manchester, and received his education at Fairfield, Lancashire, at the Moravian School. As a concession to his love of drawing his parents allowed him when he left school to become articled to an architect, with whom he spent five years. During this period he became an intimate friend of artist John Dawson Watson, and through Watson was encouraged to go to London, where he studied at the British Museum, the National Gallery, and at the life classes of the Artists' Society, Langham Place. Within a few weeks of arriving in the capital he had commenced exhibiting at the Old Water Colour Society (later the Royal Society of Painters in Water Colours), and in 1867 showed his first work at the Suffolk Street Gallery: *The Nosegay*. In 1868 he exhibited for the first time at the Royal Academy, showing his *Under the Willows*, following this in 1869, with *The Harpsicord*, which picture led to his election as an associate of the Old Water Colour Society, in 1870.

In 1869, Marsh was invited to visit the north by merchant at TYNEMOUTH, Alexander Shannon Stevenson, who had met him at the home of Myles Birket Foster (q.v.), at Witley, Surrey. Marsh stayed with his host at TYNEMOUTH in the company of his friend Watson, Watson's brother Thomas, and William Quiller Orchardson, and visiting nearby CULLERCOATS, like them fell in love with the village. In the following year, and still at CULLERCOATS, Marsh exhibited his first of many works associated with the village, showing his *Baiting the lines*, at the Royal Academy. This was immediately followed by several other Academy exhibits inspired by the village and its fisherfolk, including *The Missing Boats* (1871); *The signal . . .* (1872); *The Salmon Fishers*, and *The Departure* (1873), and *Anxiety* (1874). He remained attached to CULLERCOATS for the remainder of his life, visiting the village regularly in the period 1875-1882, while based in London, and making his home there in 1882-3, while working for the stained glass department of the glass works at GATESHEAD, of John George Sowerby (q.v.). Following his marriage in 1884 to the eldest daughter of F. W. Hall of RIDING MILL, he decided to make his home permanently in Northumbria, living first at ALNMOUTH, later at CULLERCOATS, where he maintained a studio for many years.

Although most of Marsh's early exhibits connected with the village were in oil, he remained deeply attached to painting in watercolour, and, indeed, became best known for his work in this medium. Two of his early CULLERCOATS' studies in watercolour, *A pilot on the look-out*, and *The Pedlar*, both painted in 1871, were reproduced in leading magazines of the day, and he exhibited more than a hundred works at the Old Water Colour Society, apart from the many watercolours which he exhibited at the Royal Academy, and at various London and provincial exhibitions, including among the latter those of the Arts Association, NEWCASTLE, and later the city's Bewick Club. At the turn of the century he moved to NEWCASTLE, and thereafter exhibited mainly at the Artists of the Northern Counties exhibitions at the city's Laing Art Gallery, where his last exhibits in 1908 were his watercolours: *Meal Time in the Field*, and *A Hertfordshire Cottage*. In addition to exhibiting at the various venues already mentioned, Marsh showed his work at the International Exhibitions in Paris in 1876 and 1889, and was represented at the Royal Jubilee Exhibitions at Manchester and NEWCASTLE, in 1887. Examples of his stained glass design work for Sowerby, consisting of two Shakesperian panels: *Lady Macbeth*, and *Ophelia*, and three of his cartoons, featuring figures symbolizing *Faith, Hope and Charity*, were exhibited at the Manchester Art & Industrial Exhibition, 1882, along with many other of the firm's products. He was also an occasional illustrator, and published *Scenery of London*, and *Cathedral Cities of France*. In addition to being an associate of the Royal Society of Painters in Water Colours, Marsh was elected a member of the Royal Society of British Artists, but resigned his membership. Represented: Laing A.G., Newcastle.

MARSHALL, Daniel Whitely (fl. late 19th cent.)

Portrait and landscape painter in oil. A chemist by profession, Marshall became well known at SUNDERLAND in his day for his portraits of local celebrities, and his landscape work. He was an occasional exhibitor at the Bewick Club, NEWCASTLE, making his debut at its 1884 exhibition with his oil: *Waiting for the master*. Sunderland Art Gallery has several examples of his work, including his portrait of John Green, author of *Tales and Ballads of Wearside*, and several local street scenes.

*MARSHALL, Ralph (c.1855- c.1945)

Amateur marine and landscape painter in oil and watercolour. Marshall was born at WEST HARTLEPOOL (now HARTLEPOOL), and worked most of his life as a carpenter in a local shipyard, painting in his spare time. He was a prolific painter and the quality of his work varied considerably. His best work compares favourably with that of John Scott (q.v.). He frequently repeated

compositions in his work, and sometimes painted in collaboration with his friend and pupil BERNARD KEENAN, whoever finished the painting adding his signature. He died at HARTLEPOOL. Represented: Gray A.G. & Museum, Hartlepool; Middlesbrough A.G.

MARTIN, David (fl. late 18th cent.)

Wood engraver. Martin was an apprentice of Ralph Beilby (q.v.), at NEWCASTLE, when Thomas Bewick (q.v.), joined the Beilby workshop. Little is known of his work except that he contributed some cuts to the *Select Fables*, of 1784, along with Bewick, and John Bewick, The First (q.v.). This book was later the subject of some dispute between Bewick and Emerson Charnley, NEWCASTLE, who advertised it in *The Printer*, 1819, as "with cuts designed and engraved upon wood by Thomas and John Bewick previous to the year 1784". This occasioned Bewick to write to the publication, saying that the cuts were ". . . executed partly by my late Brother, when he was an apprentice, and partly by 'David Martin', whom I respected as a Man, but who was obliged from inability to seek some other line of work . . .".

*MARTIN, John, K.L., H.R.S.A. (1789-1854)

Historical, biblical, portrait and landscape painter in oil and watercolour; illustrator; engraver; decorative artist. Martin was born at HAYDON BRIDGE, the son of a tanner, and received his education at the free grammar school in the village. He left school in 1803, and partly because of his desire to become an artist, his family moved to NEWCASTLE, where he was apprenticed as an heraldic painter to a coachbuilder. After only a year with his master, however, and despairing of advancing his skills as an artist while serving this type of apprenticeship, he left his employer, and with his father's encouragement, he

became a pupil in the studio of Boniface Muss (q.v.), at NEWCASTLE. Here he was taught perspective drawing and enamel painting in the company of fellow pupil John Dobson (q.v.), but his tuition came to an abrupt end when Muss decided to follow his son, Charles Muss (q.v.), to London, in 1805. Martin followed his teacher to the capital in September, 1806, and initially attempted to earn a living by selling drawings of Northumbrian views. Ackermann bought three of these, but the idea was not generally successful. About 1807, Charles Muss started up in business with a partner, and took Martin on at £2 a week for five years, on condition that he would return half his pay for tuition in glass and china painting. Muss later went bankrupt, and he and Martin obtained positions in the stained glass workshop of William Collins, in the Strand.

At the age of nineteen, Martin married, and began to combine his somewhat irregular work for Collins, with painting and teaching, but without any marked improvement in his financial circumstances. In 1811, and following two rejections of his *Clytie* by the Royal Academy, he had a *Landscape composition* accepted, and leaving Collins in 1812 as an established craftsman and instructor, he decided to become a full-time professional painter. "Ambitious of fame", he later wrote, "I determined on painting a large picture, 'Sadak', which was executed in a month." Exhibited at the Royal Academy in the year in which he left Collins, this painting launched him on a career which within five years led to his appointment as "Historical Landscape Painter to the Princess Charlotte and Prince Leopold",‡ and ten years later earned for him from Sir Thomas Lawrence, President of the Royal Academy, the description: "the most popular painter of the day, John Martin". Lawrence's tribute to Martin followed the showing at the British Institution in 1821, of the latter's

116

Belshazzar's Feast, a picture so stunning and dramatic that it had to be railed off from its crowds of jostling spectators. This painting, deliberately designed by Martin to "make more noise than any picture did before", won him a prize of 200 guineas from the Institution, but was small compensation for his disappointment at being rejected as a candidate for the Royal Academy in the previous year. Indeed, despite the fact that in 1828 Martin was the only painter besides Lawrence to be included in *Public Characters of the Present Age*, and by 1831, thanks to his mezzotint engravings of his work, his had become a household name, he was never to become a Royal Academician. In fact he once complained of the Academy ". . . as I progressed in art and reputation my places on its walls retrograded". The Academy accepted a total of eight-three of his paintings between 1811 and 1852, but its members obviously felt that though his work was unquestionably imaginative, it was rarely masterful in technical terms. In fairness to their view it must be said that Martin experienced difficulty in disposing of his major works throughout his life, and it was largely from the sale of engravings of these works, and his illustrations for books such as the poems of Milton, that he derived his main income for many years. In addition to exhibiting his work at the Royal Academy, the British Institution, the Suffolk Street Gallery, and the New Water Colour Society (later the Royal Institute of Painters in Water Colours), Martin also exhibited at the Scottish Academy and abroad, this activity leading to his election as an

honorary member of the Royal Scottish Academy, and member of the Belgian Academy, and St. Luke's Academy, Rome. He was also an occasional exhibitor at NEWCASTLE, showing work at the Northumberland Institution for the Promotion of the Fine Arts, 1822, the Northern Academy, 1829, and at various exhibitions subsequently.

Not all of Martin's work was of the sort which had earlier shocked the public; in 1837 he painted his highly successful group portrait: *The Coronation of Queen Victoria*, and from 1840 he painted a large number of pure landscapes, two such works: *Scene in a forest – twilight*, and *View in Richmond Park*, appearing at the Royal Academy with his *Sodom and Gomorrah*,# when he last exhibited there in 1852. In the autumn of 1853, and having just completed his famous trio of "Judgement Pictures" – *The Last Judgement; The Plains of Heaven*, and *The Great Day of His Wrath* – Martin left the London which he had once excited so much and went on a visit to the Isle of Man. Here he suffered a stroke in February, 1854, dying at the same time as his "Judgement Pictures" were being shown in the Victoria Rooms, Grey Street, NEWCASTLE. His work from then on gradually fell in popularity, the once famous "Judgement Pictures" only bringing £7 when they were auctioned in London some sixty-odd years later. At the present time, thanks to a succession of excellent exhibitions of his work at the Laing Art Gallery, NEWCASTLE, and at various London galleries over the past thirty years, and William Feaver's excellent book: *The Art of*

John Martin: The destruction of Sodom and Gomorrah. Oil 52½×82½. *Tyne & Wear County Council Museums, Laing Art Gallery.*

John Martin, 1975, it is probably enjoying its greatest popularity since his death. Martin's son, CHARLES MARTIN (1820-1896), was also a professional artist, and another son, ALFRED MARTIN (d.1872), did some mezzotint engraving. Several of his brothers dabbled in caricature and other types of art, but without notable success. Represented: British Museum; Victoria and Albert Museum; Tate Gallery; Carlisle A.G.; Glasgow A.G.; Laing A.G., Newcastle; Manchester City A.G.; Walker A.G., Liverpool.

‡ *Martin's title of "K.L." – Knight of the Order of Leopold – was conferred upon him by this same Prince (later first King of the Belgians), in 1833.*

*MASON, Frank Henry, R.I., R.B.A. (1876-1965)

Marine and coastal painter in oil and watercolour; illustrator and poster designer; etcher. Mason was born at SEATON CAREW, and after education at private schools, and H.M.S. Conway, became a ship's engineer. His early days at sea infected him with a lifelong love of ships, and while serving as an engineer he began to exhibit marine subjects, making his first mark with his Royal Academy exhibit of 1900: *The Power and Wealth of the Tyne*. This work was contributed from Scarborough, North Yorkshire, where he had settled to take instruction from Albert Strange at the town's School of Art, and from this base he gradually widened the exposure of his work to embrace not only the Royal Academy, but the Royal Institute of Painters in Watercolours, the Royal Society of British Artists, and several provincial venues, including the Artists of the Northern Counties exhibitions at the Laing Art Gallery, showing work from their inception in 1905. During this period, however, and notwithstanding his increasing success as an artist, he also worked as an engineer at Leeds and HARTLEPOOL, and it was not until after service in the First World War as a Lieutenant in the R.N.V.R., and as an Official War Artist, that he finally became a full-time professional artist. His later work included many fine portraits of Royal Navy, and merchant ships, coastal scenes with fishing vessels,# book illustrations, and numerous posters for the London and North Eastern Railway, and other railway companies. His marine work was particularly valued for its accuracy, and was largely executed in watercolour. He worked in London for much of his professional life, retiring to Scarborough, where he died in 1965. He was elected a member of the Royal Society of British Artists in 1904, and a member of the Royal Institute of Painters in Water Colours in 1929. An important exhibition of his work was held at the National Maritime Museum in 1973. Represented: Imperial War Museum; Cartwright Hall, Bradford; Dundee A.G.; Gray A.G. & Museum, Hartlepool; Laing A.G., Newcastle; Pannett A.G., Whitby; South Shields Museum & A.G.

MATHER, John Robert (1834-1879)

Coastal and landscape painter in watercolour. Mather was born at NEWCASTLE and spent his early years at sea, rising to the position of captain, before practising as an artist in his native town by 1862, in which year he began exhibiting at the Suffolk Street Gallery, showing: *At anchor on the lee shore – Day after the storm*. He continued to exhibit at the Suffolk Street Gallery until 1872, towards the end of this period living at WHITLEY BAY. From WHITLEY BAY he also sent work to the "Central Exchange News Room, Art Gallery, and Polytechnic Exhibition", at NEWCASTLE, in 1870, showing three marine works. He last showed his work at NEWCASTLE in 1878, when he sent seven works to the exhibition of works of local painters, at the Central Exchange Art Gallery. According to William Weaver Tomlinson, in his *Historical notes on Cullercoats, Whitley and Monkseaton*, 1893, Mather spent his final years at 49, Beverley Terrace, CULLERCOATS, dying there in 1879, aged 45 years. Represented: Shipley A.G., Gateshead.

Frank Henry Mason: On the beach near Bridlington, Yorkshire. Watercolour 14×20. *Dean Gallery.*

MATHIESON, William (d. 1900)

Landscape and coastal painter in oil and watercolour. This artist practised at NEWCASTLE, GATESHEAD, and SUNDERLAND, in the late 19th century. Amongst his earliest known exhibits are the four landscapes which he sent to the Central Exchange Art Gallery exhibition of the work of local painters, at NEWCASTLE, in 1878. His pictures in this exhibition were described in the catalogue notes as: "hard and crude, but there is great promise of future excellence". He later became a regular exhibitor at the Bewick Club, NEWCASTLE, several of his exhibits attracting favourable comment from reviewers. He died at GATESHEAD.

MAUGHAN, James Humphrey Morland (1817-1853)

Amateur landscape painter in watercolour. Maughan lived in Northumbria until 1844, when he moved to Maidstone, Kent, to work as a schoolmaster. In 1847 he joined H.M. Customs & Excise in NEWCASTLE, and in 1853 he was transferred to the London office. Two examples of his work were illustrated in *Country Life*, May 22nd, 1969, in connection with a letter to the editor. These works appeared over the title *Watery wastes*, and portrayed a coastal castle in ruins, and a river scene with bridge, and distant cathedral. He died in London.

MAWSON, Elizabeth Cameron (1849-1939)

Amateur landscape, genre and portrait painter in oil and watercolour. She was born at GATESHEAD, the daughter of businessman and later Sheriff of NEW-CASTLE, John Mawson, and was educated at Bedford College, London, before taking up art as a hobby. Within a few years of returning to Tyneside she had achieved remarkable proficiency as a painter of a wide range of subjects, and in 1878 had examples of her work shown at two major exhibitions at NEWCASTLE; the exhibition of works by local painters, at the Central Exchange Art Gallery, and the Arts Association. Three of these works shown in 1878 were landscapes with buildings; two were flower studies. In 1881 she commenced exhibiting outside Northumbria, between that date and 1893, showing examples at the Royal Academy, the Royal Scottish Academy, the Royal Institute of Painters in Water Colours, the Royal Institute of Oil Painters, the Royal Scottish Society of Painters in Water Colours, and in the provinces. She continued to exhibit at NEWCASTLE throughout her life, contributing to later exhibitions of the Arts Association, and sending occasional works to the Bewick Club. She died at GATES-HEAD. Represented: Shipley A.G., Gateshead.

McEUNE, Robert Ernest (1876-1952)

Portrait, figure, landscape and still-life painter in oil, watercolour and pastel; art teacher. He was born at GATESHEAD, and studied figure drawing and painting at the town's School of Art, under William Fitzjames White (q.v.), before attending Armstrong College (later King's College; now Newcastle University). He later took up employment as an executive of a Tyneside coal company, but continued to take a keen interest in art in his spare time, producing many paintings and drawings, and preparing book illustrations. At the beginning of the Second World War he was forced to retire due to ill-health, and resigning his coal company position he retired to Penrith, Cumberland. Here he taught art as a member of the staff of the Royal Grammar School, NEWCASTLE, while its pupils were evacuated to the town. Mc Eune first exhibited his work at the Artists of the Northern Counties exhibitions at the Laing Art Gallery, NEWCASTLE, later showing examples at the Royal Institute of Painters in Water Colours, and the London Pastel Society. He was a contributor to the "Contemporary Artists of Durham County" exhibition staged at the Shipley Art Gallery, GATESHEAD, in 1951, in connection with the Festival of Britain, and a posthumous exhibition of his work was held at this gallery in 1971, following its acquisition of a large number of his oils, watercolours, charcoal drawings and pencil sketches. Represented: Laing A.G., Newcastle; Shipley A.G., Gateshead.

McINTYRE, Joseph Wrightson (c. 1844- after 1894)

Landscape, coastal and genre painter in oil and water-colour. He was born at MORPETH, the son of itinerant Scottish born artist Joseph McIntyre, who had earlier practised at SOUTH SHIELDS. He received his early tuition in art from his father at Sheffield, later moving to London, where in 1866 he commenced exhibiting at the Suffolk Street Gallery, showing his *Clearing up after a storm*, and *Glen Tilt*. In 1871 he showed his first work at the Royal Academy: *A north-easterly gale on the Yorkshire Coast*, three years later settling at Sheffield, from which he continued to exhibit at the Royal Academy and the Suffolk Street Gallery, mainly show-ing North East of England coastal scenes, and Scottish landscapes. He also exhibited at the Royal Hibernian Academy, and in the provinces, where he was an exhibitor at the Arts Association, NEWCASTLE, in 1879 and 1882. It appears that he remained at Sheffield from c. 1875, until some time after last exhibiting his work, in 1894. Sheffield Art Gallery has his 1872 Royal Academy exhibit: *A Gleam of Hope*. His brothers, JAMES McINTYRE, and ROBERT FINLAY McINTYRE, were also professional artists, and exhibited their work.

McKELVIE, Robert (1889-1979)

Amateur landscape and architectural painter in water-colour; architectural draughtsman. Born at GATESHEAD, McKelvie showed a talent for drawing from an early age, but decided on a clerical career, instead of attempt-ing to succeed as an artist. He became an office worker in a shipyard, meanwhile attending local evening classes in art, as well as other studies. From leaving the shipyard office, and throughout his subsequent career as buyer for a Tyneside paint firm he did little drawing and painting, but on his retirement at seventy, resumed his early hobby with considerable success. Within a short while his work was included in an exhibition at DURHAM, and in 1973 he was one of several Northum-brian artists whose work was included in an exhibition in the library of St. Nicholas' Cathedral, NEWCASTLE. He died at GATESHEAD.

119

McKENDRICK, Thomas (1862-1890)
Landscape painter in watercolour. He was born at
NEWCASTLE, the son of the chairman of the Newcastle
Co-operative Society, and worked most of his life in a
city bank, painting and sketching in his spare time. He
was a member and towards the end of his life treasurer,
of the Newcastle Sketching Club, and was a frequent
exhibitor with his Club, and with the Bewick Club,
NEWCASTLE, until his death at the early age of thirty-
seven.

***McLACHLAN, Thomas Hope, R.I., R.O.I., N.E.A.C.
(1845-1897)**
Landscape and genre painter in oil and watercolour;
etcher. McLachlan was born at DARLINGTON, the son of
a banker, and received his education at Merchiston
Castle School, Edinburgh. He later studied law at
Trinity College, Cambridge, then entering Lincoln's
Inn Courts in 1865, was called to the bar in 1868.
Throughout his education, and later training for the
law, McLachlan had taken a keen interest in painting
and drawing, and after exhibiting at various London
galleries from 1875, and the Royal Academy in 1877,
he was encouraged by John Petrie and others to become
a full-time professional artist. Aware of his lack of
training, however, he first studied in Paris in the studio
of Carolus Duran, and here became much influenced
by the work of Millet. On returning to Britain he
resumed exhibiting at the Royal Academy, and in the
next twenty years exhibited widely throughout the
country, showing examples of his works at the Royal
Institute of Oil Painters, the Royal Institute of Painters
in Water Colours, the New English Art Club, and at
various London and provincial venues, including among
the latter, the Bewick Club, NEWCASTLE. Most of his
exhibits were painted in Scotland, the Lake District,
and Northumbria, and frequently featured stretches of
water, woodland or marshland, with twilit skies. He

achieved considerable success in his brief career as an
artist, becoming elected a member of the New English
Art Club in 1887, the Royal Institute of Oil Painters in
1890, and the Royal Institute of Painters in Water
Colours in 1897. In the year prior to his death at
Weybridge, Surrey, he attracted much interest when his
work was exhibited alongside that of five other painters,
in the "Landscape Exhibition", at the Dudley Gallery,
London. A typical example of his work is his *Evening
Quiet*,# in the Tate Gallery. McLachlan was later in his
life deeply interested in etching, and dry point work,
and provided illustrations for B. Hall's *Fish Tails and
some true ones*, 1897. He also exhibited his work in the
former medium, at the Royal Society of Painter-Etchers
and Engravers. Darlington Art Gallery has several
examples of his later work in oil, watercolour and
etching. His daughter, ELIZABETH HOPE
McLACHLAN, was also a talented artist, and exhibited
her work. Represented: Tate Gallery; Darlington A.G.

*McLEA, Duncan Fraser (1841-1916)
Marine, landscape and portrait painter in oil and
watercolour; draughtsman. He was born in Scotland,
the son of a drawing master. He went to sea in his
youth, and after serving for some years as a ship's mate,
decided to take up painting as a career, settling at SOUTH
SHIELDS. Here he became well known for his paintings
of local shipping and coastal scenes, and for his pen and
ink drawings of similar subjects for reproduction. He is
known to have exhibited outside Northumbria on only
two occasions, these being at the Royal Scottish Academy in 1884 and 1886. He was, however, a regular
exhibitor on Tyneside from 1878, when he showed a
total of eight works at the exhibitions of the Arts
Association, and the Central Exchange Art Gallery,
NEWCASTLE, in that year. He was an occasional exhibitor
at the Bewick Club, NEWCASTLE, and exhibited his work
at South Shields Art Club in 1892, 1893 and 1894, also

Thomas Hope McLachlan:
Evening Quiet, 1891. Oil
23×34¼. *Tate Gallery.*

120

serving as vice-president and committee member. He was an occasional portrait painter, two of his subjects being himself, and Robert F. Watson (q.v.); both of these works, together with a substantial number of his oils, watercolours and drawings, are in the collection of South Shields Museum & Art Gallery. McLea's landscape work included a number of Scottish subjects, one of these: *Close of day,#* exhibited at the Arts Association in 1879, being accounted his best work. A comparable work, however, is his study of John Thompson's shipbuilding yard, at SUNDERLAND, in the collection of Sunderland Art Gallery. Much of his later work is characterised by rather crude colouring, and indifferent draughtsmanship, this being due, it is said, to his failing eyesight. He died at SOUTH SHIELDS. His daughter, MARGARET McLEA (d.1947), was also a talented artist, and occasionally exhibited her work at the Bewick Club. Represented: South Shields Museum & A.G.; Sunderland A.G.

MEYNELL, Jack (1894-1970)

Portrait painter in oil and watercolour; draughtsman; caricaturist; illustrator. Born at SUNDERLAND, Meynell attended the town's School of Art before obtaining employment as a commercial artist with a fine art publisher on Wearside. After service in the First World War he went to London, where he eventually joined Odhams Press as a commercial artist in 1932. From Odhams he joined the *News Chronicle*, remaining there until 1947, when he joined the *Daily Express*. He worked for the *Express* until his retirement at the age of seventy, when he returned to SUNDERLAND. He died at SUNDERLAND. A large collection of portrait work in monochrome, including Sir Winston Churchill, John F. Kennedy, Hugh Gaitskill, and other famous men and women of his day, was presented to Sunderland Art Gallery in 1971.

MIDGLEY, Charles James (c.1865- c.1895)

Coastal and landscape painter in watercolour. Midgely was born on Tyneside, and practised as an artist in Northumbria throughout the late 19th century. He occasionally exhibited his work at NEWCASTLE, from 1878, in which year he exhibited his *St. Mary's Island*, at the Arts Association, and several pictures of CULLERCOATS, at the exhibition of works by local painters, at the Central Exchange Art Gallery. He was later an exhibitor at the Bewick Club, mainly showing coastal views. He may have been related to another Bewick Club exhibitor, JAMES TYNDALL MIDGLEY, of SUNDERLAND.

MILLER, James Jerome (c.1880- after 1932)

Amateur landscape and coastal painter in oil and watercolour. Miller was born at SOUTH SHIELDS, and became a painter and decorator in the town, painting in his spare time. He first commenced exhibiting his work at the Artists of the Northern Counties exhibitions at the Laing Art Gallery, NEWCASTLE, in 1910 showing his *On the beach*, and *Harvest Time*. He continued to exhibit at NEWCASTLE until the early 1930's, meanwhile exhibiting one work at the Royal Academy in 1914:

Duncan Fraser McLea: Close of Day, 1879. Oil 36×20. *Private collection.*

Stephenson's Birthplace, and sending a number of works for exhibition at the Royal Scottish Academy, the Glasgow Institute of Fine Arts, and the Walker Art Gallery, Liverpool, 1912-15. It is believed that he died at SOUTH SHIELDS. Represented: South Shields Museum & A.G.

MILLER, Joseph (fl. early 19th cent.)

Landscape painter in oil. This artist practised at STAINDROP, near BARNARD CASTLE, in the early 19th century, and sent several works for exhibition at NEWCASTLE in this period. When he exhibited *A View of Wensleydale*, and *Landscape, near Darlington*, at the Northern Academy, in 1829, W. A. Mitchell of the *Tyne Mercury* commented of Miller's first work: "The artist shows considerable skill in detail, and when he gets rid of his stiffness and village painter-like manner, he should soon rank amongst rapidly rising artists", while of the second he said: "Mr. Miller has overcome his hardness and stiffness of manner . . . we may have the best hopes of him . . .". Miller again exhibited at NEWCASTLE in 1831, showing two works at the Northern Academy, but appears to have exhibited on only one occasion subsequently, this being when he loaned his *Cottage near Middleton in Teesdale*, and *Moonlight, Gipsies*, to the "Exhibition of Arts, Manufactures & Practical Science", at NEWCASTLE, in 1840. Darlington Art Gallery has his oil: *High Force*.

MILLER, Lynn (fl. early 20th cent.)

Landscape and coastal painter in oil and watercolour. This artist practised at SOUTH SHIELDS in the early years of the present century, and regularly exhibited his work at the Artists of the Northern Counties exhibitions at the Laing Art Gallery, NEWCASTLE, from their inception in 1905, until 1936. From 1911 until 1936 he lived at RYTON. His final exhibits at the Laing Art Gallery comprised two watercolour views of Whitby Harbour, North Yorkshire. His artist son WILLIAM LYNN MILLER spent several years at RYTON, before moving to SUNDERLAND, and also exhibited his work at the Artists of the Northern Counties exhibitions. They may have been related to FREDERICK MILLER, who shared an address at SOUTH SHIELDS with Lynn Miller in the early years of the century, when also exhibiting at the Artists of the Northern Counties exhibitions.

MILLER, Robert Appleby (d.1918)

Stained glass designer; portrait painter in oil; sculptor; decorative designer. Miller practised on Tyneside in the late 19th and early 20th centuries, and occasionally exhibited his work at the Artists of the Northern Counties exhibitions at the Laing Art Gallery, NEWCASTLE, from their inception in 1905, and at the city's Pen & Palette Club, throughout his membership. His exhibits at the Laing Art Gallery included his *Northumbria*, and *Tritons* (both in plaster), 1905, and his *Head of a Girl* (oil), 1910. Following his death in March, 1918, an exhibition of his work was held at the Pen & Palette Club, together with that of one-time fellow member, RICHARD J. LEESON (d.1914). Miller was responsible for designing many items of printed matter associated with the Club, and also designed the cover of the catalogue which was used for the Artists of the Northern Counties exhibitions 1908-1925. His work in stained glass was regarded as particularly fine, and one of his designs in this field was accepted for showing at the Royal Academy in 1902.

MILNE, William (1873-1951)

Amateur landscape and coastal painter in oil and watercolour. Milne was born on Tyneside, and worked most of his life as an official of the Corporation of NEWCASTLE, painting in his spare time. He studied art as a young man under Robert Ventress (q.v.), and later became a regular exhibitor at NEWCASTLE, showing work at the city's Bewick Club, and later the Artists of the Northern Counties exhibitions at the Laing Art Gallery, and the Newcastle Society of Artists. A one-man exhibition of his work was held at the Hatton Gallery, NEWCASTLE. He died at NEWCASTLE. The Laing Art Gallery has his *River Scene at Gilsland*.

*MITCHELL, Charles William (1855-1903)

Figure and portrait painter in oil and pastel; mosaic artist. Mitchell was born at WALKER, near NEWCASTLE, the son of a shipbuilder. Following his general education and after early displaying a talent for drawing and painting, his father permitted him to study in Paris under Comte. On returning to Tyneside he was allowed to continue his interest in painting, and by the age of twenty-two had commenced exhibiting at the Royal Academy, showing: *A Duet*. Two years later he again exhibited at the Academy, showing a portrait: *Lucy*, and in the same year was one of the many Northumbrian artists who sent work to the first exhibition of the Arts Association, at NEWCASTLE. He had by now moved to London, where he continued to exhibit at the Academy until his mid-thirties, and also showed work at the Bewick Club, NEWCASTLE, but his first major artistic success came with the exhibition of his *Hypatia,#* at the Grosvenor Gallery, London, in 1885. This work was later shown at the Royal Jubilee Exhibition at Manchester in 1887, the Guildhall, London, in 1900, and more recently at the Royal Academy, London, in 1977, as part of an exhibition to mark the Silver Jubilee of Her Majesty The Queen.

Four years after first showing *Hypatia*, Mitchell left London, and virtually gave up painting to concentrate on his father's business interests, satisfying himself instead by helping to promote the arts on Tyneside. He became chairman of the School of Art Committee at the Durham College of Physical Science, NEWCASTLE, and purchased the old Academy of Arts building in the city with the object of presenting it as a home for the

Charles William Mitchell: Hypatia. Oil 96¼×60. *Tyne & Wear County Council Museums, Laing Art Gallery.*

122

John Henry Mole: The Fair on the common. Watercolour 5½×15. *Moss Galleries.*

arts on Tyneside. He spent a considerable sum of money on refitting the Academy for this purpose, later enabling several important exhibitions to be staged on its premises. He also became vice-president of the Northumberland Handicrafts Guild, and was a founder member of the Pen & Palette Club, NEWCASTLE, later serving as president. He died at NEWCASTLE at the early age of forty-eight. The Laing Art Gallery, NEWCASTLE, has his *Hypatia*, and other works, and his mosaic of the Apostles may be seen in the chancel of St. George's Church, in the Jesmond area of the city. This church was built in 1888 to the design of Thomas Ralph Spence (q.v.). A handsome memorial tablet with bronze figures was placed in the inside south wall of the church following Mitchell's death, to match his father's memorial tablet in the north wall.

MITCHELL, J. Edgar (1871-1922)

Portrait, figure and landscape painter in oil and watercolour. Mitchell's place of birth is not recorded, but is thought to have been Scotland, as it was in Dundee that he first began practising as a professional artist, by the age of twenty-two. He first exhibited his work in Scotland, where in 1893, he sent one work to the Royal Scottish Society of Painters in Water Colours. Two years later, and practising in Edinburgh, he commenced exhibiting at the Royal Scottish Academy, meanwhile sending two works to the Bewick Club, NEWCASTLE, in 1894. Just before the turn of the century he decided to make his home in Northumbria, settling eventually at NEWCASTLE, where he maintained studios in the Haymarket area of the city until his death in 1922. While practising in the city he sent four works to the Royal

Academy, commencing in 1904, with *The Village Tailor*, and after joining the Pen & Palette Club, NEWCASTLE, in 1904, became a regular exhibitor with the Club, and at the Artists of the Northern Counties exhibitions at the Laing Art Gallery, nearby. He showed work at the latter exhibitions, and at the city's Bewick Club, until his death, showing a large number of portraits of local celebrities, and North Country landscapes. Represented: Laing A.G., Newcastle; South Shields Museum & A.G.; Sunderland A.G.

MITFORD, Bertram Osbaldeston (1777-1842)

Caricaturist in line and wash. He was the owner of Mitford Castle, near MORPETH, and amused himself in leisure moments by producing crude though amusing caricatures in the manner of George Moutard Woodward (1760-1809), and copying the work of Rowlandson. He served as High Sheriff of the County of Northumberland in 1835, and in that year adopted the name "Osbaldeston". Represented: British Museum.

*MOLE, John Henry, V.P.R.I. (1814-1886)

Landscape and figure painter in oil and watercolour; miniature painter. Mole was born at ALNWICK, the son of a jobbing cabinet maker, who some years later moved his business to NEWCASTLE. Here Mole first worked as a clerk in the solicitor's office of a brother of William Wailes (q.v.), who encouraged his employee to draw when work was slack. While working as a clerk he also joined an art society at NEWCASTLE, comprising John Brown (q.v.), Thomas Hall Tweedy (q.v.), and other artists then seeking to develop their talents. This society flourished about 1830-35, and held its first

123

exhibition at T. Bamford's Long Room at Amen Corner in the town. It later moved its meeting place and exhibition venue to the Old Tower, Pink Lane, where Mole began to assume a leading role in encouraging his fellow members in their progress. Later he began to take instruction in minature painting from Thomas Heathfield Carrick, the Carlisle artist,. watercolour painting his likenesses on white marble statuary tablets in the manner of his master. He soon tired of this practice, however, and turning to landscape and figure painting as a relaxation, commenced exhibiting his work at NEWCASTLE, showing two theatrical studies, and one genre work, at the North of England Society for the Promotion of the Fine Arts, 1836.

Mole continued to exhibit at NEWCASTLE until the middle of the century, also in this period exhibiting at the Royal Academy in 1845 and 1856, the New Water Colour Society (later the Royal Institute of Painters in Water Colours), from 1845, and the Carlisle Academy in 1846 and 1850. His Royal Academy exhibits were all portraits, and, indeed, he continued to advertise himself as a portrait painter at NEWCASTLE until his election as an associate of the New Water Colour Society in 1847. Following his election as a full member of the Society in 1848, however, he gave up painting portrait miniatures in favour of landscapes with figures,# exhibiting more than 600 such works at the Society by the time of his death. He was also an occasional exhibitor of such works at the British Institution, the Suffolk Street Gallery, the Grosvenor and various other London galleries, and at NEWCASTLE, where his exhibits at the Bewick Club, in 1884, for instance, were: *Old Mill in Jesmond Dene*, and *On the Derwent, Borrowdale, Cumberland*. Most of Mole's work was in watercolour (though he did exhibit an oil: *Carrying Peat*, at the Royal Academy in 1879), its quality, and the number of his exhibits at the New Water Colour Society, leading to his election as its vice-president the year after it was authorised to style itself the Royal Institute of Painters in Water Colours. This honour came only two years short of his death at Russell Square, London, in 1886. Represented: Victoria and Albert Museum; Accrington A.G.; Cartwright Hall, Bradford; Gray A.G. & Museum, Hartlepool; Laing A.G., Newcastle; North Tyneside Public Libraries; Shipley A.G., Gateshead; South Shields Museum & A.G.; Sunderland A.G., and various provincial art galleries.

MONCK, Lady Mary Elizabeth (née Bennet) (d.1851)
Amateur landscape painter in watercolour. The daughter of the 4th Earl of Tankerville, of Chillingham Castle, CHILLINGHAM, she became in 1831 the second wife of Greek Scholar and M.P., Sir Charles Lambert Monck, of Belsay Castle, near CAMBO. A keen amateur artist from her childhood, she later received lessons from John Varley, and produced a considerable volume of watercolours and pencil sketches reflecting the influence of this artist. An illustrated memorandum containing twelve watercolours, and pencil sketches, and two other works, were included in "The Picturesque Tour" exhibition staged at the Laing Art Gallery, NEWCASTLE, in 1982.

MOORE, Anthony John (1852-1915)
Amateur marine and coastal painter in oil and watercolour. Moore was born at MONKWEARMOUTH, near SUNDERLAND, the son of an India merchant, and became a violin maker, painting in his spare time. He spent most of his life on Wearside, and exhibited his work exclusively in Northumbria, one of his earliest known exhibits being the genre work: *The Doll's Frock*, which he sent to the "Gateshead Fine Art & Industrial Exhibition", in 1883. He was later an occasional exhibitor at the Bewick Club, NEWCASTLE, and at various venues in SUNDERLAND. He died at SUNDERLAND. He was possibly the brother of J. White Moore (q.v.). Sunderland Art Gallery has a large collection of his work dated 1880-1912, and mainly consisting of shipping, river and street scenes in watercolour.

MOORE, J. White (fl. late 19th cent.)
Landscape and coastal painter in watercolour. This artist practised at SUNDERLAND and HARTLEPOOL, in the late 19th century, from which he mainly sent work for exhibition to the Bewick Club, NEWCASTLE. In 1897 he sent one work for exhibition at the Glasgow Institute of Fine Arts, while practising at HARTLEPOOL. He may have been the brother of Anthony John Moore (q.v.). Sunderland Art Gallery has his views in watercolour: *Whitburn, near Sunderland*, and *River Wear, near Hylton*.

MORTON, Andrew (1802-1845)
Portrait, figure and landscape painter in oil and watercolour. He was born at NEWCASTLE, the son of ship owner Joseph Morton, and elder brother of Thomas Morton, the surgeon. He left NEWCASTLE for London at an early age to enter the Royal Academy Schools, where in 1821 he gained a silver medal, with the Discourses of Barry, Opie and Fuseli, for the best copy of Raphael's *A Madonna and Child*. From 1821 he exhibited at the Royal Academy, the British Institution and the Suffolk Street Gallery, mainly showing portraits. He also exhibited his work at NEWCASTLE, showing portraits, and occasional landscape and genre works, at the Northumberland Institution for the Promotion of the Fine Arts, and the Northern Academy. While working at NEWCASTLE in 1826, he also showed one work at the Carlisle Academy. Morton's work in portraiture has been likened to that of Sir Thomas Lawrence, the Royal Academician, and one-time President of the Academy, and enabled him to build up a considerable demand for his work in London. Many distinguished men and women sat for him, including William IV, Sir James Cockburn, and Marianna, Lady Cockburn, Marianna Augusta, Lady Hamilton, and the Duke of Wellington. His portrait work also embraced several Northumbrian celebrities, among these Dr. Charles Hutton, painted for the Literary and Philosophical Society, NEWCASTLE, and Thomas Bigge, Mayor of NEWCASTLE. He died in London. Represented: National Portrait Gallery; Scottish National Portrait Gallery; Tate Gallery; Laing A.G., Newcastle; Literary and Philosophical Society, Newcastle; Newcastle Central Library.

MORTON, George (1851-1904)

Portrait and genre painter in oil and watercolour. Morton was born at HOUGHTON-LE-SPRING, near SUNDERLAND, and at the age of fifteen moved to NEWCASTLE to attend the Government School of Design, under William Cosens Way (q.v.). In 1873 he moved to London and entered the Royal College of Art, where he was very successful in his studies. He afterwards attended the Royal Academy Schools, where he is said to have been equally successful in pursuing his studies. In 1879 he began to exhibit his work at the New Water Colour Society (later the Royal Institute of Painters in Water Colours), and by 1884 had commenced exhibiting at the Royal Academy, and the Suffolk Street Gallery, at the former showing: *A Gentle Breeze*, and at the latter: *Idleness*. He remained an exhibitor at the Royal Academy until his death, also exhibiting his work at the Royal Hibernian Academy, the Royal Institute of Oil Painters, the New English Art Club, and at various London and provincial exhibitions, including the Bewick Club, NEWCASTLE. During the last seven years of his life Morton held the position of Deputy Principal of the Royal College of Art. His *After the Bath* was purchased by the Queen. He died at London. The Laing Art Gallery, NEWCASTLE, has his oil: *A portrait study*.

MOSSMAN, David (1825-1901)

Miniature painter; landscape and genre painter in watercolour. Mossman was born at NEWCASTLE, and first began practising as an artist in his native town, where among his earliest exhibits were the portrait miniatures which he showed at the North of England Society for the Promotion of the Fine Arts, 1852. In the following year, and still practising at NEWCASTLE, he sent his first work to the Royal Academy, exhibiting a portrait miniature of Sir John Fife. He continued to work on Tyneside for the next ten years, during which period he continued to exhibit his miniatures at the Academy, and in 1857 commenced exhibiting genre works at the Suffolk Street Gallery. By 1863 he had moved to London, remaining there until late in his life, and exhibiting his work at the Royal Academy, the Royal Hibernian Academy, the Royal Institute of Painters in Water Colours, and Royal Society of British Artists, and occasionally at NEWCASTLE, notably at the "Exhibition of Paintings and other Works of Art", 1866, and the Royal Jubilee Exhibition, 1887. While based in London he evidently paid several visits to his native Northumbria, one of his works produced on such an occasion being the *Turret at Blackcarts Farm*, 1875, which, together with a view of TYNEMOUTH, and a portrait of builder Richard Grainger, forms the collection of his watercolours in the Laing Art Gallery, NEWCASTLE. It is believed that he died in London.

MUSS, Boniface (c.1758- after 1805)

Landscape and portrait painter in oil and watercolour; drawing master. Muss was born in Piedmont, Italy, and following some success as a painter in his native country decided to emigrate to England. Arriving in London some time before 1779, he remained in the capital until 1790, when he sent a work to the Society of Artists exhibition of that year, entitled: *Landscape and ruins;*

Drawing. In the latter year, if we are to believe Eneas Mackenzie, in his *History of Newcastle* (Volume II, page 579) Muss moved to NEWCASTLE "with very respectable recommendations", and was here "well patronised as a painter and drawing master". It would appear that his main claim to fame was in the latter activity, for he was teacher of drawing not only to his son, Charles Muss (q.v.), later well known as an enamel painter, but to William Nicholson (q.v.), John Dobson (q.v.), and John Martin (q.v.), as well as the lesser known William Hodgson (q.v.). Muss's studio was in the attic of his lodgings at Newgate Street, NEWCASTLE, and here he also taught fencing and Italian. "Though extremely indolent, he was a skilful artist", says Mackenzie, "and a generous, liberal minded man, and was particularly anxious to foster rising genius". His living in NEWCASTLE (and for some time at GATESHEAD, at which he lived and practised in 1801), was too precarious, however, and when his son, Charles, took a job as a china painter in London in 1805, he decided to join him there. His second period in London is as poorly documented as his first, and it is not known when, and where, he died. His daughter is said to have been artistic, and according to Mackenzie: "painted and etched several local views", while living at NEWCASTLE. Her view of Fenham Hall may be seen in Hodgson's *History of Northumberland*.

MUSS, Charles (1779-1824)

Enamel and miniature painter; etcher; stained glass designer. Muss was probably born in London, some time after the emigration to England of his father Boniface Muss (q.v.), from Piedmont, Italy. At the age of eleven he moved with his family to NEWCASTLE, where he received tuition in drawing and enamel painting from his father. Towards the end of his ten-year stay in the town he began to practise as a miniature painter, experimenting in enamel painting in his spare time. In the early part of 1800 he moved to London, hoping to succeed as a professional artist in the capital. Later in the same year he sent his first work to the Royal Academy: *Dunkeld Cathedral*, following this in 1802 by exhibiting two miniatures: *Portrait of an Artist*, and *Portrait of a Lady*. He exhibited a further work at the Royal Academy in 1803, entitled *Psyche*, but finding it increasingly difficult to succeed as a miniature painter and occasional enameller, he two years later took a job as a china painter in London, eventually intending to set up on his own. About 1807 he started a business with a partner, later taking on as a pupil John Martin (q.v.). An exhibition which he put on in Bond Street failed, however, and he was obliged to enter the stained glass workshop of William Collins, in the Strand. His work for Collins was highly regarded, specimens being used at St. Bride's in London's Fleet Street, and at Brancepeth Castle, near DURHAM.

Muss retained his interest in enamel painting throughout his early years in London, and produced several examples for George III. Following his success in exhibiting work at the Academy from 1817, he was appointed enamel painter to George IV, while Regent. Most of his Academy exhibits from 1817, until he last exhibited in the year before his death, consisted of enamel copies of works by leading continental and English artists. Several of his enamels were of large proportions, his *Holy Family*, after Parmigianino being described as the "largest enamel ever painted". This work was purchased by George IV for 1600 guineas. He left several enamels unfinished on his death in London in 1824, which were later finished by John Martin. The National Portrait Gallery, London, has his enamel after Sir Thomas Lawrence, the Royal Academician, of Sir Francis Baring Bt., measuring 12″×9″. Thirty-three original designs for Gay's *Fables*, drawn and etched by Muss, were published in the year following his death. His sister was also a painter and etcher of some ability.

NESBIT, Charlton (1775-1838)

Wood engraver; illustrator. Nesbit was born at SWAL-WELL, near GATESHEAD, the son of a keelman, and was apprenticed to Ralph Beilby (q.v.), and Thomas Bewick (q.v.), at NEWCASTLE, in 1790, at the age of fourteen. While working for the partners he contributed a number of cuts to Bewick's *Birds*, 1797, the *Poems of Goldsmith and Parnell*, 1795, and *Le Grand's Fabliaux*, 1796 and 1800. His most notable work in engraving, however, was executed shortly after leaving Beilby and Bewick, and consisted of what was then described as one of the largest wood engravings ever attempted. His subject was *A North View of St. Nicholas' Church*, painted by his late friend Robert Johnson (q.v.), and was engraved for the benefit of Johnson's aged parents, while Nesbit was still resident and working at NEWCASTLE. The cut was published in London in 1798, and earned Nesbit

the lesser silver palette of the Society of Arts, and later its silver medal. Shortly after its publication Nesbit moved to London, where he is said to have "found the art of engraving in a miserably low state". Here, thanks to an early association with John Thurston, who allowed Nesbit to cut his designs, he quickly established a reputation as a fine reproductive engraver, and remaining in the capital until 1815, executed much fine work, notably for Ackermann's *Religious Emblems*, 1809. Following his return to SWALWELL, he continued engraving, though technically retired, thanks to an inheritance, and contributed cuts to Puckle's *The Club*, 1817, Emerson Charnley's edition of the *Select Fables*, 1820 (a portrait of Bewick drawn on the wood by William Nicholson (q.v.), and engraved by Nesbit as the frontispiece), and Northcote's *Fables*, 1828 and 1833. In 1830 he decided to return to the capital, and settling at Brompton, died there in 1838. Although his main success stemmed from his ability to interpret as wood engravings the designs on wood executed by leading artists of his day, Nesbit was evidently inventive in his work, and is credited with the introduction of cross-hatching, which it was imagined could not be done on wood. There is some suggestion also that he might himself have been capable of designing illustrations; the Natural History Society of Northumbria, NEWCASTLE, has two designs in pen and wash for *Le Grand Fabliaux*, which he may have prepared, as well as cut. Represented: Newcastle Central Library.

*NESFIELD, William Andrews, O.W.S. (1793-1881)

Landscape painter in watercolour. He was born at CHESTER-LE-STREET, the son of a local Rector, and was educated at Winchester, Trinity College, Cambridge, and Woolwich. He entered the Army in 1809, and served in the Peninsular War under Wellington, and in

William Andrews Nesfield: Bamburgh Castle, Northumberland. Watercolour 20⅞×27⅝. *Victoria and Albert Museum.*

Canada as aide-de-camp to Sir George Drummond. He retired from the army in 1816 on half-pay as a lieutenant, and taking up watercolour painting became so successful in his handling of the medium that he was elected an associate of the Old Water Colour Society (later the Royal Society of Painters in Water Colours) in the February of 1823, and in the June of the same year became a member. He exhibited with the Society from the year of his election as member, until 1851, showing some ninety-one works. The subjects of these works suggest that he made visits in this period to the Alps, Scotland, Wales, Yorkshire and Ireland, as well as to his native Northumbria. Nesfield was also a member of a party of artists who stayed at the Bolton Arms, near Bolton Abbey, Yorkshire, in 1844, in the company of David Cox. Apart from his occasional visits to Northumbria to paint, Nesfield was also an occasional exhibitor in the area; he was, for instance, among the many well known local artists such as Thomas Miles Richardson, Junior (q.v.), John Wilson Carmichael (q.v.) and Luke Clennell, who exhibited at the First Water Colour Exhibition of the Newcastle Society of Artists, in 1836. On his retirement from the Old Water Colour Society in 1852, Nesfield took up the profession of landscape gardening, and is said to have been responsible for helping to lay-out public parks in London, the Botanical Gardens at Kew, and the gardens of Alnwick and Arundel Castles. He won high esteem for his pictures of waterfalls, Ruskin in his *Modern Painters*, 1843, referring to him as: "Nesfield of the radiant cataract". He died at London. His son, WILLIAM EDEN NESFIELD, became a well known architect, and author on architectural subjects. Represented: British Museum; Victoria and Albert Museum; National Gallery of Ireland; Laing Art Gallery, Newcastle, and various provincial art galleries.

NEVILLE, Herbert W. (born c.1875)

Landscape painter in oil and watercolour; illustrator; art teacher. He was the brother, or son, of Hastings Mackelcan Neville, sometime Rector of FORD, and author of several books associated with the village. His place of birth is not recorded, but by the closing years of the 19th century he was practising at NEWCASTLE, following which , and living successively at CORNHILL, Skipton, Yorkshire, Lymington, Hants, and Birlingham, Worcs., he exhibited his work at the Royal Academy, the Royal Institute of Painters in Water Colours, the Royal Institute of Oil Painters, the Royal Society of British Artists, and at various provincial exhibitions. Among his provincial exhibits were those shown at the Bewick Club, NEWCASTLE, and later the Artists of the Northern Counties exhibitions at the city's Laing Art Gallery. Some of his work is reproduced in Hastings Mackelcan Neville's *A Corner in the North; yesterday and today with Border folk*, 1903. This work was reprinted by Frank Graham in 1980.

NEWTON, George Henry (1825-1900)

Landscape and genre painter in oil and watercolour; art teacher. He was born at DURHAM, and after displaying a talent for drawing at an early age was placed as a student at the Royal Academy Schools, where he

studied under F. S. Carey. He later studied at the Schools of the Department of Science & Art, in London, then returning to DURHAM he secured an appointment as master at the city's School of Art. He remained at the School from 1853 until his retirement, and became a regular exhibitor in London and the provinces. He exhibited at the Royal Academy and the Suffolk Street Gallery from 1858, at the former showing *The Village Lane*, (1858), and *The Fall of the Tees at Wynch Bridge*, (1859), and at the latter, a wide variety of Durham, North Yorkshire and Welsh views in watercolour. His provincial exhibits included his *Confidence and Timidity* genre work, and two Welsh Views, shown at the "Exhibition of Paintings and other Works of Art", at the Town Hall, NEWCASTLE, in 1866. He died in London.

NICHOLSON, Alice M. (1854- after 1890)

Fruit, flower and still-life painter in oil and watercolour. She was born at GATESHEAD, the daughter of a clerk, but later moved with her family to NEWCASTLE, where she pursued her education until she was eighteen. She had shown a remarkable talent for drawing from her childhood, and when she left school she studied for a time at the School of Art, at NEWCASTLE, under William Cosens Way (q.v.). When she left the School she decided to become a full-time professional artist, and with the blessing of her father, set up a studio in the Haymarket area of the town. She first began exhibiting her work in 1878, showing one work at the Arts Association, NEWCASTLE. She again exhibited at the Association in the following year, and by 1880 had commenced exhibiting outside Northumbria, showing works at the Royal Academy, the Royal Scottish Academy, the Royal Hibernian Academy, the Royal Society of British Artists, the Royal Society of Painters in Water Colours, and the Society of Women Artists. She was also an exhibitor at later exhibitions of the Arts Association, and showed work at the "Gateshead Fine Art & Industrial Exhibition", in 1883, and later the exhibitions of the Bewick Club, NEWCASTLE. Her Royal Academy contributions were entitled: *Herrings* (1884), and *Brambles* (1888). It is believed that she died at NEWCASTLE.

NICHOLSON, Charles Herbert (1900-1960)

Amateur marine, coastal and landscape painter in oil and watercolour. Nicholson was born at BLYTH, and became a master mariner and later a marine superintendent, painting in his spare time. He was largely a self-taught artist, but achieved considerable competence in his work, exhibiting examples at the Royal Academy, the Royal Scottish Academy, the Royal Society of Marine Artists, and at the Artists of the Northern Counties exhibitions at the Laing Art Gallery, NEWCASTLE. He was also an exhibitor at the "Contemporary Artists of Durham County" exhibition at the Shipley Art Gallery, GATESHEAD, staged in 1951 in connection with the Festival of Britain; his exhibits were: *Thames Barges; Beauty Passes*, and *The River*. He was a member of the Newcastle Society of Artists, although his home was for many years at NORTH SHIELDS. He died at NORTH SHIELDS. His wife was also artistically talented. Represented: North Tyneside Public Libraries.

NICHOLSON, Isaac (1789-1848)

Wood engraver. Born at Melmerby, Cumberland, Nicholson moved at the age of fifteen to NEWCASTLE, to become a pupil of Thomas Bewick (q.v.). He remained with Bewick until 1811, subsequently practising at NEWCASTLE, and closely following the style of his former master without ever equalling Bewick's ability in wood engraving. Bewick had to take Nicholson to task for copying his work, but despite this circumstance was generous enough in his autobiographical *Memoir*,‡ to describe his former apprentice as "... a good Apprentice & a good Artist – his engravings on Wood are clearly or honestly cut, as well as being accurately done from his patterns ...". Much similarity between his work and that of Bewick is to be seen in the tailpieces which he engraved for Charnley's *Select Fables*, 1820, many of which later appeared in this publisher's *Fisher's Garlands* for various years. Indeed, because so many of these portrayed riverside scenes they are commonly but inaccurately attributed to Bewick. His best known work consists of his wood engravings for Sharp's *History of the Rebellion*. He also did work for Flower's *Heraldic Visitation of the County of Durham*, Watt's *Hymns*, and Defoe's *Robinson Crusoe*. Ebenezer Landells (q.v.), and Thomas Kerr Fairless (q.v.), both studied wood engraving under Nicholson.

‡ *See p. 200, "A Memoir of Thomas Bewick, Written by Himself", 1862; edited and with an introduction by Iain Bain, Oxford University Press, 1975.*

*NICHOLSON, William, R.S.A. (1781-1844)

Portrait, genre and landscape painter in oil and watercolour; miniature painter; etcher. Nicholson was born at OVINGHAM, the son of a schoolmaster, but shortly afterwards moved with his family to NEWCASTLE, where he was educated at the town's Grammar School. On leaving school he went to work for a stationer in the town, but showing a marked talent for drawing was allowed by his father to become a pupil in the studio of Boniface Muss (q.v.), at NEWCASTLE. Here he made rapid progress in learning perspective drawing and enamel painting from Muss, and perhaps encouraged by the example of his master's son, Charles Muss (q.v.), began painting miniatures. Within a short time he had attracted several commissions in this line, but feeling that his prospects as a miniature painter might prove better at Hull, he moved there with his engraver brother, and was soon at work painting miniatures of local army officers. Later, however, he began to work on a larger scale, and returning to Tyneside, he set up as a portrait painter in oil, sending his first contribution in this medium to the Royal Academy from NEWCASTLE in 1808: *A group of portraits, etc.; servants of C. J. Brandling, Esq., M.P., Gosforth House, Northumberland*. Six years later, and having exhibited a further two portrait works at the Academy, he decided to leave NEWCASTLE, and seek his fortune in Edinburgh. Here his first task, as he communicated in a letter to the Rev. John Hodgson, sent from Edinburgh July 3rd, 1814, was to accumulate portraits of "public characters" for the first exhibition of the Edinburgh Exhibition Society. "It takes a long time to get known and connected here",

William Nicholson: Self portrait. Oil 26¾×23. *Scottish National Portrait Gallery.*

he confided in Hodgson. "They have elected me a member of the Society of Artists, which will enable me to get my pictures better placed in the Exhibition. My election I consider fortunate as the number to which the Society is limited is now full. If I once get connected here, which I flatter myself I shall be able to do, there is a much greater field here than in Newcastle".

Nicholson's faith in his ability to make good his position as a painter in Edinburgh was to prove fully justified. Within a few years of settling there he had painted many of Scotland's leading men and women, and later became a founding member of the Scottish Academy, as well as serving as its first secretary from 1826-30. Throughout his career in the Scottish capital, however, he never lost touch with his native Tyneside, and, indeed, executed many portrait commissions in the area. Two such portraits, painted before he left NEW-CASTLE, in fact helped pave the way for his acceptance as a portrait painter in Scotland when they were shown at the Edinburgh Exhibition Society in 1814; those of Thomas Bewick (q.v.), and the Rev. John Hodgson, both of which he later wrote to Hodgson, "have been much noticed". In 1816 he exhibited this same portrait of Bewick at the Royal Academy, and in 1829 sent for exhibition to the Northern Academy, NEWCASTLE, his portrait of George Gray (q.v.). Other well known Northumbrians included amongst his sitters were John Trotter Brockett, and Robert Doubleday. He exhibited at NEWCASTLE throughout his stay at Edinburgh, and though famous on Tyneside for his oil portraits of local celebrities, and the engravings made of these,‡ it was for his portraits in pencil and watercolour, and his etched likenesses in *Portraits of Distinguished Living*

128

Characters of Scotland, 1818, that he became best known in Edinburgh. His reputation as a portraitist has, however, tended to obscure the fact that he was an able landscape painter. Some of his earliest work was in this field (an example is his *The Demolition of Houses on the Site of Collingwood Street, Newcastle upon Tyne c.1808*, in the collection of the Laing Art Gallery, NEWCASTLE); while at the Royal Scottish Academy from its establishment in 1839, until his death at Edinburgh in 1844, he mainly showed landscapes. Represented: Victoria and Albert Museum; National Gallery of Scotland; Scottish National Portrait Gallery; Laing A.G., Newcastle; Newcastle Central Library.

‡ *See frontispiece to this volume for his portrait of Bewick, later engraved by Thomas Ranson (q.v.), and published in January, 1816.*

NIXON, G. Clement (1898-1975)

Amateur landscape and coastal painter in oil and watercolour. Nixon lived at WHITLEY BAY, and later nearby MONKSEATON, all his life, and was a keen amateur painter of local landscape and coastal subjects. He also exhibited his work, showing examples at the Artists of the Northern Counties exhibitions at the Laing Art Gallery, NEWCASTLE, from 1916 until late in his life. His exhibits at NEWCASTLE in 1916 were entitled: *Morning*, and *Rough Weather – North-East Coast*. He was friendly with many well known Northumbrian professional artists, including John Atkinson (q.v.), John Falconar Slater (q.v.), and George Edward Horton (q.v.), and was a member of the North East Coast Art Club, WHITLEY BAY, and the Newcastle Society of Artists. He died at MONKSEATON.

OGDEN, Rev. J. W. (fl. late 19th, early 20th cent.)

Amateur landscape painter. Ogden settled at GOS-FORTH, c.1900, apparently after his retirement as a clergyman, and contributed several works to the Artists of the Northern Counties exhibitions at the city's Laing Art Gallery, from 1906. His daughter, FANNY OGDEN, also painted, and exhibited her work at the Laing Art Gallery.

*OGILVIE, Frank Stanley (c.1856-after 1935)

Portrait, genre and landscape painter in oil and watercolour. He was born at NORTH SHIELDS, the son, or nephew, of local salt manufacturer and whiting merchant, Joseph Ogilvie, and studied art in London, and at Bushey, Herts., at the school of Sir Hubert Von Herkomer, before practising as a professional artist. He first began to exhibit his work in 1885, showing examples in London, and at the Bewick Club, NEWCASTLE. His first exhibits of note, however, were shown at the Royal Academy and the Suffolk Street Gallery, in 1888, while he was at Herkomer's. His Academy exhibit was: *The old, old story at Capri*, while at the Suffolk Street Gallery he showed another continental subject: *A picturesque washing place*. Back at NORTH SHIELDS in

the year in which these works were shown, he also exhibited at the Bewick Club, and remaining at his birthplace for the next three years, earned a considerable reputation as a portrait painter on Tyneside. Encouraged by this success he decided to practise in London, spending several years there, and at Letchworth, Herts., before returning to Northumbria, and settling first at TYNEMOUTH, later at NEWCASTLE. In this period he continued to exhibit at the Royal Academy, and also sent work to the Royal Scottish Academy, the Royal Society of British Artists, the Glasgow Institute of Fine Arts, and to various London and provincial exhibitions. He was a contributor to the Artists of the Northern Counties exhibitions at the Laing Art Gallery, NEWCASTLE, from their inception in 1905, until close to his death, showing among his several portraits, those of John Smales Calvert (q.v.), and Charles Napier Hemy (q.v.). He was the brother, or cousin, of Frederick Dove Ogilvie (q.v.). Represented: Dundee A.G.; Laing A.G., Newcastle; Middlesbrough A.G.; South Shields Museum & A.G.

OGILVIE, Frederick Dove (1850-1921)

Landscape and coastal painter in watercolour. He was born at NORTH SHIELDS, the son of local salt manufacturer and whiting merchant, Joseph Ogilvie, and worked in a solicitor's office before deciding to become a professional artist. He first began to exhibit his work in 1875, sending a coastal view: *Coldingham by the Sea, Berwickshire*, to the Suffolk Street Gallery. Two years later he exhibited at both the Royal Academy, and the

Frank Stanley Ogilvie: Cottage interior. Oil 36½×28½. *Tyne & Wear County Council Museums, Laing Art Gallery.*

Suffolk Street Gallery, at the former showing his *Winter*, and at the latter: *Tarbut – Loch Fyne*. He again exhibited at the Academy in 1878, shortly afterwards leaving NORTH SHIELDS for Scotland, where he practised successively at Edinburgh, Bonhill, Glasgow and Helensburgh, until the turn of the century, and exhibited his work at the Royal Academy, the Royal Scottish Academy, the Royal Hibernian Academy, the Royal Scottish Society of Painters in Water Colours, and at various London and provincial galleries. He also exhibited at the Bewick Club, NEWCASTLE, sending his first work in 1885, while working in Edinburgh: *The Wansbeck at Morpeth*. By 1901 he had settled at Harrogate, Yorkshire, from which he continued to exhibit at the Bewick Club, and for many years from their inception in 1905, the Artists of the Northern Counties exhibitions at the Laing Art Gallery, NEWCASTLE. About 1913 he left Harrogate and joined his brother, or cousin, Frank Stanley Ogilvie (q.v.), in London. He last exhibited his work in 1918 while practising in the capital, showing twelve works at the Laing Art Gallery in that year. He died at Bosham, Sussex. Two of his daughters, or nieces, CONSTANCE OGILVIE, and MAY OGILVIE, were also artists, the former exhibiting her work at the Royal Academy, in 1911 and 1950, and at the Royal Institute of Painters in Water Colours. Both women exhibited at the Artists of the Northern Counties exhibitions at the Laing Art Gallery, NEWCASTLE.

OGLE, Charles Frederick (*c.*1878- after 1930)

Landscape painter in oil and watercolour. He was born at GATESHEAD, the son of a draughtsman, and practised as an artist in his native town for several years in the late 19th century, before taking a studio at NEWCASTLE. He practised at NEWCASTLE from the early 1900's, contributing many landscapes to the Artists of the Northern Counties exhibitions at the city's Laing Art Gallery, from their inception in 1905, when his exhibits were entitled: *Breakers*, and *Ravensworth*.

OLIPHANT, Francis Wilson (1818-1859)

Religious, figure and portrait painter in oil; stained glass designer. He was the son of Thomas Oliphant of Edinburgh, but was born at NEWCASTLE while his parents were visiting the town. He was trained as an artist at the Edinburgh Academy of Art, and became fascinated in his youth by the revival of the Gothic Style. This led to a deep study of ecclesiastical art, and eventually an invitation from William Wailes (q.v.), to join his stained glass manufactory at NEWCASTLE. Here Oliphant soon established himself as an important member of a trio of designers which included fellow Scotsmen James Sticks (q.v.), and John Thompson Campbell (q.v.). This trio, at the instigation of Wailes, visited cathedrals and other buildings on the continent to study the best examples of stained glass, and it was very much on the basis of their subsequent efforts that their employer's business quickly established itself as one of the busiest of its kind in Britain.

While living at NEWCASTLE, Oliphant continued to take an interest in drawing and painting, and in 1840 sent a sketch to the "Exhibition of Arts, Manufactures & Practical Science", at NEWCASTLE. In the following year he sent a portrait in chalk, and a genre work: *The Mother's Knee*, to the North of England Society for the Promotion of the Fine Arts, NEWCASTLE, afterwards moving to London to work with the famous architect Pugin, on the painted windows of the New Houses of Parliament. In the period 1849-55 he exhibited at the Royal Academy, and submitted a cartoon to the competition for the decoration of Westminster Hall. His first Academy exhibit was entitled: *The Holy Family*, and was also shown at NEWCASTLE, in 1850. Outstanding among his later Academy exhibits were his large Shakesperian study of the interview of Richard II, and John of Gaunt, shown in 1852, and *Coming home – the prodigal son*, shown in 1853. In 1852 he married his writer cousin Margaret Oliphant Wilson. His later years were spent trying to improve the art of stained glass in Britain by involving himself in its actual production, as well as design, this resulting in much fine work for various educational and ecclesiastical establishments. Perhaps his most famous work of this period was the choristers' window at Ely, which he executed jointly with William Dyce, Oliphant being responsible for the original design. His work was, however, interrupted by ill-health, and he was forced to seek a warmer climate. He moved to Rome, dying there, it is said, mainly from the results of overwork. Towards the end of his life he published a short treatise entitled: *A Plea for Painted Glass*. A relative, JOHN OLIPHANT, was also an artist and practised briefly in NEWCASTLE as a portrait painter; the Shipley Art Gallery, GATESHEAD, has this artist's portrait of William Wailes.

OLIVER, Edith, R.M.S. (*c.*1885- after 1940)

Miniature painter. She was born at NEWCASTLE, and studied at the Praga School, Kensington, London, before practising at CULLERCOATS, by 1906. She first began to exhibit her work publicly at the Artists of the Northern Counties exhibitions at the Laing Art Gallery, NEWCASTLE, in 1906, later exhibiting at the Royal Academy, the Royal Miniature Society, and at various provincial exhibitions. She practised for some time in the South of England, but spent her later life at NEWCASTLE and CULLERCOATS, establishing a considerable reputation on Tyneside for her portrait miniatures. She was a member of the Royal Miniature Society.

*OLIVER, Thomas (1790-1857)

Architectural and topographical draughtsman. He was born at Jedburgh, Roxburghshire, the son of a weaver, and received his education in his native town. In 1814 he married the daughter of a stone mason at nearby Kelso, by whom he may have been employed for some time, then settling at NEWCASTLE, he was possibly employed by John Dobson (q.v.), before setting himself up as a land surveyor and architect in the town in 1821. In addition to practising as a land surveyor and architect, Oliver offered lessons in architectural and perspective drawing, and in 1829 exhibited at the Northern Academy, NEWCASTLE, one of his own works in this field which earned from W. A. Mitchell, in the *Tyne Mercury*, the comment: "A carefree, neatly finished piece of architectural drawing". Oliver is best remembered for his series of excellent maps of NEWCASTLE, rather than his architectural work, which, apart from his superb Leazes Terrace, consisted of undistinguished houses, and some commercial property. His maps were published in 1830, 1844, 1849, 1851, and in the year of his death, and provide an invaluable guide to the topography and growth of the town throughout one of its greatest phases of development. His abilities as an architectural and topographical draughtsman, however, are seen to their best advantage in his *A New Picture of Newcastle upon Tyne*, 1831, in the form of a pull-out view of NEWCASTLE from GATESHEAD, described as "Drawn on the Spot by Thomas Oliver".# He died at NEWCASTLE. His son by his first marriage, THOMAS OLIVER, JUNIOR (1824-1902), was a distinguished architect.

OLIVER, Thomas (fl.1766)

Architectural and topographical draughtsman. This artist practised at HEXHAM, and is known only via his drawing of nearby Dilston Hall, published as an engraving in 1766, with the note: "Drawn on the spot by Thos. Oliver of Hexham in Northumberland & pub.d according to A of P July 17. 1766." Oliver's original drawing survived for many years, and was sometimes exhibited at NEWCASTLE in a frame made from wood from the Old Tyne Bridge. A half scale version of the engraving published is reproduced opposite page 100, in *The Old Halls, Houses and Inns of Northumberland*, written and published by Frank Graham, 1977. He may have been related to Thomas Oliver 1790-1857 (q.v.).

OYSTON, George (c.1860- after 1897)

Landscape painter in oil and watercolour. Born at NORTH SHIELDS, the son of an engineering superintendent, Oyston practised as a professional artist in his native town throughout the 1880's, sending many works for exhibition at the Bewick Club, NEWCASTLE, in that period. He later moved to the South of England, practising in the Thames Valley, first at Walton, later at Shepperton, He continued to exhibit at the Bewick Club while working outside Northumbria, and also sent one work to the Royal Institute of Painters in Water Colours, and one work to the Royal Society of British Artists. Typical of his Bewick Club exhibits were those shown in 1885: *Harvest Time; Near the Oxford, Tynemouth; In Hollywell Dene*, and *At Dinsdale, near Darlington.*

PAE, William (b.1841)

Landscape and marine painter in oil and watercolour. He was born at NEWCASTLE, the son of a dyer from BERWICK-UPON-TWEED, who used the names "Pae", and "Pea". Nothing is known of his early artistic training, but by his early twenties he was advertising himself as a professional artist at his birthplace. He later moved to GATESHEAD, where his work enjoyed a measure of popularity in his lifetime, although he rarely sent it for exhibition. He specialised in small watercolour studies of local landscape subjects, usually featuring buildings, and occasionally painted marine subjects. He died at GATESHEAD in the late 19th century. The Shipley Art Gallery, GATESHEAD, has twenty of his local views. Represented: Shipley A.G., Gateshead; Sunderland A.G.

PALMER, Gerald (born c.1887)

Landscape painter in watercolour. This artist lived at CORBRIDGE in the first quarter of the present century. In 1907 he enjoyed a one-man exhibition of some thirty-seven of his watercolours of Venice, at the gallery of Mawson, Swan & Morgan, NEWCASTLE, later going on to exhibit at the Royal Academy, the Royal Society of British Artists, Walker's Gallery, London, and the London Salon. He also exhibited in the provinces, notably at the Artists of the Northern Counties exhibitions at the Laing Art Gallery, NEWCASTLE. In 1927 he was living in London.

PARK, John, A.R.E. (d.1919)

Landscape and coastal painter in watercolour; etcher. This artist practised at SOUTH SHIELDS in the late 19th century. He mainly exhibited his work at the Bewick Club, NEWCASTLE, but in 1885 sent one work to the Royal Academy: *Gillingham Church*, after William Müller. He was elected an associate of the Royal Society of Painter-Etchers and Engravers in 1898. He may have been related to amateur artist GEORGE H. PARK, who painted in the area around SOUTH SHIELDS, in the late 19th and early 20th centuries.

Thomas Oliver: Newcastle upon Tyne from the South, Drawn on the Spot. Engraving after the artist 4¾×15¾.

*PARKER, Henry Perlee, H.R.S.A. (1795-1873)

Portrait, figure, genre, landscape and marine painter in oil and watercolour; drawing master. Parker was born at Devonport, Devon, the son of Robert Parker (1748-1830), a wood carver and gilder who had taken up the profession of artist and art teacher. His first work in art followed a brief period as tailor and coachmaker, and consisted of portrait painting, and making drawings for his father's pupils to copy. About 1813 he was employed by C. T. Gilbert to produce illustrations for the latter's "Historical Survey of the County of Cornwall" (published in 1815). This commission required him to tour Cornwall with Gilbert, and brought him into contact with paintings in the private collections of noblemen. In 1814 he married, and settled down at Plymouth as a professional portrait painter. His work was much admired, but discouraged by his meagre income he decided to stay with relatives at SUNDERLAND for a while, to see what opportunities for a portrait painter might exist in Northumbria. He made his living at SUNDERLAND for some months painting portraits on tin, giving drawing lessons, and painting window blinds, but after visiting NEWCASTLE on several occasions he found he liked the town, and settled here for just over a quarter of a century.

Parker's years at NEWCASTLE 1815-1841 saw him become one of Northumbria's best known artists, and an active participant in the artistic life of the town. One of his first portraits was that of George Gray (q.v.), and soon he was attracting so many commissions that he and his wife were able to move to "respectable apartments in the most public street in the town" – Pilgrim Street. He then commenced painting "fancy pictures", in addition to his portraits, took on pupils, and soon made several important friendships with local artists,

including Thomas Bewick (q.v.), and Thomas Miles Richardson, Senior (q.v.), later collaborating with these two, and others, in the foundation of the Northumberland Institution for the Promotion of the Fine Arts, NEWCASTLE. In 1817 Parker exhibited his first of twenty-three works at the Royal Academy: *Dead Game*, and after selling his popular *Principal Eccentric Characters of Newcastle* to Charles John Brandling M.P., of Gosforth House, began to be patronised by some of the most important men on Tyneside. In 1822 he was appointed to the committee of the newly founded Northumberland Institution for the Promotion of the Fine Arts, NEWCASTLE, and showed thirteen works at its first exhibition; he also in this year showed his first works at the British Institution: *Fishermen selling Fish to a Cottage Girl, Coast of Devon*, and *Celebration of the Coronation of His Most Gracious Majesty George IV, on the Sand-Hill, Newcastle upon Tyne, July 19, 1821*, which latter work was purchased by the Mayor and Corporation of NEWCASTLE for one hundred guineas, and placed in the Mansion House. In the following year he again exhibited at the Royal Academy, sent a further work to the British Institution, and exhibited at the Institution for the Encouragement of the Fine Arts in Scotland, Edinburgh, the Carlisle Academy, and at NEWCASTLE. From this point forward he continued to exhibit his work widely, showing his last work at the Royal Academy in 1859, the British Institution in 1863, Edinburgh in 1839, Carlisle in 1833, and NEWCASTLE in 1866 (loan). The smuggling subjects for which he later became famous, and which led to his becoming nick-named "Smuggler Parker", were first exhibited in 1826, and continued to appear until 1850. But these were by no means his only preoccupation as an artist, his work, indeed, recording everything from

Henry Perlee Parker: Astonishing a native. Oil 30×36. Sotheby, King & Chasemore.

132

the grand to the ordinary in Northumbria for quarter of a century, and with titles ranging from *The Fancy Dress Ball at the Mansion House to celebrate the Coronation of William IV*, 1831, to *Pitmen at Play near Newcastle: Painted from Nature*, 1836. Drama also featured in his work, as with his *William and Grace Darling going to the Rescue of the Forfarshire Survivors*, painted jointly with John Wilson Carmichael (q.v.), in 1838. Perhaps his most outstanding contribution to the artistic activity of the area lay not in his paintings, however, but in his joint promotion with Thomas Miles Richardson, Senior (q.v.), of the Northern Academy of Arts, NEWCASTLE, in 1828.

Parker was throughout his life keenly aware of critical reaction to his work, and to celebrate the twentieth anniversary of his arrival at NEWCASTLE, he published in 1835 his "Critiques of Paintings by H. P. Parker . . . with etchings showing the compositions". He was also ambitious, and though he had been elected an honorary member of the Scottish Academy in 1829, yearned for yet greater recognition. In 1839 he painted a picture which accidentally opened the door to this recognition; the *Wesleyan Centenary Picture*, in anticipation of the John Wesley Centenary Conference, held at NEWCASTLE in 1840. As a result of the success of this work he was in 1841 offered the post of Drawing Master at Wesley College, Sheffield. He accepted the post, and taking his wife, two daughters, and son Raphael Hyde Parker (q.v.), with him, moved to Sheffield, never to return to NEWCASTLE again. Once settled at Sheffield, and despite his commitments at the College, he immediately began painting subjects associated with the town: *The Sheffield Milk Boys*, and *The Burial of Sir Francis Chantrey*, to name only two. Between 1842 and 1844, and now supplementimg his income by giving private drawing lessons, and taking classes at Chesterfield, as well as painting local subjects, he joined in efforts to establish a School of Design at Sheffield. This School was in due course set up in 1845, but Parker was not offered a post there, and some two years later he left the College for London, leaving Raphael Hyde to succeed him as Drawing Master. What little is known of Parker's remaining years suggests that while he continued to exhibit his work, his stay in London until his death in 1873 was not profitable, and he died penniless. A major exhibition of his work, consisting of many oils, watercolours and drawings, was held at the Laing Art Gallery, NEWCASTLE, in 1969-70. Represented: Victoria and Albert Museum; Grace Darling Museum, Bamburgh; Laing A.G., Newcastle; Newcastle Central Library; Sheffield A.G.; Shipley A.G., Gateshead; Sunderland A.G.

PARKER, Raphael Hyde (1829-1886)
Genre, portrait, landscape and marine painter in oil and watercolour; drawing master. He was born at NEWCASTLE, the son of Henry Perlee Parker (q.v.), and lived with his family in the town until his father's appointment as Drawing Master at Wesley College, Sheffield, in 1841. He learnt drawing and painting from his father, and when the latter left Sheffield for London *c*.1847, succeeded him as Drawing Master at the College. He first exhibited his work in 1848, showing his

The Itinerant Pan-Maker, and *View of the Entrance of the Port of Tyne, Northumberland*, at the Suffolk Street Gallery. He again exhibited at this Gallery in 1849, showing: *An Italian Boy displaying his white mice*, and in 1858 sent his only work to the Royal Academy: *The Sail in Sight*. He died at Sheffield, where directories up to 1884 record him as a "drawing master". Several examples of his work in watercolour were included in the "Henry Perlee Parker Exhibition", at the Laing Art Gallery, NEWCASTLE, in 1969-70, including a portrait of his father, three genre works and one landscape. An elder sister was also a talented artist, and exhibited her work at NEWCASTLE while her father practised in the town. The National Portrait Gallery, London, has his half-length portrait of his father in oil.

PARKER, Robert (fl. early 19th cent.)
Marine and coastal painter in oil. This artist practised at SUNDERLAND in the early 19th century, and exhibited his work at the Northumberland Institution for the Promotion of the Fine Arts, at NEWCASTLE, from its foundation in 1822, until 1826. His early exhibits all featured coastal views in Lincolnshire, Northumbria and Scotland, but in 1826 he exhibited a *View of Tobago, West Indies*, suggesting a visit abroad. He may have been related to Henry Perlee Parker (q.v.), who is known to have had relatives at SUNDERLAND. Indeed, it is possible that this was Parker's father, who painted marine subjects, and may have accompanied his son to SUNDERLAND, spending some years there before returning to Devonport, where he died in 1830, aged 82.

*PATTISON, Thomas William (b.1894)
Portrait, landscape and animal painter in oil and watercolour. He was born at Cardiff and is said to have shown marked artistic ability from an early age. On completing his general education he became a pupil at Armstrong College (later King's College; now Newcastle University) under Richard George Hatton (q.v.), but at the outbreak of the First World War volunteered for the Army. He served in the Royal Field Artillery from 1915-18, constantly carrying painting materials with him throughout his service. A frieze later designed by him was based on sketches, made during his service, of French peasants working in the fields at dawn. On leaving the Army he returned to Armstrong College, gaining the School Medal with distinction, in recognition of the high quality of his work. On completing his artistic training he travelled widely on the continent. In France he was greatly influenced by the work of Puvis de Chavannes – an influence of which there is evidence in his lunette for the Laing Art Gallery, NEWCASTLE, entitled: *The Building of the Castle (Newcastle upon Tyne) c.1177, A.D.* This was the first lunette completed for the gallery. Pattison served on the teaching staff of the School of Art at King's College for a number of years, combining his academic duties with the painting of a number of portrait commissions, landscapes, street scenes,# and industrial scenes. He later taught at HEXHAM, and since leaving teaching has practised as a full-time professional artist, including among his later work a wide variety of commissions, such as his portrait of Alderman Sanderson, of MORPETH, and his mural for

Thomas William Pattison: The Side, Newcastle upon Tyne. Watercolour 17×12. *Tyne & Wear County Council Museums, Laing Art Gallery.*

the County Hall, DURHAM: *The Building of Durham.* He has shown his work at the Royal Academy, the Royal Scottish Academy, and was an exhibitor for many years at the Laing Art Gallery, NEWCASTLE, notably at its Artists of the Northern Counties exhibitions. This gallery staged a major one-man exhibition of his work in 1942. Several examples of his local street scenes hang in the John George Joicey Museum, NEWCASTLE, alongside those of his contemporary and friend Byron Eric Dawson (q.v.). Represented: Laing A.G., Newcastle.

PEASE, Claude Edward, (1874-1952)
Amateur landscape painter in watercolour. He was the youngest son of Arthur Pease, M.P. for DARLINGTON, and was for many years associated with Pease and Partners Ltd., and Barclay's Bank, in the town, also serving as a director of Horden Collieries. He was a keen spare-time painter and frequently exhibited his work at the Darlington Society of Arts. He also took a strong interest in local sporting activites, and was president of the Darlington Horse and Dog Show in 1936. His home was at Selaby Hall, GAINFORD. He was the brother of Evelyn Ada Pease (q.v.). Darlington Art Gallery has his watercolour: *The view from Keodale Hotel, Durness (at midnight).*

PEASE, Evelyn Ada (1876-1950)
Amateur landscape painter in watercolour. The youngest daughter of M.P. for DARLINGTON, Arthur Pease,

she painted widely in Scotland, Yorkshire and Northumbria, and exhibited her work at the Alpine Club, London, and frequently at the Darlington Society of Arts exhibitions. She served on the committee of the latter organisation, and was for some time vice-president. Her home was for several years at Skeeby, near Richmond, Yorkshire. She was the sister of Claude Edward Pease (q.v.). Darlington Art Gallery has two of her Scottish landscapes in watercolour.

*PEEL, James, R.B.A. (1811-1906)
Landscape, portrait and figure painter in oil and watercolour. Peel was born at NEWCASTLE, the son of a wine and woollen merchant in the town. Following his education at Dr. Bruce's School, he entered an attorney's office, but soon gave up his employment to place himself as a pupil of Alexander Dalziel (q.v.), at NEWCASTLE. At the age of twenty-three he began exhibiting his work at NEWCASTLE, showing a portrait of a Rev. Syme, at the Newcastle upon Tyne Institution for the General Promotion of the Fine Arts. He again exhibited at NEWCASTLE, in 1836, showing: *Portrait of an artist*; a genre work, a double portrait, a figure study and four landscapes, and continued to exhibit in the town until the end of the decade, when he moved to London. Here he became one of the early organizers of the "independent" exhibitions, such as the Dudley and Portland Galleries, in association with the two Landseers, Ford Madox Brown, William Bell Scott (q.v.), and others. This was followed by the opening of a large gallery at Hyde Park Corner, as a free exhibition. In 1842 Peel sent the first of his some 248 works to the Suffolk Street Gallery; in 1843 he began exhibiting at the Royal Academy, and in 1844, at the British Institution. Several of the works which he sent to these exhibitions in his early career were based on historical incidents, but he quickly settled down to become a landscape painter, and most of his subsequent Royal Academy, British Institution, Suffolk Street Gallery and other London gallery contributions, were landscapes, many of which were painted in Northumbria, Wales, the Lake District and South East England.

About 1848 Peel left London, and marrying at DARLINGTON, remained in the town for about eight years. By 1860 he had returned to London, and here he remained based for the rest of his professional career, finally ceasing to exhibit in the capital in 1901, by which time he had moved to his home for his final years, Reading, Berkshire. Peel was an occasional exhibitor at NEWCASTLE in the late nineteenth century, notably at the Bewick Club, of which he was an honorary member. He was elected a member of the Royal Society of British Artists in 1871, and at the time of his death at Reading was its oldest member. He was also a Burgess of Newcastle upon Tyne, and a member of the Worshipful Company of Plumbers and Pewterers. In 1907 the Laing Art Gallery, NEWCASTLE, staged a major loan exhibition of his work. His daughter, AMY PEEL, was a talented landscape painter. Represented: Victoria and Albert Museum; Darlington A.G.; Laing A.G., Newcastle; Leeds A.G.; Shipley A.G., Gateshead; Sunderland A.G.

134

James Peel: Landscape
with cows. Oil 27½×37½.
Darlington Art Gallery.

PELEGRIN, Mariano (d.1920)

Amateur marine and landscape painter in watercolour.
He was born at NEWCASTLE, the son of Manuel Jose
Pelegrin, merchant and Argentinian Consul in the town.
He later joined his father's business, painting in his
spare time a large number of watercolours of sailing
ships, fishing boats and other craft, off the Northumbrian and North Spanish coasts. He exhibited his work
at the Bewick Club, NEWCASTLE, from the early 1890's,
and later at the Royal Society of British Artists, the
Royal Institute of Painters in Water Colours, the
Walker Art Gallery, Liverpool, and the Artists of the
Northern Counties exhibitions at the Laing Art Gallery,
NEWCASTLE, from their inception in 1905, until close to
his death. He died at NEWCASTLE. Pelegrin's father was
apparently of Spanish descent, and collected works by
artists of his native country. On his death in 1905 he
bequeathed two "Spanish School" paintings to the
Laing Art Gallery. Represented: Shipley A.G., Gateshead.

*PLACE, Francis (1647-1728)

Portrait, bird, fish, flower and still-life painter in oil,
watercolour and crayon; topographical draughtsman
and painter in watercolour; etcher; engraver; potter.
Place was born at DINSDALE, near DARLINGTON, and
spent his early life articled to an attorney at Gray's Inn,
London. In London he became a friend of Wenceslaus
Hollar, one of the earliest engravers working in England, and generally regarded as the most important
illustrator and topographer working in this country in
the seventeenth century. Hollar encouraged Place in his
efforts to master etching and topographical drawing,
influencing his style considerably in the process. Their
association was, however, interrupted for a period by
the Great Plague of London, during which Place returned to DINSDALE, not returning to the capital until
1667. On resuming their friendship Place and Hollar
worked on a variety of illustrative works in the form of
etchings, but in 1668 the latter left London on an

expedition to Tangiers, and Place later set off on the
first of what was to become a series of far-ranging
topographical tours encompassing much of Britain, and
parts of the continent. From London he went to
Rochester in Kent, and from DINSDALE he went north
to TYNEMOUTH, producing at the latter one of his earliest
known topographical works: *Tinmouth Castle and
Lighthouse, c.*1670, in pen, grey wash, and some
watercolour. DINSDALE appears to have been his base
during these early tours, but after drawing a series of
views of York about 1675, he formed an increasing
attachment for this city, eventually settling there in
1692, and spending the remainder of his life there.

In the period 1675-1700, and thanks to an inheritance
on the death of his father, Place was able to widen his
artistic activities to include portraiture in oil, crayon
and mezzotint, and to embark on several further topographical sketching tours. His mezzotint portraiture
became particularly accomplished in these years, and
must be reckoned amongst his finest artistic achievements in any medium, while his topographical drawing
gradually loosened and began to show greater assur-
ance. But while his work in portraiture – ranging from
a self-portrait in oil, to portraits in mezzotint of his
friends – was completed by 1700, his landscape work
continued until close to his death. In 1677 he travelled
in the Isle of Wight and France; in 1678 in North East
and South West England, and Wales; in 1681 he was in
France; in 1683 he was in London; in 1698-9 he toured
Ireland, and from 1700 wandered widely throughout
Yorkshire, and Northumberland, and paid a visit to
Scotland. His later travels were principally confined to
Yorkshire, his last recorded trip being to Hull in 1722,
when he was seventy-five years old. His fascination with
landscape was extraordinary in his time, and, indeed, it
has been observed that he was "the first English artist
whose main preoccupation was landscape". Some of his
work was executed for etching, but by far the greater
proportion of his landscape drawings were clearly done
for his own satisfaction, and were a radical departure

Francis Place: Gateway to Bamburgh Castle. Watercolour 5¼×16. *Tyne & Wear County Museums, Laing Art Gallery.*

from the popular imaginary landscape of his time. In addition to his interests in portraiture and topographical drawing, Place was an inventive potter, and like many members of the York Virtuosi, a man of varied interests. An exhibition of his work including his self-portrait in oil, drawings, prints, books to which he contributed illustrative work, and examples of his pottery, was staged at the City Art Gallery, York, in 1971, accompanied by a catalogue compiled by Richard Tyler which probably represents the most comprehensive study of Place's work to date. Represented: British Museum; Victoria and Albert Museum; National Gallery of Scotland; National Gallery of Ireland; Laing A.G., Newcastle; Leeds A.G.; York A.G.

POLLARD, Robert (1755-1838)

Landscape and marine painter in oil; engraver; etcher. Pollard was born at NEWCASTLE, and as an apprentice to John Kirkup, silversmith in the town, became acquainted with Thomas Bewick (q.v.), then also an apprentice. While on visits to Bewick's workplace with work from Kirkup he became interested in engraving, and was later allowed by his father to learn the art from Isaac Taylor of London. Bewick, on his first visit to London in 1776, met up with Pollard, and through him got work from Taylor, the two Tyneside men remaining friends and correspondents until Bewick's death in 1828. After leaving Taylor, Pollard is said to have become a pupil of Richard Wilson, following which he began to paint landscapes and seascapes, and exhibited two of the former at the Free Society of Artists in 1773. Engraving eventually reclaimed his interest, however, and he was subsequently successful in executing a variety of work after leading artists of the day, as well as producing many plates from his own designs, among these *The Blind Beggar of Bethnal Green*, and *Lieutenant Moody Rescues Himself from the Americans*. He practised as an engraver at Spa Fields, Croydon, also selling prints and taking an active interest in the Incorporated Society of Artists, becoming its director in 1789. One of his pupils was John Scott (q.v.). Pollard's final years were spent in poverty. Shortly before his death he handed over to the Royal Academy the records of the Incorporated Society of Artists, of which he was then the only surviving member. He died at Chelsea, London. His son, JAMES POLLARD

(1792-1867), became one of the most popular painters of the coaching era in Britain. The National Portrait Gallery, London, has a portrait of Robert Pollard, by R. Samuel, dated 1784.

PORTER, Sir Robert Ker, (1777-1842)

Military, religious, portrait and landscape painter in oil and watercolour; etcher; illustrator. He was born at DURHAM, the son of a retired army officer. His father shortly afterwards died, and together with his mother and sisters, Porter moved to Edinburgh. Here he received his earliest education, and making the acquaintance of Flora Macdonald, was so taken by a "battle-piece" in her possession that he decided to become a painter of such pictures. When he was thirteen his mother again decided to move, and settling her family in London she took him to meet Benjamin West, President of the Royal Academy. West was so struck by the promise of Robert's sketches that he immediately obtained a place for the boy at the Royal Academy Schools. His progress as an artist from this point forward was spectacular. Two years after enrolling in the Schools he exhibited his first work at the Royal Academy: *The Death of Sir Philip Sidney*. In 1793 he was commissioned to paint an altar-piece for Shoreditch Church. In the following year he painted a picture of *Christ allaying the Storm*, which he presented to the Roman Catholic Chapel at Portsea, and in 1798, *St. John Preaching*, for St. John's College at Cambridge. Throughout this period he also continued to exhibit at the Academy, showing portraits, battle-scenes, and military subjects, painted scenery for the Lyceum Theatre, and became acquainted with several rising young artists of the day, including Turner and Girtin. With Girtin, and others, Porter founded at his London rooms in 1799 what fellow member Louis Francia described on the reverse of a drawing made on the memorable day, as "the Brothers . . . a school of Historic Landscape", but which is now recognised as the forerunner of all the world's watercolour exhibiting societies.

In 1800 Porter completed in eight weeks a picture so large and spectacular that he became a celebrity overnight. Entitled: *The Storming and Capture of Seringapatam*, it measured 116' long, and contained 700 figures – seventy of which were recognisable. Other battle-scenes followed, among these the *Battle of Agincourt*, for the city of London; the *Battle of Alexandria*, and *The Death of Sir Ralph Abercrombie*. All of these works were painted while he continued to produce other military pictures, portraits, etc., for exhibition at the Royal Academy, and mastered the technique of etching. In 1804 he visited Russia, and was appointed historical painter to Tsar Alexander I. He then travelled in Finland and Sweden, in which latter country King Gustavus IV, knighted him. In 1808 he went with Sir John Moore to Spain to help expel the French from the Peninsula, and was at hand at the general's tragic death at the moment of victory at Corunna, 16th January, 1809. Following this he paid a second visit to Russia where he married the Princess Mary, daughter of Prince Theodore de Scherbatoff. On his return to England he published his best-selling "Narrative of the Campaign in Russia", 1812, and in 1813 was re-knighted by the Prince Regent. Between 1817 and 1820 he travelled in the East, producing many sketches which are in the British Museum. After this he published an account of his travels in Georgia, Persia (where he was decorated by the Shah), Armenia, Ancient Babylon, and other places, containing numerous portraits, and studies of costumes and antiquities.

In 1826 Porter was appointed British Consul at Venezuela, and for sixteen years while based at Caracas, with Bolivar and others made history as one of the founders of the Republic. While at Caracas he also continued to paint, executing three religious works: *Christ instituting the Eucharist; Christ Blessing a little Child*, and *Ecce Homo*. He also painted a portrait of Bolivar, and produced a number of sketches. In 1841 he paid his last visit to Russia, dying of apoplexy at St. Petersburgh in 1842 as he was preparing to return to England. Porter's connections with his native Northumbria were slight after he left DURHAM for Edinburgh (though it has been claimed that he and his family returned to DURHAM for some time before settling in London); he exhibited a view of Durham Cathedral at the Royal Academy in 1797, and sent a single work: *Fitz-James*, to the Northern Academy, NEWCASTLE, in 1830. There is a monument to Porter and his authoress sisters, Jane and Anna Maria, in Bristol Cathedral. Represented: British Museum; Victoria and Albert Museum; Paul Mellon Collection of British Art, Washington.

POTTS, John Joseph (1844-1933)

Amateur landscape painter in watercolour. Potts was born at NEWCASTLE, and became an accountant by profession, painting in his spare time. He first exhibited his work on Tyneside, showing one example at the "Gateshead Fine Art & Industrial Exhibition", in 1883. In the following year he commenced exhibiting at the Bewick Club, NEWCASTLE, and between 1887-89 showed two works at the Walker Art Gallery, Liverpool. Potts continued to exhibit at the Bewick Club throughout his life, also for some time serving as its honorary treasurer. He was a regular exhibitor at the Artists of the Northern Counties exhibitions at the Laing Art Gallery, NEWCASTLE, from their inception in 1905, until 1931. He died at NEWCASTLE. The Laing Art Gallery has his watercolours: *Victory Tea, Pilgrim Street, Newcastle upon Tyne*, 1919, and two Welsh landscapes.

PRIESTMAN, Francis (d.1897)

Sculptor. He was born at DARLINGTON, the youngest son of John Priestman (q.v.), and received his early tuition as a sculptor under his father. He continued working with his father after his training, later establishing a considerable reputation for the quality of his work. He predeceased his father by some two years, his obituary stating: "Mr. Priestman's skill as a sculptor secured for him the execution of numerous artistic and life-like busts of prominent local people as well as sculpture for Roman Catholic places of worship". One of his best known portrait busts is that of Edward Pease, sculptured by Priestman in 1885, and erected by public subscription in the public library at DARLINGTON built with money bequeathed by Pease. The bust now stands in the adjacent Darlington Art Gallery.

PRIESTMAN, John (1811-1899)

Sculptor; draughtsman. Priestman was born at HIGH CONISCLIFFE, near DARLINGTON. At an early age he moved into DARLINGTON, where he is said to have learnt to sculpture under a local marble mason. On completing his training he established a studio on the site of the town's Mechanics' Institute, and in 1832 paid his first visit to London, sailing from STOCKTON ON TEES. On returning to DARLINGTON he practised as a sculptor, mainly working on memorial tablets. In 1848 he was asked by local solicitor, and chief-bailiff of the town, Francis Mewburn, to complete a copy of the Temple of Vespasian, Rome, in Sienna Marble. This model remained in Mewburn's possession throughout his life, but was bought back by the artist following the solicitor's death in 1867. In 1851 Priestman paid another visit to London, with a brief from Mewburn to look at the Great Exhibition, at Crystal Palace. Here he met the famous sculptor R. Monti, who was later commissioned to sculpture a bust of Mewburn at DARLINGTON, using Priestman as assistant. The bust was an outstanding success, and copies of it in plaster were widely purchased for placing in public and other buildings. Priestman was a capable draughtsman, one of his most accomplished works in drawing being his pen and ink study of Durham Cathedral. This work he framed in gypsum for which he specially travelled to Carlisle. He lived at Blackwellgate, DARLINGTON, for some thirty-eight years, with a studio next to his home, and during this period became one of the best known sculptors in the area. He died at DARLINGTON. His son Francis Priestman (q.v.), was also a talented sculptor.

PRINGLE, Agnes (d.1934)

Portrait and figure painter in oil. She was born at GATESHEAD, and is said to have attended classes at the School of Art at NEWCASTLE, under William Cosens Way (q.v.), from the age of twelve. A brief period of tuition under Robinson Elliot (q.v.) followed, then in 1882 she entered the Royal Academy Schools. By the end of her first year at the Schools she had won a gold medal for the best drawing from the Antique, and a premium for the best drawing of a statue, and in 1883 secured the premium for the best model of a statue. In 1884 she commenced exhibiting at the Royal Academy and the Suffolk Street Gallery, later showing her work at the Royal Institute of Painters in Water Colours, the Royal Society of British Artists, the London Salon, and widely in the provinces. Among her provincial exhibits were several sent to the Artists of the Northern Counties exhibitions at the Laing Art Gallery, NEWCASTLE. She appears to have spent all her life as a professional artist based in London. She may have been related to David Pringle (q.v.), who practised at GATESHEAD. Although primarily a figure painter she occasionally produced landscapes in watercolour. A typical example of her figure work is her *Flight of Anthony and Cleopatra*, in the collection of the Laing Art Gallery, NEWCASTLE.

PRINGLE, David (fl. late 19th cent.)

Landscape painter in oil and watercolour. This artist practised at GATESHEAD in the late 19th century. He regulary exhibited his work at the Bewick Club, NEWCASTLE, from 1884, his first exhibits being described as: *Roslin Castle*, and *Warkworth Castle*. The Shipley Art Gallery, GATESHEAD, has examples of his local views dating from 1851 to 1900. These include: *Carr Hill – old houses* (1885-1900), and *Johnson's Quay* (1900). He may have been related to Agnes Pringle (q.v.).

*PROCTER, Ernest, A.R.A., N.E.A.C., I.S. (1886-1935)

Landscape, figure and religious painter in oil and watercolour; decorative painter; sculptor; art teacher. Born at TYNEMOUTH, Procter studied at Newlyn, Cornwall, under Stanhope Forbes, and at Calarossi's, Paris, before practising as a professional artist. While still at Newlyn in 1906 he commenced exhibiting his work at various London and provincial galleries. On his return from Paris he settled at Leeds, Yorkshire, and in 1909 sent his first of some forty-nine works for exhibition at the Royal Academy: *Out in the cold*. Throughout his several-year stay at Leeds Procter exhibited widely, typical titles being his *A Lake District Cottage*, shown at the New English Art Club in 1909, and his *A Brittany Antique Shop*, and *Dust*, shown as his first of many exhibits at the Artists of the Northern Counties exhibitions at the Laing Art Gallery, NEWCASTLE, in 1912. He first came to notice, however, after returning to Britain following a year spent in Rangoon in 1920, decorating the Royal Palace with his artist wife DORIS ("DOD") M. PROCTER (née Shaw) (1891-1972). From Burma he brought home a number of paintings which he exhibited in London, and gained for him an immediate reputation. On his return he settled once again at Newlyn, and began to paint local landscapes, treated in a decorative manner, both in colour and composition, later accepting commissions to paint the interiors of, and execute decorative stone carvings for, several local churches, including St. Hilary, Marazion, near St. Michael's Mount, Cornwall.

In addition to showing his work widely throughout

Ernest Procter: The Zodiac, 1925. Oil 60×66. *Tate Gallery*.

138

Britain Procter enjoyed joint exhibitions with his wife at the Leicester Galleries, London, in 1925, 1927, 1929, and in the year of his death. Examples of his work were acquired for Japan, Luxembourg, Australia, and for several British collections, including that of the Tate Gallery, for which his picture *The Zodiac#* was purchased through the Chantrey Bequest. He was a member of the International Society of Painters, Sculptors and Engravers for several years, and became a member of the New English Art Club in 1929, and an associate of the Royal Academy in 1932. He died at NORTH SHIELDS on his way to Glasgow to take up his duties as director of Studies in Design and Craft at the city's School of Art, a post which he had held for the last year of his life. A memorial exhibition of his work was held at the Laing Art Gallery in 1936, and five of his works were shown at the Royal Academy exhibition in that year. His wife became an associate of the Royal Academy in 1934, and a full member in 1942. A relative, MARGARET L. PROCTER, was also a talented artist and exhibited her work while living with the Procters at Leeds. Represented: Imperial War Museum; Tate Gallery; Bradford A.G.; Dundee A.G.; Laing A.G., Newcastle; Leeds A.G.

PRY, Paul – see HEATH, William.

PUTT, Hilda (fl. late 19th, early 20th cent.)
Genre, landscape and flower painter in oil and watercolour. This artist first practised at SOUTH SHIELDS, from which she commenced exhibiting her work at the Bewick Club, NEWCASTLE, soon after its foundation in 1884. By the middle 1890's she had moved to NEWCASTLE, from which she sent one work to the Royal Academy in 1898. She later exhibited her work at the Artists of the Northern Counties exhibitions at the Laing Art Gallery, NEWCASTLE, for several years.

*RAINBIRD, Victor Noble (1889-1936)
Landscape, street scene, coastal and figure painter in oil and watercolour; muralist; illustrator; stained glass designer. Rainbird was born at NORTH SHIELDS, and first studied art at local evening classes under Ralph Walter Liddell (q.v.). Later he attended Armstrong College (later King's College; now Newcastle University), where he studied for four years under Richard George Hatton (q.v.), and others. During his time at the College he was awarded the silver medal for the highest placed student in all subjects; he was King's Prizeman in design, with honours, and won a national silver token for figure compositions, his drawings being subsequently included in the Government exhibition of work which was staged in New Zealand, Canada and Australia. Also while at the College he commenced exhibiting his work on Tyneside, showing his oil: *Nocturne*, and watercolour: *Gathering Storm*, at the first Artists of the Northern Counties exhibition, at the Laing Art Gallery, NEWCASTLE, in 1905. He next studied at the Royal College of Art, taking a special course

Victor Noble Rainbird: Old Shields. Watercolour 10×15. *G. R. McArdle.*

under Professors Lanteri, Lethaby and Moira. Following this he became a student at the Royal Academy Schools, where he won the silver medal and £40 for life studies; the silver medal and £15 for figure composition, and the Landseer studentship and £40, tenable for two years.

At the outbreak of the First World War Rainbird enlisted as a private in the Northumberland Fusiliers, and after serving as a musketry instructor at York, was sent to serve in France. A variety of postings followed, including intelligence work, anti-aircraft service, field observation, and shock troop training. He was recommended and sent back to England for a commission, and was with the Officer's Training Corps at Ripon and Catterick, Yorkshire, when the war ended. Following his demobilisation he returned to NORTH SHIELDS to practise as a professional artist, and resumed exhibiting his work at the Artists of the Northern Counties exhibitions. He also exhibited at the North East Coast Exhibition, Palace of Arts, 1929, the Walker Art Gallery, Liverpool, 1930, and the Royal Academy in 1926 and 1930. His first Academy exhibit was entitled: *Sir Galahad*; his second: *St. Jan ter Biezon*. He also did a considerable amount of stained glass work in the years following the war, some of which was erected at NEWCASTLE, SUNDERLAND, ALLENDALE, and other parts of the British Isles. Rainbird practised at various places in the North during his brief life as a professional artist, spending periods at NORTH SHIELDS, Richmond, Yorkshire, NEWCASTLE, and finally SUNDERLAND. He also made several trips to France and Belgium to paint street scenes, and, indeed these are amongst his best known and most accomplished works. Two years before his death, and then practising at NORTH SHIELDS, Rainbird completed his largest single work – a mural decoration covering more than 1,000 square feet of wall space in the Ship Hotel, WHITLEY BAY. His last public commission while working at his birthplace was his personal impression of Earl Haig, standing at the salute, for the Mayor of TYNEMOUTH. From NORTH SHIELDS he moved to SUNDERLAND, dying there after an illness of some months, at the early age of forty-seven. Represented: Laing A.G., Newcastle; South Shields Museum & A.G.

139

*RAMSAY, James (1786-1854)

Portrait, historical, religious, genre and landscape painter in oil; etcher. He was the son of Robert Ramsay (1754-1828), carver and gilder at Sheffield, and one-time master of Francis, later Sir Francis Chantrey, the famous sculptor. At the time of Ramsay's birth at Sheffield, his father's business was very much confined to carving and gilding, but it was soon extended to dealing in prints and plaster models, and eventually became "a repository of works of art not equalled in the town". Thus Ramsay was brought up in an atmosphere of artistic activity, this being further intensified when Chantrey, then a precociously talented youth of sixteen, became an apprentice in the business in 1797. In the following year Ramsay Senior published two mezzotint portraits of well known Sheffield men, painted by Chesterfield artist E. Needham. The mezzotints were produced by John Raphael Smith, and possibly influenced by his contact with Needham and Smith, Ramsay Junior himself became attracted to a career in art. His earliest known work is his drawing of Samuel Peech, of the Angel Inn, Sheffield, and at the age of fifteen his father took him into the family business, announcing in the *Iris*, 12th February, 1801, that in addition to always having in stock "prints, transparencies, medallions and caricatures by eminent artists, the services of Ramsay Junior were available "As a Portrait and Miniature Painter". In 1803 he left Sheffield, taking with him a self portrait, and after showing it to an old friend of his father in London, Robert Pollard (q.v.), exhibited it at the Royal Academy. He was then only seventeen, and uncertain of his future in the capital, returned several times to Sheffield in the next four years.

After commencing to exhibit at the British Institution in 1807, Ramsay evidently felt confident enough of his success in London, and the capital remained his base for the next forty years. He first appears to have established connections with Northumbria with his painting in 1816 of his first portrait of Thomas Bewick (q.v.). This work may have been painted at the request of Pollard, who wrote to Bewick 9th February, 1816, stating "I should like to have a good likeness of you, either Painting or Print". In this letter he also mentioned his early acquaintance with Ramsay, and provided valuable confirmation of the artist's Sheffield origins.‡ Ramsay's portrait of Bewick was exhibited at the Royal Academy in 1816, and engraved by John Burnet in 1817. This engraving was the one most approved by the Bewick family of the many based on portraits of Bewick, and a close intimacy between the Bewicks and Ramsay followed. He began to include Northumbria more frequently in his professional visits, and on one of the earliest of these in 1819, painted two local views, *The Ruins of Tynemouth Castle and lighthouse*, and *View of the Harbour of North and South Shields*, as well as several portraits. Two years later, and again visiting the area, he was invited to join the committee of the Northumberland Institution for the Promotion of the Fine Arts, NEWCASTLE, showing at its first exhibition in 1822, portraits of fellow committee member Bewick, and President of the Institution, Edward Swinburne (q.v.). In the following year he again exhibited at the

James Ramsay: The Lost Child. Oil 36×28. *Newcastle Central Library.*

Institution, on this occasion showing yet another portrait of Bewick, and a figure of the artist (together with those of Ramsay and his wife), in *The Lost Child*.# In this same year Ramsay became anxious to advance his career, writing to a Mr. Reid, bookseller at Leith, near Edinburgh, asking the Scotsman's opinion as to whether he might hope to succeed the recently deceased Sir Henry Raeburn – "His Majesty's First Limner and Painter in Scotland". Reid's reply is not recorded, but Ramsay's continued residence mainly in London for the next twenty-four years suggests that it was not encouraging.

Between exhibiting at NEWCASTLE in 1823, and settling in the town permanently in 1847, Ramsay exhibited sporadically in the north, showing work at the Carlisle Academy in 1824, 1826 and 1828, at various exhibitions at NEWCASTLE in 1833, 1834 and 1838, and at Carlisle Athenaeum in 1846. Throughout this period, however, he paid several professional visits to northern towns, showing many portraits of local worthies in London, principally at the Royal Academy, the British Institution, and from 1824, the Suffolk Street Gallery. After moving to NEWCASTLE, and taking a house at Blackett Street, he continued to exhibit both in London and the north, showing work at the Royal Academy and the Suffolk Street Gallery, until his death seven years later; at Carlisle until 1850, and NEWCASTLE, until 1852. He died at NEWCASTLE in 1854, aged sixty-eight. Although principally regarded as a portrait painter, Ramsay produced a number of historical, religious, genre and

140

landscape works. Many of his portraits were engraved for sale, among these Thomas Bewick, G. G. Mounsey, the first reform Mayor of Carlisle, and the Rev. James Birkett, of OVINGHAM, which last he etched himself. Represented: National Portrait Gallery; Carlisle A.G.; Carlisle Old Town Hall; Hull A.G.; Laing A.G., Newcastle; Literary and Philosophical Society, Newcastle; Natural History Society of Northumbria, Newcastle; Newcastle Central Library.

‡ *Details of Ramsay's life until his arrival in London have hitherto remained a mystery, and the author is indebted to several individuals for their help in resolving them as presented in this entry.*

RANSON, Thomas Fryer (1784-1828)
Engraver; draughtsman. Ranson was born at SUNDERLAND, the son of a tailor. His parents shortly afterwards moved to NEWCASTLE, where at the age of fourteen he was apprenticed as an engraver to John Andrews Kidd (q.v.). After completing his apprenticeship he remained at NEWCASTLE for some years, and executed "several pieces with great taste and delicacy". He was still practising at Newgate Street in the town in 1811, but a year or two later moved to London, where he soon became well known for his work, and in 1814 received a silver medal from the Society of Arts for his engraving of a portrait of Sir Thomas Gresham. In 1816 he published his engraving of a portrait of Thomas Bewick (q.v.), by William Nicholson (q.v.), this work being immediately acclaimed the best portrait of Bewick executed up to that date. Two years later he became heatedly involved in a controversy respecting the forgery of bank notes, which resulted in the bank authorities taking proceedings against him. He was confined in Coldbath Fields Prison, where he engraved one of his best known works: *An interior view of Cold-Bath-Fields Prison, in which Thomas Ranson was unlawfully confined by the Bank of England for holding an alleged One Pound Note (that he paid Forty Shillings for), which was proved to be genuine in a Court of Justice. Dedicated without Permission, to the Govr. and the Company of the Thread Needle Street Paper Establishment.* He contended that the Bank had no right to impound notes which were the property of others, and that inspectors could not always distinguish between a forged and a genuine note. The resulting action was decided in his favour and he received much praise for his stand against the authority of the Bank. Ranson remained successful as an engraver for several years further, in 1821 receiving the Gold Isis Medal from the Society of Arts for his portrait of the Duke of Northumberland, and in the following year, the same medal for his engraving of Wilkie's *Duncan Gray*. He later accomplished little, however, and died in London in 1828 a man of very slender means. His brother, CUTHBERT RANSON, was a talented sculptor, and practised in London.

RATHBONE, William (b.1884)
Portrait and figure painter in oil; miniaturist in bronze; art teacher. Rathbone was born at SUNDERLAND, and studied at the town's School of Art before obtaining a post as second master at the School of Art, at DARLINGTON, in 1905. He remained at DARLINGTON until 1914,

when he was appointed Headmaster of the Preston School of Art. He exhibited his work at the Royal Academy, the Royal Miniature Society, and at the Walker Art Gallery, Liverpool. He was an associate of the Royal Miniature Society.

RAY, Richard Archibald, A.R.C.A. (1884-1968)
Landscape and figure painter in oil and watercolour; memorial and badge of office designer; art teacher. Ray was born at London, and studied at Brighton School of Art, and the Royal College of Art, before taking up his appointment as Principal of the College of Arts & Crafts at SUNDERLAND. While serving at the College, Ray remained deeply interested in painting, and also became interested in designing war and other memorials, and badges of office. He rarely exhibited his work outside SUNDERLAND, three examples being his oil: *Fraglioni Rock, Isle of Capri*, and watercolours: *Durham*, and *A New Forest Ride*, shown at the "Contemporary Artists of Durham County" exhibition, staged at the Shipley Art Gallery, GATESHEAD, in 1951, in connection with the Festival of Britain. Two examples of his memorial work are the war memorial at SUNDERLAND, and his tablet to Swann in the entrance to the town's Library and Art Gallery. Ray continued to live at SUNDERLAND following his retirement, dying there in 1968. He was an associate of the Royal College of Art. Represented: Sunderland A.G.

REAY, John (1817-1902)
Portrait and landscape painter in oil; copyist. This artist practised at NORTH SHIELDS in the middle years of the 19th century, later moving to SUNDERLAND, where he appears to have spent the remainder of his life. He first began to exhibit his work while at NORTH SHIELDS, sending examples to the North of England Society for the Promotion of the Fine Arts, NEWCASTLE, in 1838. In 1840 he sent two of his copies of the Old Masters, to the "Exhibition of Arts, Manufactures and Practical Science", at NEWCASTLE, following this by sending his portraits of W. S. B. Woolhouse, the well known mathematician of NORTH SHIELDS, Italian astronomer Galileo, and others, to a similarly titled exhibition at NEWCASTLE in 1848. When he moved to SUNDERLAND, Reay became friendly with William Crosby (q.v.), accompanying him on a visit to Antwerp to copy Old Masters, and subsequently sharing with his friend available portrait commissions in the town. It is believed that he died at SUNDERLAND. Represented: Sunderland A.G.

REAY, William (c.1837- c.1920)
Portrait and landscape painter in oil. He was born at GATESHEAD, and later worked in the local coal mines, painting in his spare time. His work at this point was varied in subject matter, and included local views and portraits, but when he and his brothers subsequently emigrated to Australia, he is said to have become a successful portrait painter there. Regrettably, his work is now little known in Australia, in which country he died in the first quarter of the present century. His miner brothers were also successful in Australia, one becoming a mine owner, the other an hotel proprietor in New South Wales.

REED, Elizabeth (fl. late 19th cent.)

Amateur landscape and coastal painter in watercolour. This artist lived at SOUTH SHIELDS in the late 19th century, and regularly sent her work for exhibition to the Bewick Club, NEWCASTLE, from the early 1890's. She mainly painted local landscape and coastal views, several of which are now in the collections of the Shipley Art Gallery, GATESHEAD, and South Shields Museum & Art Gallery. She may have been related to the ELEANOR REED who painted at SUNDERLAND in the same period, and sent ten works to Manchester City Art Gallery 1890-94.

REED, John (1811- after 1861)

Religious, landscape and figure painter in oil; copyist. Reed was born at NEWCASTLE, the son of Alderman Archibald Reed, six times Mayor of the town, and friend of Thomas Bewick (q.v.). He showed a talent for drawing and painting from an early age, and by the age of seventeen had commenced showing his work at the Northern Academy, NEWCASTLE. In 1829 his exhibit at the Academy: *The Head of Jupiter* (a drawing for which he had received the large silver medal of the Society of Arts), was highly praised by W. A. Mitchell, in the *Tyne Mercury*, and he continued to exhibit exclusively in his native town until 1835, when he showed his *The Assumption of the Virgin*, after Murillo, at Liverpool. In 1839 he began exhibiting in London, at the British Institution showing: *The Falconer* – a work which he had already shown at the First Exhibition of the North of England Society for the Promotion of the Fine Arts, NEWCASTLE, in 1838, along with fifteen copies of works by various European masters. He showed his first work at the Royal Academy in 1849: *The Wounded Brigand*, having by then made his home in the capital. He continued to live in London until his marriage in 1858, when he moved to Douglas, Isle of Man. He sent his last exhibit to the Royal Academy while living on the island: *Fête Champêtre – autumn; mountains of Cadore in the distance*, shown in 1861. It is believed that he died shortly after exhibiting this work. His brother, ARTHUR REED (d. 1883), was a talented amateur artist, and an occasional exhibitor at NEWCASTLE.

REID, Andrew (1823-1896)

Engraver; lithographer; draughtsman. Born at NEW-CASTLE, the son of David Reid, partner in a well known local jewellers, Reid was apprenticed at fourteen to Mark Lambert (q.v.), in the Lambert engraving workshop in the town. After completing his apprenticeship he gained experience in lithography and general printing, with Day & Son, London, principally working on railway plans. Returning to NEWCASTLE in 1845 he commenced business as an engraver, but later became increasingly interested in printing, and was responsible for publishing many publications associated with the area, some of which he illustrated himself, and engraved the plates. Notable amongst his local interest works was his *Handbook to Newcastle*, first published in 1864, but revised and reprinted in 1886. For this work by Dr. John Collingwood Bruce, he provided a large number of drawings which he indicated as having been drawn by himself, and in many instances provided the wood or other engravings. Reid took a great interest in art outside his engraving and printing activities, and was associated with the foundation and running of the Arts Association, NEWCASTLE, with Joseph Crawhall, The Second (q.v.), as well as serving on the committee of the School of Art in the town for several years. Reid's company became the largest of its kind at NEWCASTLE, his sons Philip and Sidney joining him in 1889, and their newly styled business Andrew Reid, Sons & Co., soon after buying out his old master's company, M. & M. W. Lambert. He died at NEWCASTLE.

REID, James Eadie (fl. late 19th, early 20th cent.)

Portrait, figure and landscape painter in oil and water-colour. Reid practised as a professional artist in Nor-thumbria in the late 19th, and early 20th centuries, and while living at WHITLEY BAY, exhibited at the Artists of the Northern Counties exhibitions at the Laing Art Gallery, NEWCASTLE, for several years. He later moved to London, where he exhibited at the London Salon from 1908-1917. In 1910 he published a book on artist John Everett Millais, in *The Makers of British Art* series. The Shipley Art Gallery, GATESHEAD, has his portrait of Canon W. Moore Ede, M.A., D.D., Rector of GATESHEAD 1881-1907.

*REID, John W. M., A.R.C.A. (born c.1890)

Sculptor; landscape painter in oil and watercolour; draughtsman. Reid studied at the Royal College of Art,

John W. M. Reid: St. George and the dragon. *Haymarket, Newcastle upon Tyne*. Bronze.

142

and later took up the appointment of Master of Sculpture at Armstrong College (later King's College; now Newcastle University). After service in the First World War he returned to the College, remaining there until the late 1920's, and executing as his major work on Tyneside, a figure of St. George, in bronze#, for the grounds of St. Thomas's Church, Haymarket, NEW-CASTLE. This monument to officers and men of the 6th Battalion of the Northumberland Fusiliers, stands just to the right of the church entrance, and was unveiled in 1924. The enamel plaque on the central stone pedestal was executed by RENE BOWMAN, of NEWCASTLE, while the carved stone decorations for the whole pedestal were carried out by WILLIAM CURRIE of BIRTLEY, near GATESHEAD. Reid exhibited both works of sculpture and landscapes at the Artists of the Northern Counties exhibitions at the Laing Art Gallery, NEWCASTLE, for several years from 1922. He was an associate of the Royal College of Art.

RICHARDS, Albert F. (1859-1944)

Landscape and coastal painter in watercolour. Richards was born at Bridport, Dorset, but later moved to Northumbria, where he first settled at JARROW, near SOUTH SHIELDS, later at ROKER, near SUNDERLAND. He first began exhibiting his work while living at JARROW, showing his *Coquet Island from Warkworth Beach*, and *Coquet Island from Amble*, at the Artists of the Northern Counties exhibition at the Laing Art Gallery, NEWCASTLE, in 1908. He continued to exhibit at NEW-CASTLE throughout his life, showing his last work at the Artists of the Northern Counties exhibition in the year of his death, at ROKER. Sunderland Art Gallery has several examples of his work, including *Sea at South Shields*, and *Summer Haze*.

RICHARDSON, Arthur, R.B.A. (1865-1928)

Landscape and seascape painter in oil and watercolour; art teacher. He was born at NEWCASTLE, the son of leather tanner David Richardson, and appears to have studied in London before practising as a professional artist in the capital at the age of twenty-two. He first began exhibiting his work in the provinces, while living at NEWCASTLE, showing examples at the city's Bewick Club, in 1885. Later, he moved to London, from which he commenced exhibiting at Liverpool and Manchester. In 1889 he sent his first work to the Royal Academy: *A Groyne at Leigh, Essex*. The following year he returned to NEWCASTLE, and from there sent his second work to the Academy: *Ryton Church*, and further works to the city's Bewick Club. By the mid-1890's he had settled in Gloucestershire, from which he continued to exhibit at the Bewick Club, and in 1897 sent one further work to the Academy. By the turn of the century, however, and then working as an art teacher at Cheltenham, he was exhibiting his work almost exclusively at the Royal Society of British Artists, and in 1904 was elected a member of that Society. He occasionally exhibited at the Bewick Club, and at the Artists of the Northern Counties exhibitions at the Laing Art Gallery, NEW-CASTLE, in the early years of the century, and last exhibited at the Royal Society of British Artists, in 1919. It is believed that he died at Dawlish, Devon. His sister, Edith Richardson (q.v.), was also a talented artist. He was the father of the distinguished stage and film actor, Sir Ralph Richardson. Represented: Cheltenham A.G.; Laing A.G., Newcastle.

*RICHARDSON, Charles (1829-1908)

Landscape and seascape painter in oil and watercolour; drawing master. He was born at NEWCASTLE, a son of Thomas Miles Richardson, Senior (q.v.), by his second marriage, and practised as a professional artist and drawing master in the town after some tuition from his father, and possibly his elder brother, Henry Burdon Richardson (q.v.). He first began to exhibit his work at NEWCASTLE, showing two examples at the exhibition of pictures by living artists at the North of England Society for the Promotion of the Fine Arts, in 1852. Three years later he sent his first work to the Royal Academy: *Old Flour Mill near Newcastle upon Tyne*, and in the following year (1856), began exhibiting at the Suffolk Street Gallery, showing a watercolour: *Scene in Borrowdale looking towards Rosthwaite*. By 1873 he had moved to London, leaving there just before the turn of the century to live at Petersfield, Hants. He remained a regular exhibitor at the Royal Academy until 1901, having by then shown some twenty-eight works, and also exhibited in this period at various London and provincial galleries. Most of his works were landscapes, in which he frequently included groups of people, horses or cattle.

Richardson sometimes collaborated with his brothers in the production of watercolours, an example being the seascape with shipping, in the Laing Art Gallery, NEWCASTLE, which he painted together with Thomas Miles Richardson, Junior (q.v.). He also worked with his brother, Henry Burdon, as a drawing master, and in 1848 jointly illustrated with him by means of watercolour, Dr. John Collingwood Bruce's lectures on the Roman Wall, his brother producing the greater number of works. Some of these were later reproduced in Dr. Bruce's *Handbook to the Roman Wall*. A later work which he illustrated independently was Sir William Lawson's *The Conquest of Camborne*, 1903. He is said to have died at Petersfield, but notices of a sale of his collection of oils and watercolours at NEWCASTLE in 1913, state his place of death as Peterborough, Huntingdonshire. These notices may have been correct, as his younger brother John Isaac Richardson (q.v.), was living there in 1908. Richardson's wife was also a talented watercolourist, and exhibited a work at the Royal Academy in 1846. Represented: National Gallery of Ireland; Laing A.G., Newcastle; Shipley A.G., Gateshead.

RICHARDSON, Rev. Charles Edward (c.1849- c.1937)

Genre and still-life painter in oil. He was the son of Thomas Richardson of CASTLE EDEN. He was educated at Trinity College, Cambridge, receiving his Bachelor of Arts degree in 1875. He was ordained into the priesthood in 1877, and spent the next thirteen years in London. About 1890, he moved back to Northumbria to become Rector of RED MARSHALL, near STOCKTON ON TEES, remaining there until 1895. Following the death of his father he moved to Kirklevington Hall, near YARM, and in 1897 commenced exhibiting at the Royal Academy, showing a still-life. He exhibited at the Academy until 1907, showing a total of eleven works, with titles such as: *Memories*; *A flaw in the title*, and *True Blue*. He died at Kirklevington Hall about 1937.

RICHARDSON, Charles W. (c.1865- after 1913)

Amateur landscape and genre painter in oil and watercolour. Richardson was born on Tyneside, and later took up a business career, painting and sketching in his spare time. He first worked at NEWCASTLE, where he exhibited at the city's Bewick Club from 1885. He later took up a managerial post at MIDDLESBOROUGH, where he became one of the founder members of the Cleveland Sketching Club, with John Smales Calvert (q.v.). He became a regular exhibitor with the Club, later showing work at the Artists of the Northern Counties exhibitions at the Laing Art Gallery, NEWCASTLE. He regularly showed his work at NEWCASTLE from 1905 until the outbreak of the First World War, showing a wide range of landscape and genre works, some with continental themes. His first exhibits in 1905 were entitled: *Carr's Glen, Co. Antrim*, and *The Tyne at Wylam*. Represented: Middlesbrough A.G.

RICHARDSON, Christopher (1709-1781)

Sculptor; stone mason. Richardson's place of birth is not known, but is thought to have been Northumbria. His best known work in the area is the statue of British Liberty on top of the column in Gibside Park, ROWLANDS GILL, near GATESHEAD, which was erected over a seven-year period as part of the landscaping of the park begun by George Bowes in 1729. The column is 140' in height, and Richardson's 12' statue on top was worked in situ. He worked from a solid block of stone which was hoisted to the top of the column, protecting himself from the elements meanwhile, within a wooden shed erected for this purpose. His payment for his mammoth task, which took about four months, was £40. The figure of *Liberty* holds what appears to be a staff in its hand with a cup on top, both being made of copper. The cup has long been a target for local marksmen believing that it is made of gold, or that it contains coins of this precious metal. Richardson's later work in Northumbria included carvings in stone for Alnwick Castle, and for the coat of arms on the Town Hall, BERWICK-UPON-TWEED. Most of his subsequent work was executed in other parts of Britain. He died at Doncaster, Yorkshire, and was buried there.

RICHARDSON, Edith (1867- after 1929)

Landscape and genre painter in oil and watercolour; decorative artist; illustrator. She was born at NEWCASTLE, the daughter of leather tanner David Richardson, and studied at Armstrong College (later King's College; now Newcastle University), and in Paris, before becoming a professional artist on Tyneside. By her early twenties she had become a regular exhibitor at the Bewick Club, NEWCASTLE, and in 1899 sent her first works to the Royal Academy: *The Path*, and *The Boy and the Winds*. In 1900, and still living at the family home in the Elswick area of NEWCASTLE, she again exhibited at the Academy, showing: *White Butterflies*. Later in this same year she moved to Hertfordshire, where she apparently spent the remainder of her life. She exhibited only one further work at the Academy following her move, but throughout the early years of the century she was a regular exhibitor at various London and provincial establishments, including the Royal Institute of Painters in Water Colours, the London Salon, the Walker Art Gallery, Liverpool, and the Laing Art Gallery, NEWCASTLE, whose Artists of the Northern Counties exhibitions she contributed to from their inception in 1905. She was the author of several books, some of which she illustrated herself. She was still living in Hertfordshire in 1929. Her brother Arthur Richardson (q.v.), was also a talented artist.

144

Edward Richardson: Tynemouth Priory and Lighthouse, from the North, 1872. Watercolour 12×23½. *Tyne & Wear County Council Museums, Laing Art Gallery.*

*RICHARDSON, Edward (1810-1874)

Landscape painter in oil and watercolour. He was born at NEWCASTLE, the second son of Thomas Miles Richardson, Senior (q.v.), and practised as a professional artist from an early age, following some tuition from his father. Unlike his elder brother George Richardson (q.v.), and younger brother Thomas Miles Richardson, Junior (q.v.), however, he did not exhibit his work until relatively late in life, and then first in London. Here he moved in his early thirties, and commenced exhibiting in 1856, sending his *Watermill, Castleton of Braemar, Aberdeenshire*, to the Royal Academy, and a number of works to the New Water Colour Society (later the Royal Institute of Painters in Water Colours). He exhibited at the Academy on only one further occasion, this being in 1858, when he showed a view of *Boppart on the Rhine*, but continued to exhibit at the New Water Colour Society until his death, showing a total of 187 works, and becoming elected an associate member in 1859. He painted several continental views in addition to his many Northumbrian and Scottish works, but it is not clear whether he actually travelled abroad. He appears to have spent most of his later life based at London, but paid occasional visits to his native Tyneside. He died in the same year as his younger half-brother, Henry Burdon Richardson (q.v.). A sale of his watercolours was held at Christie's in 1864; the remainder at the same establishment in 1875. Represented: Victoria and Albert Museum; City A.G., Manchester; Laing A.G., Newcastle; Newport A.G.; South Shields Museum & A.G.; Williamson A.G., Birkenhead.

*RICHARDSON, George (1808-1840)

Landscape, genre, architectural and seascape painter in watercolour. He was born at NEWCASTLE, the first son of Thomas Miles Richardson, Senior (q.v.), and by the age of fourteen was advertising his services as "historical and landscape painter" in a local directory. By the age of eighteen he was also offering "Drawing Classes for Figure, Landscape and Animal Painting". He first worked as a painter and drawing master at Brunswick Place, later opening an Academy at Blackett Street with his younger brother, Thomas Miles Richardson, Junior (q.v.). He also gave private lessons, and offered evening tuition to those who could not attend his day classes. He first exhibited his work at the age of fifteen, sending a *Study of a Plaster Cast* to the 1823 exhibition of the Northumberland Institution for the Promotion of the Fine Arts, NEWCASTLE. He continued to exhibit at the Northumberland Institution throughout its short life, also sending one work to the Carlisle Academy in 1825: *Boy Dressing after Bathing*. In 1828 he began exhibiting at the British Institution, and the Northern Academy, NEWCASTLE, and in this year also sent one further work to the Carlisle Academy. He continued to exhibit at the British Institution, the Northern Academy, and the Carlisle Academy, for the next five years, also showing two works at the New Water Colour Society (later the Royal Institute of Painters in Water Colours). He exhibited at the Newcastle upon Tyne Institution for the General Promotion of the Fine Arts from its foundation in 1832, and was also an exhibitor at the First Exhibition of Paintings and Sculpture of the Newcastle Society of Artists, in 1835, and its First Water Colour Exhibition, in 1836, while practising at DARLINGTON. He exhibited at NEWCASTLE until close to his death from consumption in 1840, his last recorded exhibits being the eight watercolours which he sent to the North of England Society for the Promotion of the Fine Arts, in 1839; these comprised several views taken in North Yorkshire, a view near ALNWICK, a view of Carlisle Cathedral and Castle, and one continental view. He occasionally exhibited continental views but

George Richardson: Doune Castle, near Stirling.
Watercolour 15¼×12⅝. *Victoria and Albert Museum.*

is not known to have travelled abroad. He died at NEWCASTLE, a lottery of his works being held subsequently for the benefit of his widow. Represented: Victoria and Albert Museum; Laing A.G., Newcastle.

RICHARDSON, George Bouchier, F.S.A. (1822-1877)

Wood engraver; landscape and architectural painter in watercolour; art teacher. The son of Moses Aaron Richardson (q.v.), and nephew of Thomas Miles Richardson, Senior (q.v.), he was born at NEWCASTLE, and received tuition in drawing and painting from his uncle before becoming a wood engraver in the town. He practised as a wood engraver at NEWCASTLE, until 1850, meanwhile taking a keen interest in antiquarian matters, and producing many pictures of "decaying streets and buildings in his native town". He became a member of the Society of Antiquaries, NEWCASTLE, in 1848, and later became a Fellow of the Society of Antiquaries, London. He produced wood engravings for a variety of locally published works, notably the *Reprints of Rare Tracts*, published by his father, but following the latter's departure for Australia in 1850, until he himself went there four years later, he mainly concerned himself with printing. Arriving in Melbourne some time in 1854, he obtained a position as a proof reader, then via a succession of sub-editorial posts became editor of the *Wallaroo Times*. In 1874 he left Wallaroo and settled in Adelaide, where he taught music, drawing and watercolour painting until his death in 1877. The Society of Antiquaries, NEWCASTLE, has

two portfolio volumes of his sketches of local old buildings, and the city's Central Library, a single volume of sketches of buildings and landscapes in Northumberland and on Tyneside. He was the elder brother of John Thomas Richardson (q.v.).

RICHARDSON, Henry Burdon (1826-1874)

Landscape, antiquarian and marine painter in watercolour; drawing master. He was born at NEWCASTLE*, a son of Thomas Miles Richardson, Senior (q.v.), by his second marriage. After some tuition from his father, and possibly his elder half-brothers, George Richardson (q.v.), Edward Richardson (q.v.), and Thomas Miles Richardson, Junior (q.v.), he practised as a professional artist and drawing master in the town, joined for a period by his younger brother Charles Richardson (q.v.). In 1848 he was given his first important commission: the production of a series of watercolour drawings of the Roman Wall to illustrate the lectures on this subject of Dr. John Collingwood Bruce. Most of these watercolours were first executed on the spot in sepia and washed with colour subsequently, and collectively comprise a work of major topographical accomplishment. Several were later reproduced in Dr. Bruce's *Handbook to the Roman Wall*. In 1850 he issued an announcement that he would give "lessons in Landscape and Marine Painting" either at his own home, or the homes of pupils. With him at this time lived his younger brother Charles, who also gave classes in drawing. In this year he also exhibited in London for the first time, showing a *Scene in Borrowdale*, at the Suffolk Street Gallery. He again exhibited at the Suffolk Street Gallery in 1851, showing a *Seapiece*, and in 1853 sent his first work to the Royal Academy: *Deck of the Hotspur, East Indiaman*.

Richardson exhibited little in his later life, showing one further work at the Royal Academy in 1861: *Near Dunkeld, Perthshire*, and one work at the Suffolk Street Gallery, in 1862: *View in Borrowdale*. He exhibited infrequently at NEWCASTLE, among his few known exhibits being the three works which he sent to the exhibition of pictures by living artists at the North of England Society for the Promotion of the Fine Arts, in 1852. Some confusion has existed regarding Richardson's exhibiting dates, but it is clear from his date of birth as confirmed in the Census Return referred to below, that he could not have been the "Henry Burdon Richardson" said to have exhibited continental views at the Royal Academy, and the Suffolk Street Gallery 1828-1834. He died at NEWCASTLE at the early age of forty-eight. Represented: Laing A.G., Newcastle; Shipley A.G., Gateshead.

* His place of birth has previously been given as WARKWORTH, but his mother's Census Return for 1851 shows it as NEWCASTLE.

RICHARDSON, Henry (Harry) (c.1867- c.1928)

Landscape painter in oil and watercolour; art teacher. Richardson was born at DURHAM and appears to have become a largely self-taught artist before practising professionally in the city by the early 1880's. He first began exhibiting his work publicly in 1879, showing his *Sketch in Durham Cathedral*, at the Arts Association, NEWCASTLE. He later became a regular exhibitor at the city's Bewick Club, at which his first exhibit in 1884 was entitled: *Durham Cathedral from the Prebends Bridge.* He continued to exhibit at the Club until the 1890's, and subsequently exhibited several works at the Artists of the Northern Counties exhibitions at the Laing Art Gallery, NEWCASTLE. He died at DURHAM.

*RICHARDSON, John Isaac, R.I., R.O.I. (1836-1913)
Landscape and subject painter in oil and watercolour. He was born at NEWCASTLE, a son of Thomas Miles Richardson, Senior (q.v.), by his second marriage, and according to Algernon Graves in his *Dictionary of Artists*, etc., (see Bibliography), exhibited at the Royal Academy from the age of ten. The work first shown was: *Laon attempting the Rescue of Cythna . . .*, an ambitious work for a child of his tender years, and one can only assume he must have been helped more than considerably in its execution by one of his artist relatives, or that Graves was incorrect in attributing this, and the several other works which followed it from an address at Islington, to this particular Richardson. He was certainly still living at NEWCASTLE at the age of fourteen,‡ when Graves gives his address as Islington, and was, indeed, still living in the town as late as 1857, according to local trade directories. Significantly, from the time that he was definitely in London, his exhibits at the Royal Academy, the British Institution and the Suffolk Street Gallery were different in character to those earlier attributed to him; landscape works featuring people, cattle and agricultural activities, and painted in Northumbria, Cumbria and Scotland. Once settled in the capital he soon began to take an interest in its artistic affairs. By the middle 1860's he had joined a committee which led in 1865 to the foundation of the Dudley Gallery, and he was later elected a member of the Royal Institute of Painters in Water Colours, and the Royal Institute of Oil Painters. He mainly exhibited his work with the first of these two Institutes, showing some sixty-nine works, but was also an occasional exhibitor at the latter, and exhibited considerably in London at various exhibitions. He also exhibited in the provinces, though infrequently in NEWCASTLE. According to his obituaries he died at Peterborough, Huntingdonshire, his home for several years, and not his native Northumbria, as is frequently claimed. He was the youngest and last surviving son of Thomas Miles Richardson, Senior. Represented: Laing A.G., Newcastle.

‡ *His mother's Census Return for 1851 shows him living with the family at 20, Ridley Place, NEWCASTLE, and still at school.*

RICHARDSON, John Thomas (1835-1898)
Landscape and animal painter in oil and watercolour; engraver. He was born at NEWCASTLE, the eighth child of Moses Aaron Richardson (q.v.), and younger brother of George Bouchier Richardson (q.v.), and received his first tuition in art from his father, and uncle Thomas Miles Richardson, Senior (q.v.). He is said to have been a remarkably gifted artist as a child, his uncle sending for him one day when he was twelve, to sketch into a large picture in oil a team of horses drawing a huge tree trunk from a forest. The boy's sketch was then faithfully followed by Richardson when completing this work. John Thomas joined his father in the family's move to Australia in 1850, later practising as an artist and engraver until his death at Richmond, near Melbourne, in 1898.

RICHARDSON, Moses Aaron (1793-1871)
Etcher. He was born at NEWCASTLE, the younger brother of Thomas Miles Richardson, Senior (q.v.), and later became a well known printer and publisher in the town, also dabbling in bookselling, bookbinding, picture cleaning, and selling artists' colours. His shop, "Richardson's Repository of Arts", specialised in pictures and engravings, but he is best known for his local history publications and directories, among the former, his eight-volume *Local Historian's Table Book*, 1838-46, and *Reprints of Rare Tracts*, which latter were illustrated by his eldest son, George Bouchier Richard-

John Isaac Richardson:
Unloading Hay in the
Dales. Watercolour 7¼×12.
Bill Minns.

147

Thomas Miles Richardson, Senior: Newcastle from Gateshead Fell. Oil 56×92. *Tyne & Wear County Council Museums, Laing Art Gallery.*

son (q.v.). In 1834 he started to publish in parts by subscription *The Castles of the . . . Border, A Series of Views*, drawn and engraved in mezzotint by his elder brother, but the project was abandoned after the publication of two parts. His work in etching was mainly confined to reproducing by this process drawings executed for publication by his brother, these including several views of old buildings in and around NEWCASTLE. In 1850 he emigrated to Australia, leaving his son to run his printing business, and took a job as a rate collector in Prahran, a suburb of Melbourne. He died at Melbourne in 1871. His eighth child, John Thomas Richardson (q.v.), was also a talented artist.

*RICHARDSON, Thomas Miles, Senior, H.R.S.A. (1784-1848)

Landscape, marine and figure painter in oil and watercolour; illustrator; engraver; lithographer; etcher. Richardson was born at NEWCASTLE, the son of a school master. As a child he showed a passionate love of drawing, and while staying with relatives at ALNWICK, made his first studies "from nature" in watercolour, at the age of eleven. Impressed by his talents as an artist, his parents later placed him as an apprentice of Tyneside engraver Abraham Hunter (q.v.), but Hunter died shortly afterwards, and by his own choice Richardson became apprenticed to a firm of cabinet makers at NEWCASTLE. He soon found that he did not like the work, however, and consoling himself by pursuing his artistic studies in his spare time, he spent a miserable seven years in his chosen trade, only escaping it with the death of his father in 1806, and his appointment in

the latter's place as master of St. Andrew's Charity School, NEWCASTLE. But his long hours of working in damp conditions as a cabinet maker had left him with symptoms of consumption, and acting on medical advice he absented himself from his school duties and went on a sea trip to London. Here he was walking along the Strand one day when he saw in a window a watercolour of Conway Castle by David Cox, which so impressed him that he returned to NEWCASTLE with a renewed enthusiasm for painting. During a second visit to London some time later he saw his first Royal Academy exhibition, and when he returned to NEWCASTLE, he was prevailed upon by surgeon William Fife to become a drawing master, accepting as his first two pupils Fife's sons William and John. Other pupils soon followed, and for the next six years he was both master at St. Andrew's, and a drawing master.

By 1813 Richardson felt that he might be able to support himself and his growing family by his work as a drawing master alone, and leaving St. Andrew's he at first devoted himself entirely to this profession. Within a few months, however, he was leaving his classes to go on painting expeditions, and with the acceptance of his *A View of the Old Fish Market, Newcastle*, by the Royal Academy in 1814, he began increasingly to rely on painting for a living. His work at first attracted little attention, and in an effort to supplement his income from painting and teaching drawing, he made his first of several forays into the field of illustration, in 1816 producing with William Dixon (q.v.), a series of aquatint views of places of interest at NEWCASTLE. This work was not successful, and for the next six years he struggled on as a painter, becoming increasingly frustrated by the absence at NEWCASTLE of a suitable place at which he and fellow artists might show their work. He decided to remedy this situation, and together with Thomas Bewick (q.v.), Henry Perlee Parker (q.v.), John Dobson (q.v.), and others, founded the Northumberland Institution for the Promotion of the Fine Arts, holding its first exhibition at his home in Brunswick Place, NEWCASTLE, in 1822. He remained one of the most prominent exhibitors at this Institution throughout its six-year life, also from 1822 showing further works at the Royal Academy, and in 1824 commencing to exhibit at the British Institution. But by the Northumberland Institution's exhibition of 1827 he had become completely disillusioned with its success as a means of promoting the sale of his paintings, and in that year he began to exhibit his work even more widely outside Northumbria, sending his first examples to the Royal Scottish Academy and the Suffolk Street Gallery, and also making appearances at the exhibitions of the Old Water Colour Society (later the Royal Society of Painters in Watercolours), and the New Water Colour Society (later the Royal Institute of Painters in Water Colours).

Late in 1827 those principally involved in the running of the Northumberland Institution decided to found an Academy in the town to take over its role as an exhibition venue for the area. Its construction was financed jointly by Richardson and Parker, with a grant from the Corporation, and was designed by John Dobson. Named "The Northern Academy of Arts", and built on the town's Blackett Street, the Academy staged its first exhibition in June, 1828. Some of the biggest names in contemporary British Art sent work to this, and subsequent exhibitions of the Academy, but by 1832 it found itself in considerable financial difficulties and had to be wound up, with Richardson and Parker obliged to pay off a large mortgage. During his four years of helping to run the Academy Richardson embarked on a number of other ventures, notably in 1830, when he painted, and exhibited with "dioramic effects" at NEWCASTLE, four large pictures, and was responsible with others for the foundation of the Northern Society of Painters in Water Colours. Undaunted by the failure of the Academy, and the Northumberland Institution before it, he next helped to found the Newcastle upon Tyne Institution for the General Promotion of the Fine Arts, and in 1836 took a leading part in the formation of the Newcastle Society of Artists. But none of these later art promoting ventures absorbed his time as fully as those in which he had been involved in the 1820's, and concentrating on his painting, he was successful in 1833, in selling to the Corporation what is widely regarded as his finest landscape: View of Newcastle from Gateshead Fell,# for which he received 50 guineas. A second success came with the purchase by the Corporation in 1835 of his View of the Side, Newcastle, the Procession of the High Sheriff of Northumberland going to meet the Judges, and with his work now widely recognised, he was able to live his remaining years at NEWCASTLE in moderate prosperity.

Richardson last exhibited at the Royal Academy and the Royal Scottish Academy, in 1845, and in the following year sent his final exhibit to the British Institution. Always a keen supporter of North Country art exhibitions, he continued to exhibit at NEWCASTLE until just short of his death, and exhibited at Carlisle from 1824 until 1846, showing his earlier works at the Carlisle Academy, and his last work in the town, at Carlisle Athenaeum. His last known exhibits were those shown at an exhibition of works mainly by members of his family, staged at his home at Blackett Street, in September 1847. He died at NEWCASTLE six months later, following a painful illness lasting seven weeks. Richardson's interest in illustration continued throughout his life, his aquatint work with William Dixon, referred to earlier, being followed by The Castles of the English Borders, 1833, for which he mezzotint engraved the plates of his drawings himself; a series of etchings of the Antiquities of Newcastle, and the several plates which he drew and lithographed for the Sketches of Shotley Bridge Spar on the River Derwent, published by his son, Thomas Miles Richardson, Junior (q.v.), in 1839. He is best known, however, for his superb work in oil and watercolour, most of it portraying Northumbrian, Scottish and Lake District scenery. Few honours came the way of this remarkable artist and man who did so much to encourage and promote the work of fellow Northumbrian artists; he was elected an honorary member of the Scottish Academy in 1829, and an associate of the New Water Colour Society in 1840. He married twice, having by his first wife: George Richardson (q.v.), Edward Richardson (q.v.), and Thomas Miles Richardson, Junior (q.v.), and by his second wife: Henry Burdon Richardson (q.v.), Charles Richardson (q.v.), and John Isaac Richardson (q.v.). He was the elder brother of Moses Aaron Richardson (q.v.), and the uncle of George Bouchier Richardson (q.v.), and John Thomas Richardson (q.v.). A major loan exhibition celebrating the artistic achievements of his immediate family was held at the Laing Art Gallery, NEWCASTLE, in 1906. Represented: British Museum; Victoria and Albert Museum; National Gallery of Ireland; Cartwright Hall, Bradford; Derby City A.G.; Grosvenor Museum, Chester; Laing A.G., Newcastle; Leeds City A.G.; Manchester City A.G.; Portsmouth City Museum; Reading A.G.; Shipley A.G., Gateshead; Sunderland A.G.; Walker A.G., Liverpool.

*RICHARDSON, Thomas Miles, Junior, R.W.S. (1813-1890)
Landscape and figure painter in oil and watercolour; lithographer. He was born at NEWCASTLE, the third son of Thomas Miles Richardson, Senior (q.v.), and first exhibited his work at the age of fourteen, when he sent a Sketch in Pencil after Cooper R.A., to the town's Northumberland Institution for the Promotion of the Fine Arts, in 1827. From this point forwards, and evidently coached closely by his father, he was a regular exhibitor of work at NEWCASTLE, showing examples at the First Exhibition of the Northern Academy in 1828, and all its succeeding exhibitions, and later at the various exhibitions of the institutions for the promotion of the fine arts which flourished in his native town. He first exhibited outside Northumbria in 1830, when he sent two works to the Carlisle Academy. In 1832 he

Thomas Miles Richardson, Junior: Dunstanburgh Castle, Northumberland. Watercolour 8½×22. *Christopher Wood Ltd.*

commenced exhibiting in London, showing: *Feeding the Shelty*, at the British Institution. In 1834 he showed at the Suffolk Street Gallery a scene from Sir Walter Scott's *Tale of the Betrothed*, and in 1837 exhibited for the first time at the Royal Academy, choosing a Northumbrian scene: *Prudhoe Castle, with the River Tyne – sunset*.

In 1837 Richardson made his first of many trips abroad, visiting France, Switzerland, Italy, Germany and Holland, and later produced an imperial folio work of lithographs entitled: *Sketches on the Continent . . . .* Eleven of the lithographs for this work were produced by himself, this leading to his involvement in another illustrative work employing this process: *Sketches of Shotley Bridge Spa on the Derwent*, published jointly with his father in 1839. He remained based at NEW-CASTLE until after his election as an associate of the Old Water Colour Society in 1843, when he moved to London. He was elected a member of the Old Water Colour Society (later the Royal Society of Painters in Watercolours) in 1851, and from then on exhibited almost exclusively with the Society, eventually showing some 702 works. Thomas Miles Richardson, Junior, is generally regarded as second only to his father in his skill as a watercolourist, his relatively few oils, which he produced mainly between 1832-1848 during his early period of exhibiting at London, being altogether too few to provide a fair basis for comparison. Much of his watercolour work differed widely in subject matter from that of his father, however, with an emphasis on highly coloured continental views which enjoyed a popularity far beyond anything achieved by his father's more restrained British views. His *Como*, for instance, reached £315 in a sale room in 1876, and his *Sorrento*, £310, in 1878 – while he was still living. On his death at London in 1890 his unsold works were sold at Christie's. Represented: British Museum; Victoria and Albert Museum; Blackburn A.G.; Darlington A.G.; Derby A.G.; Gray Museum & A.G., Hartlepool; Laing A.G., Newcastle; Shipley A.G., Gateshead; Sunderland A.G., and various provincial art galleries.

RICHARDSON, William Dudley (1862-1929)
Landscape and architectural painter in watercolour. He was born at DARLINGTON, and educated at Scarborough, North Yorkshire and later in Switzerland. He spent much of his time on the continent painting buildings, and showed his work at the Royal Academy, the Walker Art Gallery, Liverpool, and the Paris Salon. Darlington Art Gallery has several of his continental watercolours, painted shortly before his death in 1929. He is believed to have spent his final years living at DARLINGTON, from which in 1928, and 1929, he sent works to the Artists of the Northern Counties exhibitions at the Laing Art Gallery, NEWCASTLE.

*RIDLEY, Matthew White (1837-1888)
Landscape, portrait and genre painter in oil and water-colour; illustrator; etcher. He was born at NEWCASTLE, the son of a draughtsman, and is said to have worked in an architect's office before entering the Royal Academy Schools as a probationer at the age of nineteen. On completing his studies at the Schools under Smirke and Dobson he spent some years in Paris, where he became the first pupil of Whistler, and formed friendships with several important artists of the day, including Fantin-Latour, who painted Ridley's portrait. He then returned to London, where he founded his own art school. While running the school he began painting and exhibiting river, dock, harbour,# genre scenes and portraits, and later became a regular illustrator for several leading publications, including Cassell's *Family Magazine*, and *The Graphic*. He first began exhibiting his work publicly at the Suffolk Street Gallery in 1857, showing: *The Neapolitan Piper*; in 1860 he sent his first work to the British Institution: *The Boquet*, and in 1862 he exhibited for the first time at the Royal Academy, showing among his four works: *Seaham Harbour*, and *High Level Bridge, Newcastle upon Tyne*. He continued to exhibit at the Royal Academy until the year of his death, and also sent work to a number of other London and provincial exhibitions, including among the latter those of the Arts Association, NEWCASTLE, from 1878. In the

150

year following his death in London in 1888, his students and admirers founded in his memory The Ridley Art Society. This Society still flourishes today, and has mounted several important exhibitions of his work. Ridley's work in illustration has been applauded for its social realism, and is said to have been admired by Vincent Van Gogh. Represented: Tate Gallery, and various provincial art galleries.

ROBERTSON, Annie Theodora (b.1896)

Landscape painter in oil. She was born at Bradford, and studied at Sunderland College of Art, and Manchester, before making her home at GATESHEAD. She has exhibited her work at the Federation of Northern Art Societies exhibitions at the Laing Art Gallery, NEWCASTLE, and was one of the several Northumbrian artists whose work was included in this gallery's exhibition of "Paintings and Drawings of living Northern Artists selected from the Five Northern Art Galleries", in 1956. Two examples of her work: *Bright Interval*, and *End of Summer*, were included in the "Contemporary Artists of Durham County" exhibition, staged at the Shipley Art Gallery, GATESHEAD, in 1951, in connection with the Festival of Britain. The Shipley Art Gallery has her oil: *Bedburn*.

ROBERTSON, David Thomas (1879-1952)

Landscape, animal and portrait painter in oil and watercolour. Robertson was born at DARLINGTON, of Scottish parents, but moved to SUNDERLAND as a child. Here he became a largely self-taught artist, and practised in the town until his death in 1952. Robertson was a close friend, and possibly a pupil of John Atkinson (q.v.), and shared the latter's marked preference for painting horses and cattle. He exhibited his work exclusively in Northumbria, where he was a regular exhibitor at the Artists of the Northern Counties exhibitions at the Laing Art Gallery, NEWCASTLE, and

enjoyed special showings of his work at SUNDERLAND in 1922, and NEWCASTLE in 1924. Represented: Laing A.G., Newcastle; Shipley A.G., Gateshead; South Shields Museum & A.G.; Sunderland A.G.

ROBERTSON, Thomas (1823-1866)

This artist was born at ALNWICK, and later practised in the town before moving to Glasgow, where he died in 1866. Nothing is known of his work.

ROBINSON, Francis (1830-1886)

Landscape painter in oil. Born at DURHAM, Robinson received his education at the Blue Coat School, and was subsequently apprenticed to a tailor at his birthplace. He was strongly interested in drawing, however, and while still an apprentice studied under Forster Brown (q.v.), at evening classes at the Mechanics' Institute. Here he won several prizes for his work, and after working some time as a tailor, he decided to change his profession to that of artist. He soon became well known throughout the County for his landscapes, finding many clients among the aristocracy and wealthy businessmen, and receiving a number of offers to advance his career elsewhere. But Robinson remained attached to his native Northumbria all his life, only ceasing to paint its river valleys, hills and villages when towards the end of his life he suffered several paralytic strokes, with a consequent effect upon his artistic output. He died at DURHAM, and was buried in St. Margaret's churchyard.

*ROBINSON, George Finlay (1816-1902)

Landscape and coastal painter in watercolour; engraver; lithographer. Robinson was born at WHICKHAM, near GATESHEAD, and at fourteen was apprenticed to William Collard (q.v.), at NEWCASTLE. While with Collard he learnt the art of engraving, and became skilled at drawing, contributing several examples of his work to

Matthew White Ridley:
The Pool of London, 1862.
Oil 25½×36. *Tate Gallery.*

his master's publications. He also in his early years developed a keen interest in painting in watercolour, and became a member of an art society at NEWCASTLE, comprising John Henry Mole (q.v.), Thomas Hall Tweedy (q.v.), John Brown (q.v.), and other artists then seeking to develop their talents. This society flourished about 1830-35, and held its first exhibition at T. Bamford's Long Room at Amen Corner in the town. It later moved its meeting place and exhibition venue to the Old Tower, Pink Lane, where Mole began to assume a leading role in encouraging his fellow members in their progress. In 1839, and meanwhile having married a girl from Skelton, Cumberland, Robinson began to exhibit his work, showing his *View of the Tyne from Bensham*, and *Dunston on Tyne*, at the North of England Society for the Promotion of the Fine Arts, NEWCASTLE. Two years later he joined the staff of Mark Lambert (q.v.), taking over from John Wilson Carmichael (q.v.), the latter's role as "chief draughtsman" to the Lambert engraving company. Shortly after joining the company he began experimenting with lithography on behalf of his employers, and for the next half century combined the duties of draughtsman, engraver and lithographer for Lambert, and later his son, Mark William Lambert.

Although Robinson exhibited his work from his early twenties, it was in the last twenty-five years of his life that he engaged most frequently in this activity. In 1878 he showed at the Arts Association, NEWCASTLE, two studies of Coniston Water painted while visiting relatives of his wife, and at the first exhibition of the city's Bewick Club, in 1884, three further Lake District views: *The Old Mill, Borrowdale*; *Sweden Bridge, Ambleside*, and *Slate Bridge, Patterdale*. Most of his life was spent at NEWCASTLE, but following his retirement in the early 1890's, he moved to nearby GOSFORTH, from which he continued to exhibit at the Bewick Club until his death

in 1902. Robinson was one of the many Northumbrian artists who found themselves attracted to CULLERCOATS for their subject matter, and made many sketches of the village from 1842. One of these sketches is reproduced opposite page seventy-one of William Weaver Tomlinson's *Historical Notes on Cullercoats, Whitley and Monkseaton*, 1893, and an engraving of the village by Robinson was published by his employers, M. & M. W. Lambert, about 1844. It is said that Henry Hetherington Emmerson (q.v.), served a brief apprenticeship as an engraver under Robinson, and that John Surtees (q.v.), made his "first sketch from nature" in Robinson's company. He is today probably one of Northumbria's least known watercolourists, and as yet unrepresented in any local public collection.

*ROBINSON, Gerrard (1834-1891)

Wood carver; landscape, figure and decorative painter; illustrator. Northumbria's outstanding wood carver of the nineteenth century, Robinson was born at NEWCASTLE, the son of a blacksmith, and displayed a talent for drawing from an early age. His elder brother John Ewbanks Robinson (q.v.), gave him his first lessons in art, but following the discovery of his talents by the chairman of the town's Government School of Design, he was admitted as a pupil to the School, under William Bell Scott (q.v.). In 1848 he left the School and became apprenticed to Thomas Hall Tweedy (q.v.), the wood carver and gilder at NEWCASTLE, and in 1855 became foreman of the latter's workshop. In the next seven years he accomplished some of his finest work, including his famous Shakespeare Sideboard, completed within the Tweedy workshops, and exhibited under its proprietor's name, and the even more famous Chevy Chase Sideboard, which is said to have been largely completed at his home in his spare time. The latter work was first exhibited at NEWCASTLE, in 1863, the year after Robinson left Tweedy, and was hailed as a triumph of workmanship by the *Newcastle Daily Chronicle*; ". . . surely so wondrous a piece of furniture never passed from the hands of an artist", commented this newspaper.

Shortly after the work was shown, Robinson left NEWCASTLE, and set up as wood carver in London. Here he quickly built up a fashionable clientele for his wood carvings, and was a successful teacher of his skills. In 1866, however, he gave up this successful business, and returned to NEWCASTLE, hoping to take over his former employer's business. But Tweedy gave up the business without first giving Robinson an opportunity to purchase it and he was obliged to start from scratch. The demand for wood carving began to wane in the late 1860's, and although he had secured much work to begin with, notably from William Wailes (q.v.), who employed him extensively on work for Saltwell Tower, GATESHEAD, Robinson's diffidence as a businessman led to the eventual collapse of his business. He was helped by friends such as his former pupil, Seymour Lucas, the Royal Academician, and managed to supplement his income from these friends by teaching carving at NEWCASTLE, and illustrating childrens' books, but he died so impoverished at NEWCASTLE in 1891, that he was buried in a public grave. His son, Henry Thomas Robinson (q.v.), with whom he spent his final years, was also a gifted wood carver and painter. The John George Joicey Museum, NEWCASTLE, has a large permanent display of Robinson Senior's work, including his famous Tam O' Shanter series of carvings, and his *Otter Hunt*, based on Landseer's famous painting, and the Shipley Art Gallery, GATESHEAD, has his Shakespeare Sideboard, exhibited at the Great Exhibition of 1862#, and several other pieces exhibited on this occasion. The Victoria and Albert Museum has a smaller version of his Shakespeare Sideboard.

ROBINSON, Henry Thomas (1872-1952)

Wood carver; landscape painter in oil and watercolour. He was born at NEWCASTLE, the son of Gerrard Robinson (q.v.), and served his apprenticeship as a carver under his father. On his father's death in 1891, he carried on in business at Pine Street, NEWCASTLE, where he is said to have specialised in "carving for hearses, coffins, and circus things". His business failed about 1900 and he went to work as a carver at the Co-operative Wholesale Society furniture works at PELAW, near GATESHEAD, remaining there until his retirement about 1938. Robinson retained a strong interest in painting and drawing throughout his career as a wood carver, exhibiting examples of his work in this field at the Bewick Club, NEWCASTLE, from an early age, and later showing at the Artists of the Northern Counties exhibitions at the city's Laing Art Gallery. He did little carving to his own design while employed at PELAW, but did occasionally exhibit works carved in his spare time, a notable example being the work for which he was awarded Second Prize in the Artisan's Section of the North East Coast Exhibition, Palace of Arts, 1929, losing First Prize to William Robinson (q.v.). He died at PELAW. Represented: John George Joicey Museum, Newcastle; Shipley A.G., Gateshead.

ROBINSON, John Ewbanks (c.1830- after 1860)

Engraver; landscape painter in watercolour; draughtsman. He was born at NEWCASTLE, and later served an apprenticeship as an engraver with Mark Lambert (q.v.), before following this profession in the town. He was an accomplished draughtsman and watercolourist from his youth, and while serving his apprenticeship gave lessons to his younger brother, Gerrard Robinson (q.v.). He is believed to have worked for Lambert for several years before following his profession independently, and his later work as an artist outside engraving is little known. He died on Tyneside.

Gerrard Robinson: Shakespeare Sideboard. Oak 108×84×38. *Tyne & Wear County Council Museums, Shipley Art Gallery.*

153

ROBINSON, William (1867-1945)

Wood carver; genre, portrait, and landscape painter in oil and watercolour. Robinson was born at GATESHEAD, and following study at Rutherford College, and the College of Physical Science, NEWCASTLE, took up employment as a wood carver with the woodcarving firm in the city owned by Ralph Hedley (q.v.). Here he was responsible for much of the ecclesiastical carving of the firm for some thirty-eight years, while maintaining a keen interest in painting and drawing genre and landscape subjects, possibly encouraged by his employer. The first work which he exhibited was, indeed, in the latter field, and he soon became a well known exhibitor at the Bewick Club, NEWCASTLE, and later the Rutherford College Art Club, and other art clubs on Tyneside. In 1907 he exhibited at the Northumberland Handicrafts Guild, NEWCASTLE, one of his earliest known wood carvings – a carved panel of floral design, and from this point forward he exhibited both wood carvings and paintings, showing his work at the Artists of the Northern Counties exhibitions at the Laing Art Gallery, NEWCASTLE, and the city's Benwell Art Club. His most outstanding exhibition success came in 1929, when his *The Bird's Nest* wood carving, exhibited in the Artisan's Section of the North East Coast Exhibition, Palace of Arts, was awarded First Prize, the Second Prize going to Henry Thomas Robinson (q.v.), son of Gerrard Robinson (q.v.). Robinson lived at NEWCASTLE for many years, but retired to GATESHEAD, where he died in 1945. The Shipley Art Gallery, GATESHEAD, has his *The Bird's Nest*, and his other exhibit at the North East Coast Exhibition: *Natural Foliage Panel*, as well as a collection of his paintings and drawings. Examples of his work for Hedley may be seen at St. Nicholas Cathedral, NEWCASTLE, the Parish Church of St. Chad, GATESHEAD, and Seaton Hirst Parish Church, SEATON DELAVAL.

ROBINSON, W. R. (fl. 1810-1875)

Portrait, genre and landscape painter in oil and watercolour; lithographer. This artist first practised at Richmond, Yorkshire, from which in 1831 he sent a number of landscape works to the Northern Academy, NEWCASTLE. He was still practising at Richmond in 1838, when he sent eight works to the first exhibition of the North of England Society for the Promotion of the Fine Arts, NEWCASTLE, but by 1844 he had moved to SUNDERLAND. In the middle 1840's he was practising at DURHAM, from which in 1846 he sent three genre works to Carlisle Athenaeum, but he appears to have spent his later life at SUNDERLAND. His *View of Durham Cathedral from Crossgate Peth*, 1844, was included in the "Historic Durham" exhibition at the DLI Museum & Art Centre, DURHAM, in 1980, together with examples of his work in lithography. Represented: British Museum; Sunderland A.G.

ROBSON, Edward (fl. late 18th, early 19th cent.)

Landscape painter in oil and watercolour; etcher. William Hylton Dyer Longstaffe (q.v.), in his *History and Antiquities of the Parish of Darlington*, published in 1854, says of Robson that he was an "amiable and accomplished botanist" who "was fond of landscape

painting in both oil and watercolours, and used to rise at four o'clock to gratify his taste, which was . . . much repressed at the time, as a useless acquisition to the business of life". In 1817, Robson "to delight his nephews", wrote a small volume: *Hartlepool and Seaton*, which contains small etchings of views associated with the towns. These etchings are believed to have been executed by Robson.

ROBSON, Featherstone (1880- d. before 1941)

Landscape painter in oil and watercolour; illustrator. He was born at HEXHAM, and was apprenticed in his youth to a saddler called English, at SOUTH SHIELDS, studying at the town's School of Art in his spare time. Here he made rapid progress as a student, and shortly after showing two of his watercolours of local views at the Artists of the Northern Counties exhibition at the Laing Art Gallery, NEWCASTLE, in 1905, he abandoned his trade as saddler, and moved to London to become a colour illustrator for several city printers. By 1918 he had settled at Barnet, Herts., and commenced exhibiting his work in London, showing one work at the Royal Academy, and two works at the Royal Institute of Oil Painters, before emigrating to Canada some time after 1923 to take up a post with a colour printer. His work in Canada became well known, and he spent the rest of his life there.

*ROBSON, George Fennel, P.O.W.S. (1788-1833)

Landscape painter in watercolour. Robson was born at DURHAM, the eldest son of a wine merchant, and began to show an interest in art at the age of four. At this early point in his life he began to make careful outlines of the wood engraved illustrations by Thomas Bewick (q.v.), in the *History of Quadrupeds*, later loitering in the company of visiting artists, and finally taking drawing lessons from a teacher named Harle. He quickly found that he could draw more ably than his master, however, and with five pounds in his pocket was allowed by his father to seek his fortune in London. Arriving in the capital at the age of about seventeen he quickly became friendly with several other rising young artists of the day, and in 1807 exhibited his first works at the Royal Academy: *High Force Cataract: a fall of the River Tees*; *View on Ettersgill Beck, Teesdale, Durham*, and *Distant View of Durham Cathedral from Shincliffe*. A year later he published *A View of Durham* which proved so successful that he was able to repay the borrowed five pounds, and embark on a prolonged visit to Scotland, where he fell in love with the wild and rugged scenery of the Highlands.

Scottish subjects thereafter predominated amongst Robson's exhibits, and it was probably the successful exhibition of the first of these at the Royal Academy early after his return from Scotland, which led to his election as a member of the Old Water Colour Society (later the Royal Society of Painters in Watercolours), in 1813. In the year after his election he published a volume of soft ground etchings depicting his Scottish tour, and from 1813 to 1820, he was a prolific exhibitor with his society, mainly showing scenes in the Grampian and Perthshire Highlands. In many of these scenes the cattle depicted were added by animal painter Robert

George Fennel Robson: Durham Cathedral from Prebends Bridge. Watercolour 19×30¼. *Bowes Museum.*

Hills, and the two artists worked together in many other instances, adding passages to each other's compositions, and exhibiting their work jointly. Seven years after becoming a member of the Old Water Colour Society, Robson was elected to its Presidency. He was then the youngest artist ever to hold this appointment, and had clearly established a reputation as one of Britain's leading watercolourists, though not by Ruskin's estimation in the "front rank". He exhibited almost exclusively with the Society until his death, showing a total of 651 works, many of which he "previewed" at his home, and frequently sold before sending them for exhibition. Robson visited many parts of Britain apart from the Highlands of Scotland for his subject matter, touring the Lake District and Ireland in 1827, various parts of England for his "Picturesque Views of English Cities", published in 1828, and in the year of his death, Jersey with Robert Hills. He was on his way to paint in his native Northumbria in 1833, when he took ill on a fishing smack, and though attended by a doctor at STOCKTON ON TEES, died at his home in London a few days later. He was buried at DURHAM, a subject second only to his beloved Highlands, in his affections as a painter, and of which he produced some of his most accomplished works.# Represented: British Museum; Victoria and Albert Museum; Blackburn A.G.; Bowes Museum, Barnard Castle; Cartwright Hall, Bradford; Laing A.G., Newcastle; City A.G., Manchester; National Gallery of Scotland; Newport A.G.; Portsmouth City Museum; Ulster Museum, Belfast; Warrington A.G.; Williamson A.G., Birkenhead.

ROBSON, Thomas (fl. 1808-1861)
Engraver; lithographer. Robson practised at SUNDERLAND from 1808-1861, initially as an engraver, later expanding his business to embrace letterpress and lithographic printing. In 1830 he wrote the text and engraved the plates for the *British Herald*, and the *History of Heralds*, but he later concentrated mainly on printing.

ROGERS, John George (1886-1967)
Amateur landscape and still-life painter in oil and watercolour. Born at BISHOP AUCKLAND, Rogers was for fifty-five years a painter and decorator at DARLINGTON, painting local landscapes, and occasional still-life works in his spare time. He is said to have received tuition in art privately before exhibiting his work, which he commenced in his early twenties by showing examples at the Darlington Society of Arts. In 1926 he began exhibiting his work at NEWCASTLE, showing his oil: *Still-life*, at the Artists of the Northern Counties exhibition at the city's Laing Art Gallery. He remained a regular exhibitor at NEWCASTLE, and DARLINGTON for much of his life, also showing examples of his work in other provincial towns and cities. He is said to have exhibited several works at the Royal Academy in his later life, and one of his oils: *Flower Piece*, was included in the "Contemporary Artists of Durham County" exhibition, staged at the Shipley Art Gallery, in 1951, in connection with the Festival of Britain. His work is represented in several overseas collections.

ROOKE, Caroline Mary (b. 1848)
Landscape painter in watercolour. This artist painted at EMBLETON, in the late 19th and early 20th centuries, and regularly exhibited her work in the latter period, at the Dudley Gallery, London, the Society of Women Artists, and at the Artists of the Northern Counties exhibitions at the Laing Art Gallery, NEWCASTLE.

ROSE, Jeannie Morrison (c. 1868- after 1928)
Landscape, portrait and genre painter in oil and watercolour. This artist practised at NEWCASTLE in the late 19th and early 20th centuries, and regularly exhibited her work from 1890, showing examples at the Royal Society of British Artists, the Royal Miniature Society, the Royal Society of Artists, Birmingham, the Glasgow Institute of Fine Arts, the Walker Art Gallery, Liverpool, and elsewhere in the provinces, including the Bewick Club, NEWCASTLE. After 1903, she exhibited

155

mainly at the last named venue, and at the Artists of the Northern Counties exhibitions at the Laing Art Gallery, NEWCASTLE, showing as her first exhibits in 1905: *The Smithy*, in oil, and *La Gagnante*, in watercolour. She remained a regular exhibitor at NEWCASTLE until 1928.

ROSE, Robert Traill, S.S.A. (1863-1942)
Landscape and figure painter in oil and watercolour; engraver; lithographer; illustrator. Rose was born at NEWCASTLE, but left his birthplace at an early age to study at Edinburgh School of Art. Following his artistic education he remained in Edinburgh for many years, later moving to Tweedsmuir, Peebleshire. He was a frequent exhibitor at the Royal Scottish Academy throughout his professional career, and also showed his work at the Royal Scottish Society of Painters in Water Colours, the Society of Graphic Arts, and at various London and provincial galleries. Influenced by William Morris and Walter Crane, Rose worked mainly as a book illustrator. Among his works were: *The Book of Job*; *Omar Khayyàm; Edinburgh Vignettes*, and *Childrens' Dante*. The National Gallery of Scotland has several of his drawings for illustrations, including work prepared in the form of pen drawings for *The Book of Job*, which was published in Edinburgh in a limited edition in 1902. He was a member of the Scottish Society of Artists. He died at Edinburgh.

ROSS, Christina Paterson, R.S.W. (1843-1906)
Landscape and genre painter in watercolour. She was born at BERWICK-UPON-TWEED, the daughter of Royal Scottish Academician, ROBERT THORBURN ROSS (1816-1876), during her father's short period as a professional artist in the town. After receiving tuition from her father, she also became a professional artist, practising mainly at Edinburgh, and exhibiting her work widely throughout Britain. She exhibited at the Royal Academy, the Royal Scottish Academy, the Royal Hibernian Academy, the Royal Institute of Painters in Water Colours, the Royal Scottish Society of Painters in Water Colours, and at several provincial exhibitions, including those held at NEWCASTLE, in the late 19th century. Among her exhibits at NEWCASTLE, were her watercolours: *Staithes, Yorkshire*; *The Young Fisherman*, and *Durham Cathedral*, shown at the city's Bewick Club, in 1884. She was elected a member of the Royal Scottish Society of Painters in Water Colours in 1900, and died at Edinburgh six years later. She was the sister of Joseph Thorburn Ross (q.v.).

ROSS, Joseph Thorburn, A.R.S.A. (1849-1903)
Landscape and portrait painter in oil and watercolour. He was born at BERWICK-UPON-TWEED, the son of Royal Scottish Academician, ROBERT THORBURN ROSS (1816-1876), during his father's short period as a professional artist in the town. After receiving tuition from his father, he also became a professional artist, and practised at Edinburgh until his death in 1903. He exhibited his work at the Royal Academy, the Royal Scottish Academy, the Royal Institute of Painters in Water Colours, and at several provincial exhibitions, including those held at NEWCASTLE about 1880, showing

both British and continental subjects. He was an associate of the Royal Scottish Academy. His sister, Christina Paterson Ross (q.v.), was also a talented artist. Represented: National Gallery of Scotland.

ROWE, Thomas William (c.1835- after 1878)
Sculptor; draughtsman. Rowe was born at SOUTH SHIELDS, and later practised as a sculptor in the town. While at SOUTH SHIELDS he commenced exhibiting his work at the Royal Academy, showing two portrait busts: *The Hon. Mrs. Geo. Denham*, and *Miss Wood*. His most notable exhibit, however, was his bust of Thomas Salmon, the first Clerk of SOUTH SHIELDS, which he showed at the Royal Academy in 1868, and subsequently presented to the Town Hall. After leaving SOUTH SHIELDS he practised in London, and continued to exhibit at the Royal Academy until 1878.

RUSHTON, Alfred Josiah, A.R.C.A. (b.1864)
Portrait, figure and landscape painter in oil; art teacher. Rushton was born at Worcester, and studied at Birmingham School of Art, and at the Royal College of Art before becoming a professional artist. Just after the turn of the century he was appointed Second Master of the Leeds School of Art, leaving this appointment in 1905 to become Principal of the School of Art at WEST HARTLEPOOL (now HARTLEPOOL) in succession to Edwin Ely Denyer (q.v.). He first began exhibiting his work publicly when he sent a genre work: *I do like my butter*, to the Suffolk Street Gallery, in 1875/6. In 1880 he sent his first of three works to the Royal Academy: *Fanny; a portrait*. He exhibited little in Northumbria while living at HARTLEPOOL, preferring to exhibit his work in London and Birmingham. He last exhibited at the Royal Academy in 1908, showing a work entitled: *In the Garden*. He retired from his post as Principal of the School of Art at HARTLEPOOL in 1930. He was an associate of the Royal College of Art. Represented: Gray A.G. & Museum, Hartlepool.

RUSHTON, George Robert, R.I., R.B.A. (1869-1947)
Landscape painter in oil and watercolour; muralist; stained glass designer. Rushton was born at Birmingham, and later studied art in his native town, and in London. About 1895 he moved to Tyneside, where he married the sister of Sydney Ash (q.v.). He later settled at NEWCASTLE, where he did stained glass designs, and mural work, and in 1897 sent his first work for exhibition to the Royal Academy: *The Widow*. In 1900 he received his Art Master's Teaching Certificate, later gaining a teaching post at Armstrong College (later King's College; now Newcastle University), under Richard George Hatton (q.v.), and remaining at the College until 1906. He later practised as a landscape painter, working mainly in watercolour, and painting extensively in Berkshire, East Anglia, Sussex, Northumbria, and on the continent. On leaving NEWCASTLE he first settled at Ipswich, in Suffolk, and from there commenced exhibiting his work widely, showing examples at the Royal Academy, the Royal Society of British Artists, the Royal Institute of Painters in Water Colours, and several London and provincial exhibitions, including among the latter, the Artists of the Northern Counties

exhibitions at the Laing Art Gallery, NEWCASTLE. He was a regular exhibitor at NEWCASTLE from the 1920's until his death at Ipswich in 1947. Rushton was elected a member of the Royal Institute of Painters in Water Colours in 1929, and a member of the Royal Society of British Artists in 1938. Represented: Laing A.G., Newcastle, and several provincial and overseas galleries.

RUTHERFORD, Charles (fl. late 19th, early 20th cent.)
Coastal and landscape painter in oil and watercolour. This artist practised at NORTH SHIELDS, and NEWCASTLE in the late 19th and early 20th centuries, and was a regular exhibitor at the Bewick Club, NEWCASTLE, and later the Artists of the Northern Counties exhibitions at the city's Laing Art Gallery. Most of his works were in oil, and featured views along the Northumbrian coastline, and occasional inland views. He had a gallery at The Side, NEWCASTLE, for many years, at which he occasionally allowed brother artists to stage exhibitions, as with the exhibition staged there by Harry James Sticks (q.v.), in 1895. Rutherford commonly signed his work with an interlocked "C" and "R".

RUTHERFORD, Isabella – see DOBSON, Mrs. Isabella.

RUTLEDGE (ROUTLEDGE), William (c.1865- after 1918)
Portrait, landscape and coastal painter in oil and watercolour. Born at SUNDERLAND, Rutledge practised as a professional artist in the town from his early twenties, and commenced exhibiting his work in 1881, by showing his *Girls Hoeing*, at the Arts Association, NEWCASTLE. He exhibited exclusively at NEWCASTLE for the next few years, showing work at the city's Bewick Club from

1884, but after moving to London by 1892, he began to exhibit his work at the Royal Institute of Oil Painters, and the Royal Society of British Artists, as well as in the provinces. In 1897 he sent his only work to the Royal Academy: *The wind and the waves*, some four or five years later returning to SUNDERLAND, where he practised until his death, and exhibited his work only at NEWCASTLE. Here he was an exhibitor at the Artists of the Northern Counties exhibitions at the city's Laing Art Gallery, from their inception in 1905, for thirteen years. Sunderland Art Gallery has his oils: *Walt Whitman*, and *Portrait of a Young Girl*; and watercolour: *Whitburn Foreshore*.

*RYOTT, James Russell (d.1851)
Animal, sporting, landscape and portrait painter in oil and watercolour. Ryott practised in NEWCASTLE during the first half of the 19th century, living and working for much of this period in the town's Northumberland Street. He was an acquaintance of Thomas Miles Richardson, Senior (q.v.), Henry Perlee Parker (q.v.), and John Wilson Carmichael (q.v.), and regularly exhibited his work alongside that of these three artists at exhibitions held at NEWCASTLE from the early 1820's. He first exhibited his work publicly when he showed horse portraits at the 1824 exhibition of the Northumberland Institution for the Promotion of the Fine Arts, NEWCASTLE. He again showed a horse portrait at the 1826 exhibition of the Institution, and went on from showing at the Institution to become a regular exhibitor at the Northern Academy, NEWCASTLE, from its foundation in 1828, and at the exhibitions of the various institutions for the promotion of the arts which flourished in the town subsequently. Most of these works were of animal or sporting subjects,# but he occasion-

James Russell Ryott: Otter Hunt with riders and figures, 1827. Oil 16½×21. *Woburn Abbey Antiques Centre.*

ally showed genre works, and landscapes. One of his best known works was a painting of Newcastle Races, depicting the Grand Stand filled to capacity during a close race. The Laing Art Gallery, NEWCASTLE, has two of his landscape works in oil: *The Keep, Newcastle upon Tyne*, and *Newgate, Newcastle upon Tyne*. He was the father of William Ryott (q.v.).

RYOTT, William (1817-1883)

Landscape painter in oil. The son of James Russell Ryott (q.v.), he was born at NEWCASTLE, and worked most of his life as a foreman painter with the London & North Eastern Railway Company, painting landscapes in his spare time. From 1866 he occasionally sent his work for exhibition at NEWCASTLE, two works shown at the exhibition of works by local painters, at the town's Central Exchange Art Gallery, in 1878, earning in the catalogue notes, the comment: ". . . both good specimens of his work indicating careful study, fidelity in colour, and much minuteness of detail . . .". He died at GATESHEAD, where for some time previously he had lived in the town's Hutt Street, and advertised himself as a professional artist. Three of his works were included posthumously in the "Gateshead Fine Art & Industrial Exhibition", 1883, and a similar number of his works were included in the inaugural exhibition of the Bewick Club, NEWCASTLE, in the following year; these latter comprised his oils: *Ashness Bridge, near Keswick*; *Near Bardon Mill*, and *On the Derwent*. Represented: Shipley A.G., Gateshead.

SCHMALZ, Herbert Gustave – see CARMICHAEL, Herbert.

SCOTT, John (1774-1827)

Engraver; draughtsman. Scott was born at NEWCASTLE, and served an apprenticeship as a tallow chandler, meanwhile amusing himself by drawing in pencil, and pen and ink. A local carver and gilder who had seen his drawings, encouraged him to try his hand at engraving, and when he was finished his apprenticeship he was engaged by Abraham Hunter (q.v.), to engrave profiles of the king, queen, and dauphin of France, for Angus' *History of the French Revolution*, published in 1796. Hunter refused to pay for this work, claiming that artists were never paid for their first piece, but confident of his abilities as an engraver, Scott went to London, and seeking out Robert Pollard (q.v.), was engaged by his fellow townsman for a year. His initial attempts to succeed as an engraver were not encouraging but from the turn of the century, and for the next twenty years, he was one of the most popular engravers of sporting works of his day, providing plates for the *Sportman's Cabinet*; Daniel's *Rural Rides*, and *A Series of Horses and Dogs*, among publications of this kind, and also engraving illustrations for Britton's *Cathedral of Antiquities*, and Westall's *Illustrations of the Book of Com-*

mon Prayer. He is best remembered, however, for his two large engravings, *Breaking Cover*, and *The Death of the Fox*, after Gilpin and Reinagle, for which he was presented with a gold medal by the Society of Arts, in 1811, and his many engraved illustrations of dogs, mainly in the *Sportsman's Cabinet*, which was first published in 1803, and reprinted in 1820. Scott suffered a paralytic stroke in 1821 and on the advice of his medical attendants returned to NEWCASTLE for a few months. On his return to London he was faced with financial ruin, but the president and members of the Royal Academy raised a subscription to enable him to resume work. In 1823 he published an engraved portrait of his mother, Mary Scott, but this appears to have been his last work of any significance before his death at Chelsea, London, in 1827. A portrait of Scott was painted by Jackson, and engraved by Fry.

*SCOTT, John (1802-1885)

Marine and landscape painter in oil. Scott was born at SOUTH SHIELDS, and spent his early years at sea before becoming a pupil of John Wilson Carmichael (q.v.). Like his master, Scott became predominantly a painter of marine subjects, but unlike Carmichael, remained all his life on Tyneside. Here he became a popular painter of ship studies, including among his subjects colliers, keel boats, tugs and wrecks, and occasionally tackling major public events involving shipping, like his *Opening of Tyne Dock*, 1859. One of his notable works in ship portraiture was his painting of Garibaldi's ship the *Commonwealth*, which work was sent to Italy as a present to the Italian patriot. His work in ship portraiture is, indeed, regarded as important; "an excellent and productive specialist in portraits of merchantmen off points of land as far apart as Dover and Cape Town", says C. H. Ward Jackson, in his *Ship Portrait Painters*, published by the National Maritime Museum, 1978, doubtlessly basing his view on scrutiny of the several fine works by Scott in the Museum's collection, and dated 1851-1870. Scott was also skilled in making models of ships, yachts and other vessels, and in 1851 won a medal at the Great Exhibition in London in a competition organised by the Duke of Northumberland. He exhibited sparingly, among his few exhibits being his view of *The Castle Fort from Shields Bar*, shown at the 1843 exhibition of the North of England Society for the Promotion of the Fine Arts, NEWCASTLE. However, Scott's marines achieve high prices when sold at auction, based on his competence as an artist alone. He painted until quite late in life, dying at the age of eighty-three years at the home of his daughter, at SOUTH SHIELDS, just as the great days of the sailing ship were drawing to a close. Represented: National Maritime Museum; Laing A.G., Newcastle; Shipley A.G., Gateshead; South Shields Museum & A.G.

SCOTT, Septimus Edwin (1879- after 1952)

Landscape, portrait and genre painter in oil and watercolour; poster designer; illustrator. Born at SUNDERLAND, Scott studied at the Royal College of Art before practising as a professional artist at his birthplace by 1900. In 1902 he moved to London, and practising there for the next thirty-seven years, exhibited his work at

John Scott: The Old England leaving the Tyne. Oil 26¼×35½. *Anderson & Garland.*

the Royal Academy, the Royal Society of British Artists, the Royal Institute of Painters in Water Colours, the Royal Institute of Oil Painters, and at various London and provincial galleries. About 1939 he moved to Brighton, Sussex, from which he continued to exhibit his work at the Royal Academy until 1952. He was elected an associate of the Royal Society of British Artists in 1919, a member of the Royal Institute of Oil Painters in 1920, and a member of the Royal Institute of Painters in Water Colours in 1927, resigning his membership of the last named body in 1932. It is believed that he died at Brighton.

*SCOTT, William Bell, H.R.S.A. (1811-1890)

Historical, landscape, portrait and figure painter in oil and watercolour; illustrator; engraver; etcher. The son of a famous Scottish engraver, and the younger brother of artist David Scott (1806-1849), he was born at Edinburgh, and received his early tuition in art in his father's studio, and at the Trustees' Academy in the city. In 1831 he spent some time in London, drawing the marbles in the British Museum, then returning to Edinburgh he once more worked for his father, and in 1833 commenced exhibiting his engravings at the Scottish Academy. In 1837, and by then having shown both engravings and works in oil at the Academy, he decided to seek his fortune as a painter in London. His first success came with his exhibition at the Suffolk Street Gallery in 1840, of his *The Jester*; *The Wild Huntsman*, and *King Alfred disguised as a Harper* . . . . A year later he sent his first work to the British Institution: *Bell ringers and Cavaliers celebrating the entrance of Charles II into London, on his Restoration*, and in 1842 he commenced exhibiting at the Royal Academy, showing his *Chaucer with his friend and patron, John of Gaunt* . . . . Shortly after exhibiting this work at the

Royal Academy, and in the same year showing his British Institution exhibit at the Scottish Academy, Scott entered a competition sponsored by the Government to encourage design in historical painting, and though he did not feature among its prize winners, his contribution was recognised to be of sufficient merit to lead to his appointment as director of the Government School of Design, NEWCASTLE.

Scott's tuition at NEWCASTLE, 1843-1863, was one of the major influences on the development of artistic talent in Northumbria in this period. Many young artists later to become well known both locally and nationally received tuition at his hands, Charles Napier Hemy (q.v.), Henry Hetherington Emmerson (q.v.), and George Blackie Sticks (q.v.), to name only three. Indeed, such was the attraction of the School to these young men that Thomas Miles Richardson, Senior (q.v.), was once provoked to complain that it was taking pupils who would normally have gone to him. Scott also produced some of his best work while in Northumbria: atmospheric seashore scenes painted at TYNEMOUTH while visiting Alice Boyd (q.v.), and her brother Spencer; bustling street scene drawings such as his *The Bigg Market*, in the Laing Art Gallery, Newcastle; several of his best known imaginative works, and most important of all, perhaps, his series of eight large canvases depicting scenes from Northumbrian history, for the inner hall of Wallington Hall, near CAMBO. These canvases were commissioned from him through the influence of Lady Pauline Trevelyan (q.v.), who had first become acquainted with his work through her reviews for the Scottish newspapers. Scott was offered the commission in March, 1856, and accepting it gladly he at once resolved the subject matter, and began making preliminary sketches of each scene. Every character depicted should be based on a real person, he

159

William Bell Scott: The Nineteenth Century: Iron and coal. Oil 74×74. *National Trust.*

decided, this leading to the portrayal of Lady Pauline as a terrified Briton watching the approach of the Danish galleys in one work, while in another he used the figure of his new friend and pupil, Alice Boyd, as Grace Darling. He was only paid £100 for each of these pictures, but his association with Lady Pauline, and her husband Sir Walter Calverley, furnished an introduction to his idol Ruskin, and gave added status to his image in the eyes of local men of influence, such as industrialist and art collector James Leathart, who began increasingly to look to Scott for advice on pictures for his Pre-Raphaelite collection.

In 1861 Gambart exhibited the eight completed Wallington canvases at the French Gallery in London,

but their reception was not entirely flattering to the artist and his patrons, and it was not until two years later that he was able to get a definite commission to paint canvases for the spandrels of the upper part of the inner hall, having already painted those of the lower part with portraits of famous Northumbrians. In 1863 an opportunity arose to resign his position at NEW-CASTLE, and move back to London with a small pension. Here he was at work on his eighteen canvases for the spandrels – each portraying a scene from the famous Border ballad of Chevy Chase – when Lady Pauline died in Switzerland, and though much distressed by the news he was able to complete them in time for them to be shown at the International Exhibition in Paris in

1867. They were finally erected in the following year, but Sir Walter's marriage meanwhile to Laura Capel Lofft (who was a stern critic of Scott's work), had alienated him from the home which he had helped to decorate so beautifully. Scott had continued to exhibit at the Royal Academy, the British Institution, and the Royal Scottish Academy throughout his stay at NEWCASTLE, and also contributed to several major exhibitions in the town, notably those staged in 1850 and 1852, jointly by the North of England Society for the Promotion of the Fine Arts, and the Government School of Design. After settling in London late in 1864, he remained an exhibitor at the Royal Academy until 1869, and the Royal Scottish Academy until 1870, thereafter exhibiting his work only at NEWCASTLE, where examples were shown at the Arts Association in 1878, and the Bewick Club in 1884.

Shortly after they had settled in the capital, Scott and his wife began to spend their summers at the castle home of his friend Alice Boyd, at Penkill, Ayrshire, while she spent her winters with them. This practice continued for some twenty years, whereafter Scott spent an increasing amount of time at the castle without his wife, much of this occupied writing his *Autobiographical Notes etc.* (published in 1892). He died at Penkill after a long illness, and was buried there. In addition to being a gifted painter, Scott was a talented poet, and, indeed, it was through his poetry that he first became acquainted with Pre-Raphaelite Dante Gabriel Rossetti, and subsequently began painting in the manner of the Brotherhood. He also wrote and illustrated many books, and in his later years frequently returned to engraving and etching. In 1887 he was elected an honorary member of the Royal Scottish Academy. Represented: British Museum; Victoria and Albert Museum; National Gallery of Scotland; Tate Gallery; Laing A.G., Newcastle; Literary and Philosophical Society, Newcastle; Penkill Castle, Girvan, Ayrshire; Wallington Hall, Cambo.

SELBY, Prideaux John, H.R.S.A., M.A. (1788-1867)

Amateur ornithological and botanical painter in oil and watercolour; illustrator; engraver. Selby was born at ALNWICK, and was educated at Durham Grammar School, and University College, Oxford. After spending some time at University he left without taking his degree, and took up residence at the family home at TWIZELL. He was attracted to the study of ornithology from an early age, and by the time that he was twelve or thirteen he had already composed copious notes on the commoner British Birds, illustrated with his own coloured drawings. In 1821 the first part of his nineteen-part *Illustrations of British Ornithology* appeared, at once establishing him as a highly gifted artist, and ornithologist. In 1827 he began to exhibit his bird studies, showing a work entitled *Dead Game*, at the Northumberland Institution for the Promotion of the Fine Arts, NEWCASTLE. He then became a regular exhibitor at the Scottish Academy (which had made him an honorary member in 1827), and the Northern Academy, NEWCASTLE. He continued to exhibit at Edinburgh and NEWCASTLE, for several years, mean-

while working on his *Illustrations of British Ornithology*, the whole of which was completed by 1834. Twenty-six of the some 228 plates for this work were contributed by his brother-in-law, and former pupil of Thomas Bewick (q.v.), ADMIRAL ROBERT MITFORD (1780-1870), the rest being drawn by Selby, for some time with Edward Lear as his assistant. He also engraved a considerable number of his drawings for this work, after experiencing difficulty in getting others to do this satisfactorily. The completed work was the first attempt to produce life-sized illustrations of British Birds, and simultaneously with its production he assisted Sir William Jardine in bringing out yet another book on birds: *Illustrations of Ornithology* (four volumes, 1825-1843).

Selby remained absorbed in ornithological study, writing and illustrating, for the rest of his life, adding to these interests following visits to Sutherlandshire, Scotland, those of fauna and flora, and in 1837 helping to found the *Magazine of Zoology, Botany and Geology*. He was elected a Fellow of the Royal Society of Edinburgh, of the Linnean, and other scientific societies, and in 1839 had the Master of Arts Degree conferred upon him by Durham University. In 1842 he published *British Forest Trees*, based on a broad experience gained in the plantations which he began at TWIZELL early in his life. In addition to his ornithological and other studies, his writing and illustrating, Selby took an active part in the social and political life of Northumberland, holding several offices within the County. He was an acquaintance of Thomas Bewick (q.v.), and as a member of what is today the Natural History Society of Northumbria, NEWCASTLE, was one of the several men responsible for the naming after the artist, of the Bewick's Swan. Another of his acquaintances was the famous American naturalist and ornithological illustrator, John James Audubon. Selby died at TWIZELL. A portrait study of him by Edward (Edmund) Hasting (q.v.), is reproduced earlier in this volume.

SETON,* Ernest Thompson (1860-1946)

Landscape and animal painter in oil and watercolour; wildlife illustrator. Born at SOUTH SHIELDS, Seton emigrated with his family to Canada in 1866, and later studied at several public schools in Toronto, Ontario, before attending Ontario College of Art. He subsequently studied art in London 1879-1881, and Paris 1891-1896. In London he attended the Royal Academy Schools, gaining entry by his submission of a drawing of Michelangelo's *Satyr*. In Paris he attended the studios of Gêrome; Bouguereau, and Ferrier. While studying in Paris he showed his first major painting in oil, at the Chicago World Fair, 1893. This work, entitled: *Awaited in vain*, portrayed a wolf pack in the act of devouring a dead man. On returning to North America, Seton became one of Canada's most distinguished artist-naturalists, publishing more then forty books about wild animals, and illustrating most of them himself. Among his major works were: *Birds of Manitoba*, 1891; *Life Histories of Northern Animals*, 1910, and *Woodland Tales*. His drawings are regarded as being notable not only for their accuracy, but for their strong decorative sense in the context of book design. He died at Seton Village, Santa Fé, New Mexico.

*Seton was baptized in SOUTH SHIELDS: Ernest Evan Thompson; he then changed his name to Ernest Seton Thompson to respect the wishes of his mother. Later, he changed his name to Ernest Thompson Seton.

SHAND, Christine R. (fl. late 19th, early 20th cent.)
Landscape, portrait and flower painter in oil and watercolour. This artist practised at NEWCASTLE in the late 19th and early 20th centuries, and first appears to have exhibited her work at the "Gateshead Fine Art & Industrial Exhibition", 1883, showing a charcoal drawing: *Landscape – Arran*. In the following year she commenced exhibiting her work at the Bewick Club, NEWCASTLE, showing two landscapes and two portraits, between that year (1884), and 1903, continuing to exhibit at the Club, and sending three works to the Royal Academy, three works to the Society of Women Artists' exhibitions, and various works to provincial exhibitions. She later exhibited her work exclusively at the Bewick Club, and from their inception in 1905, the Artists of the Northern Counties exhibitions at the Laing Art Gallery, NEWCASTLE. She was a regular exhibitor at the latter until 1909.

SHEARER, Jacob (fl. late 19th, early 20th cent.)
Landscape and coastal painter in oil and watercolour. Shearer is believed to have been born at SUNDERLAND, of a seafaring family, and practised as an artist in his native town in the late 19th and early 20th centuries. Sunderland Art Gallery has his oil: *Training Hulk on River Wear*, 1900.

SHEPHERD, Vincent (1750-1812)
Sculptor. Shepherd worked as architect to the Duke of Northumberland, at ALNWICK, and also executed a large amount of stone carving for his patron. In the choir of St. Michael's Church, ALNWICK, he executed some work in the latter line, which was described in the *Gentleman's Magazine*, 1812, page 601, as "a piece of Gothic trellis work, which for elegance of fancy and superiority of workmanship has seldom been equalled and perhaps never excelled". He died at ALNWICK.

SHERATON, Thomas (1751-1806)
Furniture and interior painter in watercolour; draughtsman; drawing master. Sheraton was born at STOCKTON ON TEES, and served an apprenticeship as a cabinet maker while teaching himself mathematics and drawing. He subsequently became a journeyman in his trade, remaining in the area of his birth until he was nearly forty. In 1789 or 1790, he decided to work in London, taking with him much of the manuscript of his first technical book: *The Cabinet Makers' and Upholsterers' Drawing Book*, and a large number of sketches and drawings which were eventually published as *Designs of Furniture*. This book was issued in 1790 as a collection of eighty-four folio plates made from Sheraton's drawings. This was followed by a month-by-month publication of the *Cabinet Makers' and Upholsterers' Drawing Book*, the series of which was completed in 1794. A second and enlarged edition of this part-work was

started before the completion of the first, and was followed by a third edition in 1802. The first two editions were almost identical in form, but as the section on *Drawing and Perspective* proved to be less popular than he had anticipated, he cut it down drastically in the third edition.

Sheraton's income from his book publishing brought him little money and he was obliged to support his family by giving drawing lessons. Not dismayed by this lack of reward from publishing, however, he was ready with his next work: *The Cabinet Dictionary*, within two years of the publication of the third edition of *The Cabinet Makers' and Upholsterers' Drawing Book*. It contained an explanation of terms used in the cabinet and upholstery trades, eighty-eight copper plate engravings, and a supplement on drawing and painting. In another two years he was ready with his *Cabinet Makers' and Upholsterers' and General Artists' Encyclopaedia*, intended for publication in 125 monthly parts. He died after only a few numbers had been issued. Sheraton's fame as a furniture designer is legendary. His skill as a draughtsman is not as well known. It enabled him to express his design vision much more accurately than most of his competitors. He had a thorough knowledge of linear perspective, and because he was able to draw his furniture designs in room interiors using pen and ink, and watercolour, his draughtsmanship went far beyond the requirements of a pure designer. Unfortunately none of his original drawings appear to have survived, our only knowledge of their capability being derived from a study of them in their engraved form.

*SHIELDS, Frederic James, A.R.W.S. (1833-1911)
Landscape, genre and religious painter in oil and watercolour; illustrator; muralist; stained glass designer. Born at HARTLEPOOL, Shields left the town with his family at the age of three, and settling with them in London, received his education at Clement Danes Charity School. His father later secured employment at Manchester, and joining him there at the age of fourteen Shields was apprenticed to a firm of lithographers, working for the first three years without pay. He later became a designer for Bradshaw and Blacklock's, Manchester (the Railway Guide printing firm), at 10/- per week, and from this point forward became increasingly involved in illustrative work, tackling as one of his earliest assignments *The Greyt Eggshibishun* (Manchester, 1851). On visiting the Manchester Art Treasures Exhibition in 1857, he fell under the spell of the Pre-Raphaelite works shown there, and began increasingly to work in the style of the Brotherhood, in his illustrative work, his watercolours, and later his murals and stained glass designs. The bulk of his illustrative work was executed 1860-70, and included Defoe's *History of the Plague of London*, 1862, and Bunyan's *Pilgrim's Progress*, 1864, as well as contributions to *Touches of Nature by Eminent Artists*, 1866; *Once a Week*, 1867, and *Punch*, 1867-70. In 1865 he was elected an associate of the Old Water Colour Society (later the Royal Society of Painters in Watercolours), and in addition to contributing to its exhibitions until 1893, showed work at various London and provincial galleries.

Shields did a considerable amount of mural work, notably for the Chapel of the Ascension, Bayswater, London. His mural for this Chapel was probably his greatest achievement as an artist, involving him in a visit in 1889 to Italy to "gather inspiration", and almost twenty years of work subsequently. He died at Merton, Surrey, within five months of its completion, claiming that he felt his occupation "was now gone". Tragically, the entire Chapel was destroyed by a German bomb, but his other mural work for the Duke of Westminster's Chapel at Eaton Hall, together with his stained glass windows, altar-piece, and mosaics, still survive, as do his superb windows for St. Ann's, Manchester. Shields' influence by the Pre-Raphaelite movement led him to seek out the friendship of Dante Gabriel Rossetti, and Ford Madox Brown. He spent much time in the company of these men, and present at the death of Rossetti, in 1882, "weeping hysterically", made a drawing of the artist on his death bed. His work attracted considerable interest in his lifetime, and was frequently the subject of articles in the art press. He also enjoyed a one-man exhibition at Manchester in 1907, which earned him many glowing tributes. In the year following his death two excellent books were published on Shields and his art, these being: *Life and Letters of Frederic James Shields*, by E. Mills, and *The Chapel of the Ascension*. The Gray Art Gallery & Museum, HARTLE-POOL, has a fine collection of his work. Represented: British Museum; Victoria and Albert Museum; Fitzwilliam Museum, Cambridge; Dudley A.G.; Gray A.G. & Museum, Hartlepool; Laing A.G., Newcastle; Manchester A.G.; Whitworth Gallery, Manchester University.

SHIELD, George (1804-1880)
Amateur etcher. Shield was born at TWEEDMOUTH, near BERWICK-UPON-TWEED, but worked most of his life as a master tailor at WOOLER, etching in his spare time a number of excellent studies of birds.

SHORTT, Mrs. Georgina Hastings (c.1872- after 1952)
Amateur miniature painter; religious painter in oil and watercolour; sculptor. The wife of the Rev. Joseph Rushton Shortt, she first exhibited her work while her husband was a classical lecturer at DURHAM, showing a landscape: *Durham*, at the Bewick Club, NEWCASTLE, in 1895. In 1898 her husband became Rector of SOUTH-WICK, near SUNDERLAND, and from here in 1908 she began exhibiting her work more widely, showing examples at the Royal Scottish Academy, the Royal Cambrian Academy, the London Salon, and at several provincial venues, including the Royal Society of Artists, Birmingham, the Walker Art Gallery, Liverpool, and the Artists of the Northern Counties exhibitions at the Laing Art Gallery, NEWCASTLE. She last exhibited her work outside Northumbria in 1924, but remained a regular exhibitor at NEWCASTLE until 1952, in which year she was living at EAST BOLDON, near SUNDERLAND – her home since her husband's death in 1919. Her daughter, MURIEL SHORTT, was also a talented amateur artist, and exhibited her work at NEWCASTLE.

SHOTTON, James (1824-1896)
Portrait, landscape and coastal painter in oil; copyist; art teacher. Shotton was born at NORTH SHIELDS, and after displaying a talent for drawing at an early age was entered by his parents as a student at the Royal Academy Schools. Here he became a close friend of Holman Hunt, and made excellent progress with his studies until the death of his father obliged him to return to NORTH SHIELDS. Back at NORTH SHIELDS he first found employment designing a Turkish Bath in the town for George Crawshaw. This is said to have been the first such bath in England, and was followed by another in NORTH SHIELDS, and a third in NEWCASTLE, all to Shotton's designs. While at NEWCASTLE, he resumed his studies in painting under Robinson Elliot (q.v.), later practising as a portrait painter, copyist and drawing master at NORTH SHIELDS. His earliest exhibits of note in the first capacity were the portraits of Mr. J. Hudson, and an unknown gentleman, which he exhibited at the exhibition at NEWCASTLE, in 1850, of the North of England Society for the Promotion of the Fine Arts, and the Government School of Design, and two other portraits which he showed at their joint exhibition in 1852. He later exhibited little in Northumbria, and

on only one occasion outside the area, this being when he showed a portrait of W. S. B. Woolhouse, the well known mathematician of NORTH SHIELDS, at the Royal Academy in 1863. Shotton enjoyed considerable success as a portrait painter, including the Italian patriot Garibaldi, and several local dignitaries among his sitters. He was also an able copyist, and was particularly fond of copying Turner, Raphael, Rubens, Veronese and Titian. His ability as a drawing master was also valued, securing him a position as first drawing master at the School of Art, NORTH SHIELDS. He died at NORTH SHIELDS. North Tyneside Public Libraries has a large collection of his work, including portraits, Northumbrian landscape and coastal views, and copies after Turner, etc. The Garibaldi Museum, Caprera, Sardinia, Italy, has his portrait of Garibaldi. Interestingly, the two men remained friendly for many years after it was painted, and corresponded regularly with each other.

SIMPSON, Frederick (d. 1909)

Landscape painter in watercolour; commercial designer. He was born at GATESHEAD, and at the age of fifteen joined the art staff of the printing company owned by Andrew Reid (q.v.), at NEWCASTLE, eventually rising to the position of departmental chief. While working for Reid he was responsible for designing many posters for railway and shipping companies. Several of his posters for the former portrayed scenes along the Tyne Valley, for which he painted the originals in watercolour at such places as OVINGHAM, BYWELL, etc. He died at GATESHEAD.

*SKELTON, Joseph Ratcliffe, R.W.A. (d. 1927)

Architectural, landscape and figure painter in oil and watercolour; illustrator. He was born at NEWCASTLE, the son of an engraver, and was practising as a professional artist in his native city by 1888. He subsequently practised at Hinckley, Leics., and Bristol, returning to

NEWCASTLE in the early 1890's, where he established a studio at Moseley Street. He had by then exhibited his work at the Royal Academy, in 1891 showing: *A Forgotten Author*, and had also shown works at various provincial exhibitions, including those of the Bewick Club, NEWCASTLE. He exhibited at the Bewick Club throughout his second stay at NEWCASTLE, later moving to Sundridge, near Sevenoaks, Kent, then to London. During his stay in NEWCASTLE he produced a number of views of the city and its buildings,# notable among which is the panoramic view taken from St. Mary's Place looking south, dated 1893 in the collection of the Laing Art Gallery, NEWCASTLE. He exhibited his work until 1927, showing one further work at the Royal Academy, six works at the Royal Institute of Oil Painters, one work at the Royal Society of Portrait Painters, one work at the Royal Institute of Painters in Water Colours, and various works at the Royal West of England Academy, and the Bristol Savage Club. Skelton produced illustrations for *The Graphic* from 1885-1912; *The Sketch*, 1897; *The Bystander*, 1904, and the *Illustrated London News*, 1907. He also illustrated at least one book: *Our Empire Story* (Jack, 1908). He was a member of the Royal West of England Academy, and a founder member of the Bristol Savage Club in 1904. He suffered considerable ill-health in his final years, and died in "straitened circumstances" in London, 1927. Represented: Victoria and Albert Museum; Laing A.G., Newcastle.

*SLATER, John Falconar (1857-1937)

Landscape, marine, coastal, portrait, animal, flower and street scene painter in oil and watercolour; etcher; lithographer. Born at NEWCASTLE, the son of a corn miller, Slater worked as a book-keeper in his father's mill, and spent some time running a store in the diamond fields of South Africa, before deciding in his

Joseph Ratcliffe Skelton: Corner of Pilgrim Street, and Blackett Street, Newcastle upon Tyne. Watercolour 24½×35. *Westgate Antiques.*

John Falconar Slater:
Harvesting on the coast.
Oil 36×60.
G. R. McArdle.

mid-twenties to become a professional artist. Back on Tyneside by then, and encouraged by his mother, he once more took up his boyhood practice of painting and drawing, and with little or no tuition was soon exhibiting his work. His first exhibit of note was shown at the "Gateshead Fine Art & Industrial Exhibition", in 1883, and consisted of an ambitious group portrait: *Members of the Dicky Bird Society*. In the following year he showed his first of dozens of works at the Bewick Club, NEWCASTLE, and in 1885, while practising at Ashton under Lyne, Lancashire, exhibited at the Walker Art Gallery, Liverpool, and at Manchester. Four years later he showed his first work at the Royal Academy: *The Boat Landing*, and from this point forward until his death, he was one of the most regular exhibitors of work of any Northumbrian artist of his period, showing examples at the Royal Academy until 1935, the Bewick Club until the early 1920's, and at the Artists of the Northern Counties exhibitions at the Laing Art Gallery, NEWCASTLE, from their inception in 1905, until the year of his death. For the first few years of his professional life he painted at the family home at FOREST HALL, near NEWCASTLE. Just before the close of the century, however, he established a studio in the city, painting there until 1910, when he spent some months at NORTH SHIELDS.

In 1912 Slater made his home at WHITLEY BAY, remaining here until 1925, and becoming one of the best known artists painting along the Northumbrian coastline, and a leading member and president of the North East Coast Art Club, whose headquarters were in the village. CULLERCOATS became his next and final home, and here he spent the remaining twelve years of his life, living at St. Oswin's Terrace, just off the harbour. In addition to exhibiting in London, Scotland, and the provinces, at annual and special exhibitions, Slater shared an exhibition at the Laing Art Gallery in 1934, with Francis Thomas Carter (q.v.), Thomas Bowman Garvie (q.v.), and George Edward Horton (q.v.). He also wrote considerably about art, contributing articles to the local press, and in 1914 publishing his *Odds and*

Ends from an Artist's Note Book, containing much interesting information about his attitudes and experiences as an artist. Slater was one of the most versatile and prolific artists Northumbria has ever produced, tackling virtually every type of subject, and working in a great variety of media. Much of his work was painted in oil, even when working under difficult seashore conditions, but he was equally accomplished as a watercolourist, and experimented with etching, and later lithography. His work was widely reproduced in newspapers and magazines of his day, and was the subject of several chromolithographic reproductions, notable amongst which was his panoramic painting of CULLERCOATS, 1905. He died at CULLERCOATS, and was buried at WHITLEY BAY. His sister, EDITH MAUD SLATER, was a talented amateur artist. Represented: National Maritime Museum; Laing A.G., Newcastle; Shipley A.G., Gateshead; South Shields Museum & A.G.; Sunderland A.G.

SMALE, Miss Phyllis M., S.W.A. (b.1897)

Landscape painter in oil; art teacher. She was born at DARLINGTON, and studied at the town's School of Art, and later at the Regent Street Polytechnic School of Art, London, before practising as a professional artist at her birthplace in her early twenties. She first exhibited her work in 1922, while at DARLINGTON, showing a number of landscape and other works at the Artists of the Northern Counties exhibition in that year, at the Laing Art Gallery, NEWCASTLE. About 1924 she moved to London to take up a position as teacher at the Regent Street Polytechnic School of Art, and in the following year commenced exhibiting her work in the capital, showing examples at the Royal Academy, the Royal Institute of Oil Painters, the New English Art Club and the Society of Women Artists, until 1940. She last exhibited her work at the "Contemporary Artists of Durham County" exhibition at the Shipley Art Gallery, GATESHEAD, staged in 1951, in connection with the Festival of Britain. She was then living at Esher, Surrey, and her exhibits were entitled: *The Fex Valley, Enga-*

dine; *Lakeside Corner, Buttermere*, and *A Cumberland September*. She was elected an associate of the Society of Women Artists, in 1940, and became a full member a few years later. Sunderland Art Gallery has her oil: *Wastwater*.

SMALL, Thomas Oswald (1814-1887)
Landscape, portrait and genre painter in oil and water-colour; illustrator. Small was born at NEWCASTLE, and worked as an architect in the city office of John Dobson (q.v.), before becoming a full-time professional artist. By the age of twenty he was already exhibiting at NEWCASTLE, alongside many distinguished local artists, at the Newcastle upon Tyne Institution for the General Promotion of the Fine Arts, showing a landscape, but he thereafter exhibited little, although practising quite successfully as an artist. Some of his later work included drawings for reproduction in local publications. He died at GATESHEAD.

SMART, Edmund Hodgson (1873-1942)
Portrait, genre and allegorical painter in oil and water-colour. Smart was born at ALNWICK, and studied at the Antwerp Academy, the Academie Julian, Paris, and at Bushey, Herts, at the School of Sir Hubert Von Herkomer, before practising as a professional artist. He first exhibited his work at the Bewick Club, NEWCASTLE, in 1884, while living temporarily at GATESHEAD, when his exhibits were: *An Old Cabinet Maker, Gateshead*, and *Portrait of Miss Florence A. Smart*. In the next few years, and giving his address as ALNWICK, he showed further works at the Club, later moving to London, where he quickly established himself as a successful portrait painter, and commenced exhibiting his work at the Royal Academy, the Royal Society of Portrait Painters, the London Salon, and at various provincial and overseas exhibitions, including the Paris Salon, and the Walker Art Gallery, Liverpool. His principal exhi-

bits included: *Portrait of the Lady in Black*, shown at the Royal Academy in 1906, and the Paris Salon in 1908; *My Mother*, exhibited at the Royal Academy in 1906, and the Paris Salon in 1909; *F. W. Ancott*, exhibited at the Paris Salon in 1910, and *Dr. Annie Besant*, exhibited at the Royal Academy in 1934. Smart practised in London, North America, Bermuda, and his native town, and painted portraits of some of the most famous military and political figures of his day. Much of his later life was spent in Bermuda, and at ALNWICK. Represented: National Gallery, Washington, U.S.A.; Cleveland Museum of Art, Ohio, U.S.A., and various North American collections.

*SMITH, James Burrell (1824-1897)
Landscape painter in watercolour; illustrator; drawing master. Smith was born at Middlesex City, the son of an Excise Officer from FRAMLINGTON, near MORPETH. His family moved back to Northumbria when Smith was still a boy and at an early age he was placed as a pupil under Thomas Miles Richardson, Senior (q.v.), at NEWCASTLE. At sixteen he was apprenticed to a painter and glazier named Bowman, at MORPETH, but served only two years of his apprenticeship before moving to ALNWICK to practise as a landscape painter. Here he remained some eleven years, marrying a girl from nearby ABBERWICK, and building up a considerable clientele for his watercolour work, which included a wide variety of Northumbrian and Lake District views. His patrons while at ALNWICK, included the Duke of Northumberland, for whom he prepared studies of Hulne Park, and William Davison, the local printer, who issued many engravings based on his work. He does not appear to have exhibited his work before 1850, in which year he sent three works to the Suffolk Street Gallery, and eight works to Carlisle Athenaeum. He was an exhibitor at NEWCASTLE, in 1850, and 1852, at the exhibitions staged jointly by the North of England

James Burrell Smith:
Durham Cathedral with
the Prebends Bridge.
Watercolour 24×36.
Private collection.

166

Society for the Promotion of the Fine Arts, and the Government School of Design, but from 1854 until 1881 he exhibited almost exclusively at the Suffolk Street Gallery, showing some fifty works. Most of these works featured Northumbrian, Lake District, Scottish and Welsh scenes, but included some continental views.

In 1854 Smith left ALNWICK, and entered the art establishment of Dickenson of New Bond Street, London, as an artist and teacher of drawing and painting. After leaving Dickenson's he devoted himself to water-colour painting, and is said to have secured an "extensive connection with the families of the nobility and gentry", whose children became his pupils. He also prepared illustrations for Dean Alfred and others for their contributions to periodicals. Smith spent the final years of his life in London, where he died at West Kensington. A daughter, SARAH BURRELL SMITH, was also a talented painter in watercolour, and exhibited in London. Smith's work is sometimes confused with that of John Brandon Smith, but unlike the latter he rarely painted in oil. Represented: Victoria and Albert Museum; Fitzwilliam Museum, Cambridge; National Museum of Wales; County Record Office of Gloucestershire; Laing A.G. Newcastle.

SMITH, John (James) (1841-1917)

Landscape, marine and coastal painter in oil and watercolour. Born at SUNDERLAND, Smith practised as an artist in his native town, and at nearby ROKER, until the turn of the century, following which he practised at both the latter and SOUTH SHIELDS. His first exhibits of note were his *Doe Park on the Balder*, and *Percy Beck, Lower Fall, Barnard Castle*, shown at the "Gateshead Fine Art & Industrial Exhibition", in 1883. In the following year he commenced exhibiting at the Bewick Club, NEWCASTLE, showing three Tees Valley landscapes and a flower piece. He later showed his work at the Artists of the Northern Counties exhibitions at the Laing Art Gallery, NEWCASTLE, where typical exhibits were his *Old Mill, Cleadon, South Shields* (1908); *On the Wear* (1910), and *Wreck on the Long Sands, South Shields* (1914). He was popularly known throughout his later life, as "John Smith of Roker". Sunderland Art Gallery has several of his oils and watercolours painted in the late 19th century.

SNOW, John Wray (1801-1854)

Animal and sporting painter in oil and watercolour; illustrator. Snow's place of birth is not known, but records show him to have been working in NEWCASTLE throughout the 1830's, following stays in London, and Yorkshire. Robert John Charleton (q.v.), in his *Newcastle Town*, 1885, recognises Snow as a Northumbrian artist, stating: "In Snow we had a painter of animals whose works, of great excellence, are to be seen in many houses in the neighbourhood". Certainly he had a studio in NEWCASTLE, and was a founder member of the Newcastle Society of Artists, showing large numbers of oils and watercolours at its annual exhibitions from its foundation in 1835. One of his contributions to the inaugural exhibition of the Society earned the comment in the *Newcastle Journal*, July 11th, 1835: ". . . we consider this artist's knowledge of the horse, particularly

when in full action, to be inferior to few animal painters of the day . . .". Another of his contributions to this exhibition was purchased by Sir Matthew White Ridley, of Blagdon Hall, near SEATON BURN, who became one of Snow's principal patrons in the area. He also showed work at the exhibitions of the North of England Society for the Promotion of the Fine Arts, NEWCASTLE. Much of Snow's work was reproduced in the form of engravings, amongst these his *Castle Howard Ox*, which was mezzotint engraved by J. Egan in 1833; *Harkaway, with Pedigree*, of which C. Hunt produced an aquatint in 1839; and perhaps his best known work: *The Meet at Blagdon*, painted in 1836, and mezzotint engraved by Thomas Lupton in 1840 with a dedication to Sir Matthew White Ridley. Some of his work was also reproduced in *Tattersalls British Race Horses*, 1838, and the *Illustrated London News*, in 1848. He exhibited infrequently outside NEWCASTLE, showing two examples of his work at the Suffolk Street Gallery in 1832, entitled: *Portrait of a Dog*, and *The Parting*. Represented: British Museum.

SNOWBALL, Joseph (1860-1946)

Portrait, landscape and marine painter in oil. He was born at SUNDERLAND, the son of one of the manufacturers of the well known "Sunderland Ware". His first employment was in his father's potteries, but finding the artistic requirements of his work there too limiting, he became a professional artist. By 1909 he had established a successful portrait studio in London, and was sending his work to the London Salon. In 1919 a portrait work shown at the Allied Artists' exhibition at the city's Grafton Gallery earned special comment from the *Hippodrome Magazine* (British Artists Series, November, 1919), and was accompanied by an article portraying the artist, and a landscape work featuring Durham Cathedral. The article described various of the works seen by its writer at Snowball's studio, several of which were marine works, including: *The Needles in a Storm*, and *The Wreck of the Arethusa*. Little more is known of this artist.

SOPWITH, Thomas, M.A. (1803-1879)

Topographical and architectural draughtsman; etcher. Born at NEWCASTLE, Sopwith was apprenticed as a joiner and cabinet maker in the town at the age of fourteen. He did not like the trade, however, and by studying in his spare time such subjects as architecture, cartography, etc., at the end of his apprenticeship obtained a position as a trainee land and mining surveyor at Alston, Cumberland. His employer found him so useful that he was taken into partnership, and over the next four years made plans of all the lead mines at Alston Moor belonging to the estate of Greenwich Hospital. He had taken a keen interest in drawing from his youth, and when he later returned to NEWCASTLE to set up in practice as a civil and mining engineer, he began to develop this interest further, and produced a number of pen and ink sketches of local buildings, several of which he exhibited at the Newcastle upon Tyne Institution for the General Promotion of the Fine Arts, in 1833, and later etched for Hodgson's *History of Northumberland*.

Sopwith remained at NEWCASTLE for some thirteen years, and during this period became acquainted through his profession with some of the most eminent railway and mining engineers of his day. He also wrote and published many learned treatises on subjects associated with his profession, one of the most successful of which was his *Treatise on Isometrical Drawing*, 1834, which went through several editions. About 1843 he was appointed agent of the W. B. Lead Mines of Northumberland and Durham, and thereafter lived mostly at ALLENHEADS. He later moved to London, resigning his position from the Lead Mines in 1871, and remaining in the capital until his death in 1879. Sopwith kept a journal from the age of eighteen, until within a fortnight of his death, "containing descriptions of places and people, and numerous and amusing pen and ink sketches, which would do credit to a professional artist". This journal ran to 168 large, and three small volumes, and was edited and published as *The Life and Diary of T. Sopwith*, in 1891, by his old friend B. W. Richardson. Sopwith was a member of several learned societies, and in 1857 received an honorary Master of Arts Degree from Durham University, for his writings on various subjects.

Millicent Sowerby: A Cottage Garden. Watercolour 11×6¾. *Christopher Wood Ltd.*

SOWERBY, John George (1850-1914)

Landscape and flower painter in oil and watercolour; illustrator; pressed glassware designer. He was born at GATESHEAD, the son of glassmaker and art patron John Sowerby, and succeeded to his father's position in the family business after several years' responsibility in the company for the development of new products. He was a keen amateur painter from his youth, and first exhibited his work locally when he sent five works to the first exhibition of the Arts Association, NEWCASTLE, in 1878 – an exhibition for which, together with W. De Brailsford, he produced a volume of notes. He also contributed illustrations to these notes, along with Joseph Crawhall, The Third (q.v.), Henry Hetherington Emmerson (q.v.), and Robert Jobling (q.v.). In 1879 he again showed work with the Arts Association, his exhibit: *Too Late*, provoking from Aaron Watson in his notes on exhibitors, the remark: "Of all the local artists who exhibit, Mr. John George Sowerby has made the most decided advance . . .". Also in this year Sowerby began to exhibit at the Royal Academy, showing a work entitled: *Twilight*. Altogether he showed some twenty works at the Academy, also exhibiting his work at the Royal Scottish Academy, the Royal Institute of Painters in Water Colours, and at various London and provincial galleries. He was also interested in book illustration, following his first venture in 1878 with a work jointly illustrated with Henry Hetherington Emmerson: *Afternoon Tea* (1880), and independently, *At Home* (1881); *At Home Again* (1888), and *Rooks and their neighbours* (1895). Sowerby moved from GATESHEAD to Benwell Towers, NEWCASTLE, following his father's death in 1879, but moved to the Tyne valley, near HEXHAM, when he retired from the family business due to ill-health about 1894. From Tyneside he moved to Essex, then to Surrey and Berkshire before finally settling at Ross-on-Wye, from which he sent his last work for exhibition shortly before his death in 1914. His daughter, Millicent Sowerby (q.v.), was a talented landscape painter in watercolour, and illustrator.

*SOWERBY, Millicent (1878- after 1927)

Landscape painter in watercolour; illustrator. The second eldest daughter of John George Sowerby (q.v.), she was born at GATESHEAD, and began to show a talent for painting and drawing at an early age. Encouraged by her father she began to paint landscapes in watercolour, many of which she exhibited at the Bruton Gallery, London, and the Royal Institute of Painters in Water Colours, in the years immediately following her family's move to the South of England at the turn of the century. Also in this period she began to collaborate with her elder sister Katherine Githa Sowerby (1877-1970), in the production of several childrens' books, Millicent providing the illustrations, Katherine Githa, the texts. These books included: *The Bumbletoes*, and *Childhood* (1907); *Little Plays for Little People* (1910); *Poems of Childhood* (1912), and *The Pretty Book* (1915). In 1908 she illustrated *A Child's Garden of Verses*, by Robert Louis Stevenson. Later publications for which she provided illustrations included: *The Glad Book* (1921), *The Darling Book* (1922), and *The Joyous Book* (1923) – all written by Natalie Joan, and a final

work: *Cinderella's Play-Book* (1927). Katherine Githa became famous overnight following the London production of her first play: "Rutherford & Son", in 1912.

*SPENCE, Charles James (1848-1905)

Landscape and coastal painter in watercolour; etcher. He was born at NORTH SHIELDS, the son of banker Robert Spence, and later became a partner in his father's firm. Much of his time was taken up, however, with public responsibilities associated with his birthplace, including the post of Borough Treasurer of TYNEMOUTH. Spence was keenly interested in antiquarian matters, and in addition to his public commitments served as one of the curators of the Society of Antiquaries, NEWCASTLE, and Honorary Treasurer of the town's Literary and Philosophical Society. He was also Chairman of the School of Art, Armstrong College (later King's College; now Newcastle University). Although in consequence of these various commitments he was able to spend only limited time on his hobby of watercolour painting and etching, Spence established a considerable reputation locally for his work. He was a regular exhibitor at the Arts Association, and later, the Bewick Club, NEWCASTLE, and contributed a series of etched illustrations to Dr. John Collingwood Bruce's *Handbook to the Roman Wall.* He died at Edinburgh. An exhibition of watercolours and etchings selected from his work was held at The Academy of Arts, NEWCASTLE, in the year following his death, and later at his birthplace. The Laing Art Gallery, NEWCASTLE, has a substantial collection of his watercolours, including several Northumbrian coastal and river views.# His sons Robert Spence (q.v.), and Philip Spence (q.v.), were also gifted artists.

SPENCE, Mary Emma (1857-1957)

Wood carver; decorative artist. She was born at NORTH SHIELDS, a member of the well known Spence family.* After her mother's death in 1885, she kept house for her father, and during his three years of office as Mayor of TYNEMOUTH acted as Mayoress. She continued to live on Tyneside for some years following his death, but spent much time receiving tuition in wood carving from Arthur W. Simpson of Kendal, Westmorland. She eventually moved to Hartsop, near Patterdale in Westmorland, where she pursued a variety of handicraft activities, including rug-making, embroidery and the decoration of hand painted china, until her death in a Kendal nursing home in 1957. Spence is best known for carving "Wooden Dolly" number four, in the series of wooden figures of that name which have long been associated with NORTH SHIELDS. This figure, unveiled in 1902, was initially the subject of some controversy because of its departure from the traditional "Dolly" design but soon became popular. It was replaced by "Dolly" number five some fifty-odd years later, this being carved by the well known firm of Robert Thompson of Kilburn, and placed in the town's Northumberland Square.

* See also: *Charles James Spence (q.v.), Robert Spence (q.v.), and Philip Spence (q.v.).*

SPENCE, Philip (1873- after 1940)

Landscape painter in watercolour. He was born at TYNEMOUTH, the son of Charles James Spence (q.v.), and younger brother of Robert Spence (q.v.). Details of his early artistic training are not available, but by 1902, and having joined his brother in London, he had commenced exhibiting at the Royal Academy, showing two continental landscapes: *Valley of the Domleschy, Switzerland,* and *The bed of the Nolla, Thusis.* He continued to exhibit at the Royal Academy for several years, eventually showing some seven works, but following his return to Tyneside about 1905, he exhibited mainly in the provinces. He exhibited at Liverpool, but

Thomas Ralph Spence: A Greek Festival. Oil 48×78. *Roy Miles Gallery.*

sent most of his works for exhibition to the Artists of the Northern Counties exhibitions at the Laing Art Gallery, NEWCASTLE, showing Northumbrian landscapes, frequently with buildings. He lived at GATESHEAD for most of his later life, and is believed to have died there some time after 1940. In 1939 he was responsible for the publication of a book on the Spence family, based on notes compiled by Robert Spence, and Mary Emma Spence (q.v.).

SPENCE, Robert, R.E. (1871-1964)

Landscape and subject painter in oil; etcher; illustrator. He was born at TYNEMOUTH, the son of Charles James Spence (q.v.) and elder brother of Philip Spence (q.v.), and first studied art at NEWCASTLE. He later studied at the Slade (1892-1895), and in Paris under Julian and Cormon, before becoming a professional artist in London about 1896, in which year he first began to exhibit his work in the capital and in the provinces, and obtained commissions to illustrate *The Quarto*. In 1897 he was elected an associate member of the Royal Society of Painter-Etchers and Engravers, and in 1902 became a full member. He commenced exhibiting at the Royal Academy in 1902, eventually showing some twenty-four works, but sent the bulk of his work to the exhibitions of the Royal Society of Painter-Etchers and Engravers. He is, indeed, best remembered for his work in etching, and has been described as an "important and original figure" in this field "because of his use of the etched plate for both illustrations and text in the book". His most notable achievement in etching is said to have been his illustrations for *George Fox and His Journal*. He also etched scenes from Wagner, and illustrated for several magazines. He continued to exhibit his work until 1940, in the early years of the

century sending several works to the Artists of the Northern Counties exhibitions at the Laing Art Gallery, NEWCASTLE. He died in London. Represented: North Tyneside Public Libraries.

*SPENCE, Thomas Ralph (1848-1918)

Subject and landscape painter in oil; architectural, decorative and stained glass designer; wood carver. Spence was born at Gilling, near Richmond, North Yorkshire, and practised as an architect before turning to easel painting, and a wide range of decorative arts. His father was a carpenter and joiner by trade, but also carved wood and stone as special assignments, and in spare moments painted in watercolour, and Spence may have received some instruction from his father in these activities before being placed as an architectural pupil, possibly at DURHAM. By the time that he had reached his early twenties he had worked for a number of architects, and had established himself as an architect in his own right at NEWCASTLE, following to the town Ralph Hedley (q.v.), who was also born at Gilling. Here he also began painting in earnest, sending his first work to the Royal Academy from NEWCASTLE in 1876: *A breezy morning*. He again exhibited at the Academy in 1878, and in the same year showed three works at the first exhibition of the Arts Association, NEWCASTLE. He continued to exhibit at the Association throughout its short life, and again exhibited at the Academy in 1883, meanwhile making the acquaintance of Dr. Charles Mitchell, father of Charles William Mitchell (q.v.), through whose influence he was appointed architect to the firm of Mitchell & Co., at WALKER and ELSWICK, near NEWCASTLE.

Spence's association with Mitchell lasted until the latter's death in 1895, and led to his commission to design St. George's Church, in the Jesmond area of NEWCASTLE. He also designed, and in some cases executed, the decoration for the church, the exceptions being the East and West Windows, which were designed by J. W. Brown (q.v.), the wood carving, which was executed by the firm of Ralph Hedley (q.v.), and the figures of the Apostles in the chancel in mosaic, which were designed by Charles William Mitchell. St. George's was to prove Spence's only major architectural work (he also handled work for Mitchell at his home Jesmond Towers), but it gave him a taste for architectural decoration which eventually led him to regard himself a "decorator", rather then an easel painter, even although he continued to exhibit his paintings throughout his life. He exhibited on several occasions at the Academy after the completion of the church in 1888, and also showed work at the Fine Art Society, London, and other establishments in the capital. He also exhibited widely in the provinces, including the Bewick Club, NEWCASTLE, and later the Artists of the Northern Counties exhibitions at the city's Laing Art Gallery. His diverse work in decoration included his contributions to St. George's; Mitchell's home, and a wide range of structural and applied detail for churches and private homes in many parts of Britain and abroad. His work in painting included a number of subjects, but he was especially fascinated by historical themes, in particular those from Homer's Odyssey. He painted in Italy, Greece and Spain, the Fine Art Society showing a special exhibition of his topographical sketches made in these countries, in 1910. His wife was also artistically gifted, and exhibited on at least one occasion.

SPENCE, William Geddes (1860-1946)

Coastal and landscape painter in watercolour. This artist was born on Tyneside, and painted mainly as a relaxation from his work in engineering and shipbuilding at SUNDERLAND, and NEWCASTLE. While living and working at SUNDERLAND he sent several works to the Bewick Club, NEWCASTLE, commencing in 1893 by showing: *Cullen Bay, Banffshire: Clear Afternoon*, and *Cullen Harbour, Banffshire: Cloudy Morning*. He later showed several Scottish and Northumbrian landscapes at the Club, but following his appointment to a senior management post in shipbuilding in 1897, he appears to have exhibited on only one occasion, this being at the Artists of the Northern Counties exhibition at the Laing Art Gallery, NEWCASTLE, in 1905. He retired in 1931, and moving to Barton-on-Sea, died there sixteen years later.

SPICER, Charles (1868-1934)

Landscape, sporting and genre artist in oil and watercolour. He was born at NEWCASTLE, the son of a master tailor, and after showing talent as an artist at an early age was placed as a pupil under Ralph Hedley (q.v.). His development from this point forward was so rapid that at the age of fifteen he had a picture: *A Winter's Afternoon*, accepted for the "Gateshead Fine Art & Industrial Exhibition", and at the age of seventeen showed a genre work: *The Unstopped Drain*, at the Royal Academy. He was a regular exhibitor at the Bewick Club, NEWCASTLE, from its inception, his occa-

sional sporting pictures earning him special praise, as with his exhibit in 1892, of which the local press commented: "It is called 'The Rogue', and describes an incident not infrequent at the start of a race, when one of the runners shows a little temper. There are few abler artists in this direction than Mr. Spicer; his horses are always accurately drawn, and full of movement; and the surroundings are always carefully studied and artistically depicted . . .". Despite this critical acclaim, however, Spicer later turned to journalism as a career, and while he continued to exhibit at the Bewick Club, and later showed work at other exhibitions at NEWCASTLE, he remained a journalist for the rest of his life, mainly working for newspapers based on Tyneside. He died at TYNEMOUTH in 1934, while still employed as a sub-editor for the *The Journal*, NEWCASTLE.

STANILAND, Dr. Bernard Gareth (1900-1968)

Amateur landscape, portrait, figure and abstract painter in oil and watercolour; sculptor; potter. Born at Canterbury, Kent, Staniland practised as a doctor at NEWCASTLE from his early manhood, and only became seriously interested in art after the Second World War. He had been a keen spare-time painter and sculptor for many years prior to the War, and exhibited his work on a number of occasions at the Artists of the Northern Counties exhibitions at the Laing Art Gallery, NEWCASTLE, almost from its outbreak, but in the late 1940's he enrolled in evening classes at King's College (now Newcastle University), and thereafter spent an increasing amount of time at his easel. He also became deeply involved in the activities of various local art societies, joining the Newcastle Society of Artists, the West End Art Club, and the Saville Art Group, and after founding the Federation of Northern Art Societies, serving as secretary, and later chairman. He showed his work at the Federation's exhibitions at the Laing Art Gallery throughout his life, and three examples of his work were included in the "Contemporary Artists of Durham County" exhibition, staged at the Shipley Art Gallery, GATESHEAD, in 1951, in connection with the Festival of Britain. Staniland became art critic for *The Journal*, NEWCASTLE, in 1960 and contributed articles to its pages until his death at his home in the West End of the city, in 1968. Newcastle Central Library has several volumes of his cuttings and catalogues relating to Northumbrian art exhibitions and art topics, 1950-1968.

*STANFIELD, Clarkson,‡ R.A., H.R.S.A. (1793-1867)

Marine, landscape and figure painter in oil and watercolour; scenic painter; illustrator; draughtsman. He was born at SUNDERLAND, the son of actor and author James Stanfield, who was at that time trading as a spirit merchant in the town. He showed a talent for drawing and painting from an early age, and in 1806 he was apprenticed to a local heraldic coach painter. Two years later, however, he left his master and went to sea on a Tyne collier, remaining with the ship until 1812, when he was pressed into the Navy to serve on H.M.S. *Namur*, the Sheerness guardship. While with the *Namur* he is said to have painted scenery for amateur theatricals, and after serving on the Indiaman *Warley* 1815-16, and visiting China, he obtained his first position as a professional in this field at the East London Theatre, Stepney (the "Royalty"). He later moved on to the Coburg (the "Old Vic"), then to Astley's Amphitheatre. Working for Astley's in Edinburgh in 1820-21, his father introduced him to his future professional colleague, friend, and eventual rival, David Roberts (1796-1864), and the two men worked together at the Coburg until 1822, before joining the Theatre Royal, Drury Lane. Here Stanfield soon established a reputation as "the most brilliant theatrical painter of his age", achieving particular fame for his great moving dioramas for Christmas pantomimes, several of which were based on sketches taken on his foreign tours, undertaken in the early 1820's. Meanwhile, and having already exhibited his work at the Royal Academy and the British Institution from 1820, and the Suffolk Street Gallery from 1824, he had been developing his skills as an easel artist, this development encouraged by his work in scenic painting, both in style and content.

Several of Stanfield's earliest successes as an easel artist were at the British Institution, with such titles as *Market Boat on the Scheldte* (1826), and *Wreckers off Fort Rouge, Calais in the Distance* (1828), for which latter he won the Institution's premium of £50. His first major success, however, came with his showing of a stormy seapiece at the Royal Academy in 1830, and entitled: *St. Michael's Mount, Cornwall*. This work attracted the attention of William IV, who commissioned him to paint *Portsmouth Harbour*, 1831, and *Opening of New London Bridge*, 1832. These works

paved the way to his election as an associate member of the Royal Academy in November 1832, and from this point forward his work as an easel artist, scenic painter and illustrator was in increasing demand. But the second of these activities became progressively more difficult to accommodate within his available time, and at Christmas 1834, after a row with the manager of the Drury Lane, he resigned from the Theatre, and with his respectability as an artist enhanced, he was elected a full member of the Royal Academy in the February of the following year. Based at London for the remainder of his life, Stanfield continued to make the occasional trips abroad which he had commenced earlier in his career (the Alps, 1824; Venice, 1830, and France, 1832), first travelling to Belgium in 1836; later touring Italy, 1838-9; Holland, 1843, and Southern France and Northern Spain, 1851. He also made several British tours, many of the sketches and watercolours which he produced on these, and his foreign tours, being worked up later into highly finished pieces for exhibition at the Royal Academy and the British Institution, or copied by engravers for use in books and periodicals, such as his *Coast Scenery*, 1836, and *Sketches on the Moselle, the Rhine and the Meuse*, 1838. Most of his work was shown at the Royal Academy, at which he exhibited every year except one (1839) between 1830, and his death.

Although not employed professionally in the Theatre after 1834, Stanfield continued to produce scenic work for friends, especially the actor Macready, and the

Clarkson Stanfield: Coast Scene: Castle of Ischia. Oil 56×91. *Tyne & Wear County Council Museums, Sunderland Art Gallery & Museum.*

author Charles Dickens. His undoubted love, however, was his work in oil and watercolour of dramatic coastal pieces, in which his superb abilities as a painter of the sea and ships, his skills as a topographical artist, and his flair for scenic painting, were combined in the production of some of the best work of its kind after Turner. Indeed, after Turner's death in 1851, Stanfield was recognised as the undisputed master of British marine painting, maintaining this status until his own death at Hampstead in 1867, at the age of seventy-three. In addition to enjoying the title of Royal Academician, Stanfield was from 1830 an honorary member of the Royal Scottish Academy (though all his exhibits at this Academy were sent there by collectors), and he was a founder member of the Society of British Artists in 1823, and president in 1829. He married twice, having by his second wife a son, GEORGE CLARKSON STANFIELD (1828-1878), who also practised as an artist. Stanfield's younger half-brother, WILLIAM JAMES STANFIELD (1804-1827), was also a scenic painter of some ability. A major exhibition of Stanfield's work entitled: "The Spectacular Career of Clarkson Stanfield," was presented at Sunderland Art Gallery in 1979, by Tyne & Wear Museums, accompanied by a superbly written and illustrated catalogue prepared by Pieter van der Merwe, of the National Maritime Museum. Represented: British Museum; Victoria and Albert Museum; National Maritime Museum; Aberdeen A.G.; Blackburn A.G.; Cartwright Hall, Bradford; Gloucester City A.G.; Haworth A.G.; Hove Library; Laing A.G., Newcastle; Leeds City A.G.; Manchester City A.G.; Newport A.G.; Portsmouth City Museum; Shipley A.G., Gateshead; Stalybridge A.G.; Sunderland A.G.; Ulster Museum, Belfast; and various overseas art galleries.

‡ *Stanfield's Christian names have long been given as "William Clarkson". The "William" is now known to be incorrect, and if he had another Christian name apart from "Clarkson" – given to him in honour of the famous Abolitionist – it is likely to have been "Frederick".*

STEAVENSON, Charles Herbert (c.1870- after 1930)
Amateur landscape painter in oil and watercolour; etcher; illustrator. Steavenson's place of birth is not known, but is thought to have been North Yorkshire, as it was from this area that he sent his first work for exhibition to the Dudley Gallery, London, in 1893. Also, he first worked at his profession as mining engineer in that area, before settling at GATESHEAD, where he founded a mining accessories business about 1905, and later managed several local collieries, in addition to serving on the local council. As soon as he settled at GATESHEAD he commenced exhibiting at the Artists of the Northern Counties exhibitions at the Laing Art Gallery, NEWCASTLE, showing a wide range of Scottish, North Yorkshire, Surrey, Lancashire, and Durham landscape paintings and etchings. In this period he also published a book of his illustrations: *Colliery Workmen Sketched at Work*, 1912. He was serving on the local council when he became a member of the committee of Shipley Art Gallery upon its opening in 1917, and in 1930 presented the Gallery with an example of his work: *Winter at Guisborough*, dated 1919. He died at GATESHEAD.

STEAVENSON, Mrs. Elizabeth Lucy Pease (née Robinson) (1882-1975)
Amateur landscape painter in watercolour. She was born at DARLINGTON, the daughter of well known local engineer and surveyor, Robert Robinson. In 1911 she married Dr. Charles Stanley Steavenson, and moved to MIDDLETON ST. GEORGE, near DARLINGTON, where her husband served on the County Council and as chairman of the Parish Council. A keen amateur artist and poet from her youth, she occasionally exhibited her work at DARLINGTON, and contributed verse to the *Darlington & Stockton Times* and the *Northern Echo*, both published in the town. Darlington Art Gallery has her *Coniston Lake, Afternoon*, 1929.

STEPHENSON, John Atlantic (1829-1913)
Landscape painter in oil and watercolour. Stephenson was born in mid-Atlantic, and later moved with his parents to Tyneside. He left the area for some twelve years to live in India, and shortly after his return went to work at the glass works at GATESHEAD of John Sowerby, father of John George Sowerby (q.v.). He later joined the firm of John Rogerson & Co., as a representative, painting in his spare time, and taking an active interest in the affairs of the Bewick Club, NEWCASTLE, from its foundation. Stephenson exhibited his work at the Arts Association, NEWCASTLE, from 1878, and showed one work: *Black Gate, Newcastle*, at the "Gateshead Fine Art & Industrial Exhibition", 1883; following the latter date he exhibited almost exclusively with the Bewick Club. Most of his life on Tyneside was spent at GATESHEAD, where he lived until 1908. Following this he lived at Manchester. Stephenson acquired a considerable reputation in his lifetime for his recitations in the local dialect, amongst the most popular of which was his composition: *Hawk's Men*. Several of his watercolours were exhibited at the Bewick Club in the year of his death. Represented: Laing A.G., Newcastle; Shipley A.G., Gateshead.

STEPHENSON, John Cecil (1889-1965)
Abstract, landscape and portrait painter in oil, tempera and watercolour; muralist; goldsmith and silversmith; art teacher. Stephenson was born at BISHOP AUCKLAND, and studied at Leeds School of Art, the Royal College of Art, and the Slade, before becoming a professional artist. At first he painted landscapes and portraits in a naturalistic style, but in 1932 he turned to abstract painting. He exhibited with the 7 & 5 Society in 1934, and with the London Group, the Lefevre Gallery and the Leicester Gallery, 1934-1959. He taught at the Northern Polytechnic 1922-1955. He was a talented goldsmith and silversmith. He died in London.

STEVENS, Albert George (fl. late 19th, early 20th cent.)
Landscape, coastal and genre painter in oil and watercolour. Born at BARNARD CASTLE, Stevens was educated locally before attending the Manchester School of Art, where he studied under Elias Mollineaux Bancroft, a member of the Royal Cambrian Academy. Bancroft was a regular summer visitor to Whitby, Yorkshire, and it was possibly through this teacher, and through fellow

pupil at the School, James William Booth, that Stevens was attracted to the town in 1903. Nearby Staithes was at that time a favourite haunt of artists, and it is perhaps significant that Stevens' work in oil is reminiscent of that executed by Charles Hodge Mackie, one of the older members of the Staithes Group, and an eager helper of younger artists in the development of their skills. Stevens spent the remainder of his working life using Whitby as a base, and exhibiting his work at the Royal Academy, the Royal Institute of Painters in Water Colours, and at various London and provincial galleries. He sent his first work to the Royal Academy from Whitby in 1903: *A cottage interior* – a work of which the *Newcastle Daily Chronicle*, 2nd May, 1903, remarked: "In a cottage interior, Mr. Albert G. Stevens shows an old woman in lilac hood, sitting on the longsettle under the window knitting. It is a nice little picture, natural and lifelike, in excellent tone and colour".

STEVENSON, Bernard Trevor Whitworth (b. 1899)
Landscape painter in oil and watercolour. He was born at Nottingham, but moved to NEWCASTLE in his infancy, on the appointment of his father, Arthur Charles Bernard Stevenson, as first curator of the city's Laing Art Gallery. After education at the Royal Grammar School, NEWCASTLE, he studied art at Armstrong College (later King's College; now Newcastle University),

George Blackie Sticks: Evening on the Loch. Oil 36×28. *Dean Gallery.*

under Richard George Hatton (q.v.). On completing his studies at the College, however, he decided on a career in librarianship, and worked successively at NEWCASTLE, Sheffield, and Southport. On his retirement as Borough Librarian at Southport, he returned to Northumbria, where he now lives at HALTWHISTLE. He first began exhibiting his work publicly at the Artists of the Northern Counties exhibitions at the Laing Art Gallery, NEWCASTLE, in 1919, and has since exhibited widely in Britain. He has also written art criticisms for newspapers and periodicals, and produced work as a potter. Represented: Laing A.G., Newcastle.

STEWART, Ian – see CLARK, John Stewart.

STEWART, William (1884-1965)
Landscape painter in watercolour. Stewart was born at BELLS CLOSE, near NEWCASTLE, and later studied at the city's Rutherford College, and at Armstrong College (later King's College; now Newcastle University). Although he studied architecture he did not follow the profession, and appears to have taken up another occupation, painting in his spare time. He was a member of the city's Benwell Art Club, and regularly showed his work at the Artists of the Northern Counties exhibitions at the Laing Art Gallery, NEWCASTLE. Most of his work consisted of watercolour studies of scenes in the Tyne, Derwent and Wear valleys, and along the Northumbrian coastline. A large selection of his work has recently been on show at various public libraries in NEWCASTLE. He died at LEMINGTON, near NEWCASTLE, where he had lived most of his life.

STICKS, Andrew James (b. 1855)
Stained glass designer; landscape painter in oil and watercolour. One of the five artist sons of James Sticks (q.v.), he was born at NEWCASTLE and was later apprenticed in the stained glass manufactory of William Wailes (q.v.), in the city, following his brothers William Sticks, Senior (q.v.), George Blackie Sticks (q.v.), and Henry Sticks (q.v.). He is believed to have remained with Wailes all his working life, although his name appears in local trade directories towards the end of the century as an artist, without reference to stained glass. He was a regular exhibitor at the Bewick Club, NEWCASTLE, from 1884, his first contributions being titled: *Borrowdale*; *Snowing*, and *Bamborough Castle*. While working for Wailes he was joined by his younger brother Richard D. Sticks (q.v.).

*STICKS, George Blackie (1843-1900)
Landscape painter in oil and watercolour. The most distinguished member of the Sticks' family of artists, he was born at NEWCASTLE, the son of James Sticks (q.v.), the stained glass designer and draughtsman. His early artistic training was as a designer in the stained glass manufactory of William Wailes (q.v.), at NEWCASTLE, which already employed his father, and his brother, William Sticks, Senior (q.v.). One of Wailes' requirements of his young designers was that they should excel in drawing. Sticks was placed under the tuition of William Bell Scott (q.v.), at the Government School of

Harry James Sticks:
Summer on the Wear.
Watercolour 14×20. *Dean
Gallery*.

Design at NEWCASTLE, where he is said to have "de-lighted in his studies . . . but cared little for stained glass work". He remained with Wailes until his inden-tures expired, but encouraged by his master he then embarked on a career as a full-time professional artist. Even before the expiry of his apprenticeship there had been a demand for his work, and within a short time of establishing a studio in the city he was able to claim a respectable living from his artistry.

Sticks' first painting to attract attention was his *Morning after a Storm*, shown at the "Exhibition of Paintings and other Works of Art", at the Town Hall, NEWCASTLE, in 1866. Such a picture, it was said, had not been exhibited for many a day. "Train and Swift were dead, and Sticks alone occupied the field." The painting was bought by Tyneside glassmaker John Sowerby – father of John George Sowerby (q.v.), who later became one of the major buyers of Sticks' work. Other commissions came in, and in order to satisfy his patrons he made extensive sketching tours in the Trossachs, Caithness, Skye, Arran, and the areas around Loch Lomond, Loch Katrine and Glen Tilt, in Scotland. The English Lake District also claimed his attention, but his principal subjects were taken from the wilder parts of Scotland. Heartened by the success of his early exhibiting efforts at NEWCASTLE, he sent work to the "Central Exchange News Room, Art Gallery & Polytechnic Exhibition" in the town in 1870, following this by showing regularly at the Arts Associ-ation exhibitions at NEWCASTLE, from their inception in 1878. In 1885, however, he became ambitious of wider acclaim and sent a work entitled: *Storm on the Whitley Coast, Northumberland*, to the Royal Academy, having already exhibited his work at the Royal Scottish Acad-emy from 1882. But he remained a regular exhibitor in his native city, sending works to the exhibitions of the Bewick Club until failing health caused him to virtually give up painting. According to family records, he died in 1900. Represented: Laing A.G., Newcastle; Shipley A.G., Gateshead.

STICKS, George Edward (1864-1904)
Landscape and genre painter in oil and watercolour. The eldest son of George Blackie Sticks (q.v.), and grandson of James Sticks (q.v.), he was born at NEW-CASTLE, and received his early tuition in art from his father. By the time that he had reached his teens he was sharing his father's studio in the city's Westgate Road, and accompanying him on his sketching and painting expeditions. In 1888 he sent a work in oil: *The little stranger*, to the Bewick Club exhibition, following this with several exhibits over the next few years, including his *Near Ryton*, and *On the Cumberland Fell*, contri-buted in 1891. He painted in much the same style as his father, however an early commentator on his work stated: ". . . his pictures are by no means vain imita-tions, and time alone will develop his talent". He remained a professional artist in NEWCASTLE for a number of years, dying in the city in 1904.

*STICKS, Harry (Henry) James (1867-1938)
Landscape painter in oil and watercolour. The son of Henry Sticks (q.v.), and nephew of George Blackie Sticks (q.v.), he was born at NEWCASTLE, and following some tuition from his father and uncle, practised as an artist in Northumbria throughout his life. He first began exhibiting his work publicly in his native NEWCASTLE, where he was a regular exhibitor at the Bewick Club from his early twenties. In 1894 he began to exhibit his work outside Northumbria, and a year later staged his first one-man show at the gallery in The Side, NEW-CASTLE, of artist friend Charles Rutherford (q.v.); of this show the *Newcastle Weekly Chronicle*, 30th Novem-ber, 1895, remarked: "All the works exhibited are direct studies from nature and are distinguished by poetic feeling, reverence for nature, and delicacy of manipulation . . . he has depicted with rare fidelity scenes at Blaydon, Winlaton, Wylam and thereabouts . . . Mr. Sticks has made great progress within the last few years . . .". Sticks remained a devoted recorder of Northumbrian scenery all his life, but also made annual

175

trips to the Lake District to paint. He made only one notable tour abroad, this being in 1897, when he visited Rotterdam, Gibralter, Genoa, Salonica, Turkey, Greece, Malta and Trinidad, working on a commission for a Tyneside shipping company. Sticks exhibited at the Royal Scottish Academy, the Royal Institute of Painters in Water Colours, and the Royal Society of Artists, Birmingham, until 1911, and from 1905 until his death, at the Artists of the Northern Counties exhibitions at the Laing Art Gallery, NEWCASTLE. He lived at GATESHEAD for most of his later life, while maintaining a studio at NEWCASTLE. He died at GATESHEAD. Represented: Laing A.G., Newcastle; Shipley A.G., Gateshead.

STICKS, Henry (1845-1878)

Stained glass designer; coastal and landscape painter in watercolour. One of the five artist sons of James Sticks (q.v.), and father of Harry (Henry) James Sticks (q.v.), he was born at NEWCASTLE, and was apprenticed to William Wailes (q.v.) in the Wailes' stained glass manufactory in the town, under his father. Like his brothers, and fellow apprentices, George Blackie Sticks (q.v.), and William Sticks, Senior (q.v.), he was sent by Wailes to study under William Bell Scott (q.v.) at the town's Government School of Design. He remained with Wailes all his working life, producing watercolour views of local scenery in his spare time. He exhibited these views infrequently, amongst his few known exhibits being the *Cullercoats Pier* which he sent to the "Exhibition of Paintings and other Works of Art", at

the Town Hall, NEWCASTLE, in 1866, and the "four brightly coloured sketches" which he exhibited at the Central Exchange Art Gallery exhibition of the work of local painters, at NEWCASTLE, in the year of his death.

STICKS, James (b.1813)

Stained glass designer; draughtsman. The father of William Sticks, Senior (q.v.), George Blackie Sticks (q.v.), Henry Sticks (q.v.), Andrew James Sticks (q.v.), and Richard D. Sticks (q.v.), he is believed to have been born at Edinburgh, and to have joined the stained glass manufactory of William Wailes (q.v.), at NEWCASTLE, some time before the birth of his first son William, in 1841. He eventually rose to become one of Wailes' top designers, joining fellow Scotsmen Francis Wilson Oliphant (q.v.), and John Thompson Campbell (q.v.), on visits to cathedrals and other buildings on the continent to study the best examples of stained glass, and later collaborating with the famous architect Pugin, in designing the stained glass windows for St. Mary's Cathedral, NEWCASTLE.

STICKS, Richard D. (b.1857)

Stained glass designer. One of the five artist sons of James Sticks (q.v.), he was born at NEWCASTLE, and was apprenticed to William Wailes (q.v.), in the Wailes' stained glass manufactory in the city, following his brothers William Sticks, Senior (q.v.), George Blackie Sticks (q.v.), Henry Sticks (q.v.), and Andrew James Sticks (q.v.). He is not known to have produced any artistic work outside of stained glass designs.

James Stokeld: Last Man Ashore. Oil 28×47. *Tyne & Wear County Council Museums, Sunderland Art Gallery & Museum.*

176

STICKS, William, Senior (b.1841)

Stained glass designer; draughtsman. One of the five artist sons of James Sticks (q.v.), he was born at NEWCASTLE, and was apprenticed to William Wailes (q.v.) in the Wailes' stained glass manufactory in the town. It is possible that, like his brother George Blackie Sticks (q.v.), he was sent by Wailes to study for a period under William Bell Scott (q.v.), at the town's Government School of Design. He appears to have remained with Wailes all his working life, without leaving any clearly identifiable examples of his artistry outside stained glass.

STICKS, William, Junior (1864-1937)

Stained glass designer; draughtsman; seascape and landscape painter in oil and watercolour. The son of William Sticks, Senior (q.v.), and grandson of James Sticks (q.v.), he was born at NEWCASTLE, and appears to have served an apprenticeship with William Wailes (q.v.) in the Wailes' stained glass manufactory in the town, before leaving to live in Edinburgh, just before the turn of the century. Here he worked for another well known stained glass company, Ballantyne & Son, retiring in 1934, some three years before his death. Sticks was a capable spare-time painter of seascapes and landscapes, one of which: *Entrance to Dunbar Harbour*, he sent to the Bewick Club, NEWCASTLE, in 1895, from Edinburgh. He died at Edinburgh.

*STOKELD, James (1827-1877)

Genre, landscape and marine painter in oil. He was born at SUNDERLAND, at the Queen's Head, Queen Street, where his father was landlord. His father later moved to SEAHAM to become landlord of the Ship Inn, and at fourteen Stokeld was apprenticed to a painter and glazier at SUNDERLAND. After seven years as an apprentice he went to London to study at Leigh's Academy, remaining there for five years, and supporting himself by painting and photographic work. Lack of commissions, however, eventually forced him to return to Northumbria, where he lived first at HARTLEPOOL, later at NEWCASTLE. At NEWCASTLE he was helped by former fellow apprentice William Crosby (q.v.), who invited Stokeld to return to SUNDERLAND to assist in the execution of commissions from the wife of Edward Backhouse (q.v.). He took a studio at Fowler Terrace, in the HENDON district of the town, and soon established a reputation for painting "fancy pictures".

In 1862 Stokeld sent his first work for public exhibition, to the Suffolk Street Gallery: *A Frosty Morning – Couldn't help it!* He followed this in 1863 by exhibiting at both the Suffolk Street Gallery, and the Royal Academy, his exhibit at the latter being entitled: *Whisperings of sweet nothings.* He remained an exhibitor at the Suffolk Street Gallery for the next two years, but did not again exhibit at the Academy. After 1865 he did not exhibit outside Northumbria, where amongst his few contributions to local exhibitions was the landscape which he sent to the "Central Exchange News Room, Art Gallery & Polytechnic Exhibition", NEWCASTLE, in 1870. His final years were spent in precarious financial circumstances at SUNDERLAND, where he died

John Storey: Tynemouth Priory. Watercolour 20×15. *Dean Gallery.*

in 1877, by drinking a bottle of carbolic acid following an argument with his wife. His sale of sketches in the week following his death realised £87. He regarded as his best work his large oil: *Last Man Ashore.#* This work was acquired by Tyne & Wear County Council Museums to add to Sunderland Art Gallery's substantial collection of the artist's work, in 1980. An excellent account of Stokeld's life and work may be found in William Brockie's *Sunderland Notables*, 1894. Represented: Sunderland A.G.

*STOREY, John (1828-1888)

Topographical and architectural painter in watercolour; lithographer; illustrator. Born at NEWCASTLE, the son of a schoolmaster, Storey received his education from his father, and after tuition from Thomas Miles Richardson, Senior (q.v.), practised as a professional artist at his birthplace until a few weeks short of his death. His work lay mainly in the field of topographical and architectural drawing, and was in considerable demand from local authorities and public undertakings in connection with their various development projects. Indeed, two of his most important works fell into the category of topographical studies; an imaginative piece: *Newcastle in the Reign of Elizabeth*, and an on the spot drawing: *Newcastle in the Reign of Victoria.* Apart from three works shown at the Suffolk Street Gallery 1849-51, he appears to have exhibited exclusively at NEWCASTLE, participating in several important exhibitions from 1850 until his death, including the exhibition of the North of England Society for the Promotion of the Fine Arts, and the Government School of Design, 1850; the "Gateshead Fine Art & Industrial Exhibition", 1883, and the Royal Jubilee Exhibition, 1887. Storey fell ill in the early part of 1888 and went to Harrogate, Yorkshire, to recuperate, but he died there only a few weeks later. His Elizabethan and Victorian views of NEWCASTLE, were both issued as large coloured lithographs, and are now popular collectors' pieces. The original watercolour for the former is in the Board Room of the Port of Tyne Authority's headquarters at NEWCASTLE, while that of the latter is in the meeting room of the city's Literary and Philosophical Society. Storey did several other lithographic works based on his drawings, and illustrated for the local newspapers and periodicals. Represented: Laing A.G., Newcastle; Shipley A.G., Gateshead; South Shields Museum & A.G.; Sunderland A.G.

STRAKER, Henry (Harry) (1860-1943)

Amateur landscape painter in oil and watercolour. He was born at Benwell Old House, NEWCASTLE, the son of wealthy parents, and subsequently followed the life of a gentleman, painting as a relaxation. In the early years of the century he maintained a studio in London, and exhibited his work at the Royal Academy on seven occasions. He also exhibited his work widely in the provinces while at London, but on returning to Tyneside in 1927, exhibited only at the Artists of the Northern Counties exhibitions at the Laing Art Gallery, NEWCASTLE. He died at RIDING MILL.

STROTHER-STEWART, Mrs. Ida Lillie (née Taylor) (c.1890- after 1954)

Amateur portrait, figure and landscape painter in oil and watercolour; illustrator. She was born at NEWCASTLE, the daughter of a city businessman, and was a talented artist from her childhood. She first began to exhibit her work while still unmarried, showing a theme taken from Omar Khayyam, and a portrait, at the Artists of the Northern Counties exhibition at the Laing Art Gallery, NEWCASTLE, in 1908. She continued to exhibit at NEWCASTLE for many years following her marriage to local solicitor Robert Strother-Stewart, in 1913, also contributing one work to the Royal Institute of Painters in Water Colours, and two works to the Society of Women Artists, 1919-25. Among her exhibits at NEWCASTLE were portraits of her husband and herself, and several other members of her family, illustrations of American Indian activities, and various British, continental, Middle Eastern and African landscapes and street scenes, painted while she was on holiday, or living with her husband abroad while he served in various judicial capacities. She was living at NEWCASTLE when her husband died in 1954.

STUBBS, J. Woodhouse (c.1865- c.1909)

Landscape, flower and still-life painter in oil and watercolour; art teacher. Stubbs practised as an artist at NEWCASTLE and SUNDERLAND in the late 19th and early twentieth centuries, and first exhibited his work when

he sent his *Warkworth* to the Arts Association exhibition at the former, in 1882. In 1884, he again exhibited at NEWCASTLE, showing two flower studies at the city's Bewick Club, following which he appears to have exhibited little until moving to SUNDERLAND, from which in 1893 he sent his first work to the Royal Academy: *Pansies*. In the following year he took a teaching post at the Government School of Art in the town, and from there sent a second work to the Academy, and began exhibiting at the Royal Society of Artists, Birmingham, and the Walker Art Gallery, Liverpool. He appears to have remained at the School until just before the turn of the century, when he returned to NEWCASTLE for a brief period, then moved to Norwich, Norfolk. He continued to exhibit his work at the Royal Academy, and in the provinces, while at Norwich, exhibiting for the last time in 1908. Sunderland Art Gallery has his watercolour: *Summer*, 1903.

SUMMERS, John (1896-1969)

Amateur landscape and street scene painter in watercolour; etcher. Summers was a keen spare-time painter and etcher while working in SUNDERLAND, in the first half of the present century. He mainly showed his work at the Artists of the Northern Counties exhibitions at the Laing Art Gallery, NEWCASTLE. His work in etching was particularly popular, and was reproduced in local publications, as well as being issued in limited editions by the artist. Represented: Sunderland A.G

SURTEES, John (1819-1915)

Landscape, portrait and figure painter in oil and watercolour. Born at EBCHESTER, Surtees' earliest ambition in art was to become an engraver. A career in engineering was offered to him, however, and accepting it he moved to NEWCASTLE, where he was apprenticed to R. Stephenson & Co. On settling in the town he enrolled in the evening classes of the Northumberland Institution for the Promotion of the Fine Arts. His work for Stephenson's involved him in superintending the making of a set of locomotives for America. He was rewarded on their arrival by a gift of two sovereigns, and with these bought his first box of colours, later taking them on a holiday to the Lake District along a route planned for himself and three artist companions, by Thomas Miles Richardson, Junior (q.v.). At the age of twenty-six he decided to become a full-time professional artist, and left Stephenson's to set up a studio in NEWCASTLE. In the following year (1846), he showed his first work in London: *A coastal scene with figures*, at the British Institution. By 1849, and now having moved to the capital, he had also exhibited at the Royal Academy, and the Suffolk Street Gallery. Over the next forty years Surtees exhibited regularly at the Royal Academy, and occasionally sent work to the British Institution, the Suffolk Street Gallery, and to the exhibitions of the Arts Association, NEWCASTLE, and the city's Bewick Club. He returned to NEWCASTLE in the early 1850's and appears to have spent most of his time subsequently working here, at CULLERCOATS, or in London, making extensive painting tours in between.

John Warkup Swift: Off
Flamborough. Oil 8½×15.
Darlington Art Gallery.

He became particularly fond in his later life of Welsh
scenery, painting it so successfully that two examples
were purchased by David Roberts, the Royal Academician, at a Royal Academy preview. He died at
Ashover, Derbyshire. His wife, ELIZABETH SUR-
TEES (née ROYAL), was also a talented artist, and
exhibited her work. Represented: Laing A.G., Newcastle; Shipley A.G., Gateshead; South Shields Museum & A.G.; Sunderland A.G., and various provincial
art galleries.

SWAINSTON, Laura G. (b.1861)

Genre, portrait and landscape painter in oil; etcher.
She was born at SUNDERLAND, the daughter of shipowner George Swainston, and appears to have become
a largely self-taught artist before practising in the town.
She first began to exhibit her work publicly when she
sent four oils: *The Divining Peel*; *Judith*; *The Touch of
Infinite Calm*, and *In the Cloisters*, to the Bewick Club,
NEWCASTLE, in 1886. In the following year she exhibited
her first work in London, at the Grosvenor Gallery,
and in 1890 sent the first of three works to the Royal
Academy: *A toiler of the fields*. She continued to exhibit
at the Royal Academy until 1894, also in this period
sending three works to the Royal Scottish Academy.
Nothing is known of her subsequent career.

*SWIFT, John Warkup (or Worcup) (1815-1869)

Marine and landscape painter in oil; scenic painter.
Swift was born at Hull, Yorkshire, and after some years
at sea took up painting scenery for an amateur dramatic
society. He later settled at NEWCASTLE, where he
practised as an artist until his death, achieving considerable local popularity. Six years before his death, the
Daily Chronicle, NEWCASTLE, said: "There are few more
meritorious artists in the North of England than Mr.
J. W. Swift, and few studies betray evidence of more
interest than his . . . Mr. Swift is pre-eminently a self
taught painter. Brought up at Hull amid ships and
sailors, the bias of his mind soon manifested itself, his
experience as a sailor became of immense advantage to

him in after life, for if his marine pieces are examined
they will be found to be not only admirable in the
artistic sense, but to possess the additional merit of
being technically correct . . .". Swift appears to have
exhibited his work only at NEWCASTLE, where among
his few known exhibits is an oil: *Crossing the Bar*, which
he showed at the "Exhibition of Paintings and other
Works of Art", at the Town Hall, in 1866. His work
has, however, been included in several exhibitions since
his death, both at Hull, and NEWCASTLE. Some of his
work was reproduced by means of chromolithography.
Among his chief works are: *The Channel Fleet running
into Sunderland*, and *Shields Harbour*. He died at
NEWCASTLE. Represented: Darlington A.G.; Ferens
A.G., Hull; Laing A.G., Newcastle; Shipley A.G.,
Gateshead.

*SWINBURNE, Edward (1765-1847)

Amateur landscape and figure painter in watercolour;
etcher. He was born at CAPHEATON, near CAMBO, the
younger brother of Sir John Swinburne, Bart., and
uncle of Algernon Swinburne, the poet. He was a keen
amateur painter from his youth, and travelled extensively throughout his life, sketching, making watercolour drawings, and visiting art collections. In the early
years of the 19th century he formed close friendships
with Thomas Miles Richardson, Senior (q.v.), and other
artists then practising at NEWCASTLE, and in 1822
became a founder member and president of the town's
Northumberland Institution for the Promotion of the
Fine Arts. He did not, it seems, show work at its first
exhibition in that year, but in the following year sent his
View of La Cervara, in the Appenines. He subsequently
exhibited at the Institution on several occasions, mainly
showing continental views, and remained its president
until it was succeeded by the Northern Academy. At
the first exhibition of the Academy, in 1828, and now
living with his brother at CAPHEATON, he showed two
continental views, but after again showing work at the
Academy in 1830, he appears to have lost interest in
exhibiting, and though still an active watercolourist

(Right) Edward Swinburne: Shag Rock, Torbay. Watercolour 10⅛×15⅛. *Victoria and Albert Museum. (Below)* Christopher Tate: Monument to the Rev. Robert Wasney. *St. Thomas's Church, Haymarket, Newcastle upon Tyne.* Marble.

seems to have become increasingly absorbed in etching. Several of his etchings were used in Surtees' *History of Durham*, and Hodgson's *History of Northumberland*. He spent his later years mainly in London, dying there in 1847, at the age of eighty-three. His niece, JULIA SWINBURNE (1796-1893), was also a talented amateur artist. Represented: British Museum; Victoria and Albert Museum; Laing A.G., Newcastle.

SYKES, Samuel (d. 1920)
Marine and landscape painter in oil and watercolour. This artist practised at NEWCASTLE in the late 19th and early 20th centuries, where he exhibited at the Bewick Club, and later at the Artists of the Northern Counties exhibitions at the city's Laing Art Gallery. The Shipley Art Gallery, GATESHEAD, has his oil: *The Tyne with High Level Bridge*, 1920. He may have been related to CHARLES XAVIER SYKES, another artist who practised at NEWCASTLE.

*TATE, Christopher (1812-1841)
Sculptor. Tate was born at NEWCASTLE, and served an apprenticeship under Richard George Davies (q.v.), before becoming assistant to sculptor David Dunbar, Senior, who was then working in the town. After a few years in Dunbar's studio he branched out on his own account, first turning to bust portraits, and exhibiting two of these at the Newcastle upon Tyne Institution for the General Promotion of the Fine Arts, in 1833. He continued to exhibit at NEWCASTLE throughout his short

career, mainly showing busts, but in 1836 exhibited his *Judgement of Paris*, and in 1838, his *Musidora*. He executed a number of monuments for local churches, one of the most impressive of these being one to the Rev. Robert Wasney (d. 1836), for the chancel of St. Thomas's Church, Haymarket, NEWCASTLE.# He was also responsible for carving the Royal Coat of Arms for

180

the pediment of the Theatre Royal, NEWCASTLE, designed by Benjamin Green (q.v.). He exhibited this work at the Newcastle Society of Artists exhibition in the town in 1836, together with several other pieces for the theatre, and one of his best known works: *Blind Willie*. Consumption eventually forced Tate to seek a warmer climate, and he went to Malta. Soon realising that his health was not improving there, however, he sailed home, and died shortly after his ship reached London. Just prior to his death he was working on a statue of the Duke of Northumberland, to be erected in front of the Master Mariners' Asylum at TYNEMOUTH, but this work had to be completed by his former master, Davies. Of his portrait busts, the *Gentleman's Magazine*, in its obituary of him wrote: "for execution, precision and arrangement" they could "scarcely be surpassed"; and of his *Judgement of Paris*, and *Musidora*: "they would have done credit to an artist of greater experience".

TATE, Dingwall Burn (fl. late 19th, early 20th cent.)

Landscape painter in oil and watercolour. This artist practised at SUNDERLAND, and mainly painted local scenes. Sunderland Art Gallery has several examples of his work, including his oil: *Dicky Chiltern's House, Bishopwearmouth*, and watercolours: *Roker Promenade*; *Hylton Ferry*, and *Strawberry Cottage*. He was an occasional exhibitor at the Bewick Club, NEWCASTLE.

TAYLERSON, John Edward (b.1854)

Sculptor; designer of medals. Taylerson was born at NORTON, near STOCKTON ON TEES, and studied at Faversham, Kensington and Westminster Schools of Art, before setting up as a sculptor in London. He later took a position as teacher of modelling and wood carving at Battersea Polytechnic and became a regular exhibitor at the Royal Academy, showing some thirty-seven works between 1884 and 1926. His first exhibit was: *Achilles defying Agamemnon*; his later exhibits included other classical subjects, portraits, and designs for medals. He also exhibited his work at Liverpool on a number of occasions. He died in London.

TAYLOR, Ida Lillie – see STROTHER-STEWART, Mrs. Ida Lillie.

TAYLOR, John (d. 1891)

Painter; draughtsman; wood engraver. Taylor practised as an artist and wood engraver on Tyneside for many years, dying at DUNSTON, near GATESHEAD, in 1891. Nothing more is known of him, or his work.

*TEASDALE, John (1848-1926)

Architectural and landscape painter in oil and watercolour; art teacher. Born at NEWCASTLE, the son of a shoemaker, Teasdale studied at the town's Government School of Design under William Bell Scott (q.v.), from an early age. He later won a scholarship to the South Kensington School of Art, following which he held teaching positions at Belfast, Sherborne and Doncaster. On leaving the teaching profession he returned to NEWCASTLE, where for a period of some twenty-three years he maintained the art collection of local solicitor

John Teasdale: St. Nicholas Cathedral, Newcastle upon Tyne. Oil 15×11. *Lyndhurst Antiques.*

J. A. D. Shipley, at Saltwell Park House, GATESHEAD. He also wrote for the *Newcastle Weekly Chronicle*, under the pen name "Briton", and occasionally exhibited his work, notably at the Bewick Club, NEWCASTLE. Much of his work was painted on a small scale, using body colour, and portrayed such city subjects as Plummer Tower; the Old Mill, Jesmond, and St. John's Church. Some of his line work was reproduced in local publications. Represented: John George Joicey Museum, Newcastle; Laing A.G., Newcastle; Shipley A.G., Gateshead; Sunderland A.G.

TEMPLE, William (c.1798- after 1844)

Wood engraver. Temple served an apprenticeship with Thomas Bewick (q.v.), at NEWCASTLE, 1812-1819, and in this period worked with fellow apprentices Robert Elliot Bewick (q.v.), and William Harvey (q.v.), engraving designs drawn on the wood by Bewick for his *Fables of Aesop*, 1818. He later gave up wood engraving and was for many years a linen draper at NEWCASTLE.

THOMPSON, Frank (c.1852-1926)

Landscape and genre painter in watercolour; art teacher. Thompson began his career as a professional artist in London, where in 1875/6 he showed his *Old Mill near Darlington*, at the Suffolk Street Gallery. About two years later he moved to DURHAM to take up a teaching appointment at the School of Art there, and for the next ten years exhibited only in Northumbria, showing as his first exhibits *Barnard Castle on the Tees*; *A Westmorland Cottage*, and *Nothing Like Leather*, at the Arts Association, NEWCASTLE. In 1890 he began to exhibit his work more widely, showing examples at the Royal Academy, the Royal Society of British Artists, the Glasgow Institute of Fine Arts, and at various provincial exhibitions, including those of the Bewick Club, NEWCASTLE. From 1905 until his death, however, he exhibited almost exclusively at the Artists of the Northern Counties exhibitions at the Laing Art Gallery, NEWCASTLE, showing as his last works in 1925: *Camber Castle*; *Rye*, and *Piercebridge*. He died at DURHAM. Thompson taught many young artists his skills while teaching art at DURHAM, one of his pupils being Cecil Ross Wheatley (q.v.). Represented: Darlington A.G.; Bowes Museum, Barnard Castle; Sunderland A.G.

THOMPSON, Isa – see JOBLING, Mrs. Isa.

*THOMPSON, Mark (1812-1875)
Landscape, genre and coastal painter in oil. Born on Wearside, Thompson worked as a general agent before becoming a professional artist in his late forties. While working in the former capacity at SUNDERLAND, however, he was a keen amateur painter and is believed to have taken instruction from several artists then practising in the town. After becoming a professional artist he continued to live at SUNDERLAND for some years, and in 1865 and 1866, sent work for exhibition at the British Institution, in the first year showing his *The Tees, above Middleton*, and in the second, his *Sheep Walk, Cronkley Craggs, Teesdale*. In his later years he practised at BISHOPWEARMOUTH, near SUNDERLAND, dying there in 1875. Although best known as an accomplished painter of landscapes, frequently featuring country houses, Thompson first made his name as a painter of local harbour and dock scenes, outstanding amongst which is his *The Opening of Sunderland South Docks, 1850*.# Represented: South Shields Museum & A.G.; Sunderland A.G.

THOMPSON, Stanley (b. 1876)
Landscape, genre and figure painter in oil and watercolour. Thompson was born at SUNDERLAND, and studied at the town's School of Art, and later the Royal College of Art, under Walter Crane, before practising as a professional artist. While still living in London he began exhibiting at the Royal Academy, in 1899 showing: *A Grey Day on the Wear*, and in 1900: *November . . . .* He continued to exhibit at the Academy following his move to MIDDLETON IN TEESDALE, near DARLINGTON, just after the turn of the century, and was an occasional exhibitor at the Artists of the Northern Counties exhibitions at the Laing Art Gallery,

Mark Thompson: Opening of Sunderland South Docks, 1850. Oil 48×72. *Tyne & Wear County Council Museums, Sunderland Art Gallery & Museum.*

NEWCASTLE, from their inception in 1905, until his death some time after 1929.

THOMSON, James (1789-1850)

Engraver. Born at MITFORD, near MORPETH, the son of a clergyman, Thomson showed an aptitude for drawing from an early age and his father allowed him to become apprenticed to an engraver called Mackenzie, in London. He embarked for the capital on a collier at NORTH SHIELDS, and when his ship was not heard of for nine weeks was presumed dead. On arriving safely in London he soon discovered that he disliked his master, and the style of his art, and after working closely with him for the last two years of his apprenticeship, he set up on his own. His work was almost exclusively portraiture, in which he employed the stipple technique of engraving. His best known works are: *The Three Nieces of the Duke of Wellington*, after Sir Thomas Lawrence, R.A.; an equestrian portrait of Queen Victoria, attended by Lord Melbourne, after Sir Francis Grant; *Prince Albert*, after Sir William Ross, and *The Bishop of London*, after George Richmond. He also engraved many plates for Lodge's *Portraits of Illustrious Personages*, *The Townley Marbles*, and other works. He died in London.

THORPE, Thomas (c.1812- after 1855)

Landscape painter in oil and watercolour; lithographer. Thorpe was born on Tyneside and studied painting and drawing under John Wilson Carmichael (q.v.), before becoming a professional artist at NEWCASTLE in his early twenties. He first exhibited his work by sending three landscapes to the Carlisle Academy in 1833. In the following year he commenced exhibiting at NEWCASTLE, showing several works at the Newcastle upon Tyne Institution for the General Promotion of the Fine Arts.

He remained a regular exhibitor in the town for the next twenty years, also showing work at Carlisle Athenaeum in 1850. Thorpe practised at NEWCASTLE until the late 1840's, then about 1849 moved to DARLINGTON, where he remained some four years, and became quite well known for his work. While at DARLINGTON he made several visits to Northumbrian coastal towns to take views, and later lithographed these for Jordison of MIDDLESBOROUGH, among several printers in the area. Some of his views were of HARTLEPOOL and nearby SEATON CAREW, and it was at the latter that he was last recorded working as an artist in 1855. Thorpe was one of Carmichael's most gifted pupils, the draughtsmanship evident in his series of lithographs of coastal towns being the equal of much that was produced by his master.

TODD, Herbert William (1889-1974)

Amateur landscape painter in watercolour. Todd was in business for many years at DARLINGTON as a clothier and draper, but was a keen spare-time painter in watercolour. He was a founder member of the Darlington Society of Arts, and in addition to showing work at its exhibitions, regularly exhibited at the Artists of the Northern Counties exhibitions at the Laing Art Gallery, NEWCASTLE, and was an occasional exhibitor at the Royal Institute of Painters in Water Colours. A one-man show of his work was held at Darlington Art Gallery in 1968. This Gallery has his *River Tees near Blackwell*, and *The Joiner's Shop, Lartington*. He died at DARLINGTON after living for many years at the Blackwell Hall Hotel.

*TRAIN, Edward (1801-1866)

Landscape, portrait and figure painter in oil; engraver.

Train was born at GATESHEAD, and left Tyneside at an early age to take up an apprenticeship under London engraver Edward Scriven (1775-1841), a specialist in the stipple technique. On completing his apprenticeship he returned to NEWCASTLE, where he quickly formed friendships with several of its leading gentry, including George Clayton Atkinson (q.v.), and his two brothers, whom he accompanied on their expedition to the Hebrides and St. Kilda in 1831. This expedition, perhaps, gave Train his taste for Highland scenery, for from this date forward it became his main preoccupation as a painter. By the early 1830's he was exhibiting his Highland scenes at NEWCASTLE, giving both NEWCASTLE and Edinburgh as his address, and had obviously established a market for his work in the Scottish capital. In 1841, however, and again exhibiting at NEWCASTLE he listed the town alone as his address. Train exhibited sparingly outside NEWCASTLE throughout his life, showing one work at Carlisle Athenaeum in 1850, and a few works in Edinburgh. The bulk of his work lay in the field of Scottish landscape, which he occasionally combined with theatrical or historical matter, as with his *Macbeth and the three Weird Sisters*. He was also an able portrait painter, however, including several well known Northumbrians among his sitters, and drawing a portrait of Thomas Bewick (q.v.), from Bailey's bust, for reproduction as an engraving in the *Sketch of the Life and Work of the late Thomas Bewick*, published by George Clayton Atkinson, in 1831. He died at his home at NEWCASTLE. Represented: Darlington A.G.; Hancock Museum, Newcastle; Laing A.G., Newcastle; Shipley A.G., Gateshead.

TREVELYAN, Lady Pauline (née Jermyn) (1816-1866)
Amateur flower and insect painter in oil, tempera and watercolour. The eldest daughter of a Suffolk Parson, she became in 1835 the first wife of Sir Walter Calverley Trevelyan, of Wallington Hall, near CAMBO. After settling at Wallington she began to contribute reviews of books and exhibitions to the *Edinburgh Review*, and the *Scotsman*, also continuing her girlhood practice of sketching and painting. Through her reviews she made the acquaintance of John Ruskin, and later William Bell Scott (q.v.), subsequently securing for the latter the commission to decorate the central hall at Wallington, and introducing him to the great art critic. Scott's commission mainly involved the production of large canvases to fill spaces in some of the arches of the new hall, and wishing to make every character depicted in them based on real persons, he included Pauline as a terrified Briton watching the approach of the Danish galleys. The pilasters between the arches also required decoration, and Pauline, together with LAURA CAPEL LOFFT (who later became the second Lady Trevelyan), Mrs. Mark Pattison, later Lady Dilke, and even Ruskin, painted various flowers on them in tempera. She later went on a tour of the continent with her husband and Ruskin, dying at Neuchâtel, Switzerland, in 1866. Scott's portrait of her hangs in Lady Trevelyan's Parlour at the Hall, which is open to the public courtesy of the National Trust. Several other members of the Trevelyan family were artistically gifted, including SIR JOHN TREVELYAN (1734-1828), two of whose watercolours hang at the Hall, Lady Pauline's husband SIR WALTER CALVERLEY TREVELYAN (1797-1879), who contributed illustrations to Hodgson's *History of Northumberland*, and EMMA TREVELYAN (d.1857), several of whose sketches of Wallington appear in Hodgson's work. Represented: British Museum.

TROUGHTON, Mrs. Emily Wade (née Patterson) (c.1874-1924)
Amateur marine, coastal and figure painter in oil. She was born on Tyneside, and first began painting seriously after settling at WHITLEY BAY, following her marriage to a local postman. Here she became a familiar sight around the village (then named WHITLEY), often painting local views while carriages passed her on each side. She later moved to EAST BOLDON, near SUNDERLAND, where she continued to paint until arthritis in her hands made this no longer possible. She died at SOUTH SHIELDS. An example of her work is in the Fishermen's Watch House, at CULLERCOATS, showing figures gathered at a cliff face in a storm. Represented: North Tyneside Public Libraries.

*TUCKER, James Walker, A.R.C.A., A.R.W.A. (1898-1972)
Landscape and subject painter in oil, tempera and watercolour. Tucker was born at WALLSEND, near NEWCASTLE, and received his early training in art at Armstrong College (later King's College; now Newcastle University) under Richard George Hatton (q.v.), gaining two silver medals, and a scholarship to travel France in 1922. Later in that year he entered the Royal College of Art to study under Sir William Rothenstein, and in 1927 was awarded a travelling scholarship to Italy. In 1926 Tucker acted as studio assistant to Sir William while he was working on his mural for St. Stephen's Hall, Westminster, this experience being later put to use when, on returning from Italy, the young artist was commissioned by Newcastle Corporation to paint one of the several lunettes for the Laing Art Gallery, NEWCASTLE, first shown in 1931. Tucker's subject was: *The entry of Charles I into Newcastle upon Tyne*. In 1927 he sent his first work to the Royal Academy, and in 1931 was appointed Head of Gloucester College of Art, a post which he held until his retirement in 1963. Tucker exhibited at the Royal Academy for many years, his exhibit in 1941: *The Champion*, being acclaimed picture of the year. This work sold for £200 at the private view, and was subsequently reproduced in colour. He also exhibited his work at the Royal West of England Academy, the Royal Society of Marine Painters, the New English Art Club, and at various London and provincial galleries, including among the latter the Laing Art Gallery, NEWCASTLE, whose Artists of the Northern Counties exhibitions he contributed to for several years. Tucker was an associate of the Royal College of Art, and an associate of the Royal West of England Academy. He died at Gloucester. A major memorial exhibition of his work was held at Cheltenham Art Gallery in 1974, this consisting of some ninety of his works in oil, tempera and watercolour. Represented: Cheltenham A.G.; Laing A.G., Newcastle; Shipley A.G., Gateshead.

184

TUKE, Lilian Kate (fl. late 19th, early 20th cent.)
Landscape, genre and portrait painter in oil and water-colour. This artist first practised at DURHAM, from which in 1893 she showed as one of her earliest exhibits at the Bewick Club, NEWCASTLE, her work: *A Reformatory Boy*. She continued to exhibit at the Club until the early years of the century, then began to exhibit her work more widely, showing examples at the Royal Academy, the Royal Institute of Painters in Water Colours, the Royal Society of Portrait Painters, and at the Walker Art Gallery, Liverpool. In 1906 she commenced exhibiting at the Artists of the Northern Counties exhibitions at the Laing Art Gallery, NEWCASTLE, showing her landscapes: *The Castle, Durham*, and *Dordrecht*, but after moving to London about 1914 she appears to have exhibited little on Tyneside.

TURNBULL, William (d. 1935)
Landscape, coastal and flower painter in oil and water-colour. This artist practised at CULLERCOATS, and later LOWICK, near BERWICK-UPON-TWEED, in the late 19th and early 20th centuries, and regularly exhibited his work at NEWCASTLE throughout his career. He was an exhibitor at the Bewick Club, NEWCASTLE, from the mid-1890's, and showed work at the Artists of the Northern Counties exhibitions at the city's Laing Art Gallery, for thirty years from their inception in 1905. Many of his exhibits featured Northumberland landscapes, sometimes with sheep or cattle, but he was particularly fond of painting Wallflowers, and showed many studies of these at the exhibitions. Two of his works were included in the Artists of the Northern Counties exhibition following his death early in 1935. These were entitled: *North Northumberland*, and *Old Shields*. It is believed that he died at LOWICK.

TURNER, William E. (fl. late 19th cent.)
Landscape, coastal and genre painter in oil and water-colour. This artist practised at SOUTH SHIELDS in the late 19th century, and sent several works for exhibition at the Bewick Club, NEWCASTLE, in this period. Typical titles of works shown at the Club, were: *Flowing Tide* (1891); *Waiting for a Bite* (1893), and *Clean your Step, Mum* (1894). It is possible that he was the "William Eddowes Turner", who practised at Nottingham in the late 1850's and early 1860's, and exhibited work at the British Institution, and the Suffolk Street Gallery in these periods.

TWEEDY, Thomas Hall (1816-1892)
Wood carver. Tweedy practised as a wood carver at NEWCASTLE for many years in the middle of the 19th century, at one time being accounted the most influential figure in his field in Northumbria. At various times he had as his apprentices some of the finest wood carvers the area has produced, among these Gerrard Robinson (q.v.), Ralph Hedley (q.v.), and Elijah Copland (q.v.). Tweedy was himself a proficient wood carver, but like William Wailes (q.v.), in regard to stained glass designing, preferred to recruit the best available talent, and take the credit for his workshop. His shop on the town's Grainger Street was well known for its window displays of the workshop's productions, and through the several major exhibitions of crafts which were staged in Britain and abroad in the 1850's and 1860's, his name became identified in London and Paris with some of the finest carved furniture exhibited in these cities. The golden era of his workshop was during the vogue for such furniture *c.* 1840-*c.* 1860, and helped by men like Robinson, "Tweedy" pieces became in demand from the local aristocracy. One of his most

James Walker Tucker: Harvest at Pools Farm. Oil 48×60. *Mrs. J. W. Tucker.*

generous patrons was Algernon, Fourth Duke of North-umberland, who, notwithstanding his employment of his own wood carvers, commissioned much work from Tweedy. In the late 1860's, and having earlier lost his star wood carver, Robinson, to London, Tweedy de-cided to give up wood carving, and about 1870 went into partnership with T. P. Barkas in running the Central Exchange News Room & Art Gallery in the town. Under their management, and later that of Charles Edward Barkas (q.v.), the establishment staged several successful art exhibitions, notably the exhibition of works by local painters, in 1878. Tweedy spent much of his later life at RYTON, and died at his home there in 1892. His work as a wood carver is extremely difficult to distinguish from that of his pupils, several pieces once thought to have been by his hand (the Robinson "Tam O' Shanter" series in the John George Joicey Museum, NEWCASTLE, for instance), now being attrib-uted to one or other of his apprentices.

*VALENTINE, John (fl. late 19th, early 20th cent.)

Landscape, genre and portrait painter in oil and water-colour. This artist practised at NEWCASTLE in the first half of the present century, and first commenced exhi-biting his work on Tyneside by showing his *In from the fields*; *Portrait of J. Duncan Love*, and *Portrait of Thomas Bambridge*, at the Artists of the Northern Counties exhibition at the city's Laing Art Gallery, in 1910. He remained a regular exhibitor at NEWCASTLE for the next ten years, then ceased exhibiting until the Second World War. His later exhibits were shown at the Artists of the Northern Counties exhibitions 1944-7, those in the last year comprising: *The Ford*, and *The*

Tweed at Norham. It is believed that he worked as an illustrator for the *Newcastle Daily Chronicle*, for many years. He may have been the "J. Valentine" who exhibited one landscape work at the Royal Institute of Oil Painters, in 1884. An example of his work may be seen at the one-time home of Lord Armstrong at Cragside, ROTHBURY, courtesy of the National Trust. His sister, or daughter, EDITH VALENTINE, was also artistically talented and exhibited her work.

VAUGHAN, William Steains (fl. late 19th cent.)

Amateur landscape and coastal painter in watercolour. Vaughan lived at NEWCASTLE in the late 19th century, and was a keen painter of local landscape and coastal subjects in his spare time. He also exhibited his work, showing examples in 1878, at the exhibition of works by local painters, at the Central Exchange Art Gallery, NEWCASTLE, and the town's Arts Association exhibition. His three exhibits at the former exhibition were de-scribed in the catalogue notes as "very creditable performances". He later exhibited at the Bewick Club, NEWCASTLE, for several years.

VENTRESS, Robert (c.1846-c.1925)

Landscape and coastal painter in oil and watercolour. Ventress was born on Tyneside, and practised at NEW-CASTLE as an artist, picture framer and gilder all his life, occasionally sending his paintings of local landscape and coastal views to exhibitions in Northumbria. He first exhibited his work in 1866, when he showed a *Burn Scene*, and a *Coast Scene*, at the "Exhibition of Paintings and other Works of Art", at the Town Hall, NEWCASTLE. He was an exhibitor at the "Gateshead Fine Art & Industrial Exhibition", in 1883, and was later a regular exhibitor at the Bewick Club, NEWCASTLE, and the Artists of the Northern Counties exhibitions at the city's Laing Art Gallery. He was a member of the Bewick Club, and the Benwell Art Club, NEWCASTLE. He died at NEWCASTLE.

WAILES, William (1808-1881)

Stained glass designer; landscape painter in watercolour; draughtsman. Wailes was born at NEWCASTLE, the descendant of an old Northumbrian family, and endeavoured to succeed as a landscape painter before becoming first a grocer, later a manufacturer of stained glass. Accordingly, he placed himself as a pupil under Thomas Miles Richardson, Senior (q.v.), and by 1826 was exhibiting alongside his master at the Northumberland Institution for the Promotion of the Fine Arts, NEWCASTLE, albeit only showing a copy of Richardson's *View of Durham*. He again exhibited at NEWCASTLE, in 1828 showing his *The Vale of Tyne*, at the Northern Academy, but despairing of critical acclaim he decided to become a tradesman. Again his efforts met with failure, and it was almost as a last resort that he turned to the activity by which he was later to become famous: manufacturing stained glass windows. His earlier involvement with artists stood him in good stead, however, when selecting men to help him in his new venture. His judgement in selecting artists such as Francis Wilson Oliphant (q.v.), James Sticks (q.v.), and John Thompson Campbell (q.v.), was impeccable, and remained throughout a career which was to take his name around the world as the manufacturer, and in most cases mistakenly, the designer, of the finest stained glass windows. For although we have it from Wailes' grandson, William Wailes Strang, who ultimately succeeded his grandfather in owning the business, that he "excelled in delicate Indian ink, sepia, water colour and pen and ink drawing", and that his chief hobbies were "furniture designing, house building, and landscape gardening", there is no direct evidence that he actively involved himself in the designing of his windows.*

Perhaps the best assessment of Wailes comes from the pen of William Bell Scott (q.v.), in his *Autobiographical Notes etc.* 1892, who observed: "William Wailes was the last man one would have expected to organise and succeed in this new species of art . . . . He had been in trade and was unsuccessful, his reading was the *London Journal*, and his general knowledge of art nil. Yet he had the greatest delight in grand churches, and had visited many in France. This was his inspiration; he got hold of Oliphant, built a kiln in his back shop, introduced himself to Pugin, and in a few years had a hundred men busily at work with commissions more than he could handle . . . . Had Wailes been himself a Raphael or a Titian, what might he not have accomplished . . . ." As it was, Wailes accomplished much, supervising the production of some 360 windows annually for several years, and undoubtedly dictating their style and finish to no small degree. He spent his final years living at Saltwell Tower, GATESHEAD (which he is said to have designed and built himself), a short while before his death disposing of the house and adjacent land to Gateshead Corporation, on condition that he could stay in the Tower as long as he lived. He died at GATESHEAD, and was buried in the graveyard of St. Peter's, BYWELL, which church contains several windows erected in memory of his family. The Shipley Art Gallery, GATESHEAD, has a portrait of Wailes painted by JOHN OLIPHANT, relative of Francis Wilson Oliphant.

* An exception may be the designs for the Chevy Chase window exhibited in his name at the First Water Colour Exhibition of the Newcastle Society of Artists, 1836.

WALKER, James (fl. 19th cent.)

Engraver. He practised at NEWCASTLE in the early 19th century, for some years in association with George Armstrong (q.v.).

WALKER, M. Kingston (born c.1895)

Portrait, animal, landscape and flower painter in oil and watercolour. She was born on Tyneside, and received her first tuition in art at Armstrong College (later King's College; now Newcastle University), where she won a three year scholarship. During the First World War she served as a voluntary ambulance driver, and did not resume her studies in art until 1920, when she became a pupil at the Byam Shaw and Vicat Cole Schools of Art. She returned to NEWCASTLE in the early 1920's, and there commenced exhibiting at the Artists of the Northern Counties exhibitions at the city's Laing Art Gallery, receiving much favourable comment for her work. In 1936 an exhibition of her work was held at the Walker Galleries, London. The Laing Art Gallery, NEWCASTLE, has her *Thunderstorm: L'aig De Varan, Haute Savoie.*

WALKER, Seymour, N.E.A.C. (1859-1927)

Amateur landscape painter in oil. Walker was born at WEST HARTLEPOOL (now HARTLEPOOL), and following his general education entered his family's timber firm in the town. His involvement in the day-to-day running of the firm appears to have been limited, however, enabling him to indulge his early love of painting and drawing, often in the company of successful professional artists of his day, such as Whistler, Ludovici, Lee Hankey, and fellow Northumbrian artist, Ralph Hedley (q.v.). He was also able to paint widely on the continent, where he became profoundly influenced by the work of Jean-Baptiste Corot. Walker first began exhibiting his work publicly when he sent three works to the Suffolk Street Gallery in 1887/8, from his home at SEATON CAREW. These works were entitled: *A Troopship*; *Off Hartlepool*, and *Waves*. He later exhibited at the Royal Institute of Oil Painters, the New English Art Club (of which he became member in 1889), and various provincial galleries, including the Laing Art Gallery, NEWCASTLE, whose Artists of the Northern Counties exhibitions he contributed to for several years. A major one-man exhibition of his work in oil was held at the Gray Art Gallery, WEST HARTLEPOOL, in the year before his death, this including British and continental scenes, copies after Corot, and a portrait of the artist by Emmeline Deane. He died at SEATON CAREW. A son, or nephew, J. WYLAM WALKER, of SEATON CAREW, was also a talented artist, and exhibited his work.

WALLACE, James, Senior (d.1911)

Landscape painter in oil; art teacher. Wallace is believed to have been born at BLYTH, and to have obtained his art master's certificate at South Kensington School of Art, before taking up the post of art master at the Corporation Academy, BERWICK-UPON-TWEED. Here he was teaching by 1873, and is said to have had among his pupils, Frank Watson Wood (q.v.), and his son, James Wallace, Junior (q.v.). Just before the turn of the century he resigned his teaching post at BERWICK-UPON-TWEED, and settling at London, practised as a full-time professional artist in the capital until his death in 1911. Wallace appears to have exhibited little while teaching at BERWICK-UPON-TWEED, but while at London he exhibited at the Royal Academy, the Royal Scottish Academy, the Glasgow Institute of Fine Arts, the London Salon, and in the provinces. His Royal Academy exhibits included: *A village on the Berwickshire Coast* (1899); *Evening on the Tweed* (1901), and *In the Park* (1904). His work is sometimes confused with that of John Wallace (q.v.), and James Wallace, Junior. Represented: Berwick A.G.

WALLACE, James, Junior (d.1937)

Landscape and genre painter in oil and watercolour. Wallace was possibly born at BERWICK-UPON-TWEED following his father's move to the town to teach at the Corporation Academy, and is said to have studied under his father there. He first exhibited his work while practising at BERWICK-UPON-TWEED, showing examples at the Royal Academy, the Royal Scottish Academy, the Glasgow Institute of Fine Arts, and the Artists of the Northern Counties exhibitions at the Laing Art Gallery, NEWCASTLE, between 1900 and 1918. He lived at Paisley, Renfrew, after the First World War.

*WALLACE, John (1841-1905)

Landscape and genre painter in oil and watercolour. He was born at RYTON, and on leaving the village school, joined his father's business as cartwright and joiner. At the end of his apprenticeship he continued with his father as journeyman joiner, later deciding to become a builder in the village. About 1868 he entered into several large building speculations in RYTON, eventually completing several projects which were later said to have "added much to the attractions of the old place"; notable among these was Wallace Terrace, which still stands today. In the late 1870's, however, the property market became increasingly depressed, and he gave up the building trade to devote himself to his lifelong love of painting. He studied for a short time under another local artist, then in 1880 moved to NEWCASTLE to practise as a full-time professional himself. He first began exhibiting his work publicly at the Arts Association exhibitions at NEWCASTLE, showing examples in 1880 and 1881. He subsequently became a member of the Bewick Club in the city, remaining an exhibitor with the Club until his death. One of his Club exhibits of 1885 was purchased by industrialist, art patron and father of Charles William Mitchell (q.v.), Dr. Charles Mitchell; Lady Armstrong purchased one of his 1886 Club exhibits, and, indeed, all of his exhibits in that year found purchasers. In 1890 he sent his only work to the Royal Scottish Academy, following this in 1892, by sending his first work to the Royal Academy: *Butter Washing*. He exhibited at the Royal Academy on two further occasions, in 1896 showing: *A Northumberland Dairy*, and in the year prior to his death: *Derwent Vale*. Wallace's later years at NEWCASTLE were increasingly taken up with producing black and white drawings for reproduction in local publications. He died at NEWCASTLE, several of his works appearing in the year of his death, at the first exhibition of the Artists of the Northern Counties exhibition at the city's Laing Art Gallery, including his *Jesmond Falls*, dated 1901. Represented: Laing A.G., Newcastle; Shipley A.G., Gateshead.

WALTON, George (1855-1891)

Portrait painter in oil. Born at BLENKINSOP, near HALTWHISTLE, Walton studied at the School of Art, NEWCASTLE, the Royal Academy Schools, and in Paris,

John Wallace. Quayside, Newcastle upon Tyne, 1887. Oil 29×50. *Tyne & Wear County Council Museums, Shipley Art Gallery.*

Louisa Anne, Marchioness of Waterford: The Sleeping Disciples. Watercolour 5×15¾. *Tate Gallery.*

before practising as a portrait painter on Tyneside by his early twenties. He first exhibited his work while still at NEWCASTLE, showing a portrait at the Royal Scottish Academy in 1881. In the following year he moved to London, remaining there for some six years, and exhibiting his work at the Royal Academy from 1882, the Suffolk Street Gallery in 1882/3, and the Bewick Club, NEWCASTLE from 1884. On his return to NEWCASTLE in 1888 he sent his last work to the Royal Academy, a portrait entitled: *Mrs. Chatt*, later moving to Appleby, Westmorland, where he died in 1891. He is believed to have practised briefly in Australia during his short career as a portrait painter.

WARD, William Wightman (1860-1936)

Landscape painter in oil and watercolour; etcher. He was born at NORTH SHIELDS, and left school at the age of twelve to support his family following the death of his father. While later working as a painter and decorator he attended art classes locally, and at the age of seventeen won the Queen Victoria Prize for Flower Painting. He subsequently became a master painter and decorator with premises in the town, above which he maintained a studio at which various local artists, including John Falconar Slater (q.v.), were regular visitors. He first exhibited his work at the Bewick Club, NEWCASTLE, where typical titles were his *Suffolk Landscape*, and *Marshes near Aldborough, Suffolk*, shown in 1893. He later became an occasional exhibitor at the Artists of the Northern Counties exhibitions at the Laing Art Gallery, NEWCASTLE, sending as his last works, two etchings entitled: *Old Houses, Whitby*, and *Farmstead near Preston*, from his home at TYNEMOUTH, in 1928.

WASSERMAN, John Conrad (1846- c.1884)

Amateur landscape, coastal and flower painter in oil and watercolour. He was born at SUNDERLAND, the son of a commission agent, and after training under his father, joined Shield, Fenwick & Co., merchants, at NEWCASTLE. While living at NEWCASTLE, he became keenly interested in painting, and after his marriage,

settled at CULLERCOATS, from which he sent work for exhibition in the period 1880-82, to the Royal Academy, the Royal Scottish Academy, the Glasgow Institute of Fine Arts, the Dudley Gallery, London, and the Arts Association, NEWCASTLE. His Royal Academy exhibits were entitled: *Autumn Beauties* (1880); *Dunstanborough Castle*, and *Summer Sunrise* (1882). It is believed that he died in the early 1880's. He was the husband of writer Lillias Wasserman (b.1848), who contributed articles to the *Art Journal*, and the *Northern Weekly Leader*. One of her articles in the latter, in her series *Where the North Wind Blows*, 1887, was entitled: *A Cullercoats Artist*, but does not appear to have referred specifically to her husband.

*WATERFORD, Louisa Anne, Marchioness of (Hon. Miss Stuart), H.S.W.A. (1818-1891)

Amateur religious, figure, portrait and landscape painter in oil and watercolour. She was born in Paris, the daughter of British Ambassador, Charles, Lord Stuart de Rothesay, and spent her youth in the French capital. At the age of twenty-three she married the 3rd Marquess of Waterford, and spent the next eighteen years at his family home at Curraghmore in Ireland, in the later part of this period occasionally visiting Ford Castle, FORD, which he had inherited from his mother. In 1859 her husband died following a hunting accident, and she retired to Ford Castle, and High Cliffe, on the Hampshire Coast – the latter being an old Stuart family place left her by her mother. Most of her time was spent at FORD, however, where she became deeply interested in painting, and began effecting changes to her castle home, and to the neighbouring hamlet. She built a model village just to the east of the castle grounds, a new village school, a blacksmith's forge, and an ornamental cottage, designing the last two buildings herself. Her main artistic activity while at FORD was the decoration of the school, which occupied her from its opening in 1861, until some twenty-three years later. This consisted of what look like murals, but which are actually large watercolours on paper, stretched to fit the wall spaces. The themes of these works were largely biblical, and the models for many of the figures portrayed were village children and adults who would come and sit for her in her castle studio on Saturdays. Her one-time master Ruskin was not particularly impressed by his pupil's work, saying "I expected you would have done something better", but over the years of their completion many distinguished people called to see them, including Queen Mary, Mr. Gladstone, and Sir Edwin Landseer.

After working on decorations for the school for some sixteen years, Lady Waterford began to exhibit her work, from 1877 until her death, showing examples at the Royal Hibernian Academy, the Society of Women Artists (which elected her an honorary member in 1877), the Grosvenor and Dudley Galleries, London, Manchester City Art Gallery, and the Arts Association, NEWCASTLE. Although an extremely talented artist, she was very modest about her work, once writing: "I see myself as just an amateur and no more – not altogether bad, but not good". Amateur though she was, she is represented in several important public collections, and a well received exhibition of her work was held at 8, Carlton House Terrace, London, in 1910. She died at FORD, and was buried in the graveyard of St. Michael's Church, in the castle grounds. Her grave is marked by a great recumbent stone cross which is said to have been designed by George Frederick Watts, who painted her portrait in 1838, and remained friendly with her throughout her life. The Church contains a traceried stone reredos, which was erected to her memory by subscription from the "rich and poor". FORD evidently exercised a potent influence over Lady Waterford's dormant talents as an artist, not only encouraging her to paint, but to seek tuition and approval from men like Ruskin, Dante Gabriel Rossetti, and Joseph Arthur Palliser Severn. Both village people and the surrounding Northumbrian countryside featured frequently in her work, a notable example being her *Sleeping Disciples*,# in which the Cheviot Hills are seen in the background. An interesting and lavishly illustrated account of Lady Waterford's life and work may be found in Hasting Mackelcan Neville's "Under A Border Tower", 1896. Her elder sister, VISCOUNTESS CANNING, was also a talented artist. Represented: British Museum; Victoria and Albert Museum; National Gallery of Scotland; Tate Gallery.

*WATERS, Ralph, Senior (1720-1798)

Landscape and architectural painter in oil and watercolour; draughtsman; scenic painter. Waters was born at NORTH SHIELDS, the son of a gardener, and practised as a professional artist in his native town for several years before moving to NEWCASTLE. In 1782 we find him being described in the *Newcastle Chronicle* for February 23rd of that year, as having been responsible for all the scenes painted for a presentation at the New Theatre, of the pantomime "Robinson Crusoe, or the Harlequin Friday", in a "most masterly fashion", while *Whitehead's Directory* of 1787, for the town, describes Waters and his son, Ralph Waters, Junior (q.v.), as "Painters in General, Bigg Market". Waters Senior exhibited his work on only one occasion, this being when he sent *A View of the Remains of Tynemouth Monastery taken in*

Ralph Waters, Senior: St. Nicholas' Church, Newcastle upon Tyne, from the South East. Oil 31×34½. *Tyne & Wear County Council Museums, Laing Art Gallery.*

George Anthony Waterston: Shipping at the mouth of the Tyne. Oil 19½×29½. *Dean Gallery*.

the year 1742, at the Royal Academy in 1785. Several of his paintings were, however, engraved for Brand's *History of Newcastle*, these including *Tynemouth Priory*; *View of the Port of Tyne with Clifford's Fort*; *St. Nicholas' Steeple*, and *View of the Remains of the Tyne Bridge*. The work by which he is best remembered is his view of the Sandhill, NEWCASTLE, showing the Guildhall in the early morning, with the figures of several well known local people. Waters Senior, and Junior, were close acquaintances of Thomas Bewick (q.v.) and there is evidence in the latter's account books of work undertaken on each other's behalf. Another of Waters' sons, HENRY WATERS (*c.*1759-1833), was artistically gifted, and though mainly occupied as a picture and print dealer, occasionally executed drawings, as with his drawing of St. Nicholas' Steeple, after his father, for Brand. Waters Senior died at NEWCASTLE, and is buried under the porch of the city's St. Andrew's Church.

WATERS, Ralph, Junior (1750-1817)

Landscape and architectural painter in watercolour; draughtsman; drawing master. The eldest son of Ralph Waters, Senior (q.v.), he was probably born at NEW-CASTLE following his father's move to the town from NORTH SHIELDS. He evidently worked closely with his father from his adolescence, sharing a studio with Waters Senior, in the town's Bigg Market, where *Whitehead's Directory* for 1787 not only describes them as "Painters in General", but shows Waters Junior, as "Teacher of Drawing, Pilgrim Street". Waters Junior was, indeed, a prolific draughtsman, and began exhibiting his work at the Royal Academy a year before his father, in 1784, showing *The new bridge from the south, with a view of Newcastle upon Tyne*, and three other topographical works. He again exhibited at the Academy in 1785, showing two topographical, and two architectural, drawings, but following this it would appear that much of his time was taken up with teaching drawing at the school for young ladies kept by his

Edinburgh-born wife, at Pilgrim Street, or preparing drawings for reproduction, thereby leaving him little time to concern himself with exhibiting. He died at NEWCASTLE, and is buried in the interior of the city's St. Andrew's Church, where a tablet still stands in his memory. His younger brother HENRY WATERS (*c.*1759-1833), was also artistically gifted.

WATERSONE, James S. (fl. early 20th cent.)

Landscape and coastal painter in oil and watercolour. Watersone practised as an artist at NEWCASTLE in the early 20th century, and regularly exhibited his work at the Artists of the Northern Counties exhibitions at the city's Laing Art Gallery, from their inception in 1905, until 1922. In the period 1904-10 he also showed one work at the Royal Scottish Academy, and one work at the Walker Art Gallery, Liverpool.

*WATERSTON, George Anthony (*c.*1855- *c.*1918)

Landscape, coastal and marine painter in oil and watercolour. He was born at NEWCASTLE, and later practised as a professional artist on Tyneside. He exhibited his work at the Arts Association, NEWCASTLE, from 1878, the city's Bewick Club from 1884, and the Artists of the Northern Counties exhibitions at the Laing Art Gallery, NEWCASTLE, from their inception in 1905, until 1911. About 1909 he moved to Wreay, near Carlisle, Cumberland, where he is believed to have spent the remainder of his life. His exhibits included: *Sunrise* (Arts Association, 1879); *Entering the Harbour* (Bewick Club, 1893), and *Winter, Cumberland* (Artists of the Northern Counties exhibition, 1908).

WATKINS, Mrs. Kate (fl. late 19th cent.)

Amateur landscape and genre painter in oil. She exhibited three works at the Royal Academy, two works at the Glasgow Institute of Fine Arts, and two works at the Grosvenor Gallery, London, while living at DUR-HAM, in the second half of the 19th century. Her works were shown 1850-1888.

191

WATSON, Hugh Thomas (fl. 19th cent.)
Landscape, figure, animal and sporting painter in water-colour; engraver; lithographer. This artist first practised at ALNWICK, from which he exhibited several landscape works at the Northern Academy, and the Northern Society of Painters in Water Colours, NEWCASTLE 1828-30. By 1833 he had moved to NEWCASTLE, where he continued in membership of the Society of Painters in Water Colours, and also became a member of the Newcastle Society of Artists. He was a regular contributor to the exhibitions of both of these societies, and also showed works at the exhibitions of the various art promoting organisations which flourished at NEWCASTLE in the 1830's, but he appears to have worked increasingly as an engraver and lithographer towards the end of this period, and on into the 1840's. His watercolour work consisted of Northumbrian and Scottish views, and a small number of animal and sporting subjects, such as his *Newcastle Races*, which is reproduced in colour as an engraving, in *Historic Newcastle*, by Frank Graham, 1976.

WATSON, James (fl. late 19th, early 20th cent.)
Landscape, coastal and genre painter in oil and water-colour. This artist practised at NEWCASTLE in the late 19th and early 20th centuries, and was a regular exhibitor at the city's Bewick Club, and later the Artists of the Northern Counties exhibitions at its Laing Art Gallery. In 1900 he sent one work to the Royal Academy: *A cottage garden*, but thereafter exhibited exclusively in Northumbria, and only until the outbreak of the First World War. He was particularly fond of painting along the Yorkshire coast, but also painted elsewhere in Yorkshire, and in Northumbria and Wales. He was still practising at NEWCASTLE in the 1920's.

*WATSON, James Finlay (1898-1981)
Amateur landscape painter in oil and watercolour; commercial designer. Born at SOUTH SHIELDS, Watson moved to SUNDERLAND in 1906, where he later studied

James Finlay Watson: Derwent Valley Farm, 1947. Watercolour 11×14¾. *Tyne & Wear County Council Museums, Sunderland Art Gallery & Museum.*

art at the evening classes run by the town's School of Art. He enlisted in the Army in the First World War, and although deprived of an eye while in action he subsequently worked for the local Gas Board for fifty years as advertising and display officer, and was able to follow his spare-time relaxation of painting and drawing. He was for many years a member of the Sunderland Art Club, and exhibited his work widely in the North East and in the Midlands, examples being shown at the Artists of the Northern Counties exhibitions at the Laing Art Gallery, NEWCASTLE, and the "Contemporary Artists of Durham County" exhibition at the Shipley Art Gallery, GATESHEAD, staged in 1951, in connection with the Festival of Britain. Following his retirement he devoted himself entirely to art, and in 1980 enjoyed a one-man show of his work at WASHINGTON, near SUNDERLAND. He died at SUNDERLAND. Represented: Sunderland A.G.

WATSON, Mary (1875-1925)
Amateur portrait, figure and landscape painter in oil and watercolour; draughtsman. She was born at NORTH SHIELDS, the daughter of iron merchant James Watson. She was a talented artist from her childhood, and following tuition from several local artists she began to exhibit her work at the Walker Art Gallery, Liverpool, and the Bewick Club, NEWCASTLE. She later exhibited at the Artists of the Northern Counties exhibitions at the Laing Art Gallery, NEWCASTLE, contributing nine black and white drawings to the first exhibition in 1905, and a number of continental and British landscapes, to subsequent exhibitions. She was a cousin of Ernest Procter (q.v.).

WATSON, Robert (1755-1783)
Historical, portrait and genre painter in oil. Watson was born at NEWCASTLE, and began his career in art by being apprenticed to a coach painter in the town. His master's mismanagement of the business led to its downfall, however, and Watson left NEWCASTLE, and travelling to London secured admission to the Royal Academy Schools. Here he is said to have been a model student, working hard at mastering anatomy and perspective, drawing copiously from the Antique, and visiting every collection of pictures to which he could gain access. In 1778 he was awarded the gold medal or pallet of the Society for the Encouragement of Arts for the best historical drawing of the year, and showed six works at the Royal Academy, which included both portraits and historical subjects. Encouraged by this success he decided to branch out into art criticism, and in the spring of 1780 published a brochure entitled *An Anticipation of the Exhibition of the Royal Academy*, in which he described "with piquancy and force some well-known performances of eminent contemporary painters". The brochure was so well received that he quickly became befriended by many of London's most influential men – among these Sir William Fordyce, Dr. Samuel Johnson, and Sir Joshua Reynolds. Although settled in London, Watson paid visits to his birthplace every year. On one such visit he read of a controversy being conducted between a Dr. Priestley and a Dr. Price on

Robert F. Watson:
Evening on the beach near
Marsden, South Shields.
Oil 15×20.
D. Kirkup.

Materialism. He became so interested in this subject that in 1781 he published a volume entitled *An Essay on the Nature and Existence of the Material World*, addressed to the two doctors. Shortly after its publication he obtained for himself an appointment as an engineer to the British Army in India, and arriving there in 1783, assisted in the defence of Fort Osnaburgh. The British garrison at the Fort was obliged to capitulate, but on "honourable terms" obtained by Watson. He died shortly afterwards, following an attack of fever.

*WATSON, Robert F. (1815-1885)

Marine, coastal, landscape and portrait painter in oil and watercolour. Watson was born at NORTH SUNDER-LAND, the son of a lighthouse keeper on the Inner Farne Islands, and is said to have been artistically talented from his youth, gaining a silver epergne from the Duke of Northumberland for his work when he was only in his teens. He later moved to NEWCASTLE, where he received tuition from Thomas Miles Richardson, Senior (q.v.), and later John Wilson Ewbank (q.v.), before practising as a professional artist in the town. He first exhibited his work at NEWCASTLE, showing his *The remnant of a wreck*, at the Newcastle Society of Artists' exhibition in 1836. He remained at NEWCASTLE until the early 1840's, meanwhile continuing to exhibit his work in the town, and finding a friend and patron in Tyneside poet and sailmaker, Robert Gilchrist (1797-1844). Watson and Gilchrist made several excursions in a vessel named the *Vesta*, in which the latter had an interest, calling at the Farne Islands, and Edinburgh, the poet later commissioning his friend to paint *The Vesta passing the Bass Rock*, and what is believed to have been the only portrait of Grace Darling ever executed in oil, from life.

After Gilchrist's death in 1844, Watson went to London, where he commenced exhibiting at the Royal Academy and the Suffolk Street Gallery in 1845, and the British Institution in 1846. London appears to have remained his base for the next twenty years, during which period he regularly exhibited at the establishments just named, mainly showing shipping, coastal and landscape scenes, including his *Erebus and Terror under the command of Sir John Franklin, leaving the coast of Britain, on the Arctic expedition in 1845* (Royal Academy, 1849); *A Squall, the return to Shields* (British Institution, 1856), and *A Stream from the hill above Rothbury* (Suffolk Street Gallery, 1862). The last named work was exhibited by Watson during a period of residency at TYNEMOUTH, a place at which he appears to have spent much time from the early 1850's. About 1865 he settled at SOUTH SHIELDS, spending the remainder of his life in the town, and exhibiting only on Tyneside, where examples of his work were shown at the Arts Association, NEWCASTLE, from 1878, and at the city's Bewick Club, at its inaugural exhibition in the year before his death. In 1911 his works *Thrum Mill, Rothbury*; *Sketches*; *Rainbow*, and *Table Rocks, Whitley Bay*, were shown at the South Shields Arts Club Exhibition. Represented: Grace Darling Museum, Bamburgh; Laing A.G., Newcastle; North Tyneside Public Libraries; Sunderland A.G.

WATSON, William Peter, R.B.A. (d.1932)

Genre and landscape painter in oil; art teacher. He was born at SOUTH SHIELDS, and studied at the Royal College of Art, and at the Academie Julian, Paris, before practising as a professional artist and art teacher in London. He first began to exhibit his work shortly after settling in the capital, showing his *Topsy*, and *Sweet pale Margaret*, at the Royal Academy, in 1883. Later, he commenced exhibiting at the Royal Society of British Artists, the Royal Institute of Oil Painters, the Royal Society of Artists, Birmingham, the Royal Hibernian Academy, and widely in the provinces, including the Walker Art Gallery, Liverpool, Manchester City Art Gallery, and the Bewick Club, NEWCASTLE. He showed some seventy-seven works at the Royal Society of British Artists, and was elected a member of that

193

body in 1891. During the early part of his career in London, Watson was in charge of evening classes at the Royal College of Art, and established a considerable reputation for his work as a painter. After the turn of the century, and while continuing to exhibit in Britain, he showed work widely abroad, and several examples were purchased for overseas collections. His later Royal Academy exhibits included: *Day Dreams* (1889); *A Village Belle* (1897), and *When the Heart is Young* (1901). Typical exhibits at the Royal Society of British Artists were: *In Sight at Last*; *A Master Mariner*; *Sunny Days*, and *An East Anglian Port*. He was a gold medallist at the Hobart International Exhibition, and participated in the Japan-Britain Exhibition, 1910, among several other overseas exhibitions. He lived at Bosham, Sussex, in his later years, dying there in 1932. His first wife, LIZZIE MAY WATSON (née Godfrey), was also a professional artist. Represented: National Gallery, Hobart, Tasmania, and various British and overseas collections.

WATTS, Mrs. Jane (née Waldie) (1792-1826)

Amateur landscape and architectural painter in oil and watercolour; illustrator. She was the daughter of George Waldie, one of whose three homes was Forth House, NEWCASTLE. Here he, and his family, spent a great part of each year, and became friendly with the family of Thomas Bewick (q.v.), while they were living nearby. It is doubtful that Jane Waldie was born at NEWCASTLE, but she is known to have spent the first five summers of her life at TYNEMOUTH, and to have attended a boarding school at NEWCASTLE until the age of fifteen. She then attended an academy at Edinburgh, where she showed such an aptitude for drawing and painting that her father later took her on a tour of the great galleries of Italy and France, and the picturesque scenery of Switzerland and Southern Germany. On returning to England she developed into an accomplished though retiring amateur painter of landscapes and architectural pieces, contributing several works in these categories to the Royal Academy and the British Institution anonymously, until 1817, when she showed at the latter her *Tower of the Fair Gabrielle . . .*; *The Tomb of Rousseau . . .*, and *View on the coast of Northumberland; rising gale*. She again declared her name when showing her *View of Lake Albano, near Rome*, at the Royal Academy, in 1820, maintaining this practice while exhibiting at NEWCASTLE, following her marriage in 1821 to Captain George Edward Watts R.N. Her brief married life was spent at Langton Grange, near DARLINGTON, where she died in 1826. Most of her exhibits at the Northumberland Institution for the Promotion of the Fine Arts 1822-1826, were continental subjects. In addition to being an accomplished artist she was an able writer, and published at least three books.

WAY, William Cosens (1833-1905)

Landscape, coastal and genre painter in watercolour; art teacher. Way was born at Torquay, the son of an artist, and studied under his father until he was twenty-four. He then went to London, where he was persuaded by the fruit painter Leitch, to take his art master's certificate at South Kensington School of Art, meanwhile supporting himself by painting. After six years he obtained his certificate, and was recommended by the authorities at South Kensington, to their counterparts at NEWCASTLE, for a position as assistant master at the town's Government School of Design. Way took up his post in January, 1862, and when William Bell Scott (q.v.), two years later resigned the directorship of the School, his assistant assumed this role, retaining it for the next thirty-two years. About the same time as taking over from Scott, Way also assumed responsibility for the directorship of the School of Art at SUNDERLAND, holding this position until 1889, when his School at NEWCASTLE became affiliated to the Durham College of

William Cosens Way: Coast Scene, Cornwall. Watercolour 15×20. *Dean Gallery*.

194

Physical Science. He was also for some time master of art classes at NORTH SHIELDS, and at the Grammar School at NEWCASTLE, eventually retiring from all his official teaching duties in 1895, on an annuity from the College. After leaving the School of Art, as it had then become, he practised as an artist and art teacher at NEWCASTLE until his death.

Way's influence as an artist while he taught at NEWCASTLE was second only to that exerted by Thomas Miles Richardson, Senior (q.v.), in the first half of the century, and like his predecessor was mainly in the medium of watercolour painting. His work was shown widely in his lifetime, examples apearing at the Royal Academy from 1867 until his death, and at the New Water Colour Society (later the Royal Institute of Painters in Water Colours), the Suffolk Street Gallery, and at various London and provincial galleries, for several long periods in between. He also exhibited his work at NEWCASTLE, showing examples at the Arts Association from 1878-1882, and the Bewick Club from 1884 until the turn of the century. Ten of his works were included in the first Artists of the Northern Counties exhibition at the Laing Art Gallery, NEWCASTLE, in 1905, a few weeks after his death at his home in the city's St. George's Terrace. Represented: British Museum; Victoria and Albert Museum; Laing A.G., Newcastle; Shipley A.G., Gateshead; Sunderland A.G.

WEDDELL, William (d. 1878)
Cattle and landscape painter in oil; copyist. An example of this artist's work appeared at the exhibition of works by local painters at the Central Exchange Art Gallery, NEWCASTLE, in 1878, a note in the catalogue of the exhibition commenting: "W. Weddell, a well known artist, who departed this life during the present year, is the producer of No. 259; this work displays fine feeling; cattle, men and trees, all displaying the effects of wind and drenching rain. Weddell was known among the cognescenti as the 'Morland of the North', his fidelity in copying nature so true to the original that it was difficult to distinguish between Morland and Weddell-Morland". Nothing more is known of this artist, except that he was a friend of John Wilson Ewbank (q.v.), in the latter's later days on Tyneside, and that his name appears in trade directories related to NEWCASTLE in the 1860's as a professional artist working in the town. A genre work entitled: *The long grace*, which was loaned to the "Exhibition of Paintings and other Works of Art", at the Town Hall, NEWCASTLE, in 1866, and described as by "Weddell", may have been an example of his work.

WEIR, Stephen (1818-1881)
Landscape painter in oil; art teacher. He was born at NEWCASTLE, and according to his obituary in a local newspaper, spent his early life as a shoemaker in the town. He had been interested in painting from his youth, however, and eventually abandoned his trade to become a teacher at the Government School of Design, NEWCASTLE. After leaving his teaching post he became a full-time professional artist. Weir exhibited his work sparingly, showing one example at the exhibition in 1852 at NEWCASTLE, staged jointly by the North of England Society for the Promotion of the Fine Arts, and the town's Government School of Design, and another at the Arts Association exhibition in 1878. His obituary claimed that he "attained considerable eminence as an artist", but like his son William Weir (q.v.), he does not appear to have exhibited outside Northumbria. He may have been related to the William Weir (d.1865), who practised at NEWCASTLE in the middle of the 19th century, before moving to London, where he established himself as a successful genre painter.

WEIR, William (1840-1881)
Landscape painter in oil. The eldest son of Stephen Weir (q.v.), he was born at GATESHEAD, and became a professional artist at NEWCASTLE, following some tuition from his father. He appears to have exhibited his work exclusively at NEWCASTLE, where among his few known exhibits were the works he sent to the Arts Association exhibitions from 1878, until his death in 1881. A landscape work was, in fact, on display at the 1881 exhibition when he died, this being entitled: *Head of Loch Achray*. He was about to take up a professional appointment in London when he died. His father predeceased him by only a few months. He may have been related to the William Weir (d.1865), who practised at NEWCASTLE in the middle of the 19th century, before moving to London, where he established himself as a successful genre painter.

WELCH, George W. (1853-1906)
Amateur genre painter. Welch was for some twenty-eight years lay clerk to Durham Cathedral, but was throughout his life a keen amateur artist. He exhibited his work at the Bewick Club, NEWCASTLE, while living at DURHAM, showing several works associated with the Cathedral, among these: *A Doorkeeper in the House of the Lord* (1890), and *A Chorister Wanted* (1891). He retired to NEWCASTLE at the early age of fifty-two, and died in the following year at GOSFORTH, near NEWCASTLE. Welch was a tenor singer of exceptional talent, and was an Associate of the Royal College of Music.

WELSH, William (b. 1870)
Landscape and still-life painter in oil and watercolour. Welsh was born at Edinburgh, but lived from his early childhood, until the outbreak of the First World War, at NEWCASTLE. He first exhibited his work while studying at the School of Art, NEWCASTLE, showing several examples at the exhibitions of the Bewick Club. He later exhibited at the Artists of the Northern Counties exhibitions at the city's Laing Art Gallery, and on moving to Middlesex by 1919, commenced exhibiting at the Royal Academy, the Royal Institute of Painters in Water Colours, the Paris Salon, and various London and provincial galleries. The Laing Art Gallery has his watercolour: *Entrance to Fowey Harbour*.

WHEATLEY, Cecil Ross (1892-1967)
Landscape painter in watercolour; cartoonist; illuminator; art teacher. He was born at CHESTER-LE-STREET, the son of artist James Wheatley, and descendant of Francis Wheatley, the Royal Academician famous for

his *Cries of London*. Educated at Bede College, Dur-HAM, where he obtained his teaching certificate, Wheatley taught at a council school near his birthplace, then became an art master at his old College, and an assistant at the Boys' Model School, which then stood in its grounds. When the Model School closed he became art master at Whinney Hill School, DURHAM. He was later appointed headmaster of Neville's Cross Junior School in 1936. He terminated his connection with Bede College in 1950 after thirty-six years' service. In 1957 he retired from his post at Neville's Cross Junior School, where he served for twenty-one years. A pupil in his youth of Frank Thompson (q.v.), Wheatley retained a lifelong interest in watercolour painting, many of his works featuring Northumbrian and Lake District views. He was President of the Durham & District Artists Society from its foundation in 1941, until his death. One of his particular friends was Ralph Johnson (q.v.), with whom he was co-founder of the Society. Wheatley exhibited at the Artists of the Northern Counties exhibitions at the Laing Art Gallery, NEWCASTLE, for more than quarter of a century, and exhibited every year with the Durham & District Artists Society until its dissolution in 1967. Besides painting in watercolour, Wheatley was an accomplished illuminator and cartoonist. He died at DURHAM. Represented: Durham Old Town Hall.

*WHITE, Colonel George Francis (1808-1898)

Amateur landscape painter in watercolour. White was born at Chatham, and claimed to be fifteenth in descent from King Edward III, who died in 1377. His father was Major Henry White of the Grenadier Guards, and Adjutant of the 74th Highlanders. The White family lived in the County of Essex, but was a branch of the White's of REDHEUGH, near GATESHEAD. White served with the 31st Regiment in India, until 1846, his sketches made in 1829-31-32, appearing in *Views in India Chiefly Among the Himalayan Mountains*, 1837. Turner and Prout used White's sketches of the Himalayas as the basis for a series of engravings of this subject, and an exhibition of his work was held in London. On retiring from the Army, White settled at DURHAM, where he continued to sketch local scenes while serving as Second

George Francis White: The Fortune-teller. Miniature 5×7. *L. J. Cole.*

Chief Constable of Durham, and later Deputy Lieutenant of the County. Several years before his retirement from public life he was presented with a portrait of himself by Clement Burlison (q.v.). His wife ANN WHITE, and daughter ELLA WHITE, were also talented artists. Represented: Shipley A.G., Gateshead.

WHITE, Henry (fl. late 18th, early 19th cent.)

Wood engraver. White came to NEWCASTLE from London in 1804, to complete his apprenticeship under Thomas Bewick (q.v.), following the death of his master, Lee. While with Bewick he engraved the principal designs after John Thurston, for an edition of Burns's poems published by Catnach & Davison, ALNWICK, 1808, and also handled some of the tailpieces for this work with fellow apprentices Isaac Nicholson (q.v.), and Edward Willis (q.v.). After completing his apprenticeship he returned to London, where he engraved illustrations for *Puckle's Club*, 1817, William Yarrell's *A History of British Fishes*, 1836, and Major's edition of *Walton's Angler*, 1824. According to Bewick, in his autobiographical *Memoir*,‡ White "chiefly turned his attention, to the imitation of sketchy cross hatching on Wood, from the inimitable pencil of Mr. Cruikshanks, & perhaps some other artists in this same way – Henry White appears to have taken the lead of others who followed that manner of cutting . . .".

‡ *See pp. 199-200, "A Memoir of Thomas Bewick, Written by Himself", edited and with an introduction by Iain Bain, Oxford University Press, 1975.*

WHITE, William Fitzjames, A.R.C.A. (born c.1861)

Landscape painter in oil and watercolour; art teacher. White was born at LOWICK, near BERWICK-UPON-TWEED, the son of a schoolmaster, and first found employment as an elementary school teacher under the Leeds School Board. While teaching at Leeds he became interested in art, studying at the city's School of Art in his spare time. Later he was appointed a student in training at the Royal College of Art, and here he proved so successful in his studies that he was awarded several honours. On completing his studies he was appointed headmaster of Hereford School of Art, remaining there for two years before taking up the appointment as first headmaster of the new School of Art at GATESHEAD, in 1886. He remained at the School for twenty-five years, retiring in 1911, to live in Dorsetshire. While living at GATESHEAD he was a regular exhibitor at the Bewick Club, NEWCASTLE, and later the Artists of the Northern Counties exhibitions at the city's Laing Art Gallery. He also became interested in natural history illustration, and illustrated *Nests & Eggs of British Birds*, by Charles Dixon, 1896, and works of a similar nature for other collectors. He was an associate of the Royal College of Art.

WHITFIELD, Joshua (1884-1954)

Amateur landscape painter in oil and watercolour. Born at DUNSTON, near GATESHEAD, Whitfield began his working life as a costs clerk with Parsons Marine Steam Turbine Company, on Tyneside, later joining Doxford & Sons of SUNDERLAND, in the same capacity. In 1945

Samuel Wild: The Avenue. Watercolour 12×20. *Tyne & Wear County Council Museums, Shipley Art Gallery.*

he was appointed commercial manager of the firm, holding this position until his retirement four years later. Whitfield was a keen amateur painter all his life, and after studying art for five years, taught at evening classes at Rutherford College, NEWCASTLE. While working at SUNDERLAND, he was treasurer of the Stanfield Art Society 1926-36; vice-president of the Sunderland Art Club 1951, and secretary 1952. He exhibited his work almost exclusively in Northumbria, contributing examples to the Artists of the Northern Counties exhibitions at the Laing Art Gallery, NEWCASTLE, and to various exhibitions at SUNDERLAND and SOUTH SHIELDS. He died at EAST HERRINGTON, near SUNDERLAND. Represented: Sunderland A.G.

WHITTLE, Thomas (d. 1731)

Religious painter in oil; sculptor. Whittle is believed to have been the "natural son of a gentleman of fortune", and to have taken his name from that of his birthplace, near OVINGHAM. He left home at an early age, and making his way to CAMBO, some miles distant, was engaged by a miller, remaining with his employer several years. Later, he discovered he had a talent for painting, and wandering the North of England over the next ten or fifteen years, painted several works for churches in the area, including those at HARTBURN, near CAMBO, and PONTELAND, near NEWCASTLE. He also visited Edinburgh, where he executed in stone as a joke a figure of the devil, which won him considerable celebrity when he subsequently demolished it with a hammer. His works in oil and stone have all vanished, but his work as a poet and ballad writer survives in a volume published by a school teacher at CAMBO, in 1815. Most of this work was related to Northumbrian themes, notable among which is his *The Mitford Galloway*. He died in 1731 and was buried in the graveyard of St. Andrew's Church, HARTBURN, whose parish register records him as "Thomas Whittle of East Shaftoe, an ingenious man". EAST SHAFTOE is near CAMBO.

WILD, Rosina Beatrice (b. 1898)

Amateur portrait, landscape and flower painter in watercolour. She was born at GATESHEAD, the daughter of Samuel James Wild (q.v.), and received tuition from her father, and at the School of Art, GATESHEAD, before exhibiting her work. She exhibited her work at the Artists of the Northern Counties exhibitions at the Laing Art Gallery, NEWCASTLE, from 1928, and at the Gateshead Art Club, from its foundation. Two of her works were shown at the "Contemporary Artists of Durham County" exhibition, staged at the Shipley Art Gallery, GATESHEAD, in 1951, in connection with the Festival of Britain.

*WILD, Samuel James (1863-1958)

Landscape, portrait and still-life painter in oil and watercolour; art teacher. Wild was born at GATESHEAD, and studied at the schools of NEWCASTLE, GATESHEAD and SOUTH SHIELDS, and at the Royal College of Art, before practising as a professional artist. He later became an art teacher, serving at Newcastle Modern School, Leamington Secondary School, and evening classes at GATESHEAD. He first began exhibiting his work publicly at the Bewick Club, NEWCASTLE, later becoming a regular exhibitor at the Artists of the Northern Counties exhibitions at the city's Laing Art Gallery. He was a member of the Newcastle Society of Artists, and a founder member of Gateshead Art Club, at the age of eighty-five. His earlier work was mainly landscape, but as he grew increasingly infirm he turned to portrait and still-life painting. He was an exhibitor at the age of eighty-eight, at the "Contemporary Artists of Durham County" exhibition, staged at the Shipley Art Gallery, GATESHEAD, in 1951, in connection with the Festival of Britain. His exhibits were: *Ruined Hut, Saltwell*, and *Saltwell Grove*. He died at GATESHEAD. His daughter Rosina Beatrice Wild (q.v.), and a relative, W. D. WILD, were both talented amateur artists. Represented: Shipley A.G., Gateshead.

197

WILKINSON, George (fl. late 19th, early 20th cent.)
Landscape painter in oil and watercolour. This artist practised at SHOTLEY BRIDGE, near CONSETT, in the late 19th and early 20th centuries, later settling at NEWCASTLE, where he was still painting in the early 1930's. He exhibited his work at the Bewick Club, NEWCASTLE, and later at the Artists of the Northern Counties exhibitions at the city's Laing Art Gallery. His exhibits at the former included his *Early Autumn on the Derwent at Shotley Bridge* (1890), and at the latter his *Tyne near Wylam* (1927).

WILKINSON, Samuel (d. 1803)
Amateur landscape and architectural draughtsman; illustrator. Wilkinson was born at DARLINGTON, and ran a hostelry for much of his life, drawing and painting in his spare time. Most of his drawing was related to antiquarian subjects, and he is credited by George Algernon Fothergill (q.v.), in *A pictorial Survey of S. Cuthbert's Darlington*, 1905, with having produced a drawing upon which was based the "first published picture of Darlington's most ancient building". One of his best known views, however, is that of the town from Park Lane, published as an engraving by John Bailey (q.v.), two years after the production of his St. Cuthbert's view. This view of the town was published in 1760, a section later appearing in the *History and Antiquities of the Parish of Darlington*, by William Hylton Dyer Longstaffe (q.v.), 1854. Wilkinson, who is referred to frequently in Longstaffe's book, retired from the hostelry business in 1772.

George Barclay Wishart: Bottle Bank, Gateshead, 1925. Watercolour 18×9½. *Tyne & Wear County Council Museums, Shipley Art Gallery.*

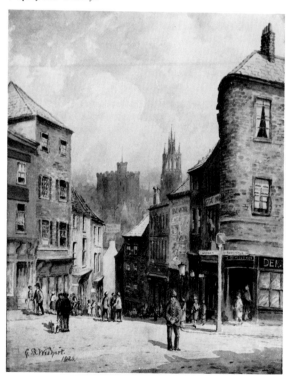

WILLIS, Edward (fl. late 18th, early 19th cent.)
Wood engraver. Born on Tyneside, a cousin of George Stephenson, the engineer, Willis served an apprenticeship with Thomas Bewick (q.v.), at NEWCASTLE, 1798-1805. His best known work consists of his tailpiece engravings for the edition of Burns's poems published by Catnach & Davison, ALNWICK, 1808. Other tailpieces for this work were engraved by fellow apprentices Isaac Nicholson (q.v.), and Henry White (q.v.), the latter also engraving the principal designs after John Thurston. A note in Bewick's workshop engraving book, in the Laing Art Gallery, NEWCASTLE, states of Willis, at the end of his time: "never a cross word passed between us", while in his autobiographical *Memoir*,‡ he says: "I had a great regard for Edward Willis on account of his regular good behaviour while he was under my tuition – he has now been long resident in London".

‡ *See p. 199, "A Memoir of Thomas Bewick, Written by Himself", edited and with an introduction by Iain Bain, Oxford University Press, 1975.*

WILSON, Robert Arthur, A.R.C.A., S.G.A. (b.1884)
Landscape and subject painter in oil, tempera and watercolour; etcher; lino-cut artist; art teacher. Wilson was born at SUNDERLAND, and studied at the town's School of Art, and later at the Royal College of Art, and the Academie Julian, Paris, before practising as a professional artist in London. He remained based at London most of his professional life, and worked as an art instructor at London and Surrey schools for many years, in addition to handling a wide variety of artistic commissions, including mural painting, and book illustration. He did not begin to exhibit his work until quite late in life, sending examples to the Royal Academy, the Society of Graphic Artists, and to various London and provincial galleries from 1927. He contributed three works to the "Contemporary Artists of Durham County" exhibition, staged at the Shipley Art Gallery, GATESHEAD, in 1951, in connection with the Festival of Britain. These works comprised: *Cobnor Point*; *Sails near Bosham*, and *Morris Dancers in Surrey*. He was an associate of the Royal College of Art, and a member of the Society of Graphic Artists. His wife, STELLA LOUISE WILSON (née Perken), has also practised as an artist, and widely exhibited her work. Represented: Victoria and Albert Museum; Sunderland A.G.

*WISHART, George Barclay (1873-1937)
Landscape painter in watercolour; architectural draughtsman. He was born at GATESHEAD, and became an engineer at Clarke Chapman & Co., in the town, painting in his spare time. In the depression of 1926 he was obliged to leave his employment as an engineer, and for the rest of his life was able to devote himself to his main interests in life of art and music. He made frequent visits to the Highlands of Scotland, and to Switzerland, to paint, but the bulk of his work featured Tyneside scenes. He exhibited his work at the Bewick Club, NEWCASTLE, from their inception, in 1884, showing *A Summer Evening at Hexham*, and later became a regular exhibitor at the Artists of the Northern Counties exhibitions at the Laing Art Gallery, NEWCASTLE. He

last exhibited at the latter in 1921, showing two water-colours: *The Tyne from Bill Quay*, and *North Shields*. In his final years Wishart suffered eye failure due to cataracts, and while obliged to give up painting he was still able to indulge his love of music, writing many compositions which were played by his own orchestra. He died at GATESHEAD. Represented: Shipley A.G., Gateshead.

WOOD, Charles (1866-1887)
Scenic painter. He was employed as a scenic painter at the Tyne Theatre, NEWCASTLE, but drowned in the River Tyne at ELSWICK, near NEWCASTLE, while bathing.

WOOD, Frank Watson (1862-1953)
Marine, coastal, landscape and portrait painter in oil and watercolour; illustrator; art teacher. Wood was born at BERWICK-UPON-TWEED, where he is said to have studied under James Wallace, Senior (q.v.), before attending South Kensington School of Art, and the Academie Julian, Paris. On completing his studies in 1883, he was appointed second master at the School of Art, NEWCASTLE, under William Cosens Way (q.v.), remaining with the School until it was affiliated to the Durham College of Physical Science in 1889. He then held the post of headmaster of the School of Art at Hawick, Roxburgh, 1889-99, deciding just before the turn of the century to give up teaching to become a full-time professional artist. He first went to Ports-mouth, Hants., where he became much influenced by the work of marine artists then practising at the port, then returning to BERWICK-UPON-TWEED, he began painting local river and shipping scenes. He later spent many years at Edinburgh, where he established a considerable reputation as an artist before eventually retiring to Strathyre, Perth, where he died in 1953. Wood first began exhibiting his work at NEWCASTLE, showing examples at the city's Bewick Club from 1885, until after his move to Hawick. In 1889 he commenced exhibiting his work outside Northumbria, contributing to the Royal Scottish Academy, the Royal Scottish Society of Painters in Water Colours and the Glasgow Institute of Fine Arts for several years into the 20th century, and in 1902 only to the Royal Academy, when his work *A Border Link* was shown. While showing much of his later work in Scotland, he never forgot his one-time connections with NEWCASTLE, and was a contributor to the Artists of the Northern Counties exhibitions at the city's Laing Art Gallery for many years. His life as a professional artist was highlighted by a number of noteworthy occurrences, among these his presence on board H.M.S. *Queen Elizabeth* at the time of the surrender of the German Fleet in 1918, which gave him the opportunity to make sketches of several German ships before they were scuttled, and his accom-paniment of George VI and Queen Elizabeth on their Canadian tour of 1939, which he illustrated. His work was mainly in watercolour, but some oils are known. Represented: National Maritime Museum; Berwick A.G.; Dundee A.G.

WOOD, George Septimus (1860-1944)
Amateur landscape and coastal painter in oil and

James Wood: Old Pant at the head of The Side, Newcastle upon Tyne. Watercolour 11½×9. *Private collection.*

watercolour. Wood was born at NORTH SHIELDS, and worked all his life in the drapery trade in the town, painting in his spare time. He mainly exhibited his work at NEWCASTLE, where examples were shown at the Bewick Club from 1885, and the Artists of the Northern Counties exhibitions at the Laing Art Gallery from 1909. He was a founder member of the art club at TYNEMOUTH, and regularly exhibited his work at this club. He died at WALLSEND near NEWCASTLE.

*WOOD, James (d.1860)
Landscape and street scene painter in watercolour; miniature painter. Wood practised as a professional artist at NEWCASTLE in the first half of the 19th century, where he first advertised his services as a painter of portrait miniatures. Much of his work in this early period, however, consisted of local street scene painting in watercolour, many of his works featuring ancient buildings at NEWCASTLE, with figures.# Many examples of his work in this field are known, and are generally small in scale, and treated as vignettes, much in the manner of John Teasdale (q.v.). In the middle of the century he moved to SUNDERLAND, where he appears to have reverted to his earlier activity of miniature painting. He died at BISHOPWEARMOUTH, near SUNDER-LAND, in 1860.

WOOD, Robert (1852-1899)
Landscape painter in oil and watercolour; illustrator. Wood was born at Hall's Hill, near WOODBURN, in Redesdale, the son of a farmer. Following his education at a local school he was apprenticed to a joiner and builder at WOODBURN, but in 1875 he decided to move

199

to NEWCASTLE. Here he saw two watercolours by Thomas Miles Richardson, Senior (q.v.), and after reading details of Richardson's life he decided to become an artist. Some two or three years later he purchased the business of a picture framer and gilder at NEWCASTLE, and made such a success of it that he was thereafter able to devote much of his time to painting. He first exhibited his work publicly when he showed a view of WOODBURN at the Arts Association exhibition at NEWCASTLE, in 1879. He followed this by becoming a regular exhibitor at the city's Bewick Club, one of his exhibits – a large watercolour of Bamburgh Castle – proving so attractive that it was purchased by Sir Matthew White Ridley. Shortly after this he also began to show his work outside Northumbria, examples being accepted by the Royal Institute of Painters in Water Colours, the Royal Scottish Academy, and various London and provincial galleries. In 1887 he staged an exhibition of almost fifty of his drawings at NEWCASTLE, many of which featured HOLY ISLAND, off the Northumbria coastline. Wood's work also included many drawings for local newspapers and other publications. Towards the end of his life he became increasingly involved in picture dealing. He died at NEWCASTLE. His watercolour of St. Mary's Island is reproduced in William Weaver Tomlinson's *Historical Notes on Cullercoats, Whitley and Monkseaton*, 1893 (reprinted by Frank Graham, 1980).

WOOD, Ruth Mary (b. 1899)

Illustrator; decorative artist. She was born at SOUTH SHIELDS, and studied at Exeter School of Art and at the British Museum, before becoming an instructor at the former, in lettering and illumination. She has lived for many years at Honiton, Devon. In 1934 she exhibited an example of her work at the Royal Society of Artists, Birmingham.

WOOD, Walter Scott (born c. 1900)

Amateur landscape and coastal painter in oil and watercolour; etcher. Wood worked as a plumber at NORTH SHIELDS for much of his life, painting and etching in his spare time. He occasionally showed his work at the Artists of the Northern Counties exhibitions at the Laing Art Gallery, NEWCASTLE, where typical exhibits were his *Collywell Bay* (watercolour), and *Shields Harbour* (etching), shown in 1928.

WOODHOUSE, John (born c. 1800)

Portrait painter in oil; silhouette artist. Born at ALNWICK, Woodhouse was practising as a portrait painter at NEWCASTLE by his early twenties. Within a few years he had built up a considerable reputation for his silhouette work, earning from Eneas Mackenzie, in his *History of Newcastle*, 1827 (pp. 588-9), the observation that, as a "profile painter in shade", he "possesses, in remarkable degree, the faculty of retaining the exact forms of objects for a length of time after he has seen them. In some instances he has produced correct and striking likenesses of persons after their death". Woodhouse practised at NEWCASTLE throughout the third decade of the nineteenth century, later moving to NORTH SHIELDS.

WORNUM, Ralph Nicholson (1812-1877)

Portrait painter in oil; art writer. He was born at THORNTON, near DURHAM, and was initially intended for the bar. In 1834, however, he decided to make art his profession and studied for five years in Munich, Dresden, Rome and Paris. On his return to England in 1840 he settled in London, where he wrote and published his *Epochs of Painting*, and worked for some time as a lecturer in the Government Schools of Design, while trying to succeed as a portrait painter. His work for the first Westminster Hall competition was selected for praise, but in 1846 he embarked on his catalogue of the National Gallery, and following his appointment that year as Keeper, he increasingly devoted his time to writing about the history and practice of art. He died in London.

WORRELL, Abraham Bruiningh van, R.A.H.B. (1787–after 1857)

Landscape, cattle and fruit painter in oil and watercolour; lithographer. He was born at Middleburgh, in the Zeeland province of Holland, where he was practising as a professional artist by 1812. He later moved to London, settling there for the next nineteen years, and exhibiting his work at the Royal Academy, the British Institution, the Old Water Colour Society (later the Royal Society of Painters in Watercolours), and the Suffolk Street Gallery. In 1827 he also exhibited for the first time at NEWCASTLE, where his works appeared at the "Exhibition of Works by the Ancient Masters", staged by the Northumberland Institution for the Promotion of the Fine Arts, and at the Institution's annual exhibition in that year. The subjects of his London exhibits were mainly landscapes with cattle, and from 1825 he was described in catalogues as a "Royal Academician of Holland and Belgium"; this may explain the inclusion of his work *The Circumcision*, in the "Ancient Masters" exhibition at NEWCASTLE, though his two landscapes with cattle were shown at the second exhibition with the obvious realisation on the part of its organisers that he was a living artist. Moving permanently to NEWCASTLE by 1838, Worrell showed work at the North of England Society for the Promotion of the Fine Arts, in that year, and in 1839; following this he exhibited little in the town, though he continued to exhibit in London until 1849, and sent three works to Carlisle Athenaeum in 1850. His work during his some twenty years in NEWCASTLE featured landscapes – several of which portrayed the Island of Walcheren, Zeeland, Holland; cattle studies; game and fruit. His final exhibit at the Royal Academy in 1846, was for him the rather unusual subject: *Fishermen and women of Cullercoats, in the County of Northumberland*. His studio was for some years in Blackett Street, NEWCASTLE, but he appears to have spent his final years living and working in St. James's Street, where he is recorded until 1857. His daughter, MISS E. N. VAN WORRELL, was also an artist, and exhibited her work. Represented: British Museum; Hancock Museum, Newcastle.

WRIGHTSON, Jocelyn, S.W.A. (1888-1979)

Landscape and flower painter in watercolour. She was

born at Norton Hall, near Stockton on Tees, the daughter of Sir Thomas Wrightson, J.P., Chairman of Head Wrightson; M.P. for Stockton, and later St. Pancras, London. In her childhood she moved with her family to Neasham Hall, Darlington, where her interest in painting was encouraged by her father. She later practised as a watercolourist, painting widely throughout Scotland and Dorset, and exhibiting her work on five occasions at the Society of Women Artists, of which Society she was a member. She painted a large number of watercolours of Cairo during a stay there in 1923, which are now in an Egyptian collection. She died at Shaftsbury, Dorset. She was the younger sister of Margaret Wrightson (q.v.).

*WRIGHTSON, Margaret, F.R.S.B.S., S.W.A. (1877-1976)

Sculptor. She was born at Norton Hall, near Stockton

Margaret Wrightson: The Viking, forecourt of Northumberland County Council Offices, Morpeth. Bronze.

on Tees, the daughter of Sir Thomas Wrightson, J.P., Chairman of Head Wrightson; M.P. for Stockton, and later St. Pancras, London. In her childhood the family moved to Neasham Hall, Darlington, and here an interest in art fostered in her by her father led to her deciding to become a sculptor. She was placed as a pupil at the Royal College of Art, and studied under Sir William B. Richmond, the Royal Academician, Lanteri, and in Paris. In 1906 she had her first work accepted by the Royal Academy: *Sleeping Baby*, and from this point forward regularly exhibited her work both at the Academy, and at the Society of Women Artists. She handled many important commissions in her long working life. One of the earliest of these was a commission from the late Lord Runciman to produce a statue of a Viking landing on the Northumberland Coast,# for the grounds of his home, Doxford Hall, Doxford. This commission was placed in 1912, but was not completed until 1925, possibly due to the interruption of the First World War, in which she served as a driver with the Womens' Auxiliary Ambulance Corps, serving in France. This statue, her largest work, was re-erected outside the new headquarters of Northumberland County Council, Morpeth, in April, 1981. Other commissions included the Lamb Memorial (the figure of a young boy) for the Inner Temple Gardens, London, and the figure St. George, which forms part of the war memorial at Cramlington, unveiled in 1922. In the grounds of the family home at Darlington stands another of her works: *The Slayer of the Sockburn Worm*. Some of her most notable exhibition successes occurred in her later life; at the age of eighty-six she flew to Paris at the invitation of the Sociéte des Artistes Français to receive a medal of honour in the 1962 Salon exhibition, and she received several other recognitions. She was a Fellow of the Royal Society of British Sculptors, and a member of the Society of Women Artists, as well as being for many years a member of the Darlington Society of Arts. She died in London. Her younger sister Jocelyn Wrightson (q.v.), was also a talented artist.

YATES, Richard (c.1895- after 1955)

Landscape painter in oil and watercolour. This artist practised at Newcastle from the early years of the present century, until the middle 1950's, and first exhibited his work at the Artists of the Northern Counties exhibitions at the city's Laing Art Gallery. His first exhibits, in 1916, were entitled: *Near Westerhope*, and *Winlaton Mill*.

YEATMAN, Alice Mary, R.D.S. (born c.1866- died after 1936)

Landscape and figure painter in oil and watercolour; art teacher. She was born at Sunderland, and studied at Heatherlys, and the Royal Drawing Society, before practising as a professional artist in the town. On returning to SUNDERLAND from London she began exhibiting her work widely throughout Britain, showing examples at the New Gallery, the Royal Institute of Painters in Water Colours, the Royal Scottish Academy, the Bewick Club, NEWCASTLE, and later the Artists of the Northern Counties exhibitions at the city's Laing Art Gallery. Many of her works were painted in Lincolnshire and Sussex. She was a member of the Royal Drawing Society, and was a teacher of art at SUNDERLAND for many years.

YOUNG, Charles Phillips (1870- after 1951)

Landscape and architectural painter in oil and water-colour. Young was born at Dublin, but following his artistic training at King's College (later Newcastle University), he decided to remain on Tyneside to practise as an artist. He first lived at GATESHEAD, but later moved further up the Tyne Valley, living successively at STOCKSFIELD, and HEXHAM. He mainly exhibited his work at the Artists of the Northern Counties exhibitions at the Laing Art Gallery, NEWCASTLE, but also exhibited at the Shipley Art Gallery, GATESHEAD, and at Carlisle. He enjoyed a one-man exhibition at the Shipley Art Gallery, and was an exhibitor at this gallery's "Contemporary Artists of Durham County" exhibition, staged in 1951, in connection with the Festival of Britain, showing his watercolour: *Hill Country*. He was a member of the Tyneside Art Club.

*YOUNG, John (fl. late 19th cent.)

Genre and figure painter in oil and watercolour. This artist was born on Tyneside, and practised at NEWCASTLE in the last quarter of the 19th century. He showed examples of his work at the exhibition of works by local painters, at the Central Exchange Art Gallery, NEWCASTLE, in 1878: its catalogue notes describing him as "an artist who devotes himself to Shakespearian figure painting". He also showed work at the "Gateshead Fine Art & Industrial Exhibition", in 1883, but little is known of him after that date. The Shipley Art Gallery, GATESHEAD, has his oil: *The Vagrant.* #

YOUNG, Ralph Atkinson (fl. late 19th cent.)

Amateur landscape painter in oil and watercolour. Young worked as a commercial traveller on Tyneside in the late 19th century, and while living at NEWCASTLE, and later nearby WALLSEND, was an occasional exhibitor at the city's Bewick Club. He first began exhibiting his work at the Club in the late 1880's, and subsequently served as its honorary secretary. His exhibit at the Club

John Young: The Vagrant. Oil 19×15. *Tyne & Wear County Council Museums, Shipley Art Gallery.*

in 1892 was singled out for comment in the local press, which said: "R. A. Young is represented by a pretty picture of Whittle Dene, with its old mill".

YOUNG, Thomas Bell (1900-1978)

Amateur landscape painter in watercolour. He was born at NEWCASTLE, and is said to have exhibited at the Laing Art Gallery, NEWCASTLE, while still at school, and to have received the Lord Mayor's special prize at the age of fifteen. In 1939 he moved to DARLINGTON, where he was a member of the town's Society of Arts for some thirty years, also serving on its committee. He was a member of the Border Society, and exhibited his work at the Royal Institute of Painters in Water Colours, the Artists of the Northern Counties exhibitions at the Laing Art Gallery, NEWCASTLE, and at York and Carlisle. A one-man show of his work was held at DARLINGTON in 1971. Represented: Darlington A.G.

Bibliography

Please see individual artists' entries for the titles of books, articles, newspaper comments, etc., of particular interest in connection with their lives and work, and which may not be listed below.

GENERAL WORKS (selected):

BAIN, IAIN. (Edited and with an introduction by). *A Memoir of Thomas Bewick, Written by Himself.* London, 1975. *Thomas Bewick, an Illustrated Record of his Life and Work.* Newcastle upon Tyne, 1975. *The Watercolours of Thomas Bewick and his Workshop Apprentices.* London, 1981.

CHARLETON, ROBERT JOHN. *Newcastle Town.* London, 1885. Reprinted, Newcastle upon Tyne, 1978.

COOPER, LEONARD. *Great Men of Durham.* London, 1956.

GODDARD, T. RUSSELL. *History of the Natural History Society of Northumberland, Durham and Newcastle upon Tyne, 1829-1929.* Newcastle upon Tyne, 1929.

HORSLEY, P. M. *Eighteenth Century Newcastle.* Newcastle upon Tyne, 1971.

LONGSTAFFE, WILLIAM HYLTON DYER. *History & Antiquities of the Parish of Darlington.* Darlington, 1854.

MACKENZIE, ENEAS. *History of Newcastle upon Tyne.* Newcastle upon Tyne, 1827.

MEE, ARTHUR (Editor). *The King's England: Northumberland.* London, 1952; Newcastle upon Tyne, 1953. *The King's England: Durham.* London, 1953.

MIDDLEBROOK, S. *Newcastle upon Tyne: Its Growth and Achievement.* Newcastle upon Tyne, 1950. Reprinted 1968.

PEVSNER, NIKOLAUS. *Buildings of England: Northumberland.* Harmondsworth, Middlesex, 1957. Reprinted 1970. *Buildings of England: Durham.* London, 1953.

SYKES, JOHN. *Local Records or Historical Register of Remarkable Events of Northumberland, Durham, Newcastle upon Tyne and Berwick-upon-Tweed.* Newcastle upon Tyne, 1866. Reprinted 1973.

WELFORD, RICHARD. *Men of Mark 'Twixt Tyne & Tweed.* London, 1895.

WILKES, LYALL. *Tyneside Portraits.* Newcastle upon Tyne, 1971.

DICTIONARIES:

ARCHIBALD, E. H. H. *A Dictionary of Sea Painters.* Woodbridge, Suffolk, 1980.

BENEZIT, E. *Dictionnaire des Peintres, Sculpteurs, Dessinateurs et Graveurs.* 8 vols. Paris, 1976.

BRYAN, M. *Dictionary of Painters and Engravers.* First edition: 2 vols. London, 1816. Revised edition in 5 vols. London, 1903-4.

COLVIN, HOWARD. *A Biographical Dictionary of British Architects 1600-1840.* London, 1954. Reprinted 1978.

DICTIONARY OF NATIONAL BIOGRAPHY. London, 1885-1937.

E. P. PUBLISHING. *Royal Academy Exhibitors 1905-1970.* 4 vols. A-SHAR, London, 1973-81.

FIELDING, MANTLE. *A Dictionary of American Painters, Sculptors and Engravers.* New York, 1945.

GRANT, COLONEL MAURICE HAROLD. *A Dictionary of British Sculptors from 13th-20th Century.* London, 1953.

GRAVES, ALGERNON. *The British Institution 1806-1867.* London, 1875. Facsimile edition, Bath, 1969. *A Dictionary of Artists 1760-1893.* London, 1884. Enlarged 1901. Facsimile edition, Bath 1969; *The Royal Academy of Arts 1769-1904.* 8 vols. London, 1905. Facsimile edition in 4 vols. Bath, 1970; *The Society of Artists of Gt. Britain 1760-1791; The Free Society of Artists 1761-1783.* London, 1907. Facsimile edition, Bath, 1969.

GROCE, GEORGE C. and WALLACE, DAVID H. *The New York Historical Society's Dictionary of Artists in America, 1564-1860.* New Haven, and London, 1957.

GUNNIS, RUPERT. *Dictionary of British Sculptors 1660-1851.* London, 1951. New revised edition 1964.

HALL, MARSHALL. *The Artists of Cumbria.* Newcastle upon Tyne, 1979.

HOUFE, SIMON. *The Dictionary of British Book Illustrators and Caricaturists, 1800-1914.* Woodbridge, Suffolk, 1978.

HUNT, C. J. *The Book Trade in Northumberland and Durham to 1860.* Newcastle upon Tyne, 1975.

JOHNSON, JANE. *Works exhibited at the Royal Society of British Artists 1824-1893.* Woodbridge, Suffolk, 1975.

JOHNSON, J. and GREUTZNER, A. *The Dictionary of British Artists 1880-1940.* Woodbridge, Suffolk, 1976.

MALLALIEU, HUON L. *The Dictionary of British Watercolour Artists up to 1920.* Woodbridge, Suffolk, 1976.

MALLETT, DANIEL TROWBRIDGE. *Mallett's Index of Artists.* New York, 1935. Facsimile edition, Bath, 1976.

PAVIERE, SYDNEY H. *A Dictionary of British Sporting Painters.* Leigh on Sea, 1965; *A Dictionary of Victorian Landscape Painters.* Leigh on Sea, 1968.

REDGRAVE, SAMUEL. *A Dictionary of Artists of the English School.* London, 1878. Facsimile edition, Bath, 1970.

RINDER, FRANK. *The Royal Scottish Academy 1826-1916.* London, 1917. Facsimile edition, Bath, 1975.

SPARROW, W. SHAW. *British Sporting Artists.* London, 1922. Reprinted 1965.

TURNBULL, HARRY. *Yorkshire Artists: A short dictionary.* Snape Bedale, Yorks, 1976.

WATERS, GRANT. *A Dictionary of British Artists Working 1900-1950.* Vol. 1. Eastbourne, 1975. Vol. 2 (with illustrations) 1977.

WILSON, ARNOLD. *A Dictionary of British Marine Painters.* Leigh on Sea, 1967; *A Dictionary of British Military Painters.* Leigh on Sea, 1972.

WHO WAS WHO. Vols. I-VII, 1897-1980. London.

WHO'S WHO IN ART. Nineteen editions, 1927-1980. Havant, Hants.

WOOD, CHRISTOPHER. *The Dictionary of Victorian Artists.* Woodbridge, Suffolk, 1971. Revised and enlarged edition 1978.

WOOD, LIEUTENANT J. C. *A Dictionary of British Animal Painters.* Leigh on Sea, 1973.

CATALOGUES AND OTHER PUBLICATIONS:

ART CIRCLE, NEWCASTLE UPON TYNE.
Works by Charles James Spence, 1906.

ART GALLERY, ARMSTRONG COLLEGE, NEWCASTLE UPON TYNE.
Works by Robert Jobling, 1923.

ARTS ASSOCIATION, NEWCASTLE UPON TYNE.
Exhibition catalogues 1878-1881.

BEWICK CLUB, NEWCASTLE UPON TYNE.
Exhibition catalogues 1884-1895, including *Royal Jubilee Exhibition,* 1887.

CENTRAL EXCHANGE ART GALLERY, NEWCASTLE UPON TYNE.
Central Exchange News Room, Art Gallery & Polytechnic Exhibition, 1870: *Works by local painters,* 1878; *Henry Hetherington Emmerson Exhibition,* 1895.

DARLINGTON ART GALLERY, DARLINGTON.
Catalogue of Picture Collection, 1980.

GRAY ART GALLERY & MUSEUM, HARTLEPOOL.
Catalogue of the Permanent Collection, 1923; Various exhibition catalogues 1925-1949: *John William Howey,* 1925; *Seymour Walker,* 1926; *James Clark,* 1926; *Robert Leslie Howey,* 1949.

LAING ART GALLERY, NEWCASTLE UPON TYNE.
Catalogue of the Permanent Collection of Pictures in Oil and Water Colours, with descriptive and biographical notes by C. Bernard Stevenson, Curator, 1915; Catalogue of the Permanent Collection of Water Colours, with descriptive and biographical notes by C. Bernard Stevenson, Curator, 1939.
Exhibitions of Works by Artists of the Northern Counties, 1905-1962.
Various exhibition catalogues 1906-1982: *Thomas Miles Richardson, Senior, and members of the Richardson Family, 1906; James Peel, 1907; Neils Moeller Lund, 1916; John Charlton, 1917; Myles Birket Foster, 1925; Thomas Bewick, 1928; Frank Thomas Carter, Thomas Bowman Garvie, George Edward Horton and John Falconar Slater, 1934; Ernest Procter, 1936; Ralph Hedley, 1938; William Park Atkin, 1940; Luke Clennell, 1940; Thomas Wiliam Pattison, 1942; Tyneside's Contribution to Art, 1951; Coronation Exhibitions, 1953; John Wilson Carmichael, 1968; Henry Perlee Parker, 1969-70; John Martin, 1970; Thomas Bewick, 1978; The Tyneside Classical Tradition – Classical Architecture in the North East, 1700-1850, 1980; The Decorated Glass of William and Mary Beilby, 1761-1778, 1980; Victorian and Edwardian Architecture in the North East, 1981; Luke Clennell, 1981; 'The Picturesque Tour in Northumberland and Durham, c. 1720-1830', 1982. George Edward Horton, 1982; John Wilson Carmichael, 1982.*

MECHANICS' INSTITUTION, NEWCASTLE UPON TYNE.
Exhibition of Paintings and Other Works of Art, 1866.

MOSS GALLERIES, HEXHAM.
John Atkinson Exhibition, 1981; George Horton Exhibition, 1982.

NEWCASTLE UPON TYNE INSTITUTION FOR THE GENERAL PROMOTION OF THE FINE ARTS.
Exhibition catalogues 1832-1837.

NEWCASTLE UPON TYNE CITY LIBRARIES.
Catalogue of the Bewick Collection (Pease Bequest), 1904.

NORTH EAST COAST EXHIBITION, NEWCASTLE UPON TYNE, 1929.
Catalogue of the Palace of Arts.

NORTHERN ACADEMY OF ARTS, NEWCASTLE UPON TYNE.
Exhibition catalogues 1828-1831.

NORTH OF ENGLAND SOCIETY FOR THE PROMOTION OF THE FINE ARTS, NEWCASTLE UPON TYNE.
Exhibition catalogues 1838-1843, and with the Government School of Design, 1850 and 1852.

NORTHUMBERLAND INSTITUTION FOR THE PROMOTION OF THE FINE ARTS IN THE NORTH OF ENGLAND, NEWCASTLE UPON TYNE.
Exhibition catalogues 1822-1827.

PEN & PALETTE CLUB, NEWCASTLE UPON TYNE.
Watercolours by John Hodgson Campbell, 1927.

SHIPLEY ART GALLERY, GATESHEAD.
Catalogue of Paintings and Drawings, 1951; Contemporary Artists of Durham County, 1951.

STONE GALLERY, NEWCASTLE UPON TYNE.
Drawings from the Sketchbook of the Rev. George Liddell Johnston, 1970.

SUNDERLAND MUSEUM & ART GALLERY.
Nineteenth Century North East Artists, 1974; The Spectacular Career of Clarkson Stanfield, 1979.

TYNE & WEAR COUNTY COUNCIL MUSEUMS, NEWCASTLE UPON TYNE.
Collection Handlist, Fine & Applied Art, 1980; comprising handlist to collections in Newcastle upon Tyne, Gateshead, Sunderland and South Tyneside. Note: This organisation responsible for the production of all catalogues of the art galleries within these areas from 1975; i.e. Laing Art Gallery, etc.

YORK CITY ART GALLERY, YORK.
Francis Place Exhibition, 1971.

*Key to Map**

Acklington	7G	Hexham	11D
Allendale	11C		
Allenheads	12C	Middlesbrough	15J
Alnmouth	6G	Middleton in	
Alnwick	5F	Teesdale	14D
Amble	6G	Middleton	
Ashington	7G	St. George	16H
		Monkseaton	10H
Bamburgh	3F	Morpeth	8G
Barnard Castle	15E		
Beadnell	4G	Newcastle upon	
Bedlington	9G	Tyne	10G
Belford	3F	Norham	2D
Bellingham	9C	North Shields	10I
Berwick-upon-		North Sunderland	4G
Tweed	1D	Norton	15I
Bishop Auckland	14G		
Blyth	9H		
Bowes	15E	Otterburn	7C
Bywell	11F	Ovingham	11F
Cambo	8E	Redcar	14K
Castle Eden	13I	Riding Mill	11E
Chester-le-Street	12G	Rothbury	7E
Chillingham	4E	Ryton	11G
Consett	12F		
Corbridge	11E		
Cornhill	3C	Seaham	12I
Cramlington	9G	Seahouses	4G
Craster	5G	Seaton Burn	10G
Cullercoats	10H	Seaton Carew	14J
		South Shields	10I
		Spennymoor	13G
Darlington	15H	Stanhope	13E
Doxford	5F	Stamfordham	10E
Durham	13H	Stocksfield	11F
		Stockton on Tees	15I
Ebchester	11F	Sunderland	11I
Ellingham	4F		
		Twizell	2C
Ford	3D	Tynemouth	10H
Gainford	15F		
Gateshead	11H	Wark	9C
Gosforth	10G	Warkworth	6G
		Whitley Bay	10H
Haltwhistle	10B	Woodburn	8C
Hartlepool	14J	Wooler	4D
Haydon Bridge	10C	Wylam	11F
Heddon-on-the-			
Wall	10F	Yarm	16I

* Note: Only place names set thus in artists' entries: ALNWICK, are given map location points above. Where it has not been possible to accommodate a place name on the map, the nearest large town or village has been named in the entry, and can be located by reference to the key.

204

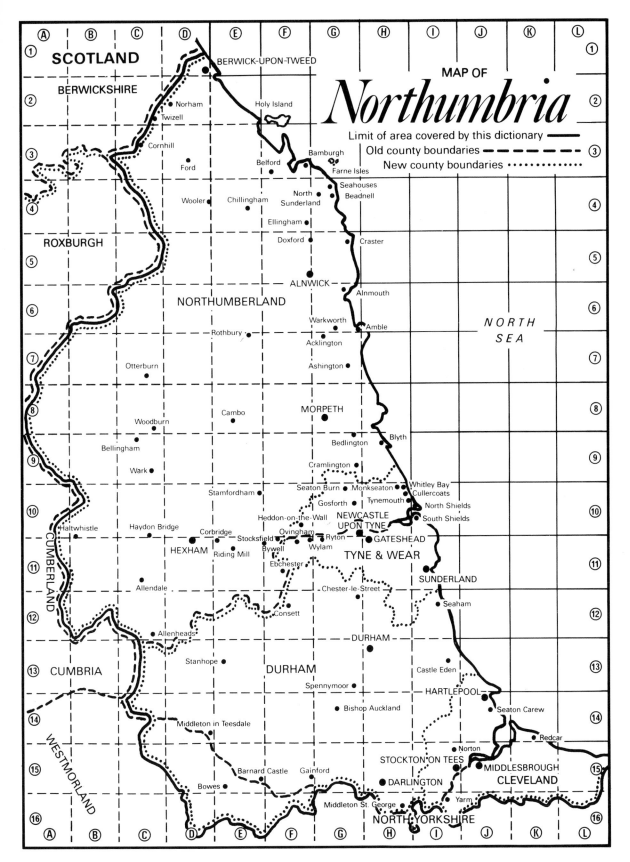

MAP OF

Northumbria

Limit of area covered by this dictionary ———
Old county boundaries – – – – – –
New county boundaries ·············

SCOTLAND

BERWICKSHIRE

ROXBURGH

NORTHUMBERLAND

Berwick-upon-Tweed
Norham
Twizell
Cornhill
Ford
Holy Island
Belford
Bamburgh
Farne Isles
Wooler
Chillingham
North Sunderland
Seahouses
Beadnell
Ellingham
Doxford
Craster
Alnwick
Alnmouth
Warkworth
Amble
Rothbury
Acklington
Otterburn
Ashington
Cambo
MORPETH
Woodburn
Blyth
Bellingham
Bedlington
Wark
Cramlington
Stamfordham
Seaton Burn
Monkseaton
Whitley Bay
Cullercoats
Gosforth
Tynemouth
North Shields
Heddon-on-the-Wall
NEWCASTLE UPON TYNE
South Shields
Haltwhistle
Haydon Bridge
Corbridge
Stocksfield
Ovingham
Ryton
GATESHEAD
HEXHAM
Bywell
Wylam
Riding Mill
Ebchester
TYNE & WEAR
Allendale
SUNDERLAND
Chester-le-Street
Seaham
Consett
CUMBERLAND
Allenheads
DURHAM
Stanhope
Castle Eden
CUMBRIA
DURHAM
HARTLEPOOL
Spennymoor
Middleton in Teesdale
Bishop Auckland
Seaton Carew
WESTMORLAND
Norton
Redcar
Barnard Castle
Gainford
STOCKTON ON TEES
MIDDLESBROUGH
Bowes
DARLINGTON
CLEVELAND
Middleton St. George
Yarm
NORTH YORKSHIRE

NORTH SEA

205

Exhibiting organisations

The following are some brief notes on the principal exhibiting organisations referred to in this dictionary:

Arts Association (Newcastle upon Tyne). Founded in 1878, this Association held important fine art exhibitions in 1878, 1879, 1880 and 1881.

Bewick Club (Newcastle upon Tyne). Founded in 1884, this Club held fine art exhibitions for forty years.

British Institution. The Institution was established in London in 1806 as a rival to the *Royal Academy*. It survived until 1867.

Carlisle Academy. Built in 1823, the Academy staged exhibitions until 1833.

Carlisle Athenaeum. Built in 1841, the Athenaeum held fine art exhibitions in 1843, 1846 and 1850.

Dudley Gallery. Established in London in 1865, it first specialised in watercolours; in 1867 it extended its exhibiting scope to include works in oil, and in 1872, works in black and white.

Free Society of Artists. Although it will be remarked later that the Society of Artists staged the first large scale exhibition of artists' work in Britain, it was in reality the Free Society which should be entitled to this claim, as the future members of the latter society seceded from the first, leaving the main body exhibiting at the same place as before. As, however, the 1760 catalogue has always been considered to belong to the *Society of Artists*, the Free Society's exhibiting life is usually stated as having started in 1761. Like the *Society of Artists* it attracted many of the nation's leading artists both before, and after, the establishment of the *Royal Academy*. It held exhibitions almost uninterruptedly until 1783. Members styled: F.S.A.

Glasgow Institute of Fine Arts. Founded in 1862, its annual exhibitions attracted artists from all over Britain. It was created Royal in 1896.

Grosvenor Gallery. Although this London gallery, founded in 1877, survived for only 13 years, it became a focal point for the Aesthetic Movement of the 1880's, and a favourite of Pre-Raphaelite followers.

Liverpool Academy of Fine Arts. Founded 1810.

Manchester Academy of Fine Arts. Founded 1859.

New English Art Club. Founded in 1885 by a body of predominantly young artists, who selected works for exhibition themselves, rather than by committee, this became one of the most important art clubs in Britain, with many outstanding artists among its members. Its first exhibition was staged at the Grosvenor Gallery in 1886. Members styled: N.E.A.C.

New Gallery. Founded in London in 1888 as a splinter of the Grosvenor Gallery, this gallery attracted many of the latter's members when the Grosvenor closed in 1890.

New Water Colour Society. This society, was founded in 1832, in competition with the *Old Water Colour Society*. In 1863 it changed its name to "Institute of Painters in Water Colours", and in 1883 it was authorised to use the title: Royal. Members styled R.I.

Northern Academy of Arts. Northumbria's first academy of the arts, this was established at Newcastle upon Tyne in 1828, and held exhibitions until 1831. These exhibitions were contributed to by artists from all over Britain.

Northumberland Institution for the Promotion of the Fine Arts in the North of England. Established at Newcastle upon Tyne in 1822, the Institution provided Northumbria with its first fine art exhibitions. These were staged from 1822 until 1827.

Old Water Colour Society. Founded in London in 1804 by a group of artists who had become dissatisfied with the *Royal Academy*, it became Royal in 1881. Members styled: R.W.S.

Pastel Society. Founded 1898.

Royal Academy of Arts. Founded in 1768, this institution has played an important part in the development of British Art for more than two centuries. Its most influential period was during the Victorian era, when its exhibitions were among the most widely discussed topics of the day. As a teaching institution, the Academy has been responsible for the early training of some of the country's best known painters, sculptors, draughtsmen and engravers. Members styled: R.A.

Royal Birmingham Society of Artists. Founded 1812.

Royal Cambrian Academy. This academy was founded in 1881, and was granted a Royal Charter in 1882. Members styled: R.Cam.A.

Royal Hibernian Academy. This academy was founded in 1822, and has included some of Ireland's finest artists among its members. Members styled: R.H.A.

Royal Institute of Painters in Oils. Founded in 1883, this institute was shortly afterwards awarded a Royal Charter. Members styled R.O.I.

Royal Institute of Painters in Water Colours: see *New Water Colour Society*.

Royal Scottish Academy. Founded in Edinburgh in 1826, it received its Royal Charter in 1839. Closely modelled on the *Royal Academy*, it was not, however, until the 1850's that it established anything like the position of its English counterpart. Members styled: R.S.A.

Royal Scottish Society of Painters in Water Colours. Founded in Glasgow in 1878, it was granted permission to term itself Royal, ten years later. Members styled: R.S.W.

Royal Society of Painter-Etchers and Engravers. Founded in 1880. Members styled: R.E.

Royal Society of Painters in Water Colours: see *Old Water Colour Society*.

Royal Ulster Academy. Founded 1879.

Royal West of England Academy. Founded 1845.

Society of Artists. One of the first societies in Britain to stage regular exhibitions of artists' work, this society was founded in 1760, and survived for 31 years. Its first exhibition in the premises of the Society for the Encouragement of Arts, Manufactures and Commerce, in London, has been described as the earliest large scale exhibition of artists' work in Britain. It subsequently established its own premises, and in the eight years before the establishment of the Royal Academy showed the work of the nation's leading artists; some continued to exhibit with the Society for the rest of its life. Fellows styled: F.S.A. (before 1791).

Suffolk Street Gallery. The exhibition venue and headquarters of the *Society of British Artists*, this London Gallery held its first exhibition in 1824, and quickly became a popular alternative to the Royal Academy for artists seeking exhibiting facilities. Its governing Society became Royal in 1887, whereafter its members were styled: R.B.A. (note that the description "Suffolk Street Gallery" is used throughout this dictionary in referring to works sent to the Society's exhibitions before 1887, and "Royal Society of British Artists", in subsequent years.